Transnational Asian American Literature

Transnational Asian American Literature

Sites and Transits

Edited by

SHIRLEY GEOK-LIN LIM,
JOHN BLAIR GAMBER,
STEPHEN HONG SOHN,
AND GINA VALENTINO

TEMPLE UNIVERSITY PRESS
Philadelphia

Temple University Press
1601 North Broad Street
Philadelphia PA 19122
www.temple.edu/tempress

Copyright © 2006 by Temple University
Published 2006
Printed in the United States of America

⊗ The paper used in this publication meets the requirements of the American
National Standard for Information Sciences—Permanence of Paper for Printed
Library Materials, ANSI Z39.48-1992

Library of Congress Cataloging-in-Publication Data

Transnational Asian American literature : sites and transits / edited by
Shirley Geok-lin Lim ... [et al.].
    p. cm.
Includes bibliographical references and index.
ISBN 1-59213-450-5 (cloth : alk. paper)
ISBN 1-59213-451-3 (pbk. : alk. paper)
    1. American literature—Asian American authors—History and criticism.
2. Emigration and immigration in literature.   3. Asian Americans—Intellectual
life.   4. Asian Americans in literature.   5. Immigrants in literature.
I. Lim, Shirley.

PS153.A84T73 2005
810.9′895—dc22   2005049680

Lines in Park chapter (pp. 236–237, 239) from "And Sing We" and "Food,
Shelter, Clothing" in Myung Mi Kim, *Under Flag* (Berkeley, CA: Kelsey St. Press,
1999). Used by permission of Kelsey St. Press.

Lines in Park chapter (pp. 244–246, 248–254) from Myung Mi Kim, *Dura*, New
American Poetry Series 28 (Los Angeles: Sun & Moon Press, 1988). Used by
permission of Sun & Moon Press.

Lines in Park chapter (p. 239) from "In a Station of the Metro", By Ezra Pound,
from PERSONAE, copyright © 1926 by Ezra Pound. Reprinted by permission of
New Directions Publishing Company.

Excerpts in Grotjohn chapter (pp. 219–232) from Kimiko Hahn's "Wax,"
"Morning Light," "Mosquito and Ant," "Jam," "The Tumbler," "Pine," "The
Downpour," "Garnet," "Guard the Jade Pass," "Orchid Root," "Radiator," and
"Croissant," from *Mosquito and Ant*, used by permission of the poet.

Lines in Islam chapter (p. 262) from Agha Shahid Ali, "Postcard from Kashmir"
from *The Half-Inch Himalayas* © 1987 by Agha Shahid Ali and reprinted by
permission of Wesleyan University Press.

2 4 6 8 9 7 5 3 1

Contents

Acknowledgments   ix

Introduction
  SHIRLEY GEOK-LIN LIM, JOHN BLAIR GAMBER,
  STEPHEN HONG SOHN, AND GINA VALENTINO   1

I. FICTION

1. Re-Signed Subjects: Women, Work, and World in the
   Fiction of Carlos Bulosan and Hisaye Yamamoto
   CHERYL HIGASHIDA   29

2. "Just Another Ethnic Pol": Literary Citizenship in
   Chang-rae Lee's *Native Speaker*
   LIAM CORLEY   55

3. The Cartography of Justice and Truthful Refractions
   Found in Karen Tei Yamashita's *Tropic of Orange*
   RUTH Y. HSU   75

4. "Valuing" Transnational Queerness: Politicized
   Bodies and Commodified Desires in Asian American
   Literature
   STEPHEN HONG SOHN   100

5. Ethical Responsibility in the Intersubjective Spaces:
   Reading Jhumpa Lahiri's *"Interpreter of Maladies"*
   and "A Temporary Matter."
   GITA RAJAN   123

6. Abjection, Masculinity, and Violence in Brian Roley's
   American Son and Han Ong's *Fixer Chao*
   ELEANOR TY   142

II.   MEMOIR/AUTOBIOGRAPHY

7.   Begin Here: A Critical Introduction to the Asian
     American Childhood
       ROCÍO G. DAVIS   161

8.   The Poetics of Liminality and Misidentification:
     Winnifred Eaton's *Me* and Maxine Hong Kingston's
     The Woman Warrior
       KATHERINE HYUNMI LEE   181

9.   Nation, Immigrant, Text: Theresa Hak Kyung Cha's
     Dictee
       SRIMATI MUKHERJEE   197

III.   POETRY

10. Kimiko's Hahn's "Interlingual Poetics" in
     Mosquito and Ant
       ROBERT GROTJOHN   219

11. "Composed of Many Lengths of Bone":
     Myung Mi Kim's Reimagination of Image and Epic
       JOSEPHINE HOCK-HEE PARK   235

12. A Way in the World of an Asian American Existence:
     Agha Shahid Ali's Transimmigrant Spacing of North
     America and India/Kashmir
       MAIMUNA DALI ISLAM   257

13. Writing Otherwise than as a "Native Informant":
     Ha Jin's Poetry
       ZHOU XIAOJING   274

     About the Contributors   295

     Index   299

Acknowledgments

WE WOULD like to acknowledge those who have shaped this project through their valuable and meticulous editing work: Janet M. Francendese and William M. Hammell at Temple University Press, who followed this book from its infancy to its final stages and provided indispensable suggestions along the way. We would also like to thank Heather Medlock at the *Studies in the Literary Imagination*, who has kindly allowed us to reprint three articles that originally appeared there. And it was through early interactions with Pearl A. McHaney that provided us with a fertile ground to begin our project.

The following scholars contributed in early stages to this project through their referee work: Nancy Abelmann (University of Illinois at Urbana-Champaign), Deepika Bahri (Emory University), Jeffrey Paul Chan (California State University, San Francisco), Juliana Chang (Santa Clara University), Monica Chiu (University of New Hampshire), Ann Choi (Rutgers University), Cheng Lok Chua (California State University, Fresno), Kandice Chuh (University of Maryland), Tim Engles (Eastern Illinois University), Cynthia Franklin (University of Hawai'i), Helena Grice (University of Wales, Aberystwyth), Ruth Hsiao (Retired (Tufts)), Sheila Hwang (Webster University), Michele Jannette (Kansas State University), Rachel C. Lee (University of California, Los Angeles), Sue-im Lee (Temple University), Yoon Sun Lee (Wellesley College), Srimati Mukherjee (Temple University), Maire Mullins (Pepperdine University), Viet Thanh Nguyen (University of Southern California), Rajeev Patke (National University of Singapore), Sangeeta Ray (University of Maryland), Karen Shimakawa (University of California, Davis), George Uba (California State University, Northridge), Fatima Wu (Loyola Marymount University), and Meiling Wu (California State University, East Bay).

The American Cultures and Global Contexts Center and its directors, Carl Gutiérrez-Jones and Giles Gunn, provided space and resources to create and complete this publication. We thank the University of California, Santa Barbara Academic Senate for their generous sponsorship. In addition, The Interdisciplinary Humanities Centers (UCSB) has continually provided its financial support to this project. We would like to also show gratitude toward Janet Mallen and Melissa Colleen Stevenson for their technical support of this project.

Lastly, the remaining editors would like thank Shirley Geok-lin Lim for her tireless, gracious mentorship.

Transnational Asian American Literature

Introduction

SHIRLEY GEOK-LIN LIM, JOHN BLAIR GAMBER,
STEPHEN HONG SOHN, AND GINA VALENTINO

Transnational Asian American Literature: Sites and Transits does
not set out to reject a U.S. nation location for Asian American writing.
Rather, this collection of essays sees the nation-formation themes, often
intrinsically tied to language strategies and formal features, as one subject
rising from a set of historical dynamics that traverse and explain the collective body of Asian American literature. A second set of dynamics comes
from the diasporic, mobile, transmigratory nature of Asian American experience, a history characterized by disparate migratory threads, unset-
tled and unsettling histories churned by multiple and different Asian ethnic immigrant groups each with a different language and cultural stock,
different value and belief systems, and different notions of literary aesthetics, albeit most largely mediated through the English language. This
continuous narrative of Asian American entry, reentry, expulsion, remi-
gration, and movement across and between borders, what Aihwa Ong
(1999) had partly captured in the phrase "flexible citizenship," which
nonetheless does not successfully express the open-ended and sometimes
exhausting nature of "temporary" societies and characters. These "immigrant" subjects are not always fugitive and furtive like the *manong* in
Bulosan's *America Is in the Heart* (1946), or queer as in Lawrence Chua's
Gold by the Inch (1998). In our use of the phrase "sites and transits"
in the volume's title, "site" also denotes attitudes and postures, the arrested moment of identity in a place and time, while "transit" denotes,
according to the *Oxford English Dictionary*, that "instance of passing or
journeying across." A transit is also the passage of a celestial body over
the meridian of a place or through the field of a telescope. In analogous
manner, Asian American transit may be said to be the passage of Asian
bodies through the field of an American-bounded lens, or the passing
of Asian stories and images over a U.S. literary place. Asian American
representations are sited in U.S. nation discourse, but representations of
Asian American transits are less place-bound and more sensitive to time

An earlier version of the Introduction appeared in *Studies in the Literary Imagination*, vol.
37:1 (2004), pp. 1–16.

dimensions: the different histories of various collectivities and individuals; the intersection of variable, even conflictual, forces rising from social, class, gender, nation ideologies all in the same fraught moment; predicaments and losses brought on by time's passage; inexorable change and movement; and so forth. The title for this book thus gestures to the complex, dialogical national and transnational formulations of Asian American imaginations as figured in their texts.

As a number of critics have noted, Asian American literary studies may be in a moment of crisis because of the very values of multiplicity and heterogeneity that had placed ethnic-identity literatures in sight in the United States. Asian American imagination, unlike that in African American writing, has no single unifying grand narrative to organize the vast materials that Asian American writers call on; it possesses no single linguistic Other, as in Latina/o writing, on which to hinge a counter tradition of stylistics. Instead, what Asian American works of imagination manifest in full are a plethora of seemingly separate threads. Threads leading to distinctively different national origins, first languages undecipherable to other Asian Americans, and cultural signs and codes of signification unintelligible to those identified as "the same" by census and academic disciplinary discourses.

Although the novels, plays, poems, and memoirs of Asian American literature do not always mark these cultural cognitive dissonances self-reflexively, it is also accurate to note that Asian American literary critics often ignore those textual sites in which such dissonances are acutely recorded. Examples might include the role of Chinese gambling houses in Carlos Bulosan's *America Is in the Heart* (1946), or the Japanese American narrator in Hisaye Yamamoto's short story "Wilshire Bus" *Seventeen Syllables,* (2001) who remains silent as the Chinese American couple, on their way to the veterans hospital, is verbally abused by a white man, drunk on spirits and triumphal anti-Asian racism. These evident imagined moments of "Asian American" cross sightings may be represented as failed, sordid, and painful. However, as Gish Jen's *Mona in the Promised Land* (1997) also imagines, there are other ways to represent these moments when ethnic identity may be confirmed, interrogated, destabilized, undermined, or blurred, as it is teased out not only in between the ethnicities that are conflated as Asian American but also in those moments that activate relations between and among other communities of identity—Jewish, Anglo-Saxon, black, or Latino.

From the inception of Asian American critical production, a number of conflicting impulses resulted in contradictory, sometimes bewildering, positions. A major formative influence on Asian American cultural discourse is the notion of a U.S. location: that Asian American literature is

above all a U.S. nation-identified production. The site of narrative perspective, albeit a narrative set in the Philippines or India or Brazil or
Korea or a dystopic future, it is always assumed, is that of the United
States of America. And for some time, despite some textual evidence to
the contrary, many critics read Asian American literature as charting a
linear developmental model of identity, plotted from immigrant entry to
successful integration, with points of conflict, reversals, epiphanies, and
so forth along the narrative route.

Increasing pressure of new immigrant national groups, the increasing presence of transnational Asian communities to whom U.S. residency may be simply one of a number of possible choices—a temporary
and provisional matter or permanent condition—the growing complex
dynamics of postcolonial flows and globalization in which the United
States as economic, cultural, and media player may be present in non-
U.S. territory and Asian presence marked in U.S. borders: these and
more associated phenomena are represented in Asian American experience and imaginations, and in like manner critical theory and readings
follow on these representations. Shirley Geok-lin Lim, in her introduction to *The Forbidden Stitch: An Asian American Women's Anthology*
(1989), noted that "As a first-generation 'Asian American woman,' for
one thing, I knew there was no such thing as an 'Asian American woman.'
Within this homogenizing labeling of an exotica, I knew there were entire
racial/national/cultural/sexual-preferenced groups, many of whom find
each other as alien as mainstream America apparently finds us. . . . [T]he
experience of being 'an Asian American woman' is an exemplar of living in difference" (10). Lisa Lowe's *Immigrant Acts* (1996) makes the
case for Asian American difference through theorizing the markers of
"heterogeneity, hybridity, multiplicity" in Asian American texts, not as
rhetorical terms but as "the material conditions that characterize Asian
American groups" (67). She argues, for instance, that "the making of
Chinese-American culture—the ways in which it is imagined, practiced,
and continued—is worked out as much 'horizontally' among communities
as it is transmitted 'vertically' in unchanging forms from one generation to
the next," and suggests Asian American identity, instead of being essentialized and fixed, is produced in a complicated, unstable fashion by "Asian
American cultural productions"; that is, it is constructed and imagined.

Kandice Chuh's *Imagine Otherwise* (2003) is the most recent formulation of these explorations into rearticulating Asian American subjects and
the interdisciplinary practices established under the term Asian American
studies. Organized around the thesis that Asian American studies need
to be retheorized as a subjectless discourse, her argument would appear
to evacuate subjects already given or assumed covered in the multiple

disciplinary practices established under an Asian American studies rubric. Her critique of the partial and reifying institutional understandings of what constitutes Asian American studies and its subjects include a criticism of approaches that take Asian American studies as part of a U.S. national project or as participating in multicultural studies or as an ethnic-identity–based discourse, or as social-science–based activism for material and political justice. Chuh's book establishes a claim for a total theory by which to frame the interdisciplinary practices undertaken and underwritten by diverse Asian Americanists. Although not denying the usefulness of sociological and empirical studies nor earlier concepts that rallied Asian American scholars around major community projects, Chuh posits instead a comprehensive response to late twentieth-century intellectual undermining of identity-based knowledge. Thus the incorporation of postcolonial, postnational, transnational, poststructuralist, and postmodernist ways of thinking—what she might call epistemes of knowing—into her radical rejection of fixed, essentialized, identity politics as characterizing the Asian American subject. Her project formulates a postsubject theory for Asian American studies; that is, what happens when we radically query the stability of unitary identity in imagining the "Asian American"? This query not only recognizes multiplicity and difference but tries to account for difference as interfaced with other differences—when difference meets itself, as Chuh says—rather than collapsed, foreclosed, and resolved into identity and sameness with the U.S. nation. The original amalgamation of the discipline being no longer appropriate, what then should replace it? Chuh takes her cue from Lisa Lowe's (*Immigrant Acts*, 1996,) and seeks to move from cultural or national identity discourses to focus on economic and social justice. This drive to move beyond cultural identity politics to economic and social justice politics motivates her study; hence, the prior position of legal judgments and legal language and the sometimes secondary position of literary works as objects of study in her book. The emphasis on difference rather than on identity allows for a new discursive space in which, while no subject is unnatural, no subject is naturalized either; that is, where the constructedness of subjects rather than their representations is analyzed. "Asian American" is therefore above all a literary sign and an abstract signifier whose signified contents are so shiftable, provisional, and undecidable that attempts to contain them will always result in incomplete narratives.

In contrast to theorizing "Asian American" as a subjectless signifier, this book reads "Asian American" as a multiplier signifier, attributed with political, social, and cultural value particularly by U.S. institutional forces such as state and federal governments, legal, educational, and cultural systems and organizations, capitalist apparatuses like banks and corporations, and so forth, whose significance in a literary and critical domain is at once capable of incorporating fresh immigrant subjectivities as well as recuperating historical multilingual texts. Its capaciousness is constructed, invented if you will, in the way that all social-cultural identities, including those now accepted as "white" and "American," are constructed, out of a combination of canny political agendas, individual imaginations, communal histories, erasures and elisions, provisional arrangements, and contingencies. "Asian American," in the literary sphere, offers a way of understanding and constructing identity mediated by textual power—that is, how language operates in these works as an agent for novel imaginaries and social transformation. This volume takes up an opening gambit, of reading Asian American writing as located and locatable in U.S. territory, sited on a discourse of nation, whether immigrant or citizen, and integrated into the dominant forms, genres, and aesthetic traditions of U.S. literature. At the same time, this critical opening acknowledges that even from the earliest outset of scholarship on Asian American writing, a nation-bounded siting was never inflexible. King-Kok Cheung and Stan Yogi's valuable *Asian American Literature Annotated Bibliography*, published in 1988, while stating its focus on "literature by Asian Americans in the United States and Canada," cautioned that "national and regional allegiances, which often vary with time, cannot be easily determined," and so included in its references the works of "overseas Chinese—be they sojourners or immigrants," "expatriates," or "regional writers" (v). Such bibliographical comprehensiveness suggests and invariably must lead to frames and theories that support a non-U.S. incorporation, which may be viewed as undermining the U.S.-claiming agenda that a number of authors and scholars like Sau-ling Wong projected for Asian American literature and studies.[1]

Before proceeding to discuss the chapters of this volume, it may be useful to contextualize the collection in a literary history. Asian American literature, covering over a century of production,[2] has shown an exponential increase in publication in recent decades. Similarly, Asian American literary criticism has expanded significantly in the past two decades. The work of literary critics has been crucial to the ways that Asian American literatures have been defined, archived, reissued, and taught at universities in the United States and internationally. Asian American literary criticism may be said to fall into distinct, although not wholly partitioned, periods and thematic categories: critical work produced prior to 1982, between 1982 and 1995, and from 1995 to the present, with thematic categories prominently shaped in the third period. The major thematic clusters that generally concern Asian American critics include the problematics of definition, particularly the relation of Asian American literature to discourses on nation, transnation, and globalization; studies on gender and sexuality; examinations of genre and form; single-author studies; and metacritical approaches in which Asian American literary criticism itself becomes the focus of study. A sixth category may be said to lie in the work of edited anthologies that cover a range of themes and deploy myriad critical strategies.

Introductions to anthologies of creative writing by Asian Americans offered the first examples of Asian American literary criticism prior to 1982. Initiating the debate on what constitutes an Asian American identity, the anthologies defined Asian American literature through the inclusion or exclusion of certain Asian American national groups. The published work was limited then to what the editors considered worthy or had access to; in the 1970s this literature was primarily by writers of Chinese or Japanese descent, with some attempt to reach Filipino American writers. The first anthology, *Asian-American Authors* (1972), edited by Kai-Yu Hsu and Helen Palubinskas, referred to only three Asian American national groups: Chinese, Japanese, and Filipino Americans. *Aiiieeeee!* (1974), a pioneering collection of Asian American writing, limited the composition of Asian American writing to these ethnic groups. Moreover, the *Aiiieeeee!* preface, distinguishing between a legitimate U.S.-born Asian American subject and a foreign-born immigrant/diasporic Asian subjectivity, valorized a cultural nationalism and argued for separatist politics. The editors (Jeffrey Paul Chan, Frank Chin, Lawson Inada, and Shawn Wong) legitimization of U.S.-born Asian American sensibility and consequent delegitimization of immigrant Asian American imaginations, while providing a rallying self-conscious call to the struggle for visibility in white-dominant U.S. society, have been widely critiqued. Indeed, the crucial value of difference as strategic theory and the many identity-based formulations it helped generate—ethnic, feminist, postcolonial and subaltern, queer, others—have not permitted such an egregiously anti-immigrant reading practice to stand. The editors' masculinist approach to defining Asian American cultural discourse, however, influenced later debate on the works by major Asian American women authors such as Maxine Hong Kingston and Amy Tan. David Hsin-Fu Wand's *Asian-American Heritage: An Anthology of Prose and Poetry* (1974), elaborating further on Asian American literature, added Korean American authors to the mix.[3] Aside from these anthologies and their introductions, the period before 1982 is relatively scant of Asian American literary criticism, reflecting the small number of Asian American writers visible in the United States then and what appears now as an unreceptive publishing industry and public.

Between 1982 and 1995 a number of Asian American literary critics began to articulate critical strategies that later critics would pick up (see King-Kok Cheung [1997], Elaine H. Kim [1982], Shirley Geok-lin Lim [1992], Amy Ling [1990], Stephen H. Sumida [1991], Sau-ling Cynthia

Wong [1993], and others). Their essays and books pushed the debate on what should constitute Asian American identity and broadened the notion of an Asian American canon. Elaine H. Kim's pioneering work, *Asian American Literature: An Introduction to the Writings and Their Social Context* (1982), initiated this fertile period in Asian American literary criticism; for example, her chapter examining gendered representations in Chinese American writing has provided an introduction to the contentious debates that have swirled around the reception of Frank Chin's and Maxine Hong Kingston's works. In this book-length study of Asian American literature, the first of its kind, Kim framed a field of study that foregrounded Asian American history to contextualize the authors and their works. Kim notes in her preface, "I have defined Asian American literature as published creative writings in English by Americans of Chinese, Japanese, Korean, and Filipino descent," and goes on to admit that "this definition is problematical" (*Asian American Literature*, 1982, xi). This admission underlines the controversy then and now concerning the composition of the canon, a controversy that may be seen to operate itself as a methodology and major mode of inquiry in the field. Two other pioneering works appeared around the same period. Houston A. Baker's *Three American Literatures: Essays in Chicano, Native American, and Asian-American Literature for Teachers of American Literatures* (1982) was one of the first critical texts to include Asian American literature as part of a literature curriculum. Baker's collection included a reprinting of the *Aiiieeeee!* preface as well as essays that usefully explicated Japanese American literature and Frank Chin's plays[4] for a classroom context. At the same time, Baker's collection demonstrated how Asian American literature can and should be read in a comparative frame with other ethnic productions.[5]

Toward the second half of this period, Asian American critical monographs began to appear. Stephen H. Sumida's *And the View from the Shore: Literary Traditions of Hawai'i* (1990), which looked at Hawaiian pastoral impulses as different phenomena from Western traditions, opened Asian American discourse to the significance of regionalism in its examination of Hawaii's colonial and postcolonial history. Sau-ling Cynthia Wong's *Reading Asian American Literature: From Necessity to Extravagance* (1993) examined the role of food, the operations of the doppelgänger as a racialized construct, and the theme of mobility in Asian American works. Offering an excellent interethnic literary study, Wong's study refigured archetypal images, myths, and themes, even those with Western resonance, in a specific Asian American history and cultural frame, and so produced an alternative and particularized rendering of Asian American subjectivity. Amy Ling's *Between Worlds: Women Writers of Chinese Ancestry* (1990) and King-Kok Cheung's

Articulate Silences: Hisaye Yamamoto, Maxine Hong Kingston, Joy Kogawa (1993) focused on analysis of gender in Asian American women's literature. Ling's study covered prose narratives written by women of Chinese or Chinese American ancestry published in English within the United States. Using feminist theories, Cheung argued that the trope of silence, which is common in a number of Asian American women's writing, reflected not only cultural specificity but also represented strategies for survival deployed by Asian American women characters. These silences thus can also be read as constitutive and formative rather than singularly destructive.

Also between 1980 and 1995, scholars began editing general collections and critical collections centering on the oeuvre of individual writers. Shirley Geok-lin Lim and Amy Ling's *Reading the Literatures of Asian America* (1992), divided into four thematic sections—the "Ambivalent Identities" of Asian American subjects, "Race and Gender" in Asian American literature, "Borders and Boundaries" of national and cultural identities, and "Representations and Self-Representations" from early to contemporary Asian American texts—was the first edited volume on Asian American literary criticism to be published, and it illustrated the growing multiplicity of inquiry and critical strategies in the field. Franklin Ng and his coeditors' collection, *New Visions in Asian American Studies: Diversity, Community, Power* (1994), while devoting a section to the study of literature with essays on Cathy Song's poetry and Amy Tan's *The Joy Luck Club*, focused chiefly on the ties between literary and cultural studies, thus underlining the interdisciplinary nature of Asian American literary criticism, where texts are examined as historical artifacts, political narratives, and social constructions. Shirley Geok-lin Lim provided a useful pedagogical tool with the publication of the edited volume *Approaches to Teaching Maxine Hong Kingston's* The Woman Warrior (1991), devoted to the explication of a single Asian American work. Elaine H. Kim and Norma Alarcón's *Writing Self, Writing Nation: A Collection of Essays on* Dictee *by Theresa Hak Kyung Cha* (1992), like Lim's edited collection, established the unique achievement of a single work in the Asian American canon.

Asian American criticism may be said to have entered a metacritical phase after 1995, when younger critics, contextualizing their analyses in the discursive tradition established by an older generation of scholars, created a field referentiality that enabled them to elaborate, refute, and reexamine texts in new and different ways. Contemporary Asian American criticism is traversed by theories associated with postmodernism, poststructuralism, psychoanalysis, and discourses on globalization, diaspora, transnationalism, and postcolonialism. Critical modes and strategies in place during the first and second phases have been modified and rearticulated. Today we find studies on form and genre, pioneering works on queer sexuality, and metacritical texts that examine Asian American literary criticism as its own subfield. The proliferation of directions in which Asian American criticism is being taken suggests that subfields need to be considered to understand the recurring critical strategies that have appeared over the course of the past quarter century. While this brief review of the field has mapped some of the themes that recur in Asian American critical studies, it does not attempt to recount the approaches found in every critical study nor does it seek to delimit certain books in a narrow analytical framework.

Lisa Lowe's *Immigrant Acts: On Asian American Cultural Politics* (1996) continued the debates on the constitution of Asian American identity as represented in literature. Because a number of her chapters appeared prior to the publication of this volume, Lowe's work bridges the periods we have been charting. Her study queries Asian American canon formation and analyzes cultural productions to illuminate sociohistorical issues significant to Asian American discourse. In Lowe's 1991 article "Heterogeneity, Hybridity, Multiplicity: Asian American Differences," her notion of the "heterogeneous and multiple positions" occupied by Asian Americans nicely sums up the varied methods and strategies Asian American critics had deployed to define an Asian American identity and literature. Susan Koshy's "The Fiction of Asian American Literature" (1996) takes up this notion in asserting that "Asian American literature" as a term is collapsing under the weight of its very heterogeneity. Other critics working in this metacritical fashion also view Asian American identity as changeful and shifting and track these transformations through the literature. In *Imagining the Nation: Asian American Literature and Cultural Consent* (1997), David Leiwei Li examines narratives that represent the predicament of Asian American subjectivity in a nation where that subjectivity is viewed as foreign. Sheng-mei Ma's *Immigrant Subjectivities in Asian American and Asian Diaspora Literatures* (1998), in contrast to the cultural nationalist model set up by the *Aiiieeeee!* editors and prefiguring the position taken by David Palumbo-Liu in *Asian/American: Historical Crossings of a Racial Frontier* (1999), argues for a more expansive understanding of Asian American literature and identity to include immigrant subjectivity. Palumbo-Liu tracks the fluctuating formations of Asian American identity from the modernist period to the current deterritorialized and globalized era in which bounded notions of Asian American identity have begun to collapse. His use of the slash in the term "Asian/American" marks these oscillating aspects of Asian American identity. Anne Anlin Cheng's *The Melancholy of Race: Psychoanalysis, Assimilation and Hidden Grief* (2000), focusing on the importance of acknowledging and confronting racialized grief (rather than grievance), takes up psychoanalytic theory to study Asian American identity and cultural productions.

The popularity of studies on women, gender, and sexuality in Asian American critical discourse follows on the movement of third-wave feminism. Weaving feminist theories into their readings, these studies examine representations of Asian American women as they are complicated by patriarchal symbolic systems. Some studies situate the female body as the location of struggle and through which discourses on the family and nation are allegorized. Phillipa Kafka's *(Un)Doing the Missionary Position: Gender Asymmetry in Contemporary Asian American Women's Writing* (1997) explains Asian American women's identity as it is negotiated through U.S. cultural and ideological structures and specific Asian ethnic value systems. In *Her Mother's House: The Politics of Asian American Mother-Daughter Writing* (1999), Wendy Ho, looking at the historical and material contexts for the prose narratives by Maxine Hong Kingston, Amy Tan, and Fae Myenne Ng, analyzes the generational tensions between the mother and daughter characters to argue that these texts resist patriarchal and totalizing discourses. In *The Americas of Asian American Literature: Gendered Fictions of Nation and Transnation* (1999), Rachel Lee, positing the varying intersectionalities of Asian American identity, notes "that gender and sexuality remain instrumental to the ways in which Asian American writers conceive of and write about 'America'" (3). For Patricia P. Chu, in *Assimilating Asians: Gendered Strategies of Authorship in Asian America* (2000), Asian American novels and memoirs often confront the dissonance between the U.S. ideal of democratic inclusion and the material reality of exclusionary politics, and gender plays an enormous role in texts as authors deploy different narrative strategies to compose their subject positions. Leslie Bow's *Betrayal and Other Acts of Subversion: Feminism, Sexual Politics, Asian American Women's Literature* (2001) examines how Asian American women's bodies and sexualities are symbolically tied to discourses on the nation-state to render these women as either traitors or patriots. Like Anne Anlin Cheng's study of melancholia and race, David L. Eng's *Racial Castration: Managing Masculinity in Asian America* (2001) makes use of psychoanalytic theory to understand the strategies deployed in representations of Asian American men and the intersections of gender, sexuality, and racial identity formation. Suturing Asian American diasporic identity to queer identity, his study draws together restrictive Asian American immigration policies and their deterrence to the dispersal of Asian American sexualities in the United States to render Asian American identity as a kind of queerness. In contrast, Laura Hyun Yi Kang's *Compositional Subjects: Enfiguring Asian/American Women* (2002) examines the constructions of Asian American women's identities as they have been shaped, reconstituted, and contested in various Asian American cultural productions; and like Palumbo-Liu, she uses the slash in her title to foreground the role of immigrant subjectivity in these identity formations. Helena Grice's *Negotiating Identities: An Introduction to Asian American Women's Writing* (2002), a broad-based study that contextualizes the history of Asian American women's writing over the course of the twentieth century, surveys the thematics of genre, mother-daughter writing, biraciality, and citizenship, while Patti Duncan's *Tell This Silence: Asian American Women Writers and the Politics of Speech* (2004) builds on Cheung's 1993 monograph to examine the role of speech and silence in relation to race, gender, sexuality, and national identity in works by Kingston, Cha, Kogawa, Nora Okja Keller, and Anchee Min.

Recent critical work on form and genre includes the study of Asian American performances and drama. Scholars are also beginning to explore photography, painting and other visual arts, and staged works. Josephine Lee's *Performing Asian America: Race and Ethnicity on the Contemporary Stage* (1997), one of the first Asian American genre studies, examines themes such as masculinity, realism, and reappropriations of stereotypes in plays by Frank Chin, David Henry Hwang, Wakako Yamauchi, Genny Lim, and others. According to Rocío Davis's *Transcultural Reinventions: Asian American and Asian Canadian Short Story Cycles* (2001), the formal use of the short-story cycle by Asian American and Asian Canadian writers underlies their desire to maintain control over representations of identity. Extending the Asian American canon to compare Asian American and Asian Canadian texts, Davis argues that the fragmented short-story cycle mirrors the works' transnational, globalized, and multiethnic complexities. Her thesis seeks to revise the perception of the short-story cycle as a European invention and to study it as an Asian American and Asian Canadian form that requires the reader to participate in the process of generating meaning. In *National Abjection: The Asian American Body Onstage* (2002), Karen Shimakawa argues that since the introduction of the term "Chinaman," the Asian and Asian American body in the United States has been envisaged as the "Other" and thus incapable of cultural and social integration. Following on Lee's study of Asian American drama, Shimakawa's monograph contributes to the growing scholarship on Asian American staged productions to look at the importance of Broadway musicals as well as performance politics. In contrast, Elena Tajima Creef's interdisciplinary and multimedia study, *Imaging Japanese America: The Visual Construction of Citizenship, Nation, and the Body* (2004), an analysis of photography, graphic novels, and media representations of Japanese Americans, focuses also on literary texts, chiefly in the chapter on Mine Okubo's *Citizen 13660*.

Among studies that seek to problematize and revise earlier readings, Jinqi Ling's *Narrating Nationalisms: Ideology and Form in Asian American Literature* (1998) contends that critics had interpreted early Asian American narratives primarily through a politico-historical lens. In contrast, unifying study of form with political content and addressing a gap in the field, Ling critiques Asian American literature published before 1980 according to its formal characteristics, particularly the features associated with social realism and cultural nationalism. Viet Thanh Nguyen's *Race and Resistance: Literature and Politics in Asian America* (2002) and Kandice Chuh's *Imagine Otherwise: On Asian American Critique* (2003) are more metacritical in approach. Arguing that Asian American intellectuals have tended to overread resistance into Asian American writing to privilege oppositional politics, Nguyen notes how such readings have mistaken or inappropriately obscured the complexities in particular narratives. Chuh, focusing her argument on legal discourse in Asian American narratives, contends that essentialist nation-based ethnic identities, expunging particularities to construct a unified identity, are nonetheless collapsing in an age of globalization.

This same period has seen an increase in single-author studies, particularly studies on Maxine Hong Kingston's oeuvre, many of which have been written to serve as useful pedagogical tools. In *The Art of Parody: Maxine Hong Kingston's Uses of Chinese Sources* (1998), Yan Gao surveys the Chinese myths, folktales, and customs in Kingston's work to complicate readings of diasporic and Asian American identities. Laura E. Skandera-Trombley's edited book, *Critical Essays on Maxine Hong Kingston* (1998), an extensive collection of original and archived essays on Kingston's *Tripmaster Monkey*, *China Men*, and *The Woman Warrior*, including reviews and historical context, reinforces Maxine Hong Kingston's preeminent position in the canon. Sau-Ling Wong's edited volume, *Maxine Hong Kingston's The Woman Warrior: A Casebook* (1999), covers issues and debates surrounding the memoir, genre and gender studies, explorations of Chinese American traditions, and an interview with the author. Diane Simmons's *Maxine Hong Kingston* (1999), a collection of essays and interviews, also includes a brief version of the "Ballad of Mulan," a biographical essay, and a bibliographic history of Kingston's work. E. D. Huntley's *Amy Tan: A Critical Companion* (1998) reviews Tan's career and life and offers interpretations of *The Joy Luck Club*, *The Kitchen God's Wife*, and *The Hundred Secret Senses*. Given the growing scholarship on Winnifred Eaton, Jean Lee Cole's *The Literary Voices of Winnifred Eaton: Redefining Ethnicity and Authenticity* (2002) is a timely addition to the field in its reviews of Eaton's literary career and analyses of the shifting interpretations of her oeuvre.

Recent edited collections tend to take the form of cultural studies texts. David Palumbo-Liu's *The Ethnic Canon: Histories, Institutions, and Interventions* (1995), recalling the multiethnic scope of Baker's 1982 collection, includes criticism of works by Amy Tan and David Henry Hwang. Wendy Ng and her co-editors' *Reviewing Asian America: Locating Diversity* (1995) offers two critical essays on Kingston's work. In *Between the Lines, South Asians and Postcoloniality* (1996), Deepika Bahri and Mary Vasudeva focus on South Asian and South Asian American writing, while Geoffrey Kain's *Ideas of Home: The Literatures of Asian Migration* (1997) examines the complex and deeply formative concept of "home" in narratives by Asian American and Asian transnational authors and the linkage between constructions of self and home in the immigrant psyche. King-Kok Cheung's edited collection, *An Interethnic Companion to Asian American Literature* (1997), the first comprehensive collection covering the range of nation groupings in Asian American writing since the publication of Lim and Ling's 1992 volume, historicizes Asian American literature and theorizes the field as a whole. While *Orientations: Mapping Studies in the Asian Diaspora* (2001), edited by Kandice Chuh and Karen Shimakawa, explores theories of Asian and Asian American postcolonialism, diaspora, transnationalism, hybridity, and border crossings, Rocío G. Davis and Sämi Ludwig's edited collection, *Asian American Literature in the International Context: Readings on Fiction, Poetry, and Performance* (2002), places Asian American literary criticism further in a globalized context. Davis and Ludwig's volume reflects the growing numbers of studies of Asian American literature outside the United States, especially in Europe and Asia. The internationalist frame is also evident in the publication of *Crossing Oceans: Reconfiguring American Literary Studies in the Pacific Rim* (2004), edited by Noelle Brada-Williams and Karen Chow. Russell Leong's *Asian American Sexualities: Dimensions of Gay and Lesbian Experience* (1996) offers one of the first collections on queer Asian American identity, including an essay on Hwang's *M. Butterfly*. *Q & A: Queer in Asian America* (1998), edited by David L. Eng and Alice Y. Hom, continues the examination of queer Asian American sexualities with essays on Frank Chin and on sexuality in Sui Sin Far's writing.

These queer-, transnational-, cultural studies–oriented volumes demonstrate that even as contemporary Asian American literary criticism focuses on works by a handful of Asian American writers, critics must press on to forge new critical strategies and lenses with which to examine emerging literatures and thematics. As the critical terrain shifts, reading practices will multiply, and newer critics will refute and revise positions taken by earlier scholars.

Today, a generally accepted canon of Asian American literature has emerged that includes, but is not restricted to, works by Kingston, Frank

Chin, Theresa Cha, David Henry Hwang, Amy Tan, Carlos Bulosan, Siu Sin Far, Hisaye Yamamoto, and Joy Kogawa, just to name a few. That so much attention is focused on these authors suggests that Asian American criticism continues to be dominated by East Asian American writing. However, Asian American critical scholarship is expanding with the increasing visibility of authors from different Asian American ethnic groups—South Asian, Korean American, Vietnamese, and South-East Asian American, for example. Bahri and Vasudeva's *Between the Lines: South Asians and Postcoloniality* (1996), for example, underlines the necessity to examine other national regions in Asian America. Although inclusion in the canon cannot be based simply on the need for representation of all ethnic groups, Asian American critics nevertheless must open their readings to more recent works: works by writers such as Lawrence Chua, Lan Cao, Le Thi Diem Thuy, Kien Nguyen, Lydia Kwa, Ghalib Shiraz Dhalla, Sigrid Nuñez, and others.

Dana Takagi, addressing the neglect of queerness in Asian American criticism, notes, "while there has been a good deal of talk about the diversity of Asian American communities, we are relatively uninformed about Asian American subcultures organized specifically around sexuality" ("Maiden Voyage," 2000, 547). Russell Leong's (1996) and David Eng's (2001) collections have begun to address this neglect, but more critical inquiry is called for, considering the increasing representations of queer characters in works by Catherine Liu, Larissa Lai, Willyce Kim, T. C. Huo, Bino Realuyo, Justin Chin, Norman Wong, Helen Zia, Ameena Mair, Shyam Selvadurai, and others. Critical examinations of representations of class in Asian American writing have also been largely absent. Further, while the focus on novels and memoirs and to some extent drama has resulted in probing analyses, similar attention has not been given to Asian American poetry and visual texts. Finally, Jinqi Ling's work on the formal presentations of Asian American narratives points to the need for more studies on aesthetics in Asian American literature. Asian American literary criticism is in a fertile moment, when intersecting disciplines, identities, genres, and histories all suggest productive tensions that trouble, complicate, and multiply meanings and interpretation.

This book taps into this moment of crisis and opportunity to foreground the dense and dynamic complexity of evolving bodies of texts that, as much as they are insistently categorized as Asian American, are simultaneously interrogated and categorized as Other: Filipino, Vietnamese, South Asian, Hmong, Korean, Southeast Asian, and so forth. When the first Asian American literature anthologies appeared in the 1970s, their editors had no compunction in dividing the map of the field into Chinese and Japanese American writing, with Filipino American as a hardly visible minority, occupied by two authors, Carlos Bulosan and Jose Garcia Villa.

Today, in the first decade of the twenty-first century, no editor of a comprehensive Asian American anthology could possibly omit Korean American writing, with its rich range of talents such as Theresa Hak Kyung Cha, Chang-rae Lee, Myung Mi Kim, and more recent authors such as Suki Kim and Susan Choi. Among South Asian American authors, Bharati Mukherjee is now accompanied by writers such as Meena Alexander, Chitra Divarakuni, and Agha Shahid Ali; and Filipino American writing, besides the novels of Jessica Hagedorn and Han Ong, displays an energetic diversity of its own in anthologies such as *Brown River, White Ocean: An Anthology of Twentieth-Century Philippine Literature in English* (1993), *Returning a Borrowed Tongue: Poems by Filipino and Filipino-American Writers* (1995), and *Flippin': Filipinos on America* (1996). The publication of Southeast Asian American collections such as *Tilting the Continent: Southeast Asian American Writing* (2000) and *Bamboo Among the Oaks: Contemporary Writing by Hmong Americans* (2002), and a number of South Asian American anthologies, for example, *Our Feet Walk the Sky: Women of the South Asian Diaspora* (1993), *Living in America: Poetry and Fiction by South Asian American Writers* (1995), and *Bolo! Bolo!: A Collection of Writing by Second Generation South Asians Living in North America* (2000), testify to the desire to make visible that particular thread that had, prior to the millennium, been subdued to a Chinese plus Japanese anthological construction of the Asian American imagination.

Some of these anthologies enact other kinds of crosswriting, such as this book is proposing, for example, the transnationalism that has become more commonplace as globalization expands to encompass once territorially separated discourses into a hubbub of exchanges. *Babaylan: An Anthology of Filipina and Filipina American Writers* (Nick Carbo and Eileen Tabios, 2001) places literature by national authors of the Philippines together with writing that comes specifically out of a U.S. location. The special issue of *Manoa, Two Rivers* (Summer 2002), explicitly includes "New Vietnamese Writing from America and Vietnam" and points to a strong emergence of Vietnamese American writing currently with the authors Monique Truong, Le Thi Diem Thuy, Kien Nguyen, and Alex W. Pham. What Gore Vidal had famously termed the United States of Amnesia is clearly not what is constructed in these collections, which maintain diasporic frames, binational perspectives, and shifting, provisional, and processual dialogics. Such expressions were, of course, present from as early as Edith Eaton's reinvention of herself as Sui Sin Far in *Mrs. Spring Fragrance* (1912). These inherently multiple sensibilities and her complicated, subtly psychological, and still resonant exposition of her identity as an Eurasian, prefigure what is now more popularly termed "Hapa" identity. *Intersecting Circles: The Voices of Hapa Women in Poetry and Prose* (2000) is only one such production of the texts that foreground these particular intersections. New anthologies about queer Asian American writing suggest that the intersections of sexuality and ethnic identity must be confronted and critiqued. *Q & A: Queer in Asian America* (Eng and Hom, 1998) and *Take Out: Writing from Asian Pacific America* (Bao and Yanagihara, 2001) are part of a growing trend within Asian American writing to explore thematics of queerness and sexuality.

This book focuses broadly on Asian American literary productions published between1890 and 2001 and examines textuality, stylistics, literariness, semiotics, poetics, narrativity, and critical language theories as inflected by ethnic, gender, class, national, diasporic, or linguistic identities. Together the chapters in this collection offer an impressive range of scholarship, chiefly from younger scholars, that shows exciting new work from U.S. and international universities that addresses both earlier and very contemporary Asian American works of imagination. The volume aims to place Asian American literary studies in a late twentieth- and early twenty-first-century context, taking into account the archival and interdisciplinary work that has produced fresh texts and interpretations since the earliest anthologies appeared in the 1970s.

Theoretical intersectionalities, largely invisible prior to 1990, are now crucial modes of operation in considering the discursive powers of these ethnically identified texts. Intersections of the imagination are contextualized in a historical specificity of location—viewed simultaneously as local and global, national and transnational—and they generate vibrant complex activations of forms, stylistics, temporality, thematic representations, and even an undecidability of language and identity. As well, the Asian American canon has been opened to fresh productions; they include visual representations, documentaries, videos, films, and performances. The conventional focus on novelistic narratives has been enlarged to include concerns with the strategic tactics in postmodernist and experimentalist works.

Clearly there is a need to examine transformations in the aesthetics and reception of Asian American cultural productions. After all, much has changed and is changing about the terrain of this field of study, not simply in the numbers of successful authors and types of texts that win recognition, but in the historical horizon of their reception. Asian American writing is increasingly viewed as both U.S. bounded and situated in global, transnational, and diasporic matrices. In an increasingly globalized world, students of Asian American texts must be conscious of other borders that shape ethnicity and cultural identities. In addition, while these writers are publishing in the United States, many of them are first-generation immigrant rather than U.S.-born authors (see, e.g., Li-Young Lee, Theresa Hak Kyung Cha, Lawrence Chua, Jessica Hagedorn, and others), and their works require postcolonial and postmodern conceptualizations as well as the normalizing, historicizing embedding of texts in U.S. political and social science contexts.

This book is arranged in three sections, each focusing on a major genre, as we believe that such organization will prove the most useful classification for teachers and students. The first section, on Asian American prose narratives, examines canonical or foundational texts—the prose narratives of Maxine Hong Kingston, Winnifred Eaton, Carlos Bulosan, and Hisaye Yamamoto—as well as novelistic innovations in the works of critically significant younger Asian American authors such as Chang-rae Lee and Karen Tei Yamashita. The second section examines memoirs and autobiographies; besides the usual interest in Maxine Hong Kingston's memoirs, the section surveys the autobiographical focus on childhood and the experimental "autobiographies" of Therese Cha and Winnifred Eaton. The third section looks at emergent poetic talents: Korean American Myung Mi Kim, mixed-race Korean American Kimiko Hahn, Pakistani American Agha Shahid Ali, and immigrant Mainland Chinese American Ha Jin. Together these essays expand the arena of Asian American literary criticism, moving such criticism away from the bounded cultural nationalism that ruled the anthologies of the 1970s and 1980s, and taking on the unstable, transformative, shifting identities that arise and collapse in response to forces of nationalism as well as transnationalism and globalization.

The volume begins with Cheryl Higashida's essay, "Re-Signed Subjects: Women, Work, and World in the Fiction of Carlos Bulosan and Hisaye Yamamoto." Exploring marginal women figures in Yamamoto's short story "Yoneko's Earthquake" (1951) and Bulosan's *America Is in the Heart* (1946), Higashida is particularly interested in the representation of seemingly silent women whose peripheral positions figure histories of oppression under patriarchal domination. The chapter gives an alternative understanding of agricultural and domestic labor in these narratives, in which women, even while apparently overshadowed by the homosocial bonding of working-class Asian American, Mexican, Mexican American, and Caucasian men, are seen to have an integral role. Higashida situates Bulosan's and Yamamoto's narratives firmly in a history of Popular Front politics and a framework of resistance, while simultaneously deploying Roland Barthes' notion of readerly and writerly texts to contextualize Yamamoto's heretofore overlooked experimentalism and Bulosan's social realism. Higashida's work contributes to an Asian American critical discourse on representations about or written by women. Clearly working within the framework of Cheung's *Articulate Silences: Hisaye Yamamoto, Maxine Hong Kingston, Joy Kogawa* (1993, and Gary Okihiro's *Margins and Mainstreams: Asians in American History and Culture* (1994), Higashida's chapter is concurrent with recent Asian American gender studies that include critical works by Phillipa Kafka, Rachel Lee, Wendy Ho, Patricia Chu, Leslie Bow, Patti Duncan, Helena Grice, Laura Hyun Yi Kang, and others.

In his chapter, "'Just Another Ethnic Pol': Literary Citizenship in Chang-rae Lee's *Native Speaker*," Liam Corley, exploring the ramifications of English language usage in Asian American writing, examines how the Asian American native speaker of English can still be marked as foreign. The primacy of the visual overshadows the ability of Asian American subjects to stake their claim on English as their native language and consequentially on America as home nation. His chapter urges that language, as a contested site, must lose its association with a specific ethnicity and be recognized as offering different modalities for individuals who claim it as native. Corley makes his argument paratextually, illuminating Chang-rae Lee's position as an author who inscribes Asian American experience into the very fabric of nationhood. Lee's *Native Speaker* thus makes the claim that the U.S. nation is dependent on acknowledging the heterogeneity of U.S. citizens both in political and literary terms. Corley's extensive analysis of Chang-rae Lee's publication trajectory and the text's positioning in the market echoes Patricia Chu's argument in *Assimilating Asians: Gendered Strategies of Authorship in Asian America*. While Chu emphasizes the different narrative strategies that Asian American authors deploy to counteract stereotypical gender presentations, Corley's chapter argues that the publisher's foregrounding of *Native Speaker* as Asian American works to elide the different valences and essentializing categorizations of Asian American identity that the narrative simultaneously supports and subverts.

Ruth Hsu, in "The Cartography of Justice and Truthful Refractions Found in Karen Tei Yamashita's *Tropic of Orange*," examines the representations of Los Angeles as city space in Yamashita's novel. Hsu's use of images of mapping and cartography offers a new mode of reading Yamashita's narrative and provides an alternate mapping of urban space that moves the interpretation of the novel beyond Eurocentric concepts of cartography. Although the characters attempt to ground themselves in a definitive truth about the city, the novel's swift pacing from one episode to another denies the existence of a single reality. Hsu argues that the novel's kaleidoscopic construction discourages an essentialist reading of Los Angeles as city space, even as, amid the chaos of the dystopic metropolis, characters still find a way to connect to one another.

In "'Valuing' Transnational Queerness: Politicized Bodies and Commodified Desires in Asian American Literature," Stephen H. Sohn takes up the spectacle of male prostitution in a novel set in the Southeast Asian city of Bangkok. Chua's text provides a complex portrayal of the queer Asian American individual who, although quite politically cognizant, nevertheless engages in an exploitative relationship with a prostitute named Thong. Following Viet Thanh Nguyen's theoretical positioning, Sohn argues that the novel presents a challenge to Asian American Studies in the way that the text refuses to be categorized as a resistance narrative. While the queer Asian American protagonist struggles against the commodification of his own body as an adolescent and young adult growing up in the United States, he finds himself as an adult indulging both in sex tourism and constant drug use in Bangkok. In Southeast Asia, as an "American" subject, the protagonist is located in an inescapable loop of exploitation, replication, and hedonism where his progressive knowledge of history and politics remains inefficacious.

Drawing on the research of social scientist Zygmunt Bauman, Gita Rajan's "Ethical Responsibility in Intersubjective Spaces: Reading Jhumpa Lahiri's 'Interpreter of Maladies' and 'A Temporary Matter'" examines Lahiri's short stories through the lens of pragmatic ethics. Rajan argues that, by placing characters in uncomfortably challenging ethical conundrums, Lahiri's fictions illustrate the permeability of socially constructed codes of ethics. The stories imply that these codes have become more slippery in the age of the simulacrum in which people imagine that they are detached from their actions. According to Rajan, Lahiri's focus on "responsibility grounded in reciprocity" is part of a growing emphasis on ethics in contemporary critical research. That is, in emphasizing "the need to act ethically at every stage of life," Lahiri's works are to be read as contemporary U.S. texts distinct from earlier postcolonial or diasporic writing in which memory is engaged primarily in terms of victimization and loss.

In her chapter on abjection, masculinity, and violence, Eleanor Ty, comparing Brian Roley's *American Son* and Han Ong's *Fixer Chao*, explores the predicament of transmigrancy in the narratives of Filipino immigrants and their children. Her work is an exemplar of the discourses on globalization and its relation to representation currently ascendant in much of Asian American criticism. Arguing that Filipino immigrants and their children experience dissonance when they observe material wealth in the United States but are trapped in laboring class positions, Ty queries the troubling theme of gender subjectivity when young Filipino men find themselves stripped of masculinity in America. Attempting to gain a measure of agency, characters in these novels participate in destructive acts that place them in a temporary position of power. However, these acts cannot obtain for them the objects of wealth and power they desire, and they are finally left bereft of any sense of community and fulfillment.

Part II opens with "Begin Here: A Critical Introduction to Asian American Childhood," in which Rocío Davis notes that the sheer number of Asian American autobiographies focusing on childhood (Davis

identifies at least twenty) warrant an investigation into the function of rec-
ollected narratives of childhood in Asian American autobiography. Drawing on autobiographical genre theories, particularly on Richard Coe's
"myth of childhood," Davis examines Asian American autobiographies
from Yan Phou Lee's *When I Was a Boy in China* (1887) to contemporary
memoirs to refigure what is usually perceived as a Eurocentric approach
to genre studies. She analyzes the historical development of these autobiographies as they move from native informant sociological texts to works
that problematize Asian American identities. The portrayal of childhood
in these autobiographies exemplifies the invasion of the private sphere
by the public as well as the process of enculturation that all immigrants
experience, be they children or adults.

Katherine Hyunmi Lee's chapter, "The Poetics of Liminality and Mis-
Identification: Winnifred Eaton's *Me* and Maxine Hong Kingston's *The
Woman Warrior*," argues that these Chinese American women's autobiographies challenge and subvert masculinist preconceptions of the autobiography. Addressing identity politics represented in the autobiographies of
marginalized females, Lee's chapter forms part of a larger move to explore
valences of feminism in Asian American literature, using, for example, the
reading strategies that characterize Anne McClintock's *Imperial Leather:
Race, Gender, and Sexuality in the Colonial Context* (1995) and Sheri
Benstock's essay "Authorizing the Autobiographical" (1997). Tracing the
lineage between Eaton's and Kingston's works, she reads Kingston's memoir against Eaton's autobiographical novel *Me* (1915) to locate Eaton's
work in a broader U.S. canon. Lee uses both genre and feminist critical
theory to unpack the different, formal, often fragmented techniques—
Eaton's text anticipating narrative strategies later used in *The Woman
Warrior*—that these Asian American women autobiographers deployed
to represent their lives.

In "Nation, Immigrant, Text: Theresa Hak Kyung Cha's *Dictee*,"
Srimati Mukherjee investigates the ways in which Cha aligns herself
with Korean nationalist Yu Guan Soon to highlight the tensions between
(post)colonial and immigrant identity and to reinscribe Soon's resistance
to Japanese imperialism as a way of underscoring, through analogy, the
trauma of immigration and the resilience needed to voice the ethnic self
in the United States. Drawing upon Kumari Jayawardena's *Feminism and
Nationalism in the Third World*, Mukherjee argues that in *Dictee*, active
revolutionary work is gendered as female. Cha rejects the static female
nationalist that Spivak and others have critiqued and instead positions
women as "superobjects" in opposition to diverse manifestations of oppression. Mukherjee's chapter looks at silence and absence in the text to
analyze how these gaps represent the slow loss of ethnic identity stem-
ming from colonization and immigration. These absences are countered,

however, by biographical elements that generate a collective, feminist autobiography founded on resistance.

Robert Grotjohn's "Kimko Hahn's 'Interlingual Poetics' in *Mosquito and Ant*" incorporates Julia Chang's concept of interlingual poetics—where poetry has the potential to "change the shape and sounds of dominant languages like English by pushing the language to its limits and breaking it open or apart"—to focus on Hahn's transgressive free play of language. According to Chang, interlingual poetics serves to reimagine and invest language with radical potential and to subvert dominant modes of discourse. Hahn destabilizes normative linguistic conventions, Grotjohn notes, by forcing readers, through the act of reading poetry, to act as translators. Linking transgression and translation, Grotjohn reads Hahn's poetry in light of its subversion of dominant masculine and orientalist practices. In Hahn's poetry, males are defined by female discourse and it is the East that constructs the "West."

Josephine Nock-Hee Park, in "Composed of Many Lengths of Bone: Myung Mi Kim's Reimagination of Image and Epic," examines Kim's poetry in the tradition of American modernism, particularly in its relation to Ezra Pound's theory of the Image. In conjuring Imagism, Kim not only establishes a place for herself in the Euro-American poetic canon but also "forces the American Orientalist poetic renewal to confront the neocolonial maneuvers of American intervention in the Far East." Kim's "Dura" follows in the line of the American long poem, first introduced by Walt Whitman and later deployed by both Pound in *The Cantos* and Theresa Hak Kyung Cha in *Dictee*. "Dura" therefore serves as a rewriting of the modernist epic. Park reads "Dura" as mimetic of the Korean American poet's movement from Korea to the United States and also as representing diasporic figures in general.

Maimuna Dali Islam, in "A Way in the World of an Asian American Existence: Agha Shahid Ali's Transimmigrant Spacing of North America and of India/Kashmir," looks at Ali's poetry in relation to his life to argue that, although the poet was frequently taken as a figure who easily negotiates biculturality, the poetry, in fact, is riven with tension and anxiety. Islam draws on the postcolonial theoretical and critical work of Jahan Ramazani and Homi Bhabha to read *The Country Without a Post Office*, the collection of poetry that Ali published after having lived in the United States for some fifteen years. Islam notes the changes in Ali's poetry as it evolves from materials grounded on the narrator's knowledge of and intimacy with Kashmir to psychological distance and anxiety over betrayal of the homeland. The poet's sense of Kashmir changes from a place that exists in the present to one that exists in the past; it becomes less a home and more a memory. Finally, Islam argues, Ali's poetry loses its viability as a method for restoring a connection to that memory of an absent home.

In a similar move, Zhou Xiaojing, in her chapter "Writing Otherwise than a 'Native Informant': Ha Jin's Poetry," argues that Ha Jin's poetry complicates current, predominant strategies of identity politics. Ha Jin, unlike most better known U.S. race commentators, ascribes to universality in his words, "there is truth that transcends borders and time." Although the poet's adherence to universality may seem outmoded and even problematical, embedded as the concept is in a European Enlightenment discourse, Zhou contends that Ha Jin's representations of "universals" are ultimately subversive because they are founded in the "particulars" of Chinese cultural identity. Ha Jin's poetry embodies the possibilities of literature to reclaim the humanity of those who have been dehumanized, not by denying particularities of cultural difference or historical specificities, but by imagining what transcends these particularities.

A central assumption underlies this collection: that Asian American literature can no longer be viewed as merely a minor ethnic province of a domestic American canon. The transnational texts discussed in this volume are grounded in specific sites, but they also feature decentering themes and aesthetics that reflect the dynamics and trajectories of Asian American transits. The works of Theresa Hak Kyung Cha and Ha Jin, for example, compel critics to regard Asian American ethnicity also as a global identity formation. This rereading implicitly carries over into the materialist histories in which these texts are to be considered. Hence the title and trope of reading across sites and transits suggest the transmigratory, translational, settling and unsettling, peopling of imaginations that had always been a feature of Asian American writing (as in Eaton's and Bulosan's works), and that has become more urgently remarkable in the late twentieth century and into the twenty-first.

NOTES

1. See Sau-ling Wong's essay, "Denationalization Reconsidered: Asian American Cultural Criticism at a Theoretical Crossroads," *Amerasia Journal*, 21: 1–2 (1995): 1–28.

2. Yan Phou Lee's *When I Was a Boy in China* (1887) was discussed in Elaine H. Kim's *Asian American Literature: An Introduction to the Writings and Their Social Context* (1982)

3. See Amy Ling's "Teaching Asian American Literature" for more on these three early anthologies.

4. These essays were "An Introduction to Frank Chin's *Chickencoop Chinaman* and *The Year of a Dragon*" by Dorothy Ritsuko McDonald and "Of Place and Displacement: The Range of Japanese-American Literature" by Lawson Fusao Inada.

5. Karin Meissenburg's *The Writing on the Wall: Socio-Historical Aspects of Chinese American Literature* (1986), which provided a generalized mapping of Chinese American literature, has remained relatively neglected.

WORKS CITED

Bahri, Deepika, and Vasudeva, Mary, eds. *Between the Lines: South Asians and Postcoloniality.* Philadelphia: Temple University Press, 1996.

Baker, Houston A. Jr. ed. *Three American Literatures: Essays in Chicano, Native American, and Asian-American Literature for Teachers of American Literature.* New York: MLA, 1982.

Bao, Quang, and Yanagihara, Hanya, eds. *Take Out: Queer Writing from Asian Pacific America.* New York: Asian American Writers' Workshop, 2000.

Benstock, Shari. "Authorizing the Autobiographical," in *Feminisms: An Anthology of Literary Theory and Criticism.* Robyn R. Warhol and Diane Price Herndl, eds. (pp. 1138–1154). New Brunswick, NJ: Rutgers University Press, 1997.

Bow, Leslie. *Betrayal and Other Acts of Subversion: Feminism, Sexual Politics, Asian American Women's Literature.* Princeton, NJ: Princeton University Press, 2001.

Brada-Williams, Noelle, and Karen Chow, eds. *Crossing Oceans: Reconfiguring American Literary Studies in the Pacific Rim.* Hong Kong: Hong Kong University Press, 2004.

Carbo, Nick and Eileen Tabios. *Babaylan: An Anthology of Filipina and Filipina American Writers.* San Francisco, CA: Aunt Lute Books, 2000.

Chan, Jeffrey Paul, Frank Chin, Lawson Fusao Inada, and Shawn Wong, eds. *Aiiieeeee! An Anthology of Asian American Writers.* New York: New American Library, 1974.

Cheng, Anne Anlin. *The Melancholy of Race: Psychoanalysis, Assimilation and Hidden Grief.* New York: Oxford University Press, 2000.

Cheung, King-Kok. *Articulate Silences: Hisaye Yamamoto, Maxine Hong Kingston, Joy Kogawa.* Ithaca, NY: Cornell University Press, 1993.

Cheung, King-Kok, ed. *An Interethnic Companion to Asian American Literature.* Cambridge: Cambridge University Press, 1997.

Cheung, King-Kok, and Yogi, Stan, eds. *Asian American Literature: An Annotated Bibliography.* New York: MLA, 1988.

Chua, Lawrence. *Gold by the Inch.* New York: Grove Press, 1998.

Chu, Patricia P. *Assimilating Asians: Gendered Strategies of Authorship in Asian America.* Durham, NC: Duke University Press, 2000.

Chuh, Kandice. *Imagine Otherwise: On Asian Americanist Critique.* Durham, NC: Duke University Press, 2003.

Chuh, Kandice, and Shimakawa, Karen, eds. *Orientations: Mapping Studies in the Asian Diaspora.* Durham, NC: Duke University Press, 2001.

Cole, Jean Lee. *The Literary Voices of Winnifred Eaton: Redefining Ethnicity and Authenticity.* New Brunswick, NJ: Rutgers University Press, 2002.

Creef, Elena Tajima. *Imaging Japanese America: The Visual Construction of Citizenship, Nation, and the Body.* New York: New York University Press, 2004.

Davis, Rocío G. *Transcultural Reinventions: Asian American and Asian Canadian Short Story Cycles.* Toronto: TSAR Publications, 2001.

Davis, Rocío, and Sämi Ludwig, eds. *Asian American Literature in the International Context: Reading on Fiction, Poetry, and Performance.* Munster: Lit Verlag, 2002.

Duncan, Patti. *Tell This Silence: Asian American Women Writers and the Politics of Speech.* Iowa City: University of Iowa Press, 2004.

Eaton, Winnifred. *Me: A Book of Remembrance.* New York: Century, 1915. Jackson: University of Mississippi Press, 1997.

Eng, David L. *Racial Castration: Managing Masculinity in Asian America.* Durham, NC: Duke University Press, 2001.

Eng, David L., and Alice Y. Hom, eds. *Q & A: Queer in Asian America.* Philadelphia: Temple University Press, 1998.

Far, Sui Sin. *Mrs. Spring Fragrance and Other Writings.* Urbana and Chicago, IL: University of Illinois Press, 1995.

Gao, Yan. *The Art of Parody: Maxine Hong Kingston's Use of Chinese Sources.* New York: Peter Lang, 1998.

Grice, Helena. *Negotiating Identities: An Introduction to Asian American Women's Writing.* Manchester: Manchester University Press, 2002.

Hara, Marie and Nora Okja Keller. *Intersecting Circles: The Voices of Hapa Women in Poetry and Prose.* Honolulu, Hawaii: Bamboo Ridge Press, 1999.

Ho, Wendy. *In Her Mother's House: The Politics of Asian American Mother-Daughter Writing.* Walnut Creek, CA: Alta Mira, 1999.

Hsu, Kai-Yu, and Palubinskas, Helen. *Asian-American Authors.* Boston: Houghton Mifflin, 1972.

Huntley, E. D. *Amy Tan: A Critical Companion.* London: Greenwood, 1998.

Inada, Lawson Fusao. "Of Place and Displacement: The Range of Japanese-American Literature." *Three American Literatures: Essays in Chicano, Native American, and Asian-American Literature for Teachers of American Literature* (254–65). Houston A. Baker, Jr., ed. New York: MLA, 1982.

Jen, Gish. *Mona in the Promised Land.* New York: Vintage, 1997.

Kafka, Phillipa. *(Un)Doing the Missionary Position: Gender Asymmetry in Contemporary Asian American Women's Writing.* Westport, CT: Greenwood, 1997.

Kain, Geoffrey. *Ideas of Home: The Literature of Asian Migration.* Lansing: Michigan State University Press, 1997.

Kang, Laura Hyun Yi. *Compositional Subjects: Enfiguring Asian/American Women.* Durham, NC: Duke University Press, 2002.

Kim, Elaine H. *Asian American Literature: An Introduction to the Writings and Their Social Context.* Philadelphia: Temple University Press, 1982.

Kim, Elaine H., and Alarcón, Norma, eds. *Writing Self, Writing Nation: A Collection of Essays on Dictee by Theresa Hak Kyung Cha.* Berkeley, CA: Third Women Press, 1992.

The Kitchen Table Collective, ed. *Bolo! Bolo: A Collection of Writing by Second Generation South Asians Living in North America.* Mississauga, Onterio: South Asian Professionals' Networking Association, 2000.

Koshy, Susan. "The Fiction of Asian American Literature." *Yale Journal of Criticism* (1996): 316–46.

Lee, Josephine. *Performing Asian America: Race and Ethnicity on the Contemporary Stage.* Philadelphia: Temple University Press, 1997.

Lee, Rachel. *The Americas of Asian American Literature: Gendered Fictions of Nation and Transnation.* Princeton, NJ: Princeton University Press, 1999.

Lee, Yan Phou. *When I Was a Boy in China*. Boston: Lothrop, Lee, and Shepard, 1887.

Leong, Russell, ed. *Asian American Sexualities: Dimensions of the Gay and Lesbian Experience*. New York: Routledge, 1996.

Li, David Leiwei. *Imagining the Nation: Asian American Literature and Cultural Consent*. Stanford, CA: Stanford University Press, 1997.

Lim, Shirley Geok-lin, ed. *Approaches to Teaching Kingston's* The Woman Warrior. New York: MLA, 1991.

Lim, Shirley Geok-lin and Cheng Lok Chua, eds. *Tilting the Continent: Southeast Asian American Writing*. Moorhead, Minnesota: New Rivers Press, 2000.

Lim, Shirley Geok-lin, Mayumi Tsutakawa, and Margarita Donnelly, eds. *The Forbidden Stitch: An Asian American Women's Anthology*. Corvallis, CA: Calyx, 1989.

Lim, Shirley Geok-lin, and Ling, Amy, eds. *Reading the Literatures of Asian America*. Philadelphia: Temple University Press, 1992.

Ling, Amy. *Between Worlds: Women Writers of Chinese Ancestry*. Elmsford, NY: Pergamon, 1990.

———. "Teaching Asian American Literature." *Heath Anthology Newsletter*. Washington, DC: Georgetown University Press, 1996.

Ling, Jinqi. *Narrating Nationalisms: Ideology and Form in Asian American Literature*. Oxford: Oxford University Press, 1998.

Lowe, Lisa. *Immigrant Acts: On Asian American Cultural Politics*. Durham, NC: Duke University Press, 1996.

———. "Heterogeneity, Hybridity, Multiplicity: Asian American Differences." *Diaspora*, 1 (1991): 24–44.

Ma, Sheng-mei. *Immigrant Subjectivities in Asian American Asian Diaspora Literatures*. Albany: SUNY Press, 1998.

McDonald, Dorothy Ritsuko. "An Introduction to Frank Chin's *Chickencoop Chinaman* and *The Year of a Dragon*." *Three American Literatures: Essays in Chicano, Native American, and Asian-American Literature for Teachers of American Literature* (229–54). Houston A. Baker, Jr., ed. New York: MLA, 1982.

McClintock, Anne. *Imperial Leather: Race, Gender and Sexuality in the Colonial Contest*. New York: Routledge, 1995.

Meissenburg, Karin. *The Writing on the Wall: Socio-Historical Aspects of Chinese American Literature, 1900–1980*. Frankfurt: Verlag für interkulturelle Kommunikation, 1986.

Moua, Mai Neng, ed. *Bamboo Among the Oaks: Contemporary Writing by Hmong Americans*. St. Paul, Minnesota: Minnesota Historical Society Press, 2002.

Ng, Franklin and Judy Yung, Stephen S. Fugita, and Elaine H. Kim et al. eds. *New Visions in Asian American Studies: Diversity, Community, Power*. Pullman: Washington State University Press, 1994.

Ng, Wendy L., Soo-Young Chin, James S. Moy and Gary Okihiro, eds. *Reviewing Asian America: Locating Diversity*. Pullman, WA: Washington State University Press, 1995.

Nguyen, Viet Thanh. *Race and Resistance: Literature and Politics in Asian America*. Oxford: Oxford University Press, 2002.

Okihiro, Gary Y. *Margins and Mainstreams: Asians in American History and Culture*. Seattle: University of Washington Press, 1994.

Ong, Aiwha. *Flexible Citizenship: The Cultural Logics of Transnationality*. Durham, NC: Duke University Press, 1999.

Palumbo-Liu, David. *Asian/American: Historical Crossings of a Racial Frontier*. Stanford: Stanford University Press, 1999.

Palumbo-Liu, David, ed. *The Ethnic Canon: Histories, Institutions, and Interventions*. Minneapolis: University of Minnesota Press, 1995.

Rustomji-Kerns, Roshni. *Living in America: Poetry and Fiction by South Asian American Writers*. Boulder, CO: Westview Press, 1995.

Shimakawa, Karen. *National Abjection: The Asian American Body Onstage*. Durham, NC: Duke University Press, 2002.

Simmons, Diane. *Maxine Hong Kingston*. New York: Twayne, 1999.

Skandera-Trombley, Laura E., ed. *Critical Essays on Maxine Hong Kingston*. New York: Twayne, 1998.

Sumida, Stephen H. *And the View from the Shore: Literary Traditions of Hawai'i*. Seattle: University of Washington Press, 1991.

Takagi, Dana. "Maiden Voyage: Excursion into Sexuality and Identity Politics in Asian America," in *Contemporary Asian America: A Mulitdisciplinary Reader*. Min Zhou and James V. Gatewood, eds. New York: New York University Press, 2000.

Wand, David Hsin-Fu, ed. *Asian-American Heritage: An Anthology of Prose and Poetry*. New York: Pocket Books, 1974.

Women of South Asian Descent Collective, ed. *Our Feet Walk the Sky: Women of the South Asian Diaspora*. San Francisco, CA: Aunt Lute Books, 1993.

Wong, Sau-Ling Cynthia. *Reading Asian American Literature: from Necessity to Extravagance*. Princeton, NJ: Princeton University Press, 1993.

———. "Denationalization Reconsidered: Asian American Cultural Criticism at a Theoretical Crossroads." *Amerasia Journal*, 21: 1–2 (1995): 1–28.

———. *Maxine Hong Kingston's* The Woman Warrior: *A Casebook*. Oxford: Oxford University Press, 1999.

Yamamoto, Hisaye. "Wilshire Bus." *Seventeen Syllables and Other Stories*. New Brunswick, New Jersey: Rutgers University Press, 2003.

I.   FICTION

1   Re-Signed Subjects

Women, Work, and World in the Fiction of
Carlos Bulosan and Hisaye Yamamoto

CHERYL HIGASHIDA

THE POETICS OF INARTICULATION

In a 1950 article on the latest crop of minority writers, fellow author
Ward Moore contrasts the aesthetics of Hisaye Yamamoto's and Carlos
Bulosan's work as follows:

> Except that both are serious writers, the two have little in common. Miss
> Yamamoto, like most contributors to "little" magazines, is a classicist,
> occupied with form and texture, extremely conscious in her approach;
> Mr. Bulosan is a romantic who is so moved by the force of emotion that
> he carries his effects to his readers by sheer passion. His literary disci-
> pline is fundamental, evidently established in the very process of learning
> to put words together efficiently; Miss Yamamoto's is obviously imposed
> and clearly requires constant enforcement. She experiments, even at the
> risk of stumbling and floundering. Mr. Bulosan's footing is surer, for
> his path is narrower; she is an intellectual, he is an artist. ("A Letter,"
> 1950, 5)

Clearly impressed with Bulosan's social realism at the expense of what
is presented as Yamamoto's contrived formal experimentation, Moore
hits upon what appears to be a fundamental difference between the two
writers: the passion in Yamamoto's writing is often hidden—indeed, unrecognized by Moore—within the subtexts of her intricately constructed
narratives, while Bulosan's social realism forcefully purports to tell it like
it is. The significance of these stylistic differences becomes even clearer as
Moore presents Yamamoto's and Bulosan's views on the politics of writing. The section on Yamamoto concludes with her assertion, "I have no
message . . . I don't want to tell anybody anything. I just want to write—
because writing is the easiest thing for me to do" ("A Letter," 1950, 5).

Cheryl Higashida's "Re-signed Subjects: Women, Work and World in the Fiction of Carlos
Bulosan and Hisaye Yamamoto" originally was published in *Studies in the Literary Imag-
ination*, vol. 37:1, pp. 35–60. © Copyright 2004, Department of English, Georgia State
University. Reprinted by permission.

Yamamoto's avoidance of didacticism contrasts distinctly with Bulosan's response to the question, "Why do I write?":

> In the making of the writer there are many factors. There was always something in me yearning to know other people. And I needed to explain my people to others. Then too, I was one of those trying to organize the exploited agricultural workers, many of whom were Filipinos. Writing was merely an inevitable extension of this work.

Unlike Yamamoto, Bulosan clearly has a message; consequently, writing for him is a political weapon, an "inevitable extension" of his labor organizing and his agitation for Filipinos' civil rights. In comparison, Yamamoto—"a classicist, occupied with form and texture"—appears to divorce art and politics. The distinction between the two writers can also be framed in Roland Barthes' terms: whereas Yamamoto's nondidactic, experimental work is "writable" (playful, open, and plural), Bulosan's social realism is "readable" (closed, structured, and authoritarian).

Without eliding the important aesthetic and political differences between the two writers, both Yamamoto and Bulosan need to be studied within the multicultural politics of the Popular Front, especially as it pertains to Asian Americans.[1] Strictly speaking, the Popular Front refers to the period of left-wing coalition building with "bourgeois" organizations and individuals in response to the rise of fascism in Europe and, as many argued, the United States. At this time, new social movements came into being that drew together anti-imperialist, antilynching, pro-union, and labor feminist activists and cultural workers. Popular Front multiculturalism flourished as African and Native Americans, immigrants, and their descendants articulated a new vision of democracy through recovering and reevaluating their heritage. The Popular Front is often dated from the mid- to late 1930s, but as Michael Denning, Bill Mullen, and others have shown, it lasted through the 1940s and beyond—and the work of Yamamoto and Bulosan shaped and was shaped by this alliance in ways that call attention to the convergences as much as the divergences in their political aesthetics.

In particular, Yamamoto and Bulosan enable us to understand the interpenetration of patriarchy and capitalism. Both writers develop a poetics of what King-Kok Cheung (*Articulate Silences*, 1993) calls "articulate silence" to render the alienation wrought by the oppression and exploitation of gendered and racialized subjects. Formally and thematically, Yamamoto and Bulosan explore the culturally conditioned and socially constructed silences around sexuality, which structures several of their narratives as an absent presence. This poetics of silence is also seen in the centrality that marginal characters come to occupy, such that traces of their narratives—although nearly inaudible within the plot or *syuzhet*—articulate the historical effects of patriarchal accumulation that give rise to the story or *fabula*. In order to clarify these political and aesthetic concerns, I will now turn to one of Yamamoto's best-known stories, "Yoneko's Earthquake." This in turn will provide a model for reading Bulosan's representations of first- and third-world women in his "ethnobiography," *America Is in the Heart* (hereafter AIH), and his short story, "Homecoming."

Yamamoto has been primarily studied within the rubric of Asian American literature and feminism. Critics have identified intergenerational conflict, especially between *issei* mothers and *nisei* daughters; the subordination of Japanese American women within patriarchal structures; and the impact of racism—in its institutionalized and informal manifestations—as the major themes in her work.[2] To a much lesser extent has scholarship on Yamamoto dealt with her "awareness of classism" (Cheung, *Seventeen Syllables*, 1994, 13), as King-Kok Cheung puts it.[3] But in many of Yamamoto's short stories, and especially "Yoneko's Earthquake" (hereafter "Earthquake"), it is not just class prejudice but the historical conditions of production that are integral to the "buried plot" of the text's subtle protest against racialized patriarchy and its sympathetic portrait of a rural *issei* woman's struggles as a mother, wife, and fieldworker. The "articulate silences" voiced by "Earthquake" are certainly those of the narrator's mother, but also of Marpo, the Filipino farmhand with whom the mother has a tragic affair; furthermore, their destinies are intimately linked by their relationships to the *issei* patriarch/employer.

As Cheung observes, Yamamoto often engages in "double-telling," or "conveying two tales in the guise of one" (*Articulate Silences*, 1993, 29) through the use of an unreliable narrator, in this case a young girl, Yoneko Hosoume. When her father hires Marpo, Yoneko is immediately taken by this multitalented newcomer with the mysterious but "lovely" last name that sounds "something like Humming Wing" (Yamamoto, "Earthquake," 1988, 47). Yoneko's misrecognition of Marpo's surname exemplifies the way that the text, at its surface level, does not fully comprehend Marpo's significance to the Hosoume household, or the reasons for Marpo's presence in their lives. Yet, just as the text latently bespeaks the psychosexual dynamics among Mrs. Hosoume, Mr. Hosoume, and Marpo, it renders traces of the historical forces of twentieth-century modernity that give rise to their love triangle.

The first "irrefutable fact" that Mr. Hosoume embeds in Yoneko's mind regarding Marpo is that "Filipinos in general were an indolent lot. Mr. Hosoume ascribed Marpo's industry to his having grown up in Hawaii, where there is known to be considerable Japanese influence" (Yamamoto, "Earthquake," 1988, 48). Marpo is thus shown to be a product of early Filipino labor migration from one American possession to another, a phenomenon engendered by the displacement of peasant farmers in the Philippines and the crushing of its native industry under U.S. imperialism.[4] Mr. Hosoume's mention of "Japanese influence" alludes to Hawaii's multinational labor force even as he elides its racially segregated structure, wherein Sakadas—Filipino indentured laborers in Hawaii—were at the bottom of the pecking order (Takaki, *Strangers*, 1989, 155–157). "Earthquake" articulates the permutations of this racial hierarchy of agricultural labor within the context of the mainland. Mr. Hosoume belongs to the strata of *issei* who, by dint of industry and kinship ties, moved from farm worker to farm owner or leaser and thereby incurred the wrath of agribusiness, which campaigned for the Alien Land Acts (1913, 1919) and the anti-Japanese Immigration Act of 1924. As a result of Japanese exclusion, the farm industries began recruiting Mexicans and Filipinos (McWilliams, *Factories*, 1971, 110–116). Although Japanese farmers initially hired other Japanese for the most part, they eventually took advantage of the newer pools of cheap labor comprised by these other ethnic groups; this is why, in "Earthquake," Mr. Hosoume hires Marpo as well as the Mexicans who assist in the fieldwork "on certain overwhelming days" (Yamamoto, "Earthquake," 1988, 51). According to Ronald Takaki, many Japanese growers chose to hire Filipinos "because they were single men and could be housed inexpensively" (*Strangers*, 1989, 321), a fact that Yamamoto conveys: "[Marpo] never sat down to the Hosoume table, because he lived in the bunkhouse out by the barn and cooked on his own kerosene stove" ("Earthquake," 1988, 47). Ironically, it is precisely as a bachelor that Marpo threatens Mr. Hosoume's household dominance.

Mr. Hosoume is invested only in "Marpo the best hired man" (Yamamoto, "Earthquake," 1988, 48), but we come to know Marpo best through the eyes of Yoneko. Initially put off by the fieldhand after "read[ing] somewhere that Filipinos trapped wild dogs" (47) for food, Yoneko grows interested in "Marpo the athlete, Marpo the musician (both instrumental and vocal), Marpo the artist, and Marpo the radio technician" (48), facets that Yoneko "uncover[s]... fragment by fragment every day" (49). Yoneko's list renders the selective fragmentation of the subject under capitalism: "the objectification of [workers'] labour-power into something opposed to their total personality (a process already accomplished with the sale of that labour-power as a commodity) is now made into the permanent ineluctable reality of their daily life" (Lukács, *History*, 1973, 90). Within the "factories in the field," to use Carey McWilliams's (Factories in the Field, 1971) apt phrase, "Marpo the best hired man" must exist separately from Marpo the athlete, Marpo the musician, and so forth. And in this context, "Marpo's versatility" (Yamamoto, "Quake," 1988, 49) carries the ironic resonance characteristic of Yamamoto's work:

for Mr. Hosoume, the farmhand's versatility would reside in his ability to work crops "so diverse as to include blackberries, cabbages, rhubarb, potatoes, cucumbers, onions, and canteloupes" (p. 46). For Yoneko, on the other hand, Marpo's versatility lies in what for her are the wondrous skills developed in his leisure time, and through socializing with him, she rejects the epithet "dog-eater."

It is not only Marpo's hobbies that humanize him to Yoneko and her brother, Seigo; he genuinely cares for the Hosoumes. During the eponymous earthquake, he runs to the family in the fields and "gather[s] them all in his arms, as much to protect them as to support himself" (Yamamoto, "Earthquake," 1988, 50). After Mr. Hosoume is rendered sexually and economically impotent by his near-electrocution in the course of the earthquake, Marpo and Mrs. Hosoume work more intensely and intimately, and Marpo again protects her and the children when Mr. Hosoume physically abuses his wife.[5]

Mr. Hosoume, however, perceives Marpo's concern for the family as infringement on paternal territory, and the fieldhand must be dehumanized further in order to prevent him from usurping the roles of father, breadwinner, and, as it turns out, husband: Marpo and Mrs. Hosoume become sexually involved, resulting in Mrs. Hosoume's pregnancy and subsequent abortion. These last events are revealed through the silences of the narrative when husband, wife, and children take a mysterious weekday trip into the city. On the way, Mr. Hosoume's nervousness causes him to hit a "beautiful collie"; Yoneko looks for its body during the drive home, "but the dog was nowhere to be seen" (Yamamoto, "Quake," 1988, 54). The only other clues to what has transpired are that Marpo, like the stricken dog, "was here one day and gone the next" (p. 54), and that Mrs. Hosoume tells Yoneko, "Never kill a person, . . . because if you do, God will take from you someone you love" (56). Again the text's double-voicing surfaces to imply that "someone you love" refers to both the aborted embryo and its father; similarly, the dog run over by Mr. Hosoume symbolizes the life that he forces out of his wife's body as well as the fieldhand whom he has summarily fired. Trespassing on Mr. Hosoume's property—his home, children, and wife—Marpo has "for[gotten] his place" (54) and thus must be reminded that he is "a mere Filipino, an eater of wild dogs" (55), to be dispatched as if he were a dog.[6] It is not only racialized patriarchal domination but, more fully, the shape it takes within modern capitalism that "Earthquake" critiques. In contrast to Marpo, the "bad" because human(e) worker, "good" workers for Mr. Hosoume are shown to be inhuman: "In the afternoon [Yoneko and Seigo] had perspired and followed the potato-digging machine and the Mexican workers—both hired for the day—around the field, delighting in unearthing marble-sized, smooth-skinned potatoes that both the machine and the men had missed" (55). Here Yamamoto insinuates the reduction of the men under Mr. Hosoume's employ to potato diggers, no different from the machine: "both [are] hired for the day," "both the machine and the men had missed" the potatoes that the children dig up. This subordination of man to "a mechanical part incorporated into a mechanical system" (Lukács, *History*, 1973, 89) is what we see again in Mr. Hosoume's replacement for Marpo. The new hired hand is "an old Japanese man who wore his gray hair in a military cut and who, unlike Marpo, had no particular interests outside working, eating, sleeping, and playing an occasional game of *goh* with Mr. Hosoume" (Yamamoto, "Quake," 1988, 54). The significance of the new hand is, naturally, that he poses no sexual threat whatsoever and is a companion for Mr. Hosoume rather than for his wife. But just as importantly for Mr. Hosoume, the old man is devoid of "the human qualities and idiosyncrasies of the worker" that "appear increasingly as *mere sources of error* when contrasted with these abstract special laws functioning according to rational predictions" (original emphases, Lukács, *History*, 89). For both these reasons, this latest worker on the Hosoume farm is truly the best hired hand.

Pace Yamamoto's denial of sending any message, this "writable" text does not engage solely or primarily in a ludic formalism, and while it invites the reader's participation in its interpretation or "writing," its open-endedness does not preclude political critique. Rather, through its double narration, "Earthquake" is carefully structured to represent the effects of racialized patriarchy on the Japanese American female subject, and to convey the dehumanizing symptoms of patriarchal accumulation.[7]

RECENTERING ASIAN WOMEN

Yamamoto's male Filipino farm worker is the central subject of Bulosan's *America Is in the Heart*, subtitled "A Personal History" but more accurately conceptualized as an "ethnobiography"; as E. San Juan, Jr. has observed, its protagonist, Allos, is both autobiographical and representative of the more than 30,000 Filipinos living in California in the 1930s (*Philippine Temptation*, 1996, 137). The majority of these Pinoys—as Filipinos in the United States called themselves—worked in the factories or in the field as "nomad harvesters," in the words of proletarian poet Marie De L. Welch (McWilliams, *Factories*, 1971). The oxymoronic idea of "nomad harvesters," people who cannot settle on the very land that they cultivate, captures the contradictions within monopoly capitalism's penetration of California farming; the migrant fieldhands responsible for the crops' ripening are themselves doomed to rot, "homeless," according to Welch, even as they "send the harvest home" (8). Likewise, *AIH* bears witness to the wretched conditions of this work, but where Welch's poem renders its ceaselessness ("Move and pause and move on") and invokes an essentially passive body of laborers, Bulosan conveys the growing militancy of Pinoy workers in the 1930s.

AIH, as aforementioned, would seemingly exemplify the "readable" text: although arguably its most striking feature is its sprawling representation of what Sau-ling Wong calls unmappable, "Necessitous motion" (*Reading*, 1993, 136), Bulosan structures his narrative to persuade his readers to strike a blow against fascism in all of its forms, from the irrigated Californian desert to the beleaguered Spanish Republic, through international labor solidarity in dialectical relation to popular nationalism.[8] Thus, Bulosan purports to depict the development of a political consciousness that will lead to a truly democratic American society, one whose members will be equally represented under the law, and who will fairly share in the fruits of their labor.

But the subjects of Bulosan's collectives are predominantly male: (inter)national, cross-racial labor solidarity in AIH is cemented by homosocial bonds facilitated by first- and third-world women, who often function as vessels for male-authored agendas rather than as subjects in their own right.[9] Indeed, Bulosan's inability to imagine, let alone represent, women's subjectivities can be understood by examining two contradictory statements culled from letters to friends. In a 1938 letter to Ann Dionisio, Bulosan wrote, "Throughout my life, from my fartherest [*sic*] childhood until now, I was really never close enough to a woman to know what kind of animal she is. And this is why when writing, when talking, my thoughts of women are too idealized" (*Sound*, 1960, 5). Three years later, Bulosan would say regarding a prostitute whom he had befriended, "I have some wonderful materials from her life. I will let you know what she *is*" (original emphasis, 11). In AIH, knowledge of "Woman" is both disavowed and assumed, much as it is in these letters; female characters fall into a whore/virgin dichotomy, the terms of which rest along the same patriarchal spectrum and depend on each other for meaning and impact. This paradigm appears early in the book, when Bulosan contrasts his saintly mother with a girl who defiantly attempts to force Allos's brother Macario into marriage. The whore/virgin dichotomy becomes even more pronounced once Allos immigrates to the United States. White female writers (the Odell sisters), prostitutes with the proverbial heart of gold (Marian), and drifters (Mary, who "become[s] a symbol of goodness" (AIH, 301) to Allos and the other Pinoys with whom he lives) embody the nurturing, open-armed and warm-bosomed America that Allos seeks once he enters the brutal world of Alaskan canneries, West Coast fields, and little Manilas. Other women, however, ranging from agents provocateurs (Helen) to political opportunists (the communist Lucia Simpson) to unnamed prostitutes and dance hall girls, use their sexuality to take advantage of Filipino men, even endangering their lives. Yet regardless of whether they are virgins or whores, women in Bulosan's narrative, according to Asian American literary critic Rachel Lee, "signal a lack of personal liberty" and thus "cannot participa[te] in a free community but can only act as the equivocal sign of its absence" (*Americas*, 1999, 23).[10]

However, just as we need to probe the "articulate silences" on Pinoy life in "Yoneko's Earthquake," we should attend more carefully to the text's double-voicing of the lives of working women in the first and third worlds. Manifestly silent on the specificities of women's oppression and liberation, *AIH* can be read against its masculinist mode of cultural production for its articulation of the ways in which U.S. imperialism, monopoly capitalism, and patriarchal modes of accumulation conditioned the lives of Filipino peasant women and white female workers in the United States. Unlike Yamamoto, Bulosan does not critique patriarchy but entirely subsumes sexual oppression under economic exploitation; in representing productive and reproductive forms of labor, he does not so much as acknowledge the sexual hierarchies that engender them. Still, overemphasis on the symbolic function of women in the book obscures the traces of female subjectivities that emerge, in spite of Bulosan's male-centered and paternalistic perspective.

I follow Rachel Lee's (*Americas*, 1999) critical examination of fraternal communities in *AIH* by commencing with one of its opening passages, in which Allos's brother, Leon, has returned to the family farmland in Mangusmana after fighting in World War I. Shortly thereafter, he marries only to see his wife tied to a tree and whipped by angry peasants according to a "cruel custom" (*AIH*, 7) of punishing women who lose their virginity before marriage. For Lee, this moment is the first of many in which female sexuality is shown to disrupt brotherly unity, as the couple is forced to leave the village. Although this reading is plausible, it does not accord with the narrator's interpretation of the events: "But [the whipping] was a fast-dying custom, in line with other backward customs in the Philippines, yielding to the new ways of the younger generation that were shaping out sharply from the growing industrialism" (7). Ostensibly, the text exemplifies what Kenneth Mostern has argued to be Bulosan's problematic Americanism, whereby the Philippines are backward and "primitive" (as the narrator often describes his homeland), and hence in need of the enlightenment that only "America" can provide. This is not to say that female sexuality is purely incidental, or that the narrator indicts the patriarchal, as opposed to atavistic, premises of the custom; as Lee observes, the woman is "repeatedly denied agency over her body" (21). At the same time, the text does not fault the sexual "impurity" of Leon's wife so much as the angry, "primitive" peasants, and while the narrator reveals his own patriarchal attitude toward the woman, the form of primitivism that Bulosan chooses to criticize is one whereby the traffic in women is brutally enforced.

Furthermore, it is not only Leon and Allos who are separated as a result of the tradition of policing male ownership of women; the family as a whole is affected, as the subsequent chapter reveals. To make this distinction is not simply to split hairs but to shift the grounds from an emphasis on Filipino blood brotherhood to the family—and especially the significance of Allos's mother—as they are portrayed in the first section of the book. This is an important move for two reasons. E. San Juan, Jr., has asserted that "what most readers of *America* have ignored, by virtue of dogmatism or inertia, is the whole of part I, in particular the resourcefulness, perseverance, and courage of the peasantry, which could not be fitted into an implicit Asian-American canonical paradigm" (*Philippine Temptation*, 1996, 146). Although San Juan's own work has done much to remedy this problem, much remains to be said about the dialectical relationship between Allos's childhood in the Philippines and its impact on his maturing political consciousness in the context of Pinoy labor organizing.[11] Second, attending to the significance of Part I of *AIH* to the rest of the ethnobiography, which takes place in the United States, is crucial to a feminist reading of *AIH* given the sexual demographics of Filipino migrant labor, whereby Pinoys were heavily overrepresented compared to Pinays in Hawaii and on the mainland.[12] Here I take my cue from Gary Okihiro's thoughts on recentering women within Asian American historiography: "Asian men in America were not solitary figures moving in splendid isolation but were intimately connected to women in Asia.... Recentering women extends the range of Asian American history, from bachelor societies in Hawaii and the U.S. mainland to the villages and households in Asia, in an intricate and dynamic pattern of relations" (*Margins*, 1994, 68).

Lee has reservations about this approach to overcoming the gendered boundaries of Asian American history, contending that it does not guarantee "a practice friendly, or even attentive to women, much less a feminist critique that would interrogate gender hierarchy and gender difference" (*Americas*, 1999, 9). Nonetheless, she succinctly formulates the merits of Okihiro's proposal:

> feminist criticism reconceived on this terrain would require more than the recovery of women's histories in Asian locations: it would entail, at the minimum, an account of the enabling or disabling economic and social effects on women circumscribed by such international trade and labor routes and by the gendered terms of kinship reformulated under transnational conditions. (9)

This is precisely why I find it necessary to examine Bulosan's portraits of Filipino women in *AIH*. And while a transnational paradigm for Asian American studies might not in and of itself lead to feminist critique, such an objection does not seem to be a compelling reason for not taking advantage of its potential.[13]

To return to the passage in which Leon brings home his bride, we can see how their union is impacted by the displacement of small landholding farmers. Bulosan mentions that Leon's wife "came from a poor family in the north, in the province of Ilocos Sur" (*AIH*, 6); her origins are significant here because they speak to the fact that she hails from an area of the Philippines from which men had begun emigrating to Hawaii in droves to work on the sugar plantations.[14] According to Elizabeth Uy Eviota *(Political Economy*, 1992), the percentage of households headed by women in those regions that had lost men to the Hawaiian plantations was much larger than the national average.[15] The declining number of marriageable men might account in part for why this Ilocano woman comes to wed a man from Pangasinan. Bulosan also notes that when the woman who becomes Leon's wife arrives in Pangasinan, she "hire[s] herself to one of the farmers who had more hectares of land than the others" (*AIH*, 6). This passage alludes to the beginning of a trend consequent upon Filipino peasant land dispossession, which exacerbated the unequal sexual division of labor; when it came to staple crops like corn, which Allos's father grows, "considerably more women than men were labourers: men were usually the farmers, and women the farm workers" (Eviota, *Political Economy*, 1992, 68). The sexual hierarchy is even more pronounced when we consider a later passage in which Allos's father tries to find work on another farmer's land after selling all of his own in order to provide one of his sons with money for school: "But my father was a farmer, not a hired laborer. It humiliated him to hire himself out to someone" (*AIH*, 29). Whereas the villagers positively attribute the work of Leon's wife as a hired hand to her origins within "a thrifty and industrious people" (6), it is humiliating for a man to hold the same socioeconomic position as a woman.

Like the woman who marries Leon, Allos's mother, Meteria, is a shadowy presence at the beginning of the book. But she quickly materializes as we learn why she is away from Mangusmana, where chapter 1 takes place: Meteria resides in the town of Binalonan from which she forays into other villages to barter *boggoong* (salted fish) for food that she can then sell in the market. Women's vending was delegitimized or rendered invisible by official discourses on work in the Philippines—such work literally and figuratively did not count within the U.S. census, for example, which consistently underestimated the number of female traders—but Bulosan makes it clear that Meteria's business is integral to the family's sustenance, and in particular, to financing the education of Allos's older brother Macario.[16] In keeping with the prevalent desire for education in the Philippines at the time—a desire fostered by the U.S. regime to create a suitable workforce and to squelch nationalist rebellion—Allos's parents are "willing to sacrifice anything and everything to put [his] brother Macario through high school" (*AIH*, 14). Allos wishes to emulate his brother, but the narrative frequently illustrates Macario's elitism and his insensitivity to his family's struggles to support him. For example, upon returning home his first words to Allos concerning the younger brother's appearance were:

> "Don't you ever cut your hair, brother?"
> I was speechless. I was ashamed to say anything.
> "He needs it for protection against vicious mosquitoes and flies," said my father. "It is also his shield from the sun in hot summer." (21)

Shielded from the harsh living conditions of the rest of his family, Macario only sees Allos's long hair as a lack of civilization rather than as a necessity for doing the fieldwork that finances his schooling. Although Allos's father accepts the reified consciousness that Macario has developed through "being educated in the American way" (*AIH*, 20), his mother tries to challenge Macario when he threatens to leave school unless his parents furnish him with money that they do not possess: "'We have only one hectare left, son,' said my mother, trying desperately to make my brother understand our poverty with futile movements of her hands" (22). Enmeshed within the daily details of (re)productive work, Meteria understands the immediate impact that losing their land would have on the rest of the family. The futility of her gestures is reinforced by Allos's father, however, who obviates her protest by telling Macario that they will sell the remaining land. In response, "[Meteria's] hands leaped frantically from her lap to her mouth and stayed there, stifling the protest. In one fleeting instant, [Allos] saw her hands—big-veined, hard, and bleeding in spots" (22). Like his mother, and unlike his father and brother, Allos perceives the human cost of Macario's education, which Bulosan captures through his description of Meteria's laboring hands— the first of a recurring synechdocal image that appears throughout the book whenever Bulosan conveys the dehumanization of being reduced by the profit motives of U.S. imperialism to a "hand."[17]

Although Macario successfully completes his high school degree, he cannot keep the family land from being expropriated by an absentee landowner, and when Allos's father is relegated to tilling inhospitable ground, he sends his son to town to live with his mother. In these subsequent passages depicting Meteria's trading, we come to know her best (Allos states, "It was during this period that I came to understand my mother's heart" [*AIH*, 33]), and it is not by coincidence that, of all the spheres of her life, her business is the one in which she possesses the most autonomy. As Eviota notes, "trading as productive women's work does enable [Filipino women] to engage in a variety of social exchanges which are valuable in themselves for the opportunities they provide and which do not occur in many other sectors of work available to working-class women" (*Political Economy*, 1992, 131). Also, by accompanying his mother in her travels and interactions with other peasants, Allos finds the scaffolding for his subsequent labor radicalism: "I had come upon another world that was to become a foretaste of my later struggles for a place in the sun. Selling *boggoong* and salt with my mother gave me an opportunity to meet many people and to become a part of their lives" (*AIH*, 36).

In the course of her enterprise, Meteria counters the American individualism that Macario attempts to inculcate in Allos through the example of Robinson Crusoe: "Someday you may be left alone somewhere in the world and you will have to depend on your own ingenuity" (*AIH*, 32). In a subsequent passage, Allos learns a different lesson from Meteria as the two foray into a village "where the poorest peasants lived on a barren land" (34). There they encounter a woman who begs for some of the *boggoong* that Meteria sells. "[T]hinking of the next payment on [the family] land" (35), Meteria initially hesitates to grant the woman's request to dip her hands into the salted fish but ultimately acquiesces. When Carlos starts to laugh at the woman's pathetic maneuver, Meteria reprimands him angrily: "'Someday you will understand these things,' she said, looking up at the house" (35) where the woman runs to find rice to eat with the remnants of her *boggoong*. Phrased similarly to Macario's enunciation, Meteria's injunction contrasts directly with her older son's perspective. Instead of being concerned primarily with making money for herself and her family, she tries to sustain others who are similarly or even more impoverished: "my mother gave even to those peasants who had nothing to barter in the hope that when we came around again they would be ready to pay. We were not always able to collect everything we had loaned, but my mother kept on giving our products to needy peasants" (33). It is not only Meteria's trade but her attitude toward it—privileging collective well-being over the motives of economic man—that shapes Allos's incipient politicization.

The spirit of collectivism is further rendered in a lyrical passage in which Meteria and Allos head for the village of Puzzorobio over a slippery highway:

> We waded through this dangerous road, holding onto each other firmly to keep from falling; and sometimes in our intimate grasp we communicated a rare and lovely understanding. Maybe it would be only the sudden tightening of my mother's thumb or forefinger on my arm, but the delicate message would be transmitted and it would linger in my memory. (*AIH*, 37)

More so than his interactions with his brothers heretofore, this moment of tactile communication, signaling an "unmistakable cry for help between two suffering people" (37), metaphorizes the familial bonds that Allos will try to re-create in America once Amado, Macario, and he are separately driven there by Philippine underdevelopment. And it is from this familial tie that Allos generalizes to imagine a larger collective of workers "holding onto each other firmly to keep from falling."

Juxtaposed with the familial, peasant solidarity intimated by Meteria and Allos's journey to Puzzorobio, their vending within the village leads to the boy's first clash with the native bourgeoisie in the person of an elegantly attired girl who upsets Meteria's beans in response to her admiring gaze. As Meteria retrieves the beans, Allos distances himself from her: "I was one peasant who did not crawl on my knees and say: 'It is all right. It is all right'" (AIH, 38). For Lee (1999) this passage illustrates the mother's submission to and identification with the bourgeoisie, but it is not only Meteria who displays such attitudes: Allos will later become exasperated with Macario's subservience as a servant in a white household, as well as contend with his own longing for bourgeois trappings. Furthermore, in an earlier passage Bulosan establishes Meteria's love for beauty in order to intimate the social dimensions of art. Meteria comes across a woman "who had nothing to give except a beautiful drinking jar that she had made out of the red clay in her backyard" (AIH, 33). Immediately drawn to the pottery, Meteria "gave the woman more than the pot's value" (33). In this light, Meteria appears to be attracted by the elegant girl in the market less so out of desire to belong to the bourgeoisie; rather, she longs for a beauty that Allos "had never known her to appreciate ..., but perhaps it was because she had no time to express the finer qualities in her" (33–34). Similarly, it is not until time slows for Allos—when he is hospitalized in America for tuberculosis brought on by years of malnutrition, harsh work, and cramped accommodations—that he can develop his own artistic sensibilities. And like his mother, Allos will come to value beauty over profit-mongering.[18]

Meteria never develops the class consciousness that Allos does; she is incapable, for example, of explaining to her son the meaning of a peasant revolt organized by the Colorum Party. However, Bulosan associates ignorance not with Filipino womanhood but with the political perspective of certain segments of the peasantry. Allos's father is equally ignorant of the significance of the Tayug revolt, preferring the reformist tactic of fighting for his property in court to no avail, which leads the narrator to pose the question, "What could a poor and ignorant peasant like my father do in an organization such as the provincial government of Pangasinan?" (AIH, 58). Bulosan then shows that the answer lies not in individual lobbying in the capital but in collective, armed struggle on the land where he and his mother happen to be engaged in seasonal agricultural labor. Yet they are "so deeply absorbed in [their] work that [they are] not aware of what [is] going on" (59). The narrative, however, does not simply imply that Meteria cannot understand the revolt because she is a woman; her ignorance is overdetermined by the fact that she, like her husband, has accepted the sociopolitical hierarchies of the neocolonial regime (which is why she suggests to Allos that he use his education to become a lawyer). Nonetheless, she does prefigure and shape the young Allos's radicalization through her work and, just as importantly, through her work ethic of prioritizing concern for the livelihood of other peasants—and in this sense, Bulosan reveals some of the "intimate connections" between women in Asia and Asian men in America that Okihiro wants to recenter.[19]

The Female Subjects of *America*

Like Meteria, the women whom Allos encounters when he immigrates to America can be compellingly read as threats to homosocial struggles for a specious equality dependent upon female subordination. According to Lee's reading of *AIH*, prostitutes and dance hall workers are sexually objectified under a male gaze, while female intellectuals are extensions of the mother/martyr figure exemplified by Meteria, but both "types" of women embody that which must be excluded from male working-class collectives. However, Bulosan's representations of working women in the United States are at once simpler and more complex than this inclusion/exclusion model would suggest. Through several of his female characters, Bulosan imparts the historical conditions that differentially engender women's oppression as well as empowerment, eschewing both the arrogant assumptions of knowing the "Other" in "her" singularity and the equally debilitating refusal to think beyond one's standpoint. As I have argued with respect to Part I of *AIH*, overemphasis on the text's symbolic structures of gender obscure these microlevel portraits of women's histories, which interrogate rather than reinforce the macrolevel rhetoric of homosociality. Attending more closely to Bulosan's representations of prostitutes and white female intellectuals, we see that he (mis)recognizes rather than elides the female subjects of labor, such that sexual exploitation is subsumed under economic exploitation. Nonetheless, even as Bulosan perpetuates this patriarchal form of analysis, I would argue that his representations of radical women intellectuals do not reinforce but repudiate dominant conceptions of what are properly "men's" versus "women's" spheres of praxis.

Bulosan both recognizes and disavows the laboring subject of prostitution in the episode involving Allos's encounter with Marian, who cares for him after he is nearly lynched by vigilantes for organizing Mexican lettuce workers. Along with the Odell sisters and Mary, Marian certainly is "the caring maternal figure" that is "the singular desire thematized as 'America'" (San Juan, *Philippine Temptation*, 1996, 139). Rather than simply engaging in hypostatization, however, Bulosan double-voices this woman's history. He portrays Marian as dependent and submissive ("I'll help you. I'll work for you.... What I would like is to have someone to care for" [*AIH*, 212], she tells Allos) but also strong (after finding out a lover is married, she says, "I tried to make a new life. Without illusions, I went on my way" [211]). Before sacrificing herself for Allos, dying from syphilis after selling her body to give him money, she tells him that she had worked as a dishwasher while attending college, and then had picked hops with Mexicans and "gypsies." And it is as a *working* woman that Marian initially compels Allos's attention: "I looked at Marian's hands: it was obvious that she had done manual work. Her hands were rough; the fingers were stubby and flattened at the top. My heart ached, for this woman was like my little sisters in Binalonan. I turned away from her, remembering how I had walked familiar roads with my mother." (211) If Bulosan elides Marian's work as a prostitute, which is only mentioned and not represented, he describes the economic hardships that lead her to become a sex worker. Nonetheless, Marian is external and even antithetical to Allos's labor organizing, despite the fact that her prostitution is what supports them in their brief time together.

But it is not so much that Bulosan subscribes to an ideology of working-class organizing that excludes women per se, so much as the fact that he categorizes prostitutes with the lumpen proletariat: "The gamblers, prostitutes and Chinese opium smokers did not excite me, but they aroused in me a feeling of flight" (*AIH*, 104). And the lumpen proletariat are fundamentally antirevolutionary: just as Amado, Allos's brother who becomes a bootlegger and gambler, is incapable of fighting against fascism so long as he belongs to a class that "cheat[s] Filipino farm workers of their hard-earned money" (161), the dance hall girls are structurally positioned to take away Pinoy wages: "The girl was supposed to tear off one ticket every three minutes, but I noticed that she tore off a ticket for every minute" that a cannery worker dances with her (105). Nonetheless, in an exchange with a Lompoc businessman, Allos clarifies both that Pinoys are not inherently dissolute, and that the small gamblers and prostitutes are not the true exploiters: "Well, you bring it upon yourself," [the businessman] said tonelessly. "I mean prostitution and gambling." "I don't know what you really mean," I said. "But the gambling and the prostitution are operated by three of this town's most *respectable* citizens." (original emphasis, 163). I think it is inaccurate, then, to read Bulosan's representations of prostitutes as part of a patriarchal schema that excludes all women from the (inter)national body of workers, insofar as he asserts that those women *and* men involved with the informal economies of gambling, prostitution, and drugs contribute to the oppression of Filipino farmhands.

Bulosan's exclusion of female sex workers from the radicalized working-class body also speaks to his need to desexualize the Filipino working class, in response to the hypersexualization of Pinoys. The idea that "every Filipino is a pimp" (*AIH*, 121) reinforced racial segregation and exploitation; as Bulosan documents, whites opposed the 1931 ruling in *Roldan v. Los Angeles County* that allowed Filipinos to marry white women, while antiunion vigilantism and fears of miscegenation ran together: the white men who lynch Allos and José for organizing the Mexican lettuce pickers make a point of mutilating their genitalia. To counter this sexualized construction of the Filipino body, Bulosan invests Allos with an asexual (or even antisexual) persona; an adolescent experience with a girl who partners him in a dance leaves him "trembling with cold and sudden fear" (78), while his one sexual encounter fills him with a "nameless shame" (160). Not surprisingly, his adult relations with women in the United States are platonic. Ultimately, though, this fear of sexuality buttresses Bulosan's refusal to perceive the material realities of prostitution and sexual abuse, which at best he perceives to be the bestialization of women and men; at worst, he implies that women invite violence upon themselves.

Perhaps the closest that Bulosan comes to grappling with the problems posed by the sexual exploitation of women is in a different text altogether: his short story, "Homecoming," which links the traffic in third-world women to the international labor market as it recounts the bitter return of a young Pinoy, Mariano, to his family in the Philippines. Mariano treads toward what he thinks of as "his father's house" ("Homecoming," 90), to find himself embracing only his mother and two sisters, Francisca and Marcela; unbeknownst to him up to this point, his father died a year after Mariano left for the United States. Although excited at the prospect of being with his family, he is hobbled by inarticulacy every step of the way: "He wanted to shout to [his mother] all the sorrows of his life, but a choking lump came to his throat" (91); "[h]e wanted to say something, but did not know where to begin" (93); he tells his mother and sisters, "I wanted to write, but there was nothing I could say" (94). His sisters and mother, too, are resoundingly silent, and Mariano realizes that he cannot bring himself to tell them that he has only two years left to live due to tuberculosis. However, the worst is yet to come; as Francisca weepingly retreats to another room in response to his query as to whether they have been able to manage, Marcela, who is "tougher," looks after her sister "with hard, unsentimental eyes" (94). Mariano is "frightened, knowing what Marcela could do in a harsh world," and she confirms his fears, telling him that "Sister isn't pretty any more" (94). As he regards

Marcela, he realizes that she, too, *"was not pretty any more"* (original emphasis, 94), and it is then that Mariano understands the silence of his mother and sisters: "it dawned on him that [they] had suffered the same terrors of poverty, the same humiliations of defeat, that he had suffered in America.... This was the life he had found in America; it was so everywhere in the world" (95). In his despair, he realizes that "he could not do anything at all" (95) and so departs forever after taking one last look at his sleeping family.

As with Yamamoto's stories, "Homecoming" (hereafter *H*) is replete with articulate silences, although ones conditioned by different social circumstances than those surrounding her *issei* and *nisei* characters.[20] For Mariano, what initially renders him wordless is his failure to strike it big in America, thereby letting his family down: "He wanted to tell [his sister] the truth, but could not. How could he let them realize that he had come home because there was no other place for him in the world?" (*H*, 93). For Francisca and Marcela, the nameless shame is their need to work as prostitutes in order to support themselves and their incapacitated mother. Unable to admit their respective downfalls to each other, the family cannot unite in the realization that Mariano achieves on his own (and that serves as the message of the story): that what they perceive to be their individual failures are pieces of a larger picture of systemic poverty, defeat, and exploitation. And so Mariano, with only two years left to his life ("Two years: How much could he do in so brief a time?" [94]), leaves home for the last time.

What is striking about "Homecoming" is that it fundamentally centers on the problem of prostitution and yet cannot fully grapple with it. On one hand, Bulosan renders the wretchedness of prostitution precisely by leaving it all but unnamed, resorting to a euphemism that captures the sisters' desperation all the more forcefully. He furthermore makes it clear through Mariano's reaction that Francisca and Marcela are not to be morally or personally indicted: "he felt like smashing the whole world; he was burning with anger. He was angry against all the forces that had made his sisters ugly" *(H*, 94). The same forces that drive Mariano to the United States are what lead him to return home empty-handed, leave his family destitute, and render sex work the only viable path for his sisters to supplement their paltry income as laundresses and nursemaids. At the same time, Mariano's systemic analysis of their situation does not account for the fact that they labor within a socioeconomic structure that is not only capitalistic but patriarchal. Symptomatic of the narrative's phallocentrism is the fact that only the male protagonist comes to possess the correct understanding of the family's oppression. And having comprehended his sisters' situation, Mariano is allowed to flee from rather than struggle with it; the question of Francisca's, or at least the stronger Marcela's, coming to a political consciousness of prostitution is never raised. Nonetheless, the story conveys the message that both migrant fieldhands and prostitutes are exploited workers. The story's failed conclusion functions as a negative rather than positive call to resist collectively the degradation of Filipino women and men, whose fates are inextricably linked under global capitalism: it is because Mariano is alone that he cannot act on his newfound knowledge.

Bulosan's (mis)recognition of the laboring subject of prostitution—his registering her economic but not her sexual subordination—extends to his treatment of white female intellectuals, who (along with Marian and the vagabond, Mary) embody the good America that Allos hopes to enter. Most notably, Eileen Odell, with "her almost maternal solicitude" and lack of "disturbing sensuousness" (AIH, 234), is "the America [Allos] had wanted to find" (original emphasis, 235). Lee argues that these maternal women serve as vessels "speaking male privilege, advocating political agendas set by men, and inadvertently securing brotherly bonds even as they remain marginal to their bonding," thereby "rendering antisexist work irrelevant" (Americas, 1999, 33). The rhetoric of brotherhood that is so flagrant in the book would seem to support this claim, as in the passage where Allos describes what he sees as the significance of the novels that Eileen gives him: "These writers collectively represented to me a heroism of the spirit, . . . so gloriously had they succeeded in inspiring a universal brotherhood" (AIH, 238). Despite the fact that her sister is a proletarian writer, Eileen gives Allos only books by male authors who become part of his international brotherhood; among the other women Allos meets, Dora Travers's stated reasons for leaving for the Soviet Union have entirely to do with U.S. racism; Laura Clarendon in AIH, Bulosan's fictionalized version of proletarian writer Clara Weatherwax, is notable not for her representations of female radicalism but for featuring a Filipino hero in her novel. Such women apparently prioritize racial and economic oppression to the exclusion of sexual oppression.

Yet despite Bulosan's inability to perceive the intersectionality of gendered and racialized social formations, his portraits of the women whom he encounters in the hospital render some of the ways that, for female intellectuals "the Depression decade opened up a range of possibilities that enabled their entry into what Leslie Rabinehas called 'feminine historicity'" (cited in Rabinowitz, 39). While they were not exempt from the raging impoverishment of the general population, "[t]hirties women speak of History—with a capital 'H'—intervening into their lives and remaking them" (Rabinowitz, 39). The political exigencies and heightened awareness of systemic crises provided some women with opportunities to insert themselves into, and to rearticulate the terms of struggles of global significance. Dora Travers, a Soviet émigré, tells Allos that she is returning home to have her child of part-Filipino parentage "born in a land without racial oppression" (p. *AIH*, 227). Although Allos indicts her for abandoning America (just as he faults expatriate writers such as Hemingway and Wright), he shows how Dora politicizes motherhood to protest America's illegitimization of interracial children. In Alice Odell, Allos finds inspiration for his own desire to become an organic intellectual. Initially intimidated by what he perceives to be her "social position" (228) as a noted proletarian writer, he realizes that "her life and mine were the same, terrified by the same forces" (230). Like him, she hails from a farming family dispossessed of their land but manages to become "a writer of promise" who "was writing a novel about her starved childhood" (228)—which, of course, is what the autobiographical Allos aspires to do at this point. And she is another woman who travels to the Soviet Union in accordance with her stance on racial and economic equality. When Alice departs, she asks Eileen to look after Allos in the hospital. Eileen proves to be her sister's intellectual peer; she furnishes the bulk of the books that comprise Allos's education and discusses the Spanish Civil War with him. Allos is almost as impressed by Laura Clarendon, "a young woman who had just written a proletarian novel about the Northwest. This book, the first of its genre to appear in the early thirties, had won a national contest" (238), and most notably for Allos, features a Filipino protagonist who counters the typical "stockpile characters in entertaining stories" (239).[21] Although she does not continue to write, Allos asserts that Laura "had helped to shape" (239) the proletarian fiction movement.

Bulosan undoubtedly idealizes these women such that they figure as surrogate mothers for Allos, but they are still unmistakably represented as political subjects who participate in the struggle over the meaning of the war between Labor and Capital.[22] To characterize them as mouthpieces "speaking male privilege, advocating political agendas set by men" (Lee, *Americas*, 33) is to imply that fascism, racism, and labor organizing are primarily male rather than female concerns. Even as Bulosan evacuates women's issues from the fight for democracy, reiterates the phallocentric rhetoric of brotherhood, and naturalizes women as caregivers, he testifies to the ways in which white female radical intellectuals refuted the very logic of brotherhood that he adopts, which would segregate women from the most salient political issues of the time.

Bulosan's conflicted representations of female subjectivity result in double-voiced narratives of women's lives that are frequently at odds with each other. On one hand, we have one-dimensional figures who conform to the whore/virgin dichotomy. This reiteration of patriarchal stereotypes is symptomatic of the text's anxieties around female sexuality, anxieties due in large part to the sexualization of anti-Filipino discourses, according to which Pinoys preyed upon white women. We can read Bulosan as addressing such racist conceptions by deploying a poetics of silence to represent the "problem" of sexuality. For example, the material realities of sex work are absented from the text as a result of the fear and disgust that Allos exhibits toward women's sexuality. Thus, even as Allos's repudiation of sex challenges racist stereotypes, it leaves the patriarchal component of these stereotypes intact: women are no longer virginal prey but whorish predators; either way, they are not political subjects as men are.

Nonetheless, it is also through this poetics of silence that Bulosan breaks out of the whore/virgin binary, contributes to the recentering of Asian women within Asian America, and represents the empowerment of the first-world female intellectual. The story "Homecoming" thematizes silence in order to name prostitution as a form of women's exploitation. At the same time, this recognition of the laboring subject of the prostitute is also misrecognition, since sexual subordination is simply equated with economic exploitation. Within *AIH* itself, strong female characters emerge from and repudiate the caricatures of womanhood that populate the narrative. Meteria and Alice Odell, for example, are not simply saintly mothers but historical agents for whom experiences of oppression have dialectically engendered modes of resistance (Meteria's trading business, Alice's writing). Consequently, they lay the foundations for Allos's politicization not as hyperfeminized caregivers/nurturers/teachers, but as women who contest the ideologies of imperialism in their daily lives.

INARTICULATION: YAMAMOTO AND BULOSAN

Although Yamamoto and Bulosan would seem to be more different than similar in their aesthetics and political visions, both writers interrogate the opposition between "readable" and "writeable" texts. Yamamoto's "open-ended," "polyvocal" work in fact enacts a critique of patriarchy and capitalism, while Bulosan's social realism is ridden with historically conditioned contradictions around sexual equality that disrupt the "closed" and "authoritarian" narrative of brotherhood. In the fiction of both Yamamoto and Bulosan, we find a poetics of articulate silence that represents the gendered and racialized subjects of imperialism. The silences of "marginal" characters such as Yamamoto's Pinoy fieldhand and Bulosan's third-world women are central to these textual engagements with mutually constitutive systems of racial, sexual, and economic oppression. Furthermore, in linking the cultural and political interests of Asian and working-class America, in demanding that the United States institute at home the democracy for which it waged war abroad, Yamamoto and Bulosan helped to extend the relevance of the Popular Front multiculturalism beyond the 1930s. The interethnic and interracial forms of solidarity that they advocate in their fiction, demanding more than formal equality to include the redistribution of resources, presage what has been called "radical multiculturalism" today.

Finally, while Bulosan's Popular Front political stance has been criticized for its "universalizing vision that oftentimes occludes the specificities and differences among various political movements" (Lee, *Americas*, 1999, 35), I would argue that one of the key contradictions within *AIH* is its lack of a sufficiently universalizing vision, one that conceives of gender and sexuality as central to implementing social equality. Allos's internationalism does not substantially recognize the pressing need to contest the subordination of women, which leads Lee to argue that "[w]hile national directives on sexuality may underlie Bulosan's textual subordination of women as laboring subjects, it may also be the case that this cross-racial, egalitarian brotherhood (of labor) is secured by the objectification of women" (*Americas*, 1999, 37).

I have shown, however, that Bulosan's cross-racial, egalitarian alliances are not only or even primarily ones with brothers under the skin, but also with antifascist women who emerge as subjects situated uneasily within discourses yoking national identity and motherhood. More broadly, I want to delink historical materialism from phallocentrism, and class-based solidarity from patriarchal relations. I am not saying that historical materialism will guarantee feminist analysis, or that class solidarity will guarantee the abolition of patriarchy, but that the one is not necessarily inherent to the other, as post-Marxist feminists would imply. Moreover, to jettison totalizing analyses for partial explanatory grids would leave us without the explanatory and political force to mobilize for the liberation of all subjects oppressed, however differentially, within global capitalism. Allos's evolving perceptions of the connections between fascism in California and Spain, Mariano's realization that prostitutes and migrant fieldworkers suffer "the same terrors of poverty," and the linkage implied between Mrs. Hosoume's disempowerment and Marpo's exploitation are critical revelations that propel the reader toward a systemic understanding of oppression and resistance, as well as a fuller sense of Bulosan's and Yamamoto's craft.

NOTES

1. I thus focus on Bulosan much more than on Yamamoto. This is not due to the fact that I agree with Moore's privileging of Bulosan, but because his work, especially *America Is in the Heart*, is more overtly engaged with the Popular Front than Yamamoto's, and one of my concerns is to reexamine the significance of the Popular Front to Asian American Studies, and vice versa. That said, I recognize that Yamamoto's place within the Popular Front needs to be more fully examined.

2. See, for example, Cheung, *Articulate Silences*; Elaine H. Kim, "Hisaye Yamamoto: A Woman's View"; Robert T. Rolf, "The Short Stories of Hisaye

Yamamoto, Japanese American Writer"; and Stan Yogi, "Legacies Revealed: Uncovering Buried Plots in the Stories of Hisaye Yamamoto."

3. One prominent example of Yamamoto criticism that focuses on her conceptualization of class is Donald C. Goellnicht's "Transplanted Discourse in Yamamoto's 'Seventeen Syllables.'" Grace Kyungwon Hong examines the relationship between race and property rights in Yamamoto's memoir, "A Fire in Fontana."

4. Interestingly, Marpo's age is given as twenty-seven, and given that the setting for the story is the 1933 Long Beach earthquake, his year of birth would have been 1906, when the first Filipinos recruited to work the sugar plantations arrived in Hawaii (Cordova, Filipinos, 1983, 26). Another possible context for "Yoneko's Earthquake" is the marriage between a Pinoy and a Japanese American girl in Stockton that eventually led to a Filipino boycott of Japanese stores in the winter of 1929–30 when the girl's father attempted to have the marriage annulled (Lasker, Filipino Immigration, 1931, 17).

5. Many critics have observed that Yamamoto is not unsympathetic to the plight of issei men, and this is the case in "Earthquake." The narrator notes that this instance is "the first time [Mr. Hosoume] had ever laid hands on [Mrs. Hosoume]" (53), and we are led to understand that Mr. Hosoume's violence, though inexcusable, is his way of compensating for the fact that he is only nominally the household head after the earthquake: he "stay[s] at home most of the time" and occasionally "[has] supper on the stove when Mrs. Hosoume came in from the fields" (51). Mr. Hosoume is as much trapped within the patriarchal structure of the family as he is a perpetrator of it.

6. It is Yoneko who thinks of Marpo as a "dog-eater" after his departure, because she is hurt by what she perceives to be his abrupt desertion of her. Her willingness to readopt the racism that she had overcome earlier speaks to its prevalence and, in particular, her internalization of her father's views (he again denigrates Filipinos to Yoneko's face when she paints her nails, prompting him to tell her that she "look[s] like a Filipino" [52]). The insidiousness of this racism is further shown by the fact that Yoneko in turn teaches her brother to think of Marpo as "an eater of wild dogs."

7. I would not go so far as Donald Goellnicht does to say that Mrs. Hosoume's and Marpo's affair is a form of interracial, cross-class solidarity ("Transplanted," 1994, 189–190) because the narrative does not provide us with either of the characters' perspectives on their relationship, let alone its political implications, nor does the narrator comment on them even indirectly.

8. As many critics have noted, AIH was initially received as an immigrant Horatio Alger story celebrating the virtues of American democracy. Marilyn Alquizola (1991) resolves the seemingly competing narratives of subversion and assimilation by plausibly arguing that the latter strategically masks the former; Kenneth Mostern (1994), on the other hand, contends that AIH is ultimately unsubversive—an interpretation that dismisses, I think, the critical edge of Bulosan's Americanism. Sau-ling Wong (1993) views the narrator's political development as fundamentally at odds with the book's representations of unmappable, "Necessitous motion" (136), which forecloses any ideological closure. Similarly,

Lisa Lowe (1996) contests the book's classification as a bildungsroman, arguing that "the narrative captures the complex, unsynthetic constitution of the immigrant subject between an already twice-colonized Philippine culture, on the one hand, and the pressure to conform to Anglo-American society, on the other" (45). Wong's and Lowe's deconstructive readings usefully probe the book's ideological oscillations and contradictions, but they short-shrift its representations of radical political development.

9. See especially Rachel Lee's (1999) discussion of *AIH*. More thoroughly than critics have heretofore done, Lee's feminist intervention within scholarship on *AIH* elucidates the ways in which the text naturalizes female subordination in the process of imagining revolutionary communities.

10. Michael Denning makes a similar argument but does not explore its implications for the configuration of female subjectivity in *AIH*: "The alliance of brothers provokes a profound ambivalence: if it marks the narrative's moments of utopian solidarity, it is haunted by sexual aggression and anxiety" (*Cultural Front*, 1998, 275).

11. In addition to San Juan's numerous writings on Bulosan, see Slotkin (2000), "Igorots and Indians: Racial Hierarchies and Conceptions of the Savage in Carlos Bulosan's Fiction of the Philippines," and Campomanes and Gernes's "Two Letters from America: Carlos Bulosan and the Act of Writing" (*MELUS* 15.3 [Fall, 1988]: 15–46). As Campomanes and Gernes show, a fuller reading of the first section of *AIH* entails looking beyond the book itself and attending to the wide range of Bulosan's work, which gets overlooked as a result of *AIH*'s canonical status within Asian American letters. Timothy Libretti's (1995) dissertation chapter on *The Power of the People*, Bulosan's novel on the Huk rebellion, is another important example of Bulosan scholarship that examines the centrality of Filipino history and culture to the writer's revolutionary imagination.

12. In Hawaii, between 1906 and 1934, an already disproportionate number of Filipino men to Filipino women grew increasingly lopsided; the Third Wave of Filipino immigration (1930–34) was comprised of 13,488 men and 610 women (Cordova, *Filipinos*, 1983, 29). In the early 1940s, Carey McWilliams wrote that "[t]he present ration of men to women in the mainland Filipino population is 14 to 1, by comparison with a ration of 1.1 to 1 in the general population" (*Brothers*, 1944, 232).

13. That said, I understand Lee's caution against conflating a transnational framework with feminist analysis. For example, drawing on Julia Kristeva's notion of "woman's time" ("Women's Times," 1983, 188–213), San Juan has commented upon what he sees as *AIH*'s most original feature, its juxtaposition of realism with "[c]omedy and the flows/flights of the unconscious" (*Philippine Temptation*, 1996, 145), which redefines "the earth, the soil, and the maternal psyche/*habitus* as the ground of meaning and identity" (144). Although I would agree with San Juan's theorization of the drives motivating the narrator and their influence on the formal properties of the text, he ignores the traces that the narrative renders of the material conditions of women's work. For a critique of Bulosan's simultaneously maternalized and sexualized envisioning of the earth, see Wong (*Reading*, 1993, 120, 132).

14. Cordova periodizes the First Wave of Filipino emigrants to Hawaii as lasting from 1906–19 (*Filipinos*, 1983, 29). Allos tells us that he "must have been five years old" when Leon comes home, and if we assume that this is somewhat autobiographical, Leon's return would date around 1918, which makes sense given that he is returning from World War I. Elizabeth Uy Eviota asserts that "[b]y 1932, there were 125,000 Filipinos employed in Hawaii, most of them Ilocanos and most of them men" (*Political*, 1992, 72).

15. "In these areas [which had sent labor abroad, such as Ilocos, or which had sent labor to other provinces], the proportion of households headed by women ranged from 13 to 19 percent of the total. In the country as a whole about 11 percent of households were headed by a woman. Women heads of households put in more hours of work as they bore the double burden of both household and paid work to an even greater extent" (Eviota, *Political*, 1992, 72).

16. See Eviota (*Political*, 1992, 65–70) for a discussion of the definitions of women's productive work as they appear in the U.S. censuses between 1903 and 1960.

17. For example, when Allos first meets the white prostitute Marian, he is drawn to her in part because of her rough hands which indicate that "she had done manual work" (*AIH*, 211); seeing that Macario's hands "were hard and calloused, like my mother's" (241), leads to Allos's comprehension of "the meaning" of his parents' toil and sacrifices; reencountering his brother Amado after the latter's stints as a racketeer, Allos notices the "long scar" on his "mud-caked" hand (295, 297), which shows how he has been "roughly handled" (295).

18. Nonetheless, Bulosan later attributes Allos's "appreciation of beauty" to his experiences of snaring birds with his brother Luciano, who keeps them for their "esthetic pleasure" rather than for their usefulness (*AIH*, 53).

19. This chapter on the Tayug revolt also documents the double burden that his mother carries, engaging in wage labor and childcare simultaneously. While harvesting the rice she "stopped now and then to feed Marcela [her daughter], undoing her rough cotton blouse to her waist and putting her dark, pointed nipple into the baby's hungry mouth. Then she would put her in a makeshift hammock and go back to work" (*AIH*, 59).

20. San Juan replicates rather than explores the story's silence on prostitution in his brief reading of it, folding it back into what for him is the more pressing absence, that of the father (*Philippine*, 1996, 159–160).

21. The novel that Allos describes is Clara Weatherwax's *Marching! Marching!* (1935), which centers around the Aberdeen, Washington, strike of lumber and shipping workers, including Mario, a Pinoy. Weatherwax's book won the 1935 *New Masses* prize for the best new proletarian novel.

22. My reading of the white female intellectuals in *AIH* coincides with Lina B. Diaz de Rivera's interpretation of Helen O'Reilly, the "Woman Reader/Teacher" in Bulosan's short story, "As Long as the Grass Shall Grow." Diaz de Rivera argues that, despite Bulosan's initial association of Helen with the Virgin Mother/Mother Nature, she becomes the propagator rather than object of knowledge who links "woman reading and men laboring" ("Female Principle," 1989, 14).

Works Cited

Alquizola, Marilyn. "Subversion or Affirmation: The Text and Subtext of *America is the Heart,*"in *Asian Americans: Comparative and Global Perspectives.* Shirley Hune, Hyung-chan Kim, et al. eds. (pp. 199–209). Pullman: Washington State University Press, 1991.

Bulosan, Carlos. *America Is in the Heart.* Seattle: University of Washington Press, 1946.

———. "Homecoming," in *On Becoming Filipino: Selected Writings of Carlos Bulosan.* E. San Juan, Jr., ed. (pp. 90–96). Philadelphia: Temple University Press, 1995.

———. *Sound of Falling Light: Letters in Exile.* Ed. Dolores S. Feria. Quezon City, PI: University of Philippines Press, 1960.

Campomanes, Oscar V., and Todd S. Gernes. "Two Letters from America: Carlos Bulosan and the Act of Writing." *MELUS* (Fall, 1988): 15–46.

Cheung, King-Kok. *Articulate Silences: Hisaye Yamamoto, Maxine Hong Kingston, Joy Kogawa.* Ithaca, NY: Cornell University Press, 1993.

———, ed. *"Seventeen Syllables."* New Brunswick, NJ: Rutgers University Press, 1994.

Cordova, Fred. *Filipinos: Forgotten Asian Americans.* Dubuque, Iowa: Kendall/Hunt Publishing Co., 1983.

Denning, Michael. *The Cultural Front: The Laboring of American Culture in the Twentieth Century.* London: Verso, 1998.

Diaz de Rivera, Lina B. "The Female Principle and Woman Reading in Carlos Bulosan Story."*Dillman Review,* 37 (1989): 11–14.

Eviota, Elizabeth Uy. *The Political Economy of Gender: Women and the Sexual Division of Labor in the Philippines.* London: Zed Books, 1992.

Goellnicht, Donald C. "Transplanted Discourses in Hisaye Yamamoto's *Seventeen Syllables,*" in *Seventeen Syllables.* King-Kok Cheung, ed. (pp. 181–93). New Brunswick, NJ: Rutgers University Press, 1994.

Hong, Grace Kyungwon. "'Something Forgotten Which Should Have Been Remembered': Private Property and Cross-Racial Solidarity in the Work of Hisaye Yamamoto." *American Literature,* 71 (1999): 291–310.

Kim, Elaine H. "Hisaye Yamamoto: A Woman's View," in *"Seventeen Syllables."* King-Kok Cheung, ed. (pp. 109–17). New Brunswick, NJ: Rutgers University Press, 1994.

Kristeva, Julia. "Women's Time," in *The Kristeva Reader,* ed. Toril Moi. 188–213. Oxford, U.K.: Basil Blackwell Ltd, 1983.

Lasker, Bruno. *Filipino Immigration to Continental United States and to Hawaii.* Chicago: University of Chicago Press, 1931.

Lee, Rachel. *The Americas of Asian American Literature.* Princeton, NJ: Princeton University Press, 1999.

Libretti, Timothy. "U.S. Literary History and Class Consciousness: Rethinking U.S. Proletarian and Third World Minority Literatures." Dissertation University of Michigan, 1995.

Lowe, Lisa. *Immigrant Acts: On Asian American Cultural Politics.* Durham, NC: Duke University Press, 1996.

Lukács, Georg. *History and Class Consciousness*. Cambridge, MA: MIT Press, 1973.

McWilliams, Carey. *Brothers Under the Skin*. Boston: Little, Brown and Company, 1944.

———. *Factories in the Field*. [1939]. Santa Barbara: Peregrine Publishers, 1971.

Moore, Ward. "A Letter From Southern California." *San Francisco Chronicle*, January 15, 1950, p. 5.

Mostern, Kenneth. "Why Is America in the Heart?" *Hitting Critical Mass: A Journal of Asian American Cultural Criticism*, 2 (1994): 35–65.

Okihiro, Gary Y. *Margins and Mainstreams: Asians in American History and Culture*. Seattle: University of Washington Press, 1994.

Rabinowizt, Paula. *Labor and Desire: Women's Revolutionary Fiction in Depression America*. Chapel Hill, NC: University of North Carolina Press, 1991.

Rolf, Robert T. "The Short Stories of Hisaye Yamamoto, Japanese American Writer," in *"Seventeen Syllables."* King-Kok Cheung, ed. (pp. 89–108). New Brunswick, NJ: Rutgers University Press, 1994.

San Juan, Jr., E. *The Philippine Temptation: Dialectics of Philippines-U.S. Literary Relations*. Philadelphia: Temple University Press, 1996.

Slotkin, Joel. "Igorots and Indians: Racial Hierarchies and Conceptions of the Savage in Carlos Bulosan's Fiction of the Philippines." *American Literature*, 72 (2000): 843–66.

Takaki, Ronald. *Strangers from a Different Shore: A History of Asian Americans*. New York: Penguin Books, 1989.

Weatherwax, Clara. *Marching! Marching!* New York: The John Day Company, 1935.

Wong, Sau-ling Cynthia. *Reading Asian American Literature: From Necessity to Extravagance*. Princeton, NJ: Princeton University Press, 1993.

Yamamoto, Hisaye. "Yoneko's Earthquake," in *Seventeen Syllables and Other Stories*. (pp. 46–56). Latham, NY: Kitchen Table—Women of Color Press, 1988.

Yogi, Stan. "Legacies Revealed: Uncovering Buried Plots in the Stories of Hisaye Yamamoto," in *"Seventeen Syllables."* King-Kok Cheung, ed. (pp. 143–60). New Brunswick, NJ: Rutgers University Press, 1994.

2   "Just Another Ethnic Pol"

Literary Citizenship in Chang-rae Lee's Native Speaker

LIAM CORLEY

ON JUNE 6, 1993, THE GOLDEN VENTURE, a freighter carrying nearly three hundred illegal Chinese immigrants, ran aground only a few miles away from downtown New York City. Aware that the vessel was taking on water, crewmembers ordered the passengers to swim ashore in the choppy, cold waters. Of the two hundred or so who complied, at least eight drowned before reaching the shore. The remaining passengers were rescued by Coast Guard cutters and subsequently arrested and imprisoned by the U.S. government. Major television networks provided live coverage of the rescue and arrest operations, and thousands of U.S. citizens watched the Chinese immigrants splash to shore or be plucked from the water with gaffes and ropes.[1] Literally and figuratively, the Golden Venture of these hopeful emigrants was broken upon the forbidding shore of New York City, and their journey toward freedom and prosperity was interpreted to the U.S. public through a media spectacle of abjection.

Written around the time of the Golden Venture and published in 1995, Chang-rae Lee's Native Speaker (1995, cited as NS hereafter) includes a version of the incident at the crucial transition point of the novel. Native Speaker charts the rise and fall of a mayoral challenger who is racially marked as an immigrant in the turbulent New York political scene of the mid-1990s. John Kwang, a Korean American businessman and city council member, runs a permanent campaign for mayor in his attempt to become part of the political "vernacular.... a larger public figure who was willing to speak and act outside the tight sphere of his family" (139). Kwang's challenge to the racially insular New York political establishment leads to his eventual disgrace and exile to Korea. By depicting the infiltration of Kwang's political organization and deportation of his key

Liam Corley's "'Just Another Ethnic Pol': Literary Citizenship in Chang-rae Lee's Native Speaker" originally was published in Studies in the Literary Imagination, vol. 37:1, pp. 61–81, © Copyright (2004), Department of English, Georgia State University. Reprinted by permission.

supporters as illegal immigrants, Lee demonstrates the powerful array of forces brought to bear against the full political enfranchisement of New Yorkers who can be constructed as both racially minoritized and foreign. However, Lee complicates this reading of Kwang by framing the story of his destruction with the anti-bildungsroman of another Korean American, Henry Park, the narrator of the novel and the corporate spy who infiltrates Kwang's campaign. The self-doubts and tensions resulting from Henry's infiltration of Kwang's political organization and concurrent attempts at rapprochement with his white American wife, Lelia, restate on a microlevel the questions of political and social enfranchisement posed by Kwang's sabotaged campaign for mayor. The interplay of the domestic and political plotlines allows Lee to critique the dominant paradigms of racial enfranchisement in the United States and the status of "ethnic" literatures within the U.S. publishing industry and literary canon. The book's title draws attention to Lee's self-conscious complicity in the racial marketing of his book, and the ambiguity surrounding the identity of the novel's "native speaker" (Park? Lelia? Kwang? Lee, the author?) sharpens the edge of the novel's paratextual critique. Ultimately, the novel moves beyond New York and its political/publishing establishment to address the roles that immigrants have historically played in the literature and politics of the United States, a trajectory that Lee traces from the colonial era through the democratic vision of Walt Whitman and into the dystopic world of twentieth-century media culture.

The *Golden Venture* incident contributed to fears among the U.S. populace of an "Asian invasion" facilitated by unscrupulous snakeheads and international networks of organized criminal syndicates (Smith, "Migrant," 1997, 2). The exceptionally harsh treatment meted out to the Chinese immigrants on the *Golden Venture* was meant to serve as a warning to aspiring immigrants around the world that they were not welcome in the United States. Most of the passengers on the *Golden Venture* were imprisoned for periods extending into years, and the last of the *Golden Venture* detainees were not released until fifty-three of them were pardoned by President Bill Clinton in March 1997, nearly four years after their disastrous entry into the country. The White House press secretary's comments on the occasion of the pardon give a clear summary of the reasons for their long imprisonment: "The Administration's policy of detaining smuggled aliens has deterred smuggling by organized criminal syndicates, resulting in a sharp decrease in the number of alien smuggling vessels that have reached U.S. shores. Moreover, the newly enacted immigration bill's provisions that permit the expeditious exclusion of smuggled aliens have significantly strengthened our ability to deter alien smuggling."[2]

Although the insistent repetition of "alien" is meant to distinguish the government's policy from the reception given to legal immigrants, the treatment of the *Golden Venture* detainees is only a more extreme version of the exclusionary attitude faced by other racially marked minorities within the national culture of the United States. Lisa Lowe describes the exclusion of Asian immigrants from full participation in modern U.S. society as the result of a "national memory [that] haunts the conception of Asian American, persisting beyond the repeal of actual laws prohibiting Asians from citizenship and sustained by the wars in Asia, in which the Asian is always seen as an immigrant, as the 'foreigner-within,' even when born in the United States and the descendant of generations born here before" (*Immigrant*, 1996, 5–6). Due to the a priori construction of Asians as inescapably foreign within a domestic visual economy, brokered by the mass media and popular culture, Asian Americans are not fully naturalized into U.S. national culture. Thus, the threat of detention and expulsion aimed at "smuggled aliens" can also be used against Asian Americans who threaten in some way the economic or political dominance of citizens who are visually constructed as "native." Like all citizens of non–Anglo European descent, Asian Americans undergo a double scrutiny when attempting to enjoy the full spectrum of rights guaranteed to Americans regardless of race. Lee invokes this experience of containment, exclusion, and potential expulsion throughout his novel.

Lee prefigures the significance of the *Golden Venture* incident to the Kwang subplot by incorporating the image of a shipwreck into the narrative fulcrum point of Henry and Lelia's relationship. Separated previously by their culturally disparate responses to the death of Henry's mother and the accidental smothering of their biracial son, Henry and Lelia undergo an emotional journey of reconstruction after the death of Henry's father. This journey leads eventually to Henry's reconciliation with both Lelia and the ambivalent effects of the cultural heritage passed on to him through his familial relationships. Henry and Lelia's restored physical intimacy represents the turning point in the subplot of marital accommodation. Lee connects the scene of conjugal intimacy with the crisis of political visibility through a careful use of descriptive language that associates sex with the arrival of smuggled immigrants: "She wanted me to push down on her harder. I couldn't, so then she turned us around and pushed down on me, the slightest grimace stealing across her face. Her body yawed above me, buoyed and restless. I held on by her flat hips, angling her and helping her to let me in. Mixed-up memories, hunger. It was like lonesome old dogs, all wags and tongues and worn eyes. This was the woman I promised to love. This is my wife." (*NS*, 230)

Initially, Henry is in a traditional posture of male dominance, but Lelia demands that Henry exert more leverage—more dominance—than he is capable of in order to consummate her physical pleasure and his full penetration of her body. She therefore inverts their sexual/political roles and uses the greater (social) force afforded to white bodies to facilitate Henry's sexual penetration of her body and the consummation of her pleasure. In the moment of reversal, Lelia's body is figured as a seafaring vessel, causing her to be associated with the immigrants of the *Golden Venture* and also invoking the memory of Puritan immigration. Henry is pushed down into the floor as Lelia's body "yawed above." Buoys and angling (tacking) continue the maritime imagery as Henry "help[s] her to let me in." The crossing of boundaries is here described as a consensual act in which the Pilgrim Lelia is nonetheless a gatekeeper who must initiate a more aggressive form of hospitality in order to experience sexual union. Lee returns to this metaphor at the novel's close when Henry and Lelia ironically agree to call Henry a "long-term guest. Permanently visiting" in Lelia's apartment (347). Lelia's contractual claim to her apartment can be understood as a legal fiction that requires her to undercut her own "natural" rights in order to live with her husband, another instance in which she must acknowledge the superior status afforded to her as a white American and the concomitant need for her to restore the historical equivalence between immigrants like her and Henry within America's political and economic worlds. The definitive shift in the novel is signaled by the transition from past tense into present. Henry declares, "This is my wife," and for the rest of the novel the use of the present tense indicates the unfixed possibilities of narrative development, a syntactic expression of hope in contrast to the narration of past events, which heretofore gave the novel its determined atmosphere of helplessness and despair.

Upon this transition, Henry and Lelia reminisce freely about their pasts and speculate about their pasts' effects on the course of their lives. A barrage of past events, landmarks, and cultural icons serve to illustrate the political and historical currents that have affected Henry and Lelia's sense of themselves: World War II, the Korean War, the Statue of Liberty, Ellis Island, a ferry ride, spy thriller movies, racial slurs. In a redoubling of their physical union, they make love again. Afterward they watch the local news. The first report they watch involves the most recent in a string of cabbie murders. New York cab drivers are drawn from all nations, "recently arrived Latvians and Jamaicans, Pakistanis, Hmong" (*NS*, 246). The cabbies are an exploited immigrant labor pool, perpetually in motion as they fulfill their instrumentality as a means of transporting white subjects from work to home, and from home to work and play. The vulnerability of these immigrants to economic violence is emphasized by the physical violence that circumscribes their lives. Linguistic barriers, a theme I will treat at some length, exacerbate the problem. Henry muses, "I wonder if the Cuban [cabbie] could even beg for his life so that the killer might understand. What could he do? *Have mercy*, should be the first lesson in this city, how to say the phrase instantly in forty signs and tongues" (original emphasis, 246). An appeal to mercy is the most urgent lesson for immigrants to America, and tellingly, the linguistic barriers indigenous to the city require facility in "forty signs and tongues." Like the *Golden Venture* incident, Lee adapts the story of cabby murders from readily available news sources. Since 1990, 243 cabbies have been murdered in New York City, and the tragedies emerge into the media as "news" whenever a sufficiently large number of murders occur close enough together in time to constitute a "string." In addition to dramatizing the spectacular nature of violence against immigrants, the narration of the cabbie murders also suggests the existence of panethnic coalitions constructed by the negative force of that violence. Other instances of panethnic grouping appear in *Native Speaker,* most notably the *ggeh* managed by Kwang and Hoagland's Glimmer & Co., but these groupings are also the result of economic expediency and political contingency, negative origins that Lee appears to portray as teleologically bounded by the logic of racial exclusivism.[3]

Following the cabbie story is the fictionalized version of the *Golden Venture* incident, a "small freighter that runs aground" with fifty smuggled Chinese men who leap from the sides of the boat into the choppy waters. Lee's fictional Chinese immigrants face the same treatment as their historical models: "The drowned are lined up on the docks beneath canvas tarps. The ones who make it, dazed, soaked, unspeaking, are led off in a line into police vans" (NS, 246–247). The spectacle of shipwreck recapitulates the theme of immigrant experiences in America already associated with Henry and Lelia through Lee's description of their initial sexual rapprochement. At this point in the novel, the narrative tension flows from Henry and Lelia's sexual union into the rising subplot of Kwang's political demise. Henry and Lelia's restored intimacy is punctuated by the next news report, footage and interviews describing a bombing and double murder at Kwang's campaign headquarters. The silencing of the cabbies and the unspeaking Chinese immigrants are thematically repeated in the refusal of John Kwang's staffers to comment in the news story on the bombing of his main office. Through this litany of spectacles involving the death, silencing, and imprisonment of immigrants, the private space of rapprochement in Henry's marriage becomes linked to the public crisis of John Kwang's political fortunes. This oscillation between the personal and the private, the physical and the political, is a part of a larger strategy of articulation in which Lee's novel stands in as a commentary on New York and the fate of immigrants in the no less violent world of fact. The competition between fact and fiction, political commentary and plot development, dramatized by Lee's narrative indicates how the novel is embedded within the literary and literal context of New York, a realist and subversive narrative technique that requires attention to the historical context of New York in the 1990s in order to more fully explicate Lee's technique.

DE ROOS, NEW AMSTERDAM, AND THE PERMANENCE
OF RACIAL STRUGGLE

In early 1994, Rudolph Giuliani took over from David Dinkins as mayor of New York City. This signal transition in New York politics ushered in "Giuliani time, not Dinkins time," a phrase reportedly chanted by New York City police officers as they assaulted Abner Louima and repeatedly sodomized him with a broken-off broomstick. According to Neil Smith, the beating of Louima, a Haitian immigrant, expressed succinctly the mood of the revanchist New York politics in the mid-1990s: "Revanchism is in every respect the ugly cultural politics of neoliberal globalization. On different scales, it represents a response spearheaded from the standpoint of white and middle class interests against those people who, they believe, stole their world (and their power)" ("Which New Urbanism?" 1999, 196).[4] The attack on Louima in 1997 expressed symbolically the consummation of a politics of nativism and blame that helped determine the 1993 mayoral election. Louima's tortured body gave lurid expression in a physical register to the political climate for racially constructed immigrants. "Giuliani time" thus describes both an eruption into public discourse of violence against racially marked immigrants and a particular historical moment in which a majority of New Yorkers expressed their political and racial allegiances.

Although Rudolph Giuliani is only mentioned once by name in *Native Speaker*, "Giuliani time" is an important concept in the implicit world of the novel. Henry and his coworker Jack speculate that their employer, Dennis Hoagland, treasures a signed photograph from Giuliani in his office, a sign of Hoagland's political and cultural allegiances (*NS*, 32). Glimmer & Co., founded by Hoagland in the 1970s, is an espionage firm that focuses on immigrant populations who threaten in some way the economic or political interests of "multinational corporations, bureaus of foreign governments, [and] individuals of resource and connection" (18). Henry eventually learns that the INS is the client who has hired Glimmer & Co. to infiltrate John Kwang's campaign, and the INS uses the information provided through Henry's espionage to fulfill the general pattern of immigrant containment, brutalization, and expulsion characteristic of "Giuliani time." Instead of dealing more extensively with Giuliani, Lee establishes a *ruse* character who functions as Giuliani's stand-in. By giving the incumbent mayor a Danish name, "De Roos," Lee invokes the historical nature of New York as a long-contested site of political and linguistic allegiances as well the apartheid era government of South Africa. Founded as New Amsterdam in 1626, New York has long been the most visible site of the struggle over U.S. identity as it has been domestically and transnationally constructed.

Linguistically and ethnically diverse from its founding, the colony was held together by a common desire for profit. Conquered by the English in 1664, New York became a royal colony and grew rapidly through an influx of English settlers, but the Dutch influence persists even today, making the choice of De Roos as a character name a subtle indicator of both the permanence of ethnic difference and the dynamic of assimilation, which hides the social, economic, and political value accruing to whiteness.

Like De Roos, John Kwang makes a claim for legitimacy as the inheritor of New York's political tradition. Henry describes him as someone who didn't want to be "just another ethnic pol from the outer boroughs" (NS, 303). Instead, he would become "the living voice of the city, which must always be renewed. . . . He would stride the daises and the stages with his voice strong and clear, unafraid to speak the language like a Puritan and like a Chinaman and like every boat person in between" (304). Kwang's mark of success lies in his ability to give voice to the city as a native speaker. Language becomes the figure that equates both Puritans and Chinese as "boat person[s]," immigrants from other lands with equal claims upon the privileges of citizenship. Kwang's optimism in this regard runs up against the vested interests of Glimmer & Co.'s clients. Kwang sinks into a depression after the bombing at his headquarters, and he goes on a drinking binge that ends with a car wreck in which an underage illegal immigrant bargirl is killed. Henry's research revealing that John Kwang ran a Korean-style money club with hundreds of illegal immigrants is then leaked to the press, and Kwang's destruction is complete. In place of his dream of full political inclusion as mayor, Kwang is assaulted at his home by a crowd carrying banners reading "Smuggler Kwang" and "AMERICA FOR AMERICANS." One of them shouts, "We want our fucking future back" (331–332). Kwang's fate is largely the result of both his racial exclusion from full enfranchisement and the revanchist features of New York politics at the time. Yet Lee is careful not to paint Kwang solely as a victim of New York racism, a subject position that would have completed his emasculation as a political actor. The closing pages of the book reveal that the trigger event for Kwang's decline, the bombing and deaths at his headquarters, is ordered by Kwang himself in a fit of rage when he learns that his closest associate—another Glimmer & Co. operative—has been collecting evidence against him. Although Kwang's personal failings of rage, alcoholism, and philandering played a role in his political destruction, they would not have had such a prominent effect if the INS had not hired Glimmer & Co. to infiltrate his campaign. In his failings, Kwang is not unlike many of New York's and the United States' most successful political leaders, though the price he pays for his failings is much greater than most.

Despite his political failure, Kwang's vision of New York is more true to the city than the protests of the (presumably) white Americans who want to claim it and America exclusively as their own. As a symbol for the country, New York is a site of contestation and cultural pluralism. Home of the Statue of Liberty, Ellis Island, the Empire State Building, Wall Street, Broadway, Madison Avenue, and the United Nations, New York is used as an important symbol in both the domestic and transnational imaginary construction of nation. Each of these national and international icons maintains a dual life as representative instances of material and political connections between New York and a global urban community. New York's economic success and growth in the late eighteenth and early nineteenth centuries depended upon its participation in world systems of trade, most notably as an intermediary with China. Then as now, New York exists not solely in the domestic imagination but also as a projection of world expectations and desires. France's gift of the Statue of Liberty is a representative instance of such an exchange of approbation and obligation. Although few would go as far as Ford Madox Ford's claim in the title of his 1927 travelogue that "New York Is Not America," New York is an undeniably transitional space between the domestic and the foreign, and as such, symbolizes through its cultural centrality within the American national consciousness the hybridity of American identity.

The novel's ending display of revanchism at Kwang's home emphasizes the national fantasies that would deny historical and contemporary hybridity of American identity. The demonstrators' impassioned declarations of American purity ("America for Americans") enact what Homi Bhabha (1993) describes as the pedagogic function of the nation-state in contrast to the performative challenge brought by Kwang. In "DissemiNation: Time, Narrative, and the Margins of the Modern Nation," Bhabha analyzes modern concepts of the state as an affective and delimited unity, a homogeneity determined by its valorized history and symbols. Bhabha questions the primacy accorded to national narratives that exclude the presence of the marginal, countering their spurious portrait of domestic uniformity and tranquility with the agonistic tensions of the performative and the pedagogical. Because of the "powerful master discourse" of the pedagogical State, which busily constructs a homogenous (and wholly imagined) national origin, migrants are excluded from the cultural discourse of national construction (306).

Bhabha ultimately asks how we can recast the formative myths (narratives) of nations in a manner that accounts for the presence of marginal peoples. As the ordering principle of the nation replaces the affective ties of kin, culture, and geography, pedagogical theorists make enunciative attempts to clarify "the Other" and "the insider," much in the way that Mayor De Roos attempts to paint John Kwang as "just another ethnic pol." In the heterogeneous nation-state, dominance has been accorded to declarative and arbitrary national symbols that exclude or ignore marginal, migrant voices, which in turn leads to a despotic and imagined "homogeneity." In a remarkable gloss of Ernest Renan's aphoristic claim that a "nation's existence is . . . a daily plebiscite" ("What Is a Nation?" 1993, 19), Bhabha argues that contemporaneity and locality are more important to a nation than affective (read temporally constructed and ultimately arbitrary) ties to an envisioned or imagined past. If we construe the construction of the nation-state as iterative, liminal, and essentially performative in its contemporaneous construction, then "no political ideologies could claim transcendent or metaphysical authority for themselves" (Bhabha, "DissemiNation Time," 1993, 299). "America for Americans" would be clearly exposed as a racist ideology of exploitation and exclusion. The Statue of Liberty could be acknowledged as oscillating in the symbolic realm between the domestic matron of unifying (and homogenizing) liberty and the immigrant as naturalized foreign gift. However, before engaging in a more detailed reading of the novel as an enactment of pedagogic and performative tensions in the narration of New York as an American zone of linguistic fluency and racial homogeneity, I want to explore how Lee uses the novel to interrogate the status of "ethnic" literatures within the U.S. publishing industry and academic canon.

NEW YORK AS THE CAPITAL OF THE U.S. PUBLISHING INDUSTRY: LEE AS NATIVE SPEAKER

Native Speaker was published in 1995 as the first title under a new imprint launched by the international publishing conglomerate which became Penguin Putnam. Susan Petersen, the founding editor, and four others formed Riverhead Books with "the goal of publishing quality books in hardcover and then in trade paperback—both fiction and nonfiction, including significant religious and spiritual titles—that would open readers up to new ideas and points of view."[5] Riverhead Books was formed, then, in response to the economic imperative to incorporate potentially subaltern multicultural aesthetic and spiritual productions into the dominant national economy of entertainment commodities. Part of the salability of Riverhead's offerings required a grounding of "new ideas and points of view" in the recognizably other bodies of racially constructed minorities. Lee's *Native Speaker* played a significant role in the success of the Riverhead imprint and, consequently, in the promulgation of its particular ideology of multiculturalism, which required the commodification of minority subjects as aesthetic exemplars. Another early commercial success was James McBride's *The Color of Water*, "a poignant memoir" that relates how a Jewish woman raised her twelve mixed-race children in predominantly black neighborhoods before seeing all of them through college. In addition to Kathleen Norris's books on monastic Christianity, Riverhead's religious offerings emphasize Asian spirituality, including two books by the Dalai Lama and Thich Nhat Hanh's *Living Buddha, Living Christ*. However, Riverhead's most successful hardcover offering to date is Suze Orman's *The Courage to Be Rich*. The title and cover of the book, which features a large color photograph of blond-haired and smiling white Orman, suggest again the priorities of the publisher and the financial grounds for its promulgation of this particular brand of editorial difference.

Given *Native Speaker*'s seminal role in Riverhead Books' establishment and in Chang-rae Lee's writing career, the marketing strategies engaged to bring about this success merit close attention. How does the literary "immigrant" fare in the publishing—and, arguably, the cultural—capital of the United States? The cover of the book features three images of recognizably Asian subjects. The front cover contains a montage in which the mouth of a two-toned, gray and black image of an almost featureless and indistinct adult Asian male face is overlaid with a small photograph of an Asian child dressed in festive cowboy attire. The mixture of images suggests both the dynamics of assimilation and the effects of a childhood spent immersed in U.S. culture on the tendency of an adult Asian American toward speech or silence. The image montage also suggests how the death of Mitt, Henry and Lelia's biracial child, has affected Henry in his relationship with Lelia. The back cover of the book is almost completely covered with a black and white portrait of a debonair-looking Chang-rae Lee, clad in a stylish turtleneck and sweater ensemble, his hair rakishly tousled. His mouth is closed, and his eyes look off into the distance. The effect of the portrait is to convey an impression of Lee as a youthful (he was twenty-eight at the time of the portrait) and suave standard-bearer of a distinctly Asian American literary tradition. The white turtleneck peeping up from the dark-toned sweater provides the necessary element of contrast in the photograph: whiteness held close to the skin, yet obviously distinct. The mirroring effect of the images, front and back, emphasizes the consonance between Lee and Korean American characters in the novel. The prominence of Asian faces on the cover further serves as a guarantee of the "difference" in the contents, visual evidence that the novel will contain "new ideas" from a "new point of view."

The book's title also contains a dual signification in that it refers both to the linguistic facility of John Kwang the character and the luminous prose of Chang-rae Lee the author. Kwang's tragedy lies in the fact that his English fluency cannot erase in Mayor De Roos and the INS's eyes— and ultimately in the eyes of the mob that assails him—the interpretation that his face connotes foreignness, not nativity. Likewise, Lee's lyrical writing and mastery of craft take a back seat to the predictable marketing of the book as "Asian American" fiction, treating customary themes of immigration, "biculturalism, racial conflict, generational conflict, and resistance to U.S. hegemony" (Lee, *Americas*, 1999, 107). However, following Dorinne Kondo's notions of complicitous critique, Lee's title and choice of genre can also be seen as performing an opposition that is "both contestatory and complicit and yet still constitute[s] a subversion that matters" (*About Face*, 1997, 11). Kondo distinguishes between Western forms of orientalism, autoexoticisms by Asian subjects, and counterorientalisms, which subvert Western modes of apprehending discursively produced Asian identities. The blurred lines of significance in the different uses of stereotypes define what is potentially a very muddy project: the differentiation of subversions that matter from subversions that fail. Lee's commodification as an author within the publishing industry's code of orientalism does not, in this view, eliminate the contestatory value that may result from the counterorientalisms deployed in his text, even as certain autoexoticisms within the text ensure that *Native Speaker* is read as a novel with a commodifiable difference. Although Lee's sea passage into print occurs at a price, the characters in the text remain as evidence of a repressed reality within the national culture.

Lee has stated in interviews that while "he does not define himself as an Asian-American writer, he acknowledges that he has used the Asian-American experience for his inspiration so far."[6] *Native Speaker* enunciates this tension in its choice of genre and its sustained engagement with Walt Whitman's poem, "The Sleepers," from which the novel's epigraph is taken. *Native Speaker* can be helpfully characterized as a spy thriller novel, described by many reviewers as a "page-turner," a standard term of praise in this genre.[7] In contrast to immigrant literature, which is often read as following the pattern of *bildungsroman*, Lee's novel moves from unity to dissolution in the Kwang subplot, the portion of the novel in which the espionage genre is prevalent. The tension in this plot is maintained by a clever construction of the novel's audience as white and therefore invested in the exclusion of Asian Americans from full participation in U.S. national culture because they are visibly "foreign" and not "native." Rachel C. Lee argues that, to the degree the espionage plot engages the reader, the novel interpellates its audience into the subject position of the INS agents who hire Glimmer & Co. to investigate Kwang's campaign.[8] The assumption that Kwang has something to hide, that his success in the New York political scene masks some dirty secret that makes him a threat to the tranquility of the city, reveals both reader and revanchist government agents as invested in constructions of Asian Americans as ineradicably foreign and hence a threat to the tranquility of American society. In fact, the novel is framed by a confessional second-person address in which Henry Park interpellates the reader as the target of his infiltration: "I won't speak untruths to you. . . . I make do with on-hand materials, what I can chip out of you, your natural ore. Then I fuel the fire of your most secret vanity" (NS, 7). "You" in this case, and in the asides throughout the novel, is not primarily the immigrant subject to whom Henry would normally be assigned by Glimmer & Co. Instead, it is the representative white American who constructs his or her national identity as one that excludes racially differentiated immigrants, whose "natural ore" is a hermeneutic of suspicion toward political or social accomplishment when it is not accompanied by a white face. It is this discursively produced subject that Park targets in his narrative.

Lee performs here the same inversion charged against Henry Park by his estranged wife, that of being a "genre bug" (NS, 5). In the act of refusing to conform to expectations of commodifiably multicultural Asian American writers who are expected to write autobiographies or tortured tales of assimilation, Lee presents his spy antihero as the "most prodigal and mundane of historians" churning out "remote, unauthorized biographies" (18). Henry is here figured as a stand-in for the writers of biographical and autobiographical Asian American works that can be commodified as "simple" immigrant literature. This counterorientalist maneuver contends that the role of a writer in the employ of the late capitalist state is that of a hack, alienated from his subject material and constrained to produce the portrait already determined by those who commission the investigation at the outset. As the commodifiable Asian American writer, Henry Park's ambivalent relationship to the repressive work of Glimmer & Co. is expressed in his uneasy acquiescence to a profession that seems to suit him perfectly and yet is used against him and others with whom he comes to identify, most notably the psychiatrist Emile Luzan and John Kwang himself. Henry's eventual break with Glimmer & Co. and his refusal to reveal the most damning evidence against John Kwang represent the limited agency left to him in a profession that can be death to leave. Likewise, Lee's attempt to "turn" from the spectacle of Asian immigrant exploitation and its eventual literary recuperation within late capitalism does not succeed in allowing him to fully "extricate himself" from the "confused, the past-reading," which constructs him as a literary outsider regardless of his linguistic fluency. To fully understand, however, Lee's engagement with U.S. literary tradition, we must look more carefully at the epigraph to the novel, from which the quotations expressing Lee's authorial strategy in the previous sentence are taken.

Chang-rae Lee grew up in New York City, and that may be reason enough for his choice of setting. However, New York's status as the capital of the U.S. publishing industry inflects that choice in a way that Lee's invocation of "Walt Whitman, a kosmos, of Manhattan the son" makes explicit. Walt Whitman, poet of America, boldly claimed a universal perspective that subsumed all differences within its capacious vision. Whitman was also a rough, a dandy, a man of the city, New York. Whitman's literary star has brought him from the margins of American literary studies to the center. Throughout *Native Speaker*, Lee performs an equivalent claim to universality that depends, as Whitman's did, upon a narcissistic focus on the embodied self as the representative figure of humanity. Instead of escaping from the particularity of a "wide immigrant face," Lee focuses upon it and the contradictions it presents to an American national culture that has repressed knowledge of its hybridity and the racially based categories subsumed within the concept of abstract citizenship (NS, 343). Through his narrative, Lee revises Whitman's heritage of representative Americanness to include the immigrant experience as central.

The epigraph, taken from the fourth poem in the Sleepers cycle, is worth considering as a whole and in context to better understand how Lee accomplishes this revision:

I turn but do not extricate myself,
Confused, a past-reading, another,
but with darkness yet. (*Whitman, Leaves of Grass*, 546)

The spectacle from which Whitman here turns is a shipwreck. The image of a "beautiful gigantic swimmer swimming naked through the eddies of the sea" (546) and battered to death by the waves against the rocks on the shore in the third poem of the cycle has been transformed in the fourth poem into the more representative tragedy of a shipwreck. The poet can "hear the howls of dismay" as the passengers are cast into the waters, but he is powerless "to aid with [his] wringing fingers" (546). Though he turns away from this horrific scene of death and destruction, he is unable to escape it. In the morning, the poet is drawn back to the shore and helps to "pick up the dead and lay them in rows in a barn" (546).

Lee charges this poetic scene with multiple meanings through his numerous visual and conceptual citations of it in *Native Speaker*. The starting point for any explication of the poem's meaning within *Native Speaker* is the spectacle with which this chapter began: the wreck of the *Golden Venture* as it is fictionalized in the novel. Even as John Kwang claims a continuity with the Puritans as "boat people," so is the traumatic experience of immigration into a nativist and exclusionary society here associated with Whitman's vision of a shipwreck, a searing vision that cannot be escaped. The immigration tragedy that Henry views on television ends when "[t]he drowned are lined up on the dock beneath canvas tarps" (NS, 246–247). Order is imposed on both Whitman's and Lee's spectacles of suffering by the organization of the dead into uniform spaces. Within the novel, the comparison of the *Golden Venture* scene to Whitman's poem serves to link the spectacle of immigration to universal experiences of human suffering such as Whitman explores in "The Sleepers" cycle.[9] For Henry, this scene also links his nautically described rapprochement with his wife to the political destruction of John Kwang. As an epigraph, the passage also serves to explain how Lee, who has "turn[ed] away" from a self-definition as Asian American, which he deems limiting, cannot extricate himself from the market pressures that force him to collaborate in his own commodification as an Asian American author. Nonetheless, Lee's "wringing fingers" create a story of considerable power and beauty.

In spite of the double-bind experienced by both Kwang and Lee, of being fluent and acculturated and yet also constructed as foreign and other, Lee is able to contest the interpellation of racially marked immigrant subjects as always already excluded from the category of American by making the more controversial claim that terrorizing and exploiting immigrants is quintessentially American:

> My ugly immigrant's truth . . . is that I have exploited my own, and those others who can be exploited. This forever is my burden to bear. But I and my kind possess another dimension. We will learn every lesson of accent and idiom, we will dismantle every last pretense and practice you hold. . . . This is your own history. We are your most perilous and dutiful brethren, the song of our hearts at once furious and sad. For only you could grant me these lyrical modes. I call them back to you. Here is the sole talent I ever dared nurture. Here is all of my American education. (319–320)

Here Henry returns to the second-person form of address in order to more clearly label and indict his audience. Henry's "ugly immigrant truth" is America's, and his memoir of complicity with John Kwang's investigation and destruction is "your own history," the legacy of immigrant and racial minority scapegoating that is instantiated in "Giuliani time." The "lyrical modes" of Lee's novel participate in and subvert the circulation of orientalist marginalizations of Asian American writers as "ethnic authors" cut off from the mainstream of American literary creation in much the same way that Henry Park participates in and resists the destruction of John Kwang. Or, in the words of Walt Whitman at the end of the seventh movement of "The Sleepers" cycle, "[t]he diverse shall be no less diverse, but they shall flow and unite—they unite now" (549).

The diverse facets of U.S. national culture that flow and unite in Whitman's poem are no less diverse for being ignored by homogenizing constructions of national identity that achieve unity through the erasure in popular memory of historically vibrant instances of diversity and exchange. In this vein, Traise Yamamoto has argued that "the private contains all things that exceed normative categories. To bring these things into public culture affects the construction of the national imaginary."[10] Earlier in my discussion of revanchist New York politics and the repression of material history it entailed, I alluded to the question of performative American identities and how they reveal in the private realm historical truths that exceed the normative categories of public culture. It is to this node of theoretical explication that I wish to return in my conclusion as a means of illustrating Lee's argument in *Native Speaker* that U.S. history is repressed history.

The average citizens knows very little about U.S. history, and this ignorance is perpetuated largely because the past exists for us only as it can be strategically deployed in contemporary arguments in which it is useful to "claim transcendent or metaphysical authority" (Bhabha, "Dissemi-Nation," 1993, 299). When Lelia complains that the "average white girl has no mystery any more, if she ever did. Literally nothing to her name," Henry correctly replies, "There's always a mystery.... You just have to know where to look" (*NS*, 10). Mystery, as Lee's choice of genre emphasizes, has been displaced in U.S. national culture onto racialized others who can then be constructed as spectacle, interrogated as foreign, and treated like aliens. If, in contrast to the orientalist assumption that Lee invites by his choice of genre, the mystery at the heart of *Native Speaker* is not the legitimacy of John Kwang's campaign for mayor, then where else might we look for the target of Lee's investigation? Rejecting the standard immigrant's tale, in which interracial marriage represents the consummation of the plot, Lee instead begins *Native Speaker* with the rupture of Henry and Lelia's relationship, displacing the story of their romance into the narrative past. More private history is also encapsulated in Mitt, the fruit of their relationship, and the details of his life and death are slowly and tantalizingly revealed through hints and indirections. Mitt, whose name reminds readers of baseball, "America's game," is crushed to death by his white neighbors in a game of dog pile. Since the game occurs during Mitt's birthday party, his nativity is highlighted, and biracial Mitt expires as the symbolic representation of American hybridity that the collective weight of (perhaps) unthinking white America definitively removes. This crushing moment should be contrasted with the related but politically distinct valence of Lelia's desire to push down harder on Henry during their initial sexual rapprochement. The exploration of Henry, Lelia, and Mitt's mysterious and repressed past together provides most of the narrative tension in the first portion of the novel, and the suspenseful unraveling of their private history thus stands in for the pressing critical interrogation of the originary American family unit that they corporately represent. In such an interrogation, the symbolic role that Lelia plays as a "pure"

American native speaker can be analyzed in a manner that reveals her repressed cultural and racial heterogeneity.

Lelia's complaint about mystery and white identity is prompted by Henry's ethnographic interpretation of her surname. Her given name, however, receives less scrutiny, despite Henry's assurance that "there's always a mystery." In this case, a second look at the first syllable of Lelia's awkward given name suggests that Lee accomplishes more in this name choice than merely a parodic redoubling of consonants that are stereotypically difficult for many nonnative English speakers to pronounce. Encoded in Lelia's name is a syllabic evocation of the author's name, an association also suggested by Lelia's aspiration to be a writer, her vocation of teacher, and the beauty of her linguistic ability, all characteristics that describe Chang-rae Lee. But "Lee" is only part of Lelia's mysterious derivation and identity. Tim Engles's discussion of Lelia as the novel's symbol of normative whiteness emphasizes her role in Henry's refashioning of himself according to middle-class white norms. According to Engles's reading of the novel, Henry "resolve[s] his identity crisis by unwittingly casting himself as a white manque" ("Visions of Me," 1997, 45). His detailed analysis of Henry and Lelia's interactions highlights the ways in which Henry comes to accept many of Lelia's judgments about him as they are encapsulated in the list she gives him at the beginning of the novel, "visions of me in the whitest raw light" (NS, 1). Engles chooses to focus his reading of the novel on the "whiteness" of the light cast upon Henry throughout the book, as though Lelia represented a pure space of white, middle-class American identity—as if, in fact, there were such a thing at all. Although Engles's interpretation is compelling to a point, he fails to account for the significant evidence throughout the novel that the most careful performer of American identity, in pursuit of the perfection June Dwyer describes as the "greenhorn desire to fit in," is Lelia herself ("Speaking," 1999, 78). Far from fulfilling the role of "standard bearer" (NS, 12), which she claims for herself at the beginning of the novel, Lelia, as Henry observes, succeeds by "executing the language" (10), a figure of speech that associates death and formality with her verbal abilities.

At the point where Henry capitulates to Lelia's demand that he abandon his Korean reserve and speak openly about his fears for himself and Kwang, Lelia begins to exhibit signs of cultural and racial heterogeneity. When Henry and Lelia clean out Henry's boyhood home, during the last stage of their journey toward rapprochement, surrounded by pictures and mementos of Henry's Korean family and past, Lelia expresses her frustration at the effects of Henry's espionage work on their relationship. Lelia swings her arms to emphasize her speech and "accidentally knocked over the rest of her coffee onto the white carpet rug" (NS, 226). As the brown stain spreads over the rug, "[s]uddenly she looked exhausted, sodden in the face. 'As long as you don't get hurt, I won't care. . . . I won't say a word to you. I won't even think it'" (226). The staining of the white carpet becomes an image of Lelia's transformation as the coffee-soaked carpet is refigured in Lelia's "sodden" face. At this point, Henry reveals the name of his mark, John Kwang, the man he spies upon. "I could see her turning the words inside her head. . . . She didn't say anything, though, and I could see that she was trying her very best to stay quiet" (227). Henry recognizes her behavior as reflective of his own as a Korean man, the reserve Lelia has decried up to this point in the novel: "Ten years with me and now she was the one with the ready method" (277). Finally, "in a voice [he] hardly recognized," Lelia surrenders, both to Henry's will as her husband and to his manner of speaking. "'You just say what you want. Please say what you want'" (277). By the end of the novel, Lelia is depicted as "horsing with the language to show them [her students] that it's fine to mess it all up" (349). The novel ends with Lelia's vaunted linguistic facility challenged by the diversity acknowledged as belonging to the city. Dismissing her students by name at the end of the day, "she calls out each one as best as she can, taking care of every last pitch and accent, and I hear her speak a dozen lovely and native languages, calling all the difficult names of who we are" (349). In a "difficult" sea voyage in which she must take "care of every last pitch," Lelia finally discovers who "we" really are.

For Chang-rae Lee, who toyed at an early age with changing his own first name to something more typically American like Tom or Chuck, foreign names are no barrier to an American identity. As an authorial calling card, *Chang-rae* indicates a much different trajectory of social incorporation than Amy, Frank, or Maxine. June Dwyer, among many reviewers of *Native Speaker*, recognizes the importance of language in the novel's schema and denouement, but the significance of John Kwang's becoming "a part of the vernacular" lies in his ability, for as long as it lasts, to bring his Korean identity along with him ("Speaking," 1999, 139). Jack Kalantzakos, Henry's mentor in surveillance, describes the constitutive function of Kwang's speech this way: "'He is in the language now. The buildings and streets there are written with him. In this sense he exists'" (*NS*, 169). Yet this movement from existence in the material world to constitution in language reveals troubling contradictions within America's national culture. Kwang's existence in language "helplessly heads end on" into his construction within the visual economies of race in the United States. The novel's conclusion does not, as Dwyer claims, ask us to "listen to immigrants' incorrect but highly expressive English" ("Speaking," 1999, 82). It points out instead in a dual movement that *native speakers*, like Lelia, cannot equate their whiteness with ownership of the language unless they repress the material histories of *other native speakers* like John

Kwang. Being Korean and being a *native speaker* embody a contradiction that requires the deconstruction of white English speakers as native. Lee does this by including Henry in Lelia's work at the end of the novel and recording the "wonder in their [the immigrant children's] looks as they check again that my voice moves in time with my mouth, truly belongs to my face" (*NS*, 349). Henry performs the same challenge to prevailing constructions of U.S. identity that Lee does when his book is marketed with a picture of himself and the polysemic title, *Native Speaker*.

The claim that U.S. identities are performative through language carries many consequences for contemporary debates with Asian American cultural studies about the status of Asian Americans within U.S. national culture. Imperatives to "claim the language" and thereby claim a place within U.S. polity that have impelled the enterprise of Asian American cultural nationalism are valuable and yet incomplete. More recent emphasis on the diasporic components of Asian American identity, in which private memory is used to link public contradictions with material histories of imperialism, hybridity and exploitation, enables a broader venue for critiques of U.S. national culture as it has been constituted through repressed transnational exchanges. Vital, however, to both enterprises is the public recuperation of what Chang-rae Lee calls America's "ugly immigrant's truth": the material success and social structuring of the United States that has depended from its earliest days upon the exploitation and alienation of racially marked others. From Peter Minuit's founding of New Amsterdam on the backs of swindled Native Americans to the harsh treatment of immigrants such as those smuggled in the *Golden Venture*, "boat people" have always been a part of the American vernacular.

In the first movement of "The Sleepers," Walt Whitman calls out what he views as the constitutive elements of American identity:

> I am the actor, the actress, the voter, the politician,
> The emigrant and the exile, the criminal that stood in the box,
> He who has been famous and he who shall be famous after to-day,
> The stammerer, the well-form'd person, the wasted or feeble person.

By means of the universal "I," Whitman brings the concepts of performance and political involvement into apposition with the categories of immigrant, exile, and criminality. He associates fame with speech and the body in a shrewd evocation of the marginality that defines the performative center stage of American identity. Homi Bhabha describes how "[m]inority discourse . . . contests genealogies of 'origin' that lead to claims for cultural supremacy and historical priority." In the place of definitions of American society or literary canon, which argue for the primacy and centrality of orthodoxical white Americans, "[m]inority discourse acknowledges the status of national culture—and the people—as a contentious, performative space" ("DissemiNation," 1003, 307). The actor and the politician, the politician and the emigrant, the emigrant and the criminal—all combine in Chang-rae Lee's evocation of the "contentious, performative space" in American literary and political citizenship.

NOTES

1. See Smith, "Chinese Migrant Trafficking," 1999, pp. 1–4, for a complete description of the *Golden Venture* incident, including responses in national media.

2. Statement by the White House Press Secretary, February 14, 1997.

3. Caroline Rody further discusses Lee's ambivalent portrayal of interethnic collaboration in a paper given at the 2003 Modern Language Association convention titled, "The Interethnic Imagination in Contemporary AsiaWhitmann American Fiction." Rody associates interethnic coalitions in *Native Speaker* with similar instances of interethnic imagination in works by, among others, Gish Jen and Karen Tei Yamashita, and suggests that such groupings may grow in importance as contemporary Asian American writers grapple with the distinctive future of Asian America within an increasingly multicultural United States.

4. Smith uses *revanche*, the French word for revenge, to reference a movement of reactionary populists in France of the 1890s known as the Ligue des Patriotes. These revanchists "mixed militarism and moralism with claims about public order on the streets as they flailed around for enemies" ("Which New Urbanism?" 1999, p. 185).

5. All quotations regarding Riverhead Books history and editorial policies taken from Penguin Putnam website, www.penguinputnam.com.

6. "Chang-rae Lee, Writer on the Rise, Inspired by Questions of Belonging," Reuters News Service, November 1, 2000.

7. Taken from editorial endorsements included in the trade paperback edition.

8. Rachel Lee, in conversation.

9. Universality and Whitman is an extremely vexed subject in Whitman scholarship. While the suspect foundation of Whitman's use of himself as a representative figure is rightly interrogated by many scholars, Lee is not here invoking Whitman as an example of how an all-seeing eye colonizes the subjects it surveys. Likewise, Whitman's role in my argument about *Native Speaker* and literary citizenship should not be construed as casting Whitman into the role of unproblematic touchstone of U.S. literature and identity. This is, however, very nearly the way that Lee uses Whitman, but only, I think, in order to link Whitman to a revised understanding of American identity as inclusive of Asian American immigrants.

10. Traise Yamamoto, in conversation.

WORKS CITED

Bhabha, Homi K. "DissemiNation: Time, Narrative, and the Margins of the Modern Nation," in *Nation and Narration*. (pp. 291–322). London: Routledge, 1993.

Dwyer, June. "Speaking and Listening: The Immigrant as Spy Who Comes in from the Cold," in *The Immigrant Experience in North American Literature: Carving Out a Niche*. Katherine B. Payant and Toby Rose, eds. (pp. 73–82). Westport, CT: Greenwood, 1999.

Engles, Tim. "'Visions of Me in the Whitest Raw Light': Assimilation and Doxic Whiteness in Chang-rae Lee's *Native Speaker*." *Hitting Critical Mass*, 4.2 (Summer 1997): 27–48.

Ford, Ford M. *New York Is Not America*. London: Duckworth, 1927.

Kondo, Dorinne. *About Face: Performing Race in Fashion and Theater*. New York: Routledge, 1997.

Lee, Chang-rae. *Native Speaker*. New York: Riverhead Books, 1995.

Lee, Rachel C. *The Americas of Asian American Literature: Gendered Fictions of Nation and Transnation*. Princeton, NJ: Princeton University Press, 1999.

Lowe, Lisa. *Immigrant Acts: On Asian American Cultural Politics*. Durham, NC: Duke University Press, 1996.

Palumbo-Liu, David, and Hans Ulrich Gumbrecht, eds. *Streams of Cultural Capital* (pp. 1–21). Stanford, CA: Stanford University Press, 1997.

Renan, Ernest. "What Is a Nation?" in *Nation and Narration*. Homi K. Bhabha, ed. (pp. 8–22). London: Routledge, 1993.

Rody, Caroline. "The Interethnic Imagination of Contemporary Asian American Fiction." Presented at the Future of Asian American Literary Studies Panel. MLA Convention, San Diego, CA, December 29, 2003.

Smith, Neil. "Which New Urbanism? New York City and the Revanchist 1990s," in *The Urban Moment: Cosmopolitan Essays on the Late-20th Century City*. Robert A. Beauregard and Sophie Body-Gendrot, eds. Urban Affairs Annual Reviews 49 (pp. 185–208). Thousand Oaks, CA: Sage, 1999.

Smith, Paul J. "Chinese Migrant Trafficking: A Global Challenge," in *Human Smuggling: Chinese Migrant Trafficking and the Challenge to America's Immigration Tradition*. Paul J. Smith, ed. Significant Issues Series 19.2 (pp. 1–22). Washington, DC: Center for Strategic and International Studies, 1997.

Whitman, Walt. *Leaves of Grass*. 1891–92 ed. New York: Vintage, 1992.

The Cartography of Justice and
Truthful Refractions in Karen Tei
Yamashita's *Tropic of Orange*

RUTH Y. HSU

KAREN TEI YAMASHITA: THE UNITED STATES AND THE QUESTION OF BELONGING

I have followed Karen Tei Yamashita's narrative trajectory since I first read *Brazil-Maru* (1992) almost a decade ago. Her other works include *Through the Arc of the Rain Forest* (1990), *Tropic of Orange* (1997), and *Circle K Cycles* (2001). My main interest was Asian American novels, drama, poetry, and short stories about immigration, concentration camps, culture clash, and the terrible price Asian Americans pay for being told that they have "made it" in the United States. The price is assimilation into the mainstream, the mental contortion needed to act "Asian American" so that an individual is more American than Asian, or just Asian enough so that he or she does not upset white America with inassimilable alienness. If one were to place a pin on a map of the United States for each instance an Asian American had to make choices about how much "Asian" to put out, the map would soon be covered with pins. If one then linked all the pins with a fine piece of wire, the map would be a criss-cross of wire, to the point of covering the cartographic representation of hills and rivers, or the freeways, waterways, and roads on that map. Notably, the National Asian Pacific American Legal Consortium (NAPALC) in its "2001 Audit of Violence against Asian Pacific Americans" documented 507 bias-motivated hate crimes against Asian Pacific Americans in 2001, which represents almost a 23 percent increase from those documented in 2000. In the three-month period following September 11, 2001, alone, NAPALC and its affiliates "documented nearly 250 bias-motivated incidents and two murders targeting Asian Pacific Americans."[1]

Karen Tei Yamashita's writing, over the past decade, defies simple categorization. Three of her four novels are set outside the United States. *Brazil-Maru* is about Japanese emigrants to Brazil in the early twentieth century. *Through the Arc of the Rain Forest* fast-forwards to contemporary Brazil, confronting an encroaching global capitalism led by the

United States. The quirky narrator is Kazumasa Ishimaru's sphere, which is the size of a golf ball, that rotates on its axis and is positioned in front of Kazumasa's forehead. The story focuses on the ordinary people of Brazil (where Yamashita spent ten years), trying to make their lives count in an economic and societal structure that diminishes their humanity.[2] *Circle K Cycles*, Yamashita's most recent novel, is set in contemporary Japan, and it depicts second- and third-generation Japanese Brazilian *dekasegi* (migrant laborers) who have in recent years "returned" to Japan as contract laborers for jobs that most Japanese refuse to take.

Yamashita's writing—often humorous, almost always incisive—seeks repeatedly to undercut familiar landmarks that offer false comfort and that obfuscate the truths in direct, lived experiences, or that misdirect us from the radical creativity and imagination residing in even the most ordinary mind. Asian American cultural texts have as a whole accomplished the important task of performing a cohesive identity, of mapping out what the term "Asian American" means. We speak of, for example, shared, communal experiences in figurative tropes such as the cultural and intergenerational conflicts that appear inherent in the process of assimilation; the mother-daughter or father-son relationship, the American dream, and the model minority myth. Decidedly, Yamashita's narratives, thus far, evoke those familiar tropes or landmarks that have been staged in Asian American literature and scholarship. At the same time, her narratives explore other vistas. She not only examines familial relationships within the Asian American context but also is concerned with assimilative politics such as the Asian American encounter striving for the American dream. Ultimately, her fiction envisions experiences beyond the conventional depiction of the quintessential American immigrant. She rewrites and renews that cultural idea and defamiliarizes it. It is this process of defamiliarization that allows us to examine the archetypal American figuration of the immigrant more critically so that we might see the individuality rather than the reductive, shared discursive traits that posit a static, essentialist identity category. This process of particularization is a humanizing one; it subverts the homogenizing mythologies of nation and "the people."

TROPIC OF ORANGE: THE INNER COMPASS

We are whom others say we are; that is, we are defined by others. We define ourselves, or we are reduced to mere reflections in a hall of distorted mirrors furnished by those who would define us. We are defined—passive tense. We define ourselves—an active construction; I define myself.

I found Karen Tei Yamashita's *Tropic of Orange* engrossing the first time I read it; much as I have similarly thought of Los Angeles as a fascinating city—the fascination with the City of Angels increased the more distanced I grew from its physical location and I became more grounded in the sounds, rhythms, sights, smells, and issues of Hawai'i. Yamashita's novel reflects images of Los Angeles back to its residents, to former residents, and to those who have not been to Los Angeles physically but who have imagined themselves connected to the city by means of images found in various modes of representation: movies, television shows, the Academy Award ceremonies, posters, spoken and written words, and photographs.[3] Los Angeles, in popular imagination, exists as a mass of concrete and steel, freeways or high-rise office buildings. More importantly, particularly for this chapter, it exists as flashes of images, lines, sounds, and colors that have come to epitomize collective imaginations, in the United States and beyond, of some essential quality of Los Angeles. Los Angeles exists in still another way—from the concrete-physical[4] to the ethereal or nonphysical yet real manner—in the American and, by now, after approximately one hundred years of mass-produced images exported to all parts of the globe, non-American psyches as well. Real, in a sense, points to the way in which images or concepts may eventually materialize as action. A more interesting way to think about "real" is to think of images or concepts, uttered or not, as occurring then eventually dissipating, but only after marking, indelibly, the time and space in which it occurred, which are never the same again. It is in this sense that the ethereal or the nonphysical has a material presence; it is real. From this perspective, Los Angeles possesses a component of something I will call real, much like blackness is real, marking a distinctive location in U.S. literary and other discursive environments (Morrison, *Playing in the Dark*, 1992). Although some of the perceptions of Los Angeles are not distinct from one another, for example the physicality of the place—the afternoon heat of the sidewalk, the heady, pungent smell of car exhausts—they are part of the network of imagery about the city and its absent-presence existence. What I wish to stress is that each formulation does not merely intersect with the others; rather, the ways that Los Angeles exists are mutually constitutive and ultimately cannot be truthfully imagined or thought about as discrete or separate without in some way distorting each sphere.

This chapter examines the images of Los Angeles represented in the *Tropic of Orange*.[5] These images, I argue, seek to decenter the dominant Anglo Euro-American narratives about Los Angeles, the ones that empower and maintain the dominant image of white and Western superiority. And the novel does so by appropriating and redeploying hegemonic tropes of cartography and geography in ways that map Western colonialism and the buried sites (longitude and latitude figured in the parole of history) of prehistoric rivers, flora and fauna, and "native" resistance as well as the ongoing transgressions of African Americans, new Asian immigrants, Latino/as, just to name a few of the others who have inhabited and are inhabiting the geography—in the deep sense—of Los Angeles.[6] In the process of redrawing the map of this city, and by extension the region,

Yamashita's narrative calls into question the still predominant, dualistic paradigm of social/cultural identity (an individual's identity is the "local" scale of a "global" geography of "reality").[7] However, the alternative universe offered the reader is indeed an alternative one, better understood *not* through the lens of certain strains of postmodernism that posit a non-centered subjectivity composed merely of endless linguistic play and of endless deferral of meaning. In other words, this literary narrative may pay homage to Marquez and to magic realism, but its physics is that of quantum theory. Characterization remains within the regime of current narrative technique, even while characters' motivations and the social construction of their identities are ultimately mapped along the key principles of chaos (not the same as anarchy) and fractal theories. In this novel, characters' decisions are "unpredictable" in the sense that they no longer follow a linear route of cause and effect, limited in duration and territory. Rather, individual's decisions affect the world in ever-widening ripples of power and influence, inestimable in terms of the boundaries of time and space; actions are never discrete, single acts but "self" expressions traceable along multidimensional and centripetal swaths, partially driven yet never determined by a past history, an individual's "re-memory."[8]

In *Tropic of Orange*, the white world exists (just as Newtonian physics) in the form of the police state, or personified as the professional wrestler, supernafta[9], and most compellingly in the form of ideas or action that have for centuries subjugated much of the nonwhite world to the needs and desires of what we call the West. Yet, because the action is predominately focused on nonwhite characters the reader leaves this hypertext with the realization that in the ways that count decolonization indeed has always been in the hands of each of us, in tandem with others of like intent.

Celestial Navigation: The Big Dipper

Tropic of Orange is woven from the stories of seven major characters whose connections to one another are not apparent in the beginning of the story. Ancient hunters and gatherers used the seven stars in the Big Dipper to navigate on the oceans or to chart their journeys across land. Some of the stars in the handle and the bowl of the Big Dipper (which belongs in the larger constellation Ursa Major) lead to other important constellations.

According to Chris Dolan from University of Wisconsin:

> The Big Dipper was also a very important part of the Underground Railroad which helped slaves escape from the South before the Civil War. There were songs spread among the slave population which included references to the

"Drinking Gourd." The songs said to follow it to get to a better life. This
veiled message for the slaves to flee northward was passed along in the form
of songs since a large fraction of the slave population was illiterate. (Dolan,
"Ursa Major")

One of the seven characters in *Tropic of Orange* is Manzanar
Murakami, a Japanese American who was formerly a physician with a
secure practice but who dropped out of conventional society and popped
back up as a homeless person. He conducts symphonies gleaned from the
sounds of traffic and of other absent-present sounds/music of the city that
he alone hears. Buzzworm is an advocate for people like Manzanar, drug
addicts, and generally, the poor. Bobby Ngu, in many ways, represents
a new kind of immigrant: he is ethnic Chinese, from Singapore, posing
as a Vietnamese refugee, "with a Vietnam name speaking like a Mexican
living in Koreatown" (*Tropic of Orange*, hereafter cited as TO, 15). He
is a janitor who is married to Rafaela Cortes, a recent arrival from south
of the border. Bobby is, like most other characters in the story, under no
illusion about Los Angeles or the United States. The United States is a vast
"neighborhood," and for a character like Bobby, the means to take some
of the power in this neighborhood is through financial success. Arcangel
is five hundred years old—Yamashita's homage to Marquez but with a
tongue-in-cheek twist. Arcangel, as the name implies, is part angel, part
WWE (World Wrestling Entertainment) super showman, in turn reserved
and bombastic. He travels from Mexico north to SUPERNAFTA's (Westernized global capitalism) lair in order to challenge and perhaps deal a
mortal blow to the ogre.

On a superficial level, these characters are clichés: Bobby and Rafaela
are just another Los Angeles divorce statistic; Emi is a Japanese American
princess like so many others, marching as far away from her ancestral
heritage as her ethnic features would allow; Manzanar is simply one
among tens of thousands of homeless people in Los Angeles. They live
along the fringes of the general Los Angeles buzz; they are powerless,
ignored, largely invisible to the mainstream population. In a Hollywood
movie, these characters would appear as mere background for the real,
dramatic action of a scene; they would enable the progression of the main
heroic action, they would intimate authenticity, providing splashes of local
color, and they would remain quite invisible. The marginalization of these
characters occurs in the oral and the aural realms as well, not only the
visual, through the silencing of their voices, or the distortion of the sounds
of their words and messages (Chinglish, Spanglish, or some form of "broken" English). The characters' attempts to speak their stories unfettered
by dominant socioideological constructs are often undercut by "white
noise" (to borrow Joy Kogawa's phrase), which originates, ironically, not

simply from places of power external to these characters but from their speech, and it mediates their comprehension of reality as well.

The predictable point of *Tropic* is that one may read these lives and their seeming nonrelatedness in ways that displace, or exorcise, or better yet undo dominant socioideological paradigms. Not so predictable are the connections that Yamashita does envision among the characters and the alternative means of dislodging dominant binarisms and the tactics of erasure, silencing, and distortion. Her narrative uses the subject of cartography and the trope of migrations as metaphors to rewrite the devastating and persistent effects of the modern era of European colonialism on non-Western peoples. The narrative seeks to displace and put in its proper place the West's self-congratulatory and narcissistic history of itself, to sidestep the dominant imaginary and symbolic realms. This novel challenges readers' typical understanding and, therefore, our experiences of time, space, and an orderly universe.

Much of the novel can be interpreted through the paradigms of chaos and complexity theories in terms of the characters' experiences of time and space and the events that occur. Some characters are more prescient than others as to the chaotic and complex nature of the universe. A key point of the novel, then, has to do with how certain characters come by this consciousness and the attendant issue of the ways that Yamashita represents order in disorder and ways of understanding the world that are alien to most readers. It examines the implications of chaos and complexity theories on issues such as the materiality of race, ethnicity, class, the nation-state, as well as for the understanding of fictive narratives, for example, the ways that fiction impinges on "real" notions of "truth" and the ways that narratives (representational words and signs) may result in "real" action.

LONGITUDES AND LATITUDES, OR GRIDS OF EXILE AND ALIENATION

Tropic of Orange may be read as a critique of the ways in which the prevailing, Anglo American–centric narratives about Los Angeles constitute a history imposed by successive generations of white colonizers who have traversed, liberally and as libertines, the "American" continent, and particularly, in terms of *Tropic of Orange*, Los Angeles and the region of Mexico immediately south of the border. (The reach of the book goes beyond that region of the continental United States.) Colonizers' footprints have marked and changed our understanding and relationship to the land with their stories of progress, as if indigenous people had not evolved along with their surroundings; they are stories of marvelous machines and equally marvelous Western men with imaginations that interjected modernity into that continent, as if indigenous people were not always innovative (innovation ensures the group's survival and perpetuation). American Indians today, despite the devastating effects of Western colonialism, continue to adapt and thrive. The colonizers forced on the precontact land their own grids of reality, in both material and symbolic ways, through fences, guns, and blankets infested with killer germs or, symbolically, through deeds of ownership, or nationalistic myths of manifest destiny, or a regime of maps and travel. The land had to be defined and ordered or, rather, tamed in order to be productive. Specifically, the landscape had to be cleared of both existing flora and fauna so that it could be used as farmland, settlements, and open range for livestock, whereas, according to the settlers, prior to their arrival, the land was wild and, therefore, unproductive. The former could be easily dispatched in the name of sport or in the name of innovation in weaponry. The Native American, of course, neither myopic nor short-sighted, proved much more difficult to clear from the landscape.

Here I will focus on notions of mapping and navigation that will run as threads throughout the rest of this chapter. First, European settlers navigated the "new" continent like their mariners did the "unknown" oceans. One aspect of these voyages of "discovery" is the development of a history about these travels that characterizes these navigators in the role of the protagonist/hero. These explorers are narrated as intrepid and civilized men who endured tremendous hardship in order to advance the cause of God, or monarchical treasuries, or civilization, science, new technological inventions, and so forth. Different chapters of this book reiterate this message, each chapter phrased in a different unit of the superstructure: religion, science, philosophy, government. One of the means by which early Western colonialism succeeded was through a comprehensive and quick Western cultural/ideological sphere that penetrated the worlds through military or economic incursions secured for various colonial empires. Another means by which Western colonialism succeeded was the denial from collective consciousness of the linkages between the seizure of land, gold, and the conquest of heathen souls undertaken by Christian churches.

The elision of these connections is a mechanism of hegemony necessary to maintain the effectiveness of the various units of the superstructure. In order for a hegemonic structure to work, we must be acculturated to conceive of ourselves within that structure as citizens and not subjects, interpellated, using Althusser's term, as voluntary partners and not slaves. In other words, hegemonic discourse provides the means to rationalize our existence so that we avoid seeing our society as a form of totalitarianism, in which schools, church, government, and business are multiple expressions of a single structure and project.

Yamashita's novel, from the preceding perspective, seeks to reveal the relation or the homology among the different ideological realms of the superstructure. Emi, for instance, is a television newsroom producer who exploits her title as a "reporter" in order to get newsworthy items to sell as a commodity. She is interested in what will boost the ratings, and not news that will inform the citizenry. Emi has happily assimilated into the U.S. culture constructed from fifty years of homogenous, prefabricated network television, which is pathos or the titillating, carefully packaged fifteen-second capsules cleansed of information that may seriously disturb for the ordinary viewer/consumer the image of U.S. society as liberal, democratic, and basically sound. In contrast, Gabriel, her boyfriend, believes that his job as a newspaper columnist is to uncover crime and corruption; he is what most people think of as a "real" investigative reporter. Yet he finds it increasingly difficult to sustain this viewpoint when confronted with a popular culture that values the facile as representations of the real. The reading public wants what Gabriel rebels against and what someone like Emi can provide, just enough gore in high-definition to make dinner more interesting. Gabriel's need to uncover the truth gets redirected into the romantic quest of building his dream house in Mexico. He substitutes spiritual fulfillment with material possessions. Gabriel's dream house is never completed, because within the narrative structure of *Tropic of Orange*, such a construction project merely dissipates the productive discomfort and existential questioning that drives Gabriel's half-acknowledged search for nonmaterial truths or the reality behind the apparent physical (social, political, and economic) reality. A dream house in Mexico is not meant to be a solution to Gabriel's quietly lived yet nonetheless urgent crisis of meaning. On the obvious level, both characters' lives call into serious question the dominant trope of the model minority and its goal of the American Dream.

On another level, Yamashita's decision to name one key character, Arcangel, and two other pivotal characters the names of the important archangels Gabriel and Rafaela deserves closer scrutiny. In Judaism, Islam, and Christianity, Gabriel is one of the seven archangels and one of the four most well known among the seven. In the Bible, as a messenger of God, Gabriel announced God's plan to Mary, and he is the archangel who announces the second coming. In *Tropic of Orange*, Gabriel has become earthbound, a fallen angel, whose line of communication with God has been severed. His favorite color clothing is black, contrary to the typical iconographical representation of the archangel. Unlike the biblical Gabriel, he is uncertain about his goals. Rafaela Cortes, Bobby Ngu's estranged wife, wins an epic battle with a Mexican drug lord, an archetypal battle between good and evil. However, at a crucial point in Arcangel's wrestling match with his opponent, SUPERNAFTA, Rafaela tries to resuscitate the wounded hero by feeding him the magical orange grown from the tree in Gabriel's garden on his property in Mexico. *Tropic of Orange*, however, ends with the reader still uncertain if Rafaela succeeds in saving

Arcangel's life. Ironically, the biblical archangel Raphael is a healer. Arcangel has the power to suspend time and to bend the perception of space; at certain points in the story, he seems to follow a plan, perhaps one from God. On other occasions, he reminds the reader of an Arnold Schwarzenegger character, a showman who courts the trappings of celebrity.

In a novel that represents at times the rhythm and language of the Los Angeles streets, the echo between Arcangel and a Hollywood action-hero character can be taken in the same vein as the novel's appropriation of biblical figures, Gabriel and Raphael, as an indication of the homology between two apparently oppositional and unrelated cultural spheres. Arcangel's fate enables at least one lesson to be drawn, that conventional religious institutions can contribute little to this phase of the ongoing battle between Western neocolonialism and resistors of this next chapter of the Grand Narrative.[10] Another lesson is that cinematic heroes are certainly poor imitations of the real hero. The reader winces, for example, at the scenes in the novel in which Arcangel swings into his big-tent performance persona. Yet, did the real hero ever exist except as mythic archetypes, condensations of communal fears and hopes? In *Tropic of Orange*, there are only heroic acts by ordinary individuals; not even the angels are what we think angels should be. Perhaps, then, one can come to the conclusion that one cannot expect heroism to be someone else's business, that one must get into the ring with gloves on.

From a different vantage point with regard to *Tropic of Orange*, the mutual referentiality between sacred iconography, Arcangel, and a profane yet highly charged symbolic figure such as a cinematic action-hero reveals the homology between ideological realms. The mechanism by which those connections exist can, in one sense, be described as cross-fertilization, a borrowing of traits belonging to the figuration of the heroic in one source text by another textual community. Such a borrowing masks the relation that always existed between either separate or seemingly opposed ideological realms, such as the sacred and the profane.[11] What I have been focusing on in the preceding paragraphs on the homology among discursive registers is to ask how we might unpack the ways that psychic energies or drives of the collective unconscious can clothe themselves in metaphors that in themselves only intimate the existence and nature of those deeply hidden desires. In terms of *Tropic of Orange*, the question for the reader living in a world saturated with powerful media and print imagery and metaphors has to do with how one is to reveal and to interrupt those metaphors and the circuitry of linkages and borrowings among various homologous realms.

Tropic of Orange asks the reader to reconfigure his or her perceptions of popular U.S. and, specifically, Los Angeles culture. The narrative critiques our mundane existences constituted and fractured by the processes of cultural self-production, processes that create a sense of coherence where none (of the kind we typically think of) exists, by means of a network of imagery, wondrous signs, or rather semiotic signs, that reflect the signs we mistake for reality. In short, these signs at best merely refract the truths of existence or being. Being does not refer to the notion of an essential being, which I will discuss later when I look at meditative silence. Even then, essentialness does not mean universal or homogenous.

This novel is set purposely in a city that typically figures to itself and in the national collective imagination as the most prolific and effective producer and purveyor of popular culture. Its critique of Los Angeles is a critique of popular culture, particularly in relation to the discursive trope of the Western heroic navigator and traveler. Moreover, the narrative's inclusion of the epistemology of cartography is the condition that enables this heroic character. The power residing in this cultural figure is substantiated by the discursive structuring of the area of cartography as a pseudoscientific discipline that deserves unquestioned acceptance. Paraphrasing Edward Said in *Orientalism* (1978): Something is true because people with power say it is true. It is perhaps helpful to reiterate that the hegemonic project is one of changing the very conditions of human interaction, from one of open dialogue to one of monologue, of dislocating the ways we perceive our worlds so that we accept without question that the world has always been a certain natural, universal way.

LONGITUDES AND LATITUDES: THE CARTOGRAPHY OF EMPIRE

Tropic of Orange critiques and subverts the ideological meanings and values undergirding the epistemology of cartography and the related "scientific" fields of trigonometry, geography, meteorology, mathematics, and so on. The raison d'etre of cartography is as a handmaiden for those fields, which are both consumer and supplier of cartography. Cartography, then, needs these other fields of knowledge to provide the raw material—figures, statistics, and measurements—for the products of cartography, maps. The raw material is then translated into maps, which are merely the visual form, the confirmation that those in this discipline have worked diligently to obtain the secrets of physical reality. These fields of "knowledge" have overtaken most of the world's understanding of climate, the relationship of coastline to mountains, and ocean navigation.

The "scientific" way of knowing that is uniquely Western (a story the West revels in retelling) dams up our perceptions such that we see only what the eyes and the mind are trained to take in: the superficial elements of our environment. Even when we delve below the surface of the landscape, we merely perceive the veneer of a very complexly interrelated ecosystem that in many non-Western thought systems is constituted of many layers and types of existence, some of which cannot be accessed by means of rational thought or the five senses as they are habitually employed. The Western way of understanding the world is to essentialize based on surface features: fauna and flora behave in predictable and calculable ways, determined by a set of universal and immutable laws. The corollary of this perception is the belief that humans inherently managed to catapult ourselves beyond this natural structure. We enjoy intelligence and consciousness; we have free will. In contrast, the natural world has none of these capacities; it is mute, mechanical, and mostly inanimate and soulless. Our intelligence is evidenced by the ability, for example, to encapsulate and represent, through abstract and wondrous signs, the laws governing the physical world, down to the molecular level. Absolute order is the call of the day. In short, we have yet to get beyond the European Enlightenment. Western humans, in this view, are masters of their physical surroundings because they are intelligent enough to know how it works and because they simply are the masters. This Euro- and anthropocentric worldview permeates popular texts such as movies and "scholarly" texts. Glancing at the Internet version of the *Encyclopaedia Britannica*, I came across the following entries, arranged as hypertext, under the various headings of "Navigation" and "Latitude and Longitude" (italicized words indicate a hypertext link):

> In the 17th century, Britain, France, and other maritime countries actively began to aid the development of navigation. Astronomical observatories were established to provide almanacs. Mapmaking and the invention of required navigational instruments were also encouraged.

> In 1731 John Harrison, an Englishman, and Thomas Godfrey, an American, simultaneously invented a *quadrant* that made it possible to obtain accurate observations of *celestial bodies*. The instrument was similar to the *sextant* in common use today. The problem of fixing *longitude* was solved when *John Harrison* in England produced several *chronometers* between 1730 and 1763. Pierre LeRoy in France built an improved chronometer in 1766 (see *Watch and Clock*). Captain James Cook's voyages of discovery in the Pacific Ocean at this time proved the accuracy and reliability of navigational instruments and techniques (see *Cook, James*).

The style of the writing aims to make the content accessible to the general reading populace. At the same time, its objective and authoritative tone, as well as the formal diction, erects itself as a "scholarly" text. A significant aspect of these entries is that they assert, as unquestioned fact, the fiction that the West, specifically Britain and France, initiated and led the development of navigation and map-making. There are links to English and French inventors.[12] Noticeably, there are no links to Chinese or other Asian and Pacific mariners, who made extensive trans-Pacific journeys many hundreds of years before the Europeans and without mechanical instruments. Instead, ancient travelers journeyed using knowledge, accumulated from generations of travel, based on the positions of sun, moon, stars, and cloud formations as well as the signs offered by birds and animals and the messages they learned to *sense* from the oceans.

Through the stories of oral historians such as Buzzworm and Manzanar, *Tropic of Orange* contests the repetitive thesis of the grand history of Western superiority. Arcangel's trek from Mexico to Los Angeles, the staging ground of SUPERNAFTA, Bobby Ngu's trans-Pacific journey, and Manzanar's inner travels unmask and seek to undercut the continued presence today of those successive waves of European settlers who tramped and rolled across the land, surveyed it, mapped it out, and drew vertical and horizontal lines on the emerging maps that would show future settlers the way to more forests or lands for settlements. That act of map making symbolized their belief that land could be thought about as merely one-dimensional geography, and that those from the West had the inherent and unquestionable right to own and do to that land what they wanted. Moreover, the very act of surveying a place, of measuring or surveying heights, widths, or depths, bespeaks of the attitude that knowing an object is simply to know its physical dimensions. This object is encased in or recast as "measurements" that one can manipulate by means of the network of discursive structures of religion, politics, commerce, education, literature, and so on. The settlers, in other words, recoded the Native American's world using lines, and the language of degrees and minutes, north and south, east or west, all of which are words calibrated to Greenwich Mean Time.

Location	Longitude	Latitude
Calcutta	22° 32′ N	88° 20′ E
Tegucigalpa, Honduras	14° 6′ N	87° 13′ W
Cayenne, French Guiana	4° 56′ N	52° 27′ W
Brazzaville, Congo	4° 15′ S	15° 15′ E

What are the colonial and decolonizing stories of the locations above that have been mapped using the colonizing tools of cartography and geography? For each battle we are able to recall and redraw the mappings of conquest advanced in the grand history, many battles by groups or individuals have been permanently erased by the dominant narrative of the West.

As *Tropic of Orange* asserts, colonizers have pulled across that western portion of the North American continent nets of narrative that seek to erase the multiple ways that people of color have predated white settlers and the ways that indigenous peoples continue to play crucial roles on that continent. Yamashita's *Tropic of Orange* presents alternative experiences of time, space, and connections among humans, humans to objects, and humans to the planet in order to refigure this incomplete and distorted version of the world.

GRIDS OF RELATIONS IN *TROPIC OF ORANGE*

In stark contrast to the way that European colonizers thought the oceans to be empty territory inhabited by monsters, Epeli Hau'ofa writes:

> "Oceania" connotes a sea of islands with their inhabitants. The world of our ancestors was a large sea full of places to explore, to make their homes in, to breed generations of seafarers like themselves. People raised in this environment were at home with the sea.... *Theirs was a large world in which people and cultures moved and mingled unhindered by boundaries of the kind erected later by imperial powers.*" (emphasis added, *A New Oceania*, 8)

Most noticeable in Hau'ofa's account is the different configurations that Polynesians and Western seafarers envision of the relations between landmass and ocean, among ocean, landmass, and human beings. In Western imagery, the ocean is akin to a desert, inhospitable, a void. It separates pieces of land and societies from each other. Oceans stand in the way. As Hau'ofa points out, the Polynesians thought of the oceans as home that helped create and sustain life. Humans lived, played, and traveled freely on the seas; they were fed by it both metaphorically and literally. The ocean was certainly not to be feared or to be treated as a barrier or location to be conquered. When Hau'ofa writes about boundaries, he refers to political borders as well as metaphorical ones. As various Western countries traversed the Pacific, they used the maps they gradually created and took a colonizing attitude with regard to the constellations. Both provided them the cartographical bearings needed to set up colonies—France claims this atoll while Britain plants its flag on that island. In doing so, European powers forced drastic changes on the political landscape of the Asia and Pacific regions. Such changes accompanied equally devastating changes to other facets of the indigenous episteme. Polynesian peoples were gradually cut off from their traditions, from the ways they connect to the sea and land, from the old ways of conceiving peoplehood and community, and from their stories. Without those stories, one is also cut off from the present and the future and from other people.

Like "Our Sea of Islands," Yamashita's *Tropic of Orange* offers a different geography of reality, one that seeks to deconstruct radically the bifurcating or binary paradigms that order our reality, that bring about that disconnect from others, from our past and ones inner self. *Tropic of Orange*, for example, contains insightful depictions of the ways that gender constructions separate the sexes (Bobby from Rafaela, Emi from Gabriel), or the ways that economic hierarchies formulate labor as the Other, or the ways that racism isolates members of one family from one another (Emi refuses to meet Manzanar, her grandfather). The novel can be found very much within a location of everyday politics, the politics that normalize a permanently disenfranchised underclass, or the kind that adjudicates what is newsworthy for television consumers, or the class stratification in health care, that is, who gets it and who does not and at what cost. The book contains a dystopic representation of Los Angeles and contemporary U.S. life that reminds one of *The Blade Runner*. The future is already here.

Buzzworm, a character in Davis's *City of Quartz*, understands "how the system works." At one point, he refers to the City of Quartz as he studies a map:

> He followed the thick lines on the map showing the territorial standing of Crips versus Bloods. Old Map. 1972. He shook his head. Even if it were true, whose territory was it anyway? Might as well show which police departments covered which beats...which kind of colored people (brown, black, yellow) lived where...which corner liquor stores served which people; which houses were crack; which houses banging; which houses on welfare. If someone could put down all the layers of the real map, maybe he could get the real picture. (Davis, "Oldies—This Old House," *City of Quartz*, 1992, 80–81)

Buzzworm correctly points out the political and arbitrary nature of maps. The ruling elite decides the kinds of maps needed: we need maps showing the territory of gangs so as to be able to better control them; we need maps showing property prices; maps to the stars' homes as a means of enticing more tourists to Los Angeles. Buzzworm studies a map that is perhaps meant for police, sociologists, cultural critics, criminologists, or city planners who have to consider in their planning riots and urban unrest and how best to cordon off one segment of the city from the rest if necessary; how best to protect the wealthy citizens from the poor. The construction of this map reveals a kind of thinking in which the city is an inanimate object to be dissected and studied, somewhat like a bug under a microscope or the skull of an African in the days when measuring cranial volume was a respectable "science." This kind of map identifies the city within the national, collective imagination as a location of warring races, of high crime rates, of poverty, and of incurable gang-bangers. The thick, imaginary lines on the map that "reveal" the territories of the Bloods and the Crips interject an image of radical disconnection and alien/nation between individuals and groups. Lines placed on this text, like iron bars on windows, assert and enact separation. The most popular maps of Los Angeles are of the freeway system, which in itself has come to distinguish the city from all other U.S. cities. For most residents, the freeways are to be avoided if possible or traversed during nonpeak hours. Commuters must drive the freeways to work, ironically so that they can afford homes away from Los Angeles, the exclusive site, supposedly, of inner-city poverty and crime. They read, listen to the radio talk shows and CDs, or finish up dressing for work while inching forward on the freeway in morning rush-hour traffic. Motorists learn to endure the freeways, wrapped up in their own thoughts or the eternal (radio) buzz that Buzzworm also tunes into. One avoids eye contact with other motorists like one would fellow elevator passengers, each of us hurtling toward one's destination in isolation. In the popular imagination, the freeway system is a necessity and a nuisance, resembling a circuit board (Pynchon, *Crying of Lot*, 1978, 49). Made of concrete and steel, the freeway is one vast inanimate object that helps distinguish the haves from the have-nots. Residents become residents once they are acculturated into Los Angeles's car and freeway parole—SigAlert (*TO*, chapter 46), I-5 (*TO*, chapter 40), Traffic Window (*TO*, chapter 5). Each of these terms acts like longitude and latitude markers, coordinates that pinpoint physical and discursive locations that help construct one's racial, gender, and class identity.

Buzzworm, rooted in the streets and street-wise, assumes that if he looks hard enough he will have the "real" picture of Los Angeles. His association with Gabriel, the columnist, is driven by the belief that a complete map of Los Angeles's material reality can be assembled. His assumption is that once such a map is laid bare for all to see, the injustices will dissipate somehow. Buzzworm, therefore, mercilessly pressures Gabriel to write about the "real" stories, such as Manzanar, or the mysterious courier from Mexico. Buzzworm is in his "true" element when he becomes news anchor, uncovering and bringing the "real" stories of the city to television consumers.

In the midst of his quest to find all the pieces of the map, Buzzworm senses that there is more to that map than material reality, that there is another way people and places connect. When he looks at the city streets, they are not simply concrete and pilings. Neither are palm trees simply trees. In his sights/sitings, palm trees—tall and starkly silhouetted against the sky—are like lighthouses pointing the way to his neighborhood in the vast desert-like quality of Los Angeles. They are also "like the eyes of his neighborhood, watching the rest of the city, watching it sleep and eat and die.... They were fed by *something else*, something only the streets of his hood could offer. It was a great fertilizer, the dankest but richest of waters" (emphasis added; 33). Despite Buzzworm's sense of that absent-presence, he is unable to go beyond the conventional boundaries in which he has been inculcated, a state symbolized by the buzz from the radio that he constantly keeps in his ears and in his mind. Buzzworm listens to all the stations not so much to be able to decode the secrets of that city in order to complete that map. Ultimately, the buzz from the radio acts like "white noise" drowning out that very city and the people and their stories.

The point of *Tropic of Orange*, however, seems to be about a "truth" that is the most disconcerting of Truths. The narrative suggests that a complete picture of anything is impossible, that there is not a single reality. The story puts to flight the fantastical desire that if only we can happen upon the most singular reality, then perhaps, we have found It, the best reality to possess, among all the models of reality we imagine. Instead, in *Tropic of Orange*, the belief that one can locate a universal, irrefutable, and immutable truth inhabits the realm of desire, a yearning for certainty that cannot be fulfilled. Manzanar's vision of reality is valorized in *Tropic of Orange*. He senses an absent-presence that defies our conventional notions of order, of space and time, and also of interpersonal and alter-personal relatedness. He thinks:

> There are maps and there are maps and there are maps. The uncanny thing was that he could see all of them at once, filter some, pick them out like transparent windows and place them even delicately and consecutively in a complex grid of pattern, spatial discernment, body politic. Although one might have thought this capacity to see was different from a musical one, it was really one and the same.
>
> For what were these mapping layers? For Manzanar they began with the very geology of the land, the artesian rivers running beneath the surface, connected and divergent, shifting and swelling....
>
> On the surface, the complexity of layers would drown an ordinary person, but ordinary persons never bother to notice, never bother to notice the prehistoric grid of plant and fauna and human behavior, nor the historic grid of land usage and property, the great overlays of transport....
>
> As far as Manzanar was concerned, it was all there. A great theory of maps, musical maps, spread in visible and audible layers—each selected sometimes purposefully, sometimes at a whim, to create the great mind of music. (TO, 56–57)

Each cartographic configuration of Los Angeles represents a different time and spatial arrangement. These various configurations exist simultaneously for Manzanar; he *selects* "sometimes purposefully, sometimes at a whim" certain layers, placing them in complex patterns. This apprehension of time and space, therefore, does not see time as linear. Rather, each configuration of existence exists simultaneously and dynamically, infusing all the layers with its presence and vice versa. The prehistoric, for instance, is not in the past and dead. Manzanar can see—by selecting and placing certain layers consecutively—the rivers evolve, connect, diverge, and reconnect. Paradoxically, change is the immutable truth.

Manzanar's mapping of reality extends beyond Los Angeles to include the Pacific and cities he had never seen, to Shanghai, Ho Chi Minh City, to New Zealand, the "very last point West, and after that it was all East. Then, there was the great land mass to the south" (170)central and South America. He sees that all points on Westernized maps—the intersections of longitudes and latitudes—refract the truth and offer a fraction of reality as the whole truth. Each of those points can only be briefly captured in stasis and then only through the *bias* that time is inherently linear and space is forever static, sectioned, or wedged durations of time ("Everything was for a brief moment fixed. Fixed as they had *supposedly* always been"; emphasis added, TO, 171). The way we imagine time is analogous to the way that we think of the globe as an object that can be divided into sections by means of imaginary lines drawn on its surface and extending deep into its core.

Manzanar lives in and out, or perhaps, more accurately, on the edge of these different yet coexistent realities; he comprehends and lives in the conventional way of ordering time and space as well as the other realities. To him, human bias desires to cover "everything in layers . . . building upon building the residue, burial sites, and garbage that defined people" (TO, 171). It is the propensity to think a certain way as if it were reality that gradually builds the belief, supposedly supported by experiential evidence, that life is indeed the way we think it to be. Manzanar's ability to access the rest of the universe that is not a closed system is momentary. In this passage, his apprehension of a dynamic, ever-changing reality suddenly shifts to "irrevocably, crush itself into every pocket and crevice, filling a northern vacuum with its cultural conflicts, political disruption, romantic language with its one hundred years of solitude and its tropical sadness" (TO, 171). Conventional understandings and experiences of reality reassert themselves.

To this orchestral conductor and formerly practicing physician, reality is not static; it is a complex pattern of simultaneity, change, stability, and convergence, or rather, an enfolding of everything into everything else. On the plane of the body politic, to behold reality in such a manner is to reaffirm the analogous experiences and the enduring relationships among people, along all points of the compass. Given the focus of this book—unmistakably on the poor and people of color—the implied vision is particularly concerned with the profound relations among them both in terms of their political interests (the realm of the body politic) as well as the shared, common experiences of generations in various lands. It is these experiences that compose profound interpersonal connections that cross structural boundaries of discursive identifications or mappings of all kinds (race, ethnicity, nation, gender, sex) and of time and space without necessarily denying the materiality or the physicality of any of these cultural constructs. To apprehend reality in a realm other than that of the body politic surely urges us to reorient our inner compasses.

Tropic of Orange offers the reader two tables of content, one more conventional than the other. The first is laid out in a manner that we have come to expect, suggestive of a closed system of time and space in which fictive events happen more or less in a linear fashion. The narrative action progresses (the plot—remember Aristotle); characters mature (or not, that is, they are dynamic or static); we can trace the direct consequences of specific action, the cause and the effect (the theme; the fatal flaw; a morally ambiguous ending; and the nature of the tragedy). As in "real" life, this conventional table of contents postulates a world that is in motion, but motion that is always from some kind of chaos to order, from some form of disturbance to a resolution of that disturbance and the reinstatement of calm, from moral ambiguity to moral certainty. Even when peace or harmony (order) cannot be restored within the confines of the narrative, reasons why can always be found if one knows where to look. The deep structure of this kind of narrative paradigm is homologous to prequantum physics, in which we believe that the next set of formulae, just over the hill, or across the next ocean, can net us the complete and "real" picture of the universe. In other words, in the conventional fictive realm, characters/humans follow more or less immutable and universal laws even though we factor in so-called accidents of birth, such as country or time period.

Tropic of Orange's second table of contents, tellingly titled, "Hyper-Contexts," calls up the idea, in chaos and complexity theories, of open systems, or systems not in equilibrium. In one axis, certainly, events in the lives of the characters are arranged according to the days of the week, Monday to Sunday. These events are further arranged within this method of framing time as occurring in the lives of Rafaela, Bobby, and the other five characters. Our habitual ways of reading and formulating reality, therefore, construct these events as a progression. Event A happens to Bobby on Monday; event B happens to Bobby on Tuesday. Indeed, our understanding of meaningfulness, of (narrative) thematic significance as well as the "larger" significance of human existence mirrored in the narrative (so we believe), relies on this perception of and belief in progress. In other words, we desire that Gabriel solve the mystery of the courier from Mexico and, in the process, resolve his personal, moral dilemma. We want to move from one chapter to the next, onto the final chapter, in the hope that Bobby and Rafaela reunite (or not, depending on the individual reader's needs at the time). The implied author of *Tropic of Orange* uses events that move the plot along, that mark stages for these characters, for example, Bobby and Rafaela reunite, during that climatic scene, worthy of any Hollywood action-adventure movie, of the wrestling match between Arcangel and SUPERNAFTA. Yet, at what point or points of the plot did they end their estrangement? Even though Bobby and Rafaela move closer to each other, by gradually understanding each other better, these thoughts do not lead to their physical reunification. Instead, they cross paths in a series of coincidences or accidents. Rafaela happens across the ice chest containing human organs just as Gabriel at the same time in Los Angeles comes across what is possibly a story on drug trafficking from Mexico (which turns out to be also a story about the harvesting of human organs). She calls Gabriel after happening across a piece of news broadcast on a recently installed television belonging to her neighbor who is actually the mother of the trafficker of drugs and human organs. Rafaela in Mexico "falls" into the roles of sleuth and warrior. Certainly, her job as Gabriel's housekeeper and accidental interior designer did nothing to prepare her for what she finds in the neighbor's refrigerator. Rafaela did not have to open the refrigerator when she did, except that she felt thirsty. She did not have to open the cooler she found in the refrigerator, yet she did. Her estrangement from Bobby led her to become housekeeper of an uninhabited house in Mexico. She escapes the house in Mexico because the trafficker catches her opening the cooler. She heads back north with the help of Arcangel who happens upon Gabriel's house. Arcangel, in an apparent act of volition, travels to El Norte in order to engage in this epic battle with evil. Yet, he too can be propelled by random events: He did not have to use the route that he did, for instance, that brought him to Gabriel's property.

Other characters are similarly drawn along by random events. Emi is shot and killed by police as she sunbathes atop the news van. She decides to darken her tan just as the authorities decide to close down the Revolt of the Homeless. Emi almost meets Manzanar because she knows Gabriel, who becomes acquainted with Manzanar because of his association with Buzzworm. Buzzworm and Emi meet because they know Gabriel and because the Los Angeles freeway system shuts down due to two horrific accidents. These events happen one after another, surely. However, to say that things occur in sequential fashion is not the same as to say that things necessarily occur in a causative chain or related series of events. In fact, one is hard put to locate any inherent, deterministic logic (which can be understood as a set of rules governing whatever it is these rules are thought to govern: rules, such as the syntax of a culture) connecting the events that occur in these characters' lives other than that of a randomness of sorts.

One significant point of *Tropic of Orange* is suggested in the ways in which the trajectories of these characters' lives converge. They connect with each other either because of a decision they make—and, often, those decisions do not result in the desired consequences—or because of their association with another character, who makes a decision that sets off other unforeseen events. By the final page, each of the seven major characters is connected to at least two other characters, each of whom is in turn related to at least two other characters, and so on. Space constraints prevent me from following up further the implied author's use of fractal theory in this novel.[13] For now, I merely wish to note that the plot structure confounds one's attempt to predict what will happen to a character. The second table of contents argues for a version of the universe that is nondeterministic. The major characters begin Monday locked in their own narcissistic spheres of existence. Because we believe that unless we are cognizant of someone (for example, a friend, lover, newspaper vendor) that someone is not part of our life, these characters move about their daily affairs as if they have no connection with other persons, that their business has no relevance for others and vice versa. In short, what is the connection between or the significance of the death of an African American teenager in south-central Los Angeles with a mother in Mexico receiving a new television from her devoted son, who drives a black BMW? *Tropic of Orange* attempts to undercut this typical model of human connectivity. Not only are we connected or related to people we do not "know," we have, in a sense, always known them. Not only are we connected to so-called strangers in an ever-widening matrix of complexity that defies logical, deterministic mapping, one's actions change perhaps the texture, or the organization, or the meaning of that matrix, at specific locations, which in turn ripple out to change the totality of this nonlinear structure. In brief, small changes lead to bigger ones, although not in predictable or calculable ways. We cannot be certain what a kick-off event will accomplish elsewhere. Neither is it possible to pinpoint a particular event as the kick-off event. For instance, when exactly did Bobby and Rafaela begin to drift apart? Much in our experiences cannot be measured or accounted for if we use linear and causative reasoning.

Tropic of Orange's hypertextual construction exemplifies a nonlinear model of chaos and complexity. Characters are connected and they act but not in any predetermined way. The results (in the plural, in the true sense of plurality and not in the way that this concept is used to describe U.S. culture) of their actions surprise even them. In other words, there is no reason for a result to have come from a particular act. Yet, the universe is not a murky, swirling stew of utter incomprehensibility and disorder. Chaos or randomness does not mean a lack of pattern, just as the absence of clock-time does not mean the absence of duration. In *Tropic of Orange*, the nonlinear world is not an arbitrary world. Characters embark upon journeys that bring them, by the last page of *Tropic of Orange*, to connect to others; yet the trajectory of these journeys cannot be absolutely predicted, all of which are the logical operations of a mind trapped in a linear, closed way of conceiving the universe. In a nonlinear worldview, one may not be able to chart seamlessly cause and effect—this action caused that effect—yet, any act may contain profound significance. Any act can be a pebble dropped into a pond. Humans are agents.

Stated somewhat differently, the significance of an act is created, imagined, at a point in the now when, for example, one must reassure oneself of the efficacy of one's behavior or that one's life has meaning. Phrased reductively, history is all about the present. The present is impossible without narratives, without the artifice that is history. Universal and immutable Truth, therefore, exists, but only as the grandest aspect of the grand narrative, the ultimate delusion and self-imprisonment.

Conclusion

Tropic of Orange works out most fully a recurrent topic in Karen Tei Yamashita's novels: that there are many truths or experiences of reality. *Brazil-Maru*, for example, is five narratives interwoven, indicative perhaps of the idea that our lives are marked by patterns of convergences and divergences too intricate to be easily mapped into a single narrative on a two-dimensional surface. This is a theme that is also examined in *Through the Arc of the Rain Forest*. The implications of this idea are gradually being explored in various Western academic disciplines that pertain to those disciplines (for example, architecture, economics, geography, mathematics, physics, philosophy, urban planning). It is important to note that versions of this idea can be found in many Eastern philosophical and religious traditions of considerable lineage. It is also important to note here that this idea should not be reduced to the adage that "it's all relative" and therefore all perspectives are equal. For the purposes of this chapter, and I think this thought can be found in all of Yamashita's published work, different perspectives in the societies depicted in these fictive works obviously do not enjoy equality. In Yamashita's fictive representations of the imaginaries of Japan, Brazil, and Los Angeles, various perspectives are accorded unequal treatment depending on who advances a particular perspective. This is another way of saying that an individual's perspective exists in a material structure constituted in and ordered by a hegemonic structure and can be defined as a collective perspective arrived at not via citizenry equality but via consensus building, which typically means the less powerful are induced or persuaded to give way to the more powerful. Consensus building is not power sharing, it is the ruling elite's successful dissemination of the *perception* that everyone shares more or less equal power, that one has a meaningful stake in the status quo. Power is constantly being negotiated among the various stake holders. So far, Western hegemony has proven very resilient, primarily because it appears to have the ability and flexibility to assume various guises as a means of maintaining a consensus, which is in effect a reiteration of its own continual dominance. Therefore, in a sense, perspective is everything. Minority groups, since the first glimmerings of the notion of minority rights within the United States, have been engaged in affecting both the metaphorical and material structures of the U.S. cultural and political economies. The two spheres of U.S. hegemony cannot be separated. Indeed, the "reality" of material structures must be first won in the sphere of the representational—the cultural economy. Perspective is everything, particularly for minority groups in their efforts toward true emancipation. Emancipation has to begin with the self. Manzanar in *Tropic of Orange* is an instance of the exploration of this assertion that the next step in counterhegemony necessitates a most extreme paradigm shift, one that does not depend on the "counter" in counterhegemony. For it is this dependence on the "counter" that reinstates, in myriad ways, hegemony, just as the castaway in film *Castaway* manages to erase Friday/coconut and refocus our attention on the castaway himself, scripted as the fount of all emotions and the universe itself. Therefore, emancipation also necessitates a reconfiguration of the understandings of perspective, representational politics, and by extension identity politics.

NOTES

1. See NAPALC (2001) http://www.napalc.org/literature/annual_report/2001_Audit.htm.

2. Rachel Lee has a very insightful chapter on "In the Arc of the Rain Forest" in her book, *The Americas of Asian American Literature* (1999, 224–290).

3. In *Tropic of Orange*, Buzzworm vainly seeks to discover the answers to the secrets of Los Angeles by keeping his ears tuned to the city's numerous radio stations. He hears only a cacophony of "white" noise. Unlike for Manzanar, maps to Buzzworm are also undecipherable signs. In a pointed reference to Mike Davis's seminal "map" to Los Angeles (*City of Quartz* uncovers the machinations of power in the city), Buzzworm—perhaps wisely—doubts the printed page torn from *Quartz City* (TO 80). Unfortunately, he is too bounded in the material and Newtonian world (unlike Manzanar) to be able to see the "real picture"—Buzzworm says to no one in particular: "If someone could put down all the layers of the real map, maybe he could get the real picture" (TO, 81). *Tropic of Orange* should not be taken as merely another offering in a long list of

mappings of this madding city. It speaks to Davis's *City of Quartz*, and attempts to remap it in ways that locate Los Angeles in a global spatial scale. Publication constraints limit my ability to review in this chapter the extant academic literature on Los Angeles. Briefly, besides Davis's *City of Quartz*, which contains a very interesting discussion of various postmodernist critics' encounter with the city, see Soja's *Postmodern Geographies* and *Postmetropolis* ("Fractal City: Metropolarities and the Restructured Social Mosaic"), as well as his *Thirdspace: Journeys to Los Angeles and Other Real-and-Imagined Places* and Sawhney's *Unmasking L.A.* To locate Los Angeles in the economic and political map of globalization, see Sassen's *The Global City* (Los Angeles may be a world city but not a global one).

4. That is not the same as saying one can know what a concrete-physical thing *is*.

5. Erich Maria Remarque described Los Angeles thusly: "Real and false were fused here so perfectly that they became a new substance. . . . It devoured everyone, and whoever was unable to save himself in time, would lose his identity" (qtd. in Davis, *City of Quartz*, 1992, 50).

6. David Harvey has called for a "dialectical relationship between political-economic and socio-ecological change on the one hand and geographical knowledges on the other" (*Spaces of Capital*, 2001, 208).

7. I have drawn much insight from the following books in preparing this chapter: Arjun Appadurai's *Modernity at Large* (1996); Annette Kolodny's *The Lay of the Land* (1975); Said's *Orientalism* (1978); Mignolo's *Local Histories/Global Designs* (2000). Even though this essay does not deal with the issue of gender (which is a crucial concern), I have also found extremely helpful the following: Massey's *Space, Place, and Gender* (especially parts II and III, 1994) and McDowell's *Gender, Identity and Place* (1999).

8. Walter Benjamin, "To portray a city, a native must have other, deeper motives—motives of one who travels into the past instead of into the distance. A native's book about his city will always be related to memoirs" (qtd. in Davis, 1992,). Toni Morrison chose the word re-memory to articulate the ways in which the past must be restructured in order to end living the present by reliving past pain, for living the present through the past is to consent to one's ongoing oppression. *Beloved* is one of Morrison's many memoirs as a native. Similarly, Yamashita's native city in *Tropic of Orange* serves as the place for various characters to uncover past emotional, political, and economical landscapes in order to restructure those landscapes in liberatory ways.

9. SUPERNAFTA is a professional wrestler in the novel. His name of course comes to symbolize and represent larger global and economic forces shaping Mexico, the United States, and Canada through the North American Free Trade Agreement.

10. The West is broadly defined. It is composed of North America, western European nations and client states such as, but not limited to, Japan. I use the term "Grand Narrative" here to more broadly suggest the narrative of Western progress.

11. Stallybrass and White assert that the dominant discourse enables the setting up of opposing spheres, such as holy days versus carnivals, as a kind of othering

and as a way to rehabilitate such acts of transgression against authority (*Politics and Poetics*, 1986).

12. See the 2002 A&E special event, "Longitude" on John Harrison. This program was originally produced for television in 1999; its full title was "Longitude" and can be purchased on VHS and DVD . . . the full citation details can be found at imdb.com under "Longitude."

13. A useful discussion can be found in Philip Stehle's *Order, Chaos, Order: The Transition from Classical to Quantum Physics* (1994). Also, see Mandelbrot's *The Fractal Geometry of Nature* (1977). For complexity theory, see Mitchell Waldrop's *Complexity: The Emerging Science at the Edge of Order and Chaos* (1992).

Works Cited

Appadurai, Arjun. *Modernity at Large: Cultural Dimensions of Globalization.* Minneapolis, MN: University of Minnesota Press, 1996.

Davis, Mike. *City of Quartz.* New York: Vintage Books, 1992.

Dolan, Chris. "Ursa Major." Retrieved from http://www.astro.wisc.edu/~dolan/constellations/constellations/Ursa_Major.html.

Harvey, David. *Spaces of Capital: Towards a Critical Geography.* New York: Routledge, 2001.

Hau'ofa, Epeli. *A New Oceania: Rediscovering Our Sea of Islands.* Suva, Fiji: University of the South Pacific with Beake House, 1993.

Kolodny, Annette. *The Lay of the Land: Metaphor as Experience and History in American Life and Letters.* Chapel Hill: University of North Carolina Press, 1975.

"Latitude and Longitude." *Encyclopaedia Britannica Online.* 2002. Retrieved from http://www.britannica.com/ebi/article?eu=297359.

Lee, Rachel. *The Americas of Asian American Literature.* Princeton, NJ: Princeton University Press, 1999.

Mandelbrot, Benoit. *The Fractal Geometry of Nature.* San Francisco: W. H. Freeman, 1982.

Massey, Doreen. *Space, Place, and Gender.* Minneapolis, MN: University of Minnesota Press, 1994.

McDowell, Linda. *Gender, Identity and Place. Understanding Feminist Geographies.* Minneapolis, MN: University of Minnesota Press, 1999.

Mignolo, Walter. *Local Histories/Global Designs: Coloniality, Subaltern Knowledges, and Border Thinking.* Princeton, NJ: Princeton University Press, 2000.

Morrison, Toni. *Beloved.* New York: Knopf, 1987.

———. *Playing in the Dark: Whiteness and the Literary Imagination.* Cambridge, MA: Harvard University Press, 1992.

National Asian Pacific American Legal Consortium (NAPALC). "2001 Audit of Violence Against Asian Pacific Americans." Retrieved from http://www.napalc.org/literature/annual_report/2001.htm.

"Navigation." *Encyclopaedia Britannica Online.* 2002. Retrieved from http://www.britannica.com/ebi/article?eu=298065.

Pynchon, Thomas. *The Crying of Lot 49.* Philadelphia: Lippincott, 1966.

Said, Edward. *Orientalism*. New York: Pantheon Books, 1978.

Sassen, Saskia. *The Global City: New York, London, Tokyo*. 2nd ed. Princeton, NJ: Princeton University Press, 2001.

Sawhney, Deepak Narang, ed. *Unmasking L.A. Third Worlds and the City*. New York: Palgrave, 2002.

Soja, Edward. *Postmetropolis: Critical Studies of Cities and Regions*. Malden, MA: Blackwell, 2000.

———. *Postmodern Geographies: The Reassertion of Space in Critical Social Theory*. London: Verso, 1989.

———. *Thirdspace: Journeys to Los Angeles and Other Real-and-Imagined Places*. Malden, MA: Blackwell, 1996.

Stallybrass, Peter, and Allon White. *The Politics and Poetics of Transgression*. London: Methuen, 1986.

Stehle, Philip. *Order, Chaos, Order: The Transition from Classical to Quantum Physics*. New York: Oxford University Press, 1994.

Waldrop, M. Mitchell. *Complexity: The Emerging Science at the Edge of Order and Chaos*. New York: Simon and Schuster, 1992.

Yamashita, Karen Tei. *Through the Arc of the Rain Forest*. Minneapolis, MN: Coffee House, 1990.

———. *Brazil-Maru*. Minneapolis, MN: Coffee House, 1992.

———. *Tropic of Orange*. Minneapolis, MN: Coffee House, 1997.

———. *Circle K Cycles*. Minneapolis, MN: Coffee House, 2001.

4 "Valuing" Transnational Queerness

Politicized Bodies and Commodified Desires in Asian American Literature

STEPHEN HONG SOHN

THIS CHAPTER EXPLORES the complexities of transnationalism in relation to queer sexuality, commodification, and bodies. I will begin with a brief survey of queer Asian American literature with particular emphasis on anthologies and the attention that many anthological contributors have paid to the Asian American queer body. Taken together, queer Asian American anthologies relate a particular "body" politic in collecting literatures that resist and subvert stereotypes of queer bodies and queer sexualities. These anthologies also work to increase the visibility of queer Asian American groups with the express purpose of creating a community that can generate political coalitions and artistic camaraderie. I move then to a discussion of the field of Asian American literature, which has been altered by publications from Southeast Asian American and queer Asian American groups, especially in the form of the novel. In particular, Jessica Hagedorn's *Dogeaters* (1990) and Lawrence Chua's *Gold by the Inch* (1998) provide accounts of queer sexuality located in national and transnational spaces. This chapter focuses primarily on Chua's novel, in which the narrator finds himself traveling to Bangkok in the complicated situation of the Asian American transnational entity, physically similar to the Thai, Malay, and other Asian individuals surrounding him, but afforded a rare kind of global mobility. His failed attempts to experience genuine romantic love with the gay hustler, Thong, push him further into a disintegrating life, mediated primarily by drugs. The larger implication of this portrayal lies in the transnational scope of the Asian American, whose ambiguous locus of power renders him complicit in a kind of post-colonial exploitation and a lost subject without a coherent community to support him. Once rendered as a kind of prostitute and object of desire in the United States, he reverses this position as he engages in sex tourism in Southeast Asia. Chua's text puts forth a challenge to Asian American Studies and the politicized bodies present in queer Asian American anthologies as it presents a protagonist, who, although quite politically cognizant of both his position and the postcolonial landscape of Bangkok, nevertheless continues to engage in activities that undermine his moral superiority. The novel marks corruption in even the most well-intentioned and informed individuals.

For queer individuals, their bodies are central because they are regulated not only by larger nation-state and legal apparatuses, but also by their very own desires and struggles with and against societal mores. In an age where critical discourses on the body continue to manifest, from Michel Foucault's discussion of the body and state disciplinary institutions to Elaine Scarry's juxtaposition of the body and torture, it is a natural extension to explore the body in relation to queerness and desire. Of course, critics have extended the understanding of the queer body, from Eve Kosofsky Sedgwick's theorization of the homosocial to Judith Butler's articulations of the performativity of gender, but this particular piece aims to explore textual representations of queerness in Asian American literature and to examine how the queer body itself becomes the site of commodification, a location that is marked with a certain value. As cultural critic Dana Y. Takagi notes, "the field of Asian American Studies is mostly ignorant about the multiple ways that gay identities are often hidden or invisible within Asian American communities" ("Maiden Voyage," 2000, 32). Takagi's assertion is based on the relative complexity of queer visibility in an Asian American community that struggles to incorporate queers organically into its political project and the relative lack of critical attention given to queer issues in academia. Pratibha Parmar eloquently remarks on her own predicament as a queer Asian American: "The idea that many of us have our own self-defined sexuality is seen as subversive and threatening by the majority of the Asian community. Within our own communities our existence as lesbians and gays continues to be denied or is dismissed as a by-product of corrupting Western influences" ("Emergence," 2000, 378). As Asian American communities, both intellectually and socially, downplay the importance of queer issues, queer Asian Americans struggle to maintain their visibility and to stress that queer sexuality cannot be deemed as deviant nor culturally produced by the West.

Queer visibility requires the public presence of the body in space, whether or not that space is textually produced or physically constructed. However, queer visibility is itself fraught with dangerous possibilities ranging from hate crimes, dismissal from family units, and other such discriminatory consequences. Through literature, queer Asian Americans have constructed a space where they maintain control over representations of queerness and at the same time illuminate the complexities of queer identity as it relates to ethnicity, gender, and the body. David L. Eng and Candace Fujikane's much needed survey essay, concerning the state and history of the Asian American queer writings[1] and literature begins by noting, "Asian/Pacific gays and lesbians share problems of invisibility specific to histories fraught with Orientalist stereotypes" ("Asian American Literature," 2004, 1). Indeed, Asian Americans queers have and still continue to face destructive Orientalist stereotypes in which the Asian American queer male is perceived as an effeminate, submissive, and passive partner, while the Asian American queer female remains trapped in the assumption that her sexuality must remain primarily heterosexual. In this realm of limited categorizations, Eng and Fujikane see the need for "the recognition that Asian/Pacific gays and lesbians voice richly multiple and diverse identities" (1). Eng and Fujikane firmly root their arguments in the discourse of the body, as queer Asian Americans must "voice" their opinions and positions rather than remain silent and unseen. The body of the queer Asian American in textual representations becomes infused with a sort of political value that simultaneously redefines queer sexuality from an Asian American perspective, visibly presents this queer sexuality, and affirms the importance of freeing queer bodies from societal strictures and governmental regulations to explore desires and sexual proclivities.

Of particular interest are queer Asian American anthologies that demonstrate the importance of the queer body as an exemplar of political value. *Between the Lines: An Anthology by Pacific/Asian Lesbians of Santa Cruz, California* (1987), edited by C. Chung, A. Kim, and A. K. Lemeshewsky, is a compilation of queer Asian American writings. The conflict with visibility is evident in the number of the writers who took on pseudonyms, while others chose not to appear in photographs included in the volume. One contributor, Alison Kim, laments the limitations placed on queer bodies in a poem that metaphorically relates Asian American queerness to a chameleon's ability to change colors. Kim's lyrics point to the ways in which queer individuals can alter themselves to try to conform to societal standards but lament that in doing so, the queer body can lose its political power and presence. In publishing the volume, the contributors refuse this exclusion from the public eye. Sharon Lim-Hing's *The Very Inside: An Anthology by Asian and Pacific Islander Lesbian and Bisexual Women* (1994) sustained the strong contribution by Asian American and Asian lesbians to the literary community with the publication of this substantial volume of poetry and prose. Peou Lakhana, a Cambodian American contributor, identifies herself resolutely in the first lines of her poem as a lesbian. Lakhana's lyrics reinscribe the universality of the queer body to take on a humanist standpoint that includes queer sexuality as a natural desire. Taken together, Lakhana's and Kim's poems suggest strongly the concerns that queer individuals face in relation to their bodies, which publicly situate both queer desire and allow them to revolt against others who would deny queers their humanity. Other important anthologies of Asian American queer writings would appear in the late 1990s: *Asian American Sexualities: Dimensions of the Gay and Lesbian Experience* (1996) edited by Russell Leong; *Q & A: Queer in Asian America* (1998) edited by David L. Eng and Alice Y. Hom; *Queer Papi Porn: Gay Asian Erotica* (1998) edited by Joel Tan; and *Take Out: Queer Writing from Asian Pacific America* (2000) edited by Quang Bao and Hanya Yanagihara.

Richard Fung's piece, "Looking for My Penis" (included in both *Q & A* as well as *Asian American Sexualities*), reiterates both the risks in publicly exposing the queer body and the problems associated with representations of queer Asian American bodies in pornographic productions. He writes, "in coming out we risk losing this support" of "our families and our ethnic communities," and finds that gay representations have been populated by "images of ... *white* men and *white* male beauty" (*Q & A*, 1998, 118). First, Fung reiterates the risks of coming out in the queer Asian American community through the loss of "families and our ethnic communities." Second, Fung emphasizes the importance of finding and creating new images of the Asian American queer body that destabilize the exaltation of white gay male beauty standards and that will more publicly promote and include the queer Asian American body within erotic representations. Fung's work seeks to find depictions of queer desire and bodies that redefine and rearticulate gay male beauty from an Asian American point of view. In a similar vein, Joel Tan's anthology takes as its motivation the desire to "depict real, unsanitized, images of gay Pilipino, Asian, Pacific Islander sex. I want to wrap humanity—a body, a character, and a history—around the objects of *my* desire as a response to the racism in the gay community and the homophobia in our own ethnic communities" (*Queer Papi*, 1998, 10). Appearing as a central focus of this anthology, the Asian American queer body possesses a political value as a receptacle for erotic power. By opening up sexualized portrayals of queer bodies, Tan's anthology critiques the stereotypes that have been perpetuated about queer Asian Americans, locates the particularities of queer Asian American history, and combats the obstacles the queer Asian American community faces in its own ethnic groups. *All* the anthologies take this stance, to include a diversity of queer Asian American voices and writings that resist, complicate, and undermine the control of nation-state apparatuses over their bodies as seen in the hegemonic representations that have imprisoned queer Asian Americans in homophobic caricatures, and finally, to challenge their relative exclusion from the Asian American community as a whole. As Cecilia Tan notes of queer Asian American writers: "We are the pioneers. We have to carve out the territory that the next generation will inhabit. We'll have to teach them how to survive in the land we create. But let's make it a big land where individualism—not conformity to genre expectations or mainstream tastes—defines success" ("Queer Asian Writing," 1999, 15). In the struggle for recognition, these anthologists have set out to create a community of writers and artists who will serve as a model for others to follow.

This recent proliferation of queer Asian American writings and political articulations of the queer body and desire requires an increased vigilance on the part of Asian American Studies scholars. One of the few book-length texts to extensively critique queer Asian American writings is David L. Eng's *Racial Castration: Managing Masculinity in Asian American* (2001). His reading of R. Zamora Linmark's *Rolling the R's* explores coalition-building across sexuality and ethnicity, noting that "While the disparate ethnic affiliations of the immigrant adolescents who populate Linmark's novella threaten to divide further their tenuous loyalties, it is precisely sexuality—an obsessive queer sexuality that permeates *Rolling the R's* from beginning to end—that binds them together as a social group with a common sense of purpose and esprit de corps" (Eng, *Racial Castration*, 2001, 225). Eng's thesis revolves around the creation of a new coalition between Asian American subjectivity and queerness; Asian Americans coalesce under the political cause of queerness due to the ways that Asian American sexuality has always been rendered as "deviant" through various laws and restrictions. For Eng, queerness offers a political vantage point that does not collapse the myriad national, class, ethnic, and gender affiliations of the increasingly complicated conceptualization of who and what can be termed Asian American. This discourse is powerful both in the way it would inscribe queerness as a central politic with Asian American communities and academic circles, but also in the way that it attempts to bridge the divide between race and queer sexuality. Critic Crystal Parikh has more specifically argued that Asian American masculinity might be read in terms of "queer aesthetics, an alternative articulatory space of gender and sexuality," a reading enabled by her analysis of works by David Mura and David Wong Louie that contest "the heteronormative logic through which Asian-American masculinity has been formulated" ("Masquerade," 2002, 863). Parikh's insights offer ways to appraise the heteronormative and masculinist rhetoric that has helped to construct Asian American male gender identities as heterosexual. These related readings, however, must contend with issues best epitomized in Eng's cautionary note, that the "disparate ethnic affiliations . . . threaten to divide" the youths of Linmark's fictional work. The very basis of Eng's notion of coalition building relies on the affirmation and creation of a queer Asian American community, one that both identifies as queer and builds relationships through that queerness. This possibility is precarious because of the dangers in being visibly out and also because such coalitions must occur in a space that nurtures the development of such a community (where individuals can meet and form cohesive relationships between each other).

Linmark's *Rolling the R's* is one of many Asian American novels that expanded and complicated the representations of queer Asian Americans and their respective bodies in the past few years.[2] Jessica Hagedorn's novel, *Dogeaters* (1990), too, contains representations of various queer characters, including one of the major characters, Joey Sands, who possesses erotic authority as an attractive hustler. Sau-ling Cynthia Wong advances that Joey is a "mixed homosexual prostitute with the adaptability of a chameleon" ("Denationalization," 1995, 11) who maintains a job as a disc jockey, while having been brought up as a pickpocket, sometimes prostitutes himself, and later becomes connected to the guerrilla movement. Certainly, Joey's ability to navigate the multifaceted urban world of sexual tourism, nightclubs, and prostitution confers this chameleon-like feature of his character. Joey seems to retain a certain power over those individuals he comes in contact with during prostitution: "Sometimes I'll steal from them, just to make a point. . . . I never keep what's given to me as a gift; I like to let them know how little their trinkets are really worth, what kind of dope I bought with their money" (Hagedorn, *Dogeaters*, 1990, 37). Here, Joey turns the table on individuals who seek to demonstrate their economic superiority over him and construct him as an individual who is dependent on them for material survival. In Joey's mind then, buying becomes a sort of statement that temporary material gain is a superfluous byproduct of his prostitution; he is with them because he wants to be. In this sense, Joey believes he commands an agency in the sex tourism trade. He further exerts a sexual power over his johns, employing his body to entice customers to do his bidding. Through his sexual power and youthful physical attractiveness, Joey meets transnational entities: the American G.I. Neil, an Australian man who eyes Joey lasciviously, as well as Rainer, a German director who visits Manila during an international film festival featuring his movies. These individuals attempt to gain Joey's favor by buying him various things (e.g., fashionable American foods like hamburgers) or taking him to special locations (mansions in Manila).

Joey's erotic power, however, is problematized by exploring it from the vantage point of these transnational elites like Rainer. Joey laments, "I don't mind when he [Rainer] takes real pictures of me with that fancy camera of his, which he's done all week: *Joey Swimming. Joey and Cup of Coffee. Joey Lighting a Cigarette. Joey Bored. Joey Brooding*" (Hagedorn, *Dogeaters*, 1990, 149). Here, Hagedorn again exposes the downside of the sex trade; the sexual encounter with the exotic "other" becomes commodified. As Rainer takes pictures of Joey, he clearly objectifies Joey's queer body, consuming him in filmic slide reels. Therefore, the deployment of the body and sexuality is not simply Joey's to control; his attractiveness exerts its own force that causes johns to capitalize on his existence. In this way, Joey remains enslaved to his physical beauty to provide for his well-being. Consequently, in a transnational perspective, the queer body takes on new complicated formations. Hagedorn's text begs a number of questions: What is the queer body's political value in the face of physical deprivation and commodification? And further, how can we understand the queer Asian American figure in transnational space, especially in relation to building queer communities? Hagedorn provides a political outlet for Joey Sands as he becomes a guerrilla warrior ensconced in the mountains beyond Manila, yet, strangely his sexuality becomes cleaved, almost absent from the text. The novel therefore produces a strange and strained relationship between the political value of the queer body and the inexorable alterations that late capitalism produces on queer individuals in transnational spaces.

Lawrence Chua's first novel, *Gold by the Inch*, is a challenge (especially to the politically lucid interventions made by queer Asian American anthologies, to Asian American studies in general, and to the politically engaged coalition building theorized by David L. Eng) in its articulation of the strained connections between the queerness, politics, and the body and in its representation of a politically ambivalent, queer Asian American protagonist. The book is fragmented, destabilizing, and at times opaque in its characterization of this unnamed narrator, whose motivations and obsessions sometimes cannot fully be explained. Reviewer Shirley N. Quan notes of Chua's novel: "The images are often graphic and disturbing, giving this story a hard and realistic edge" ("Review," 1998, 136). And subtly, the text portrays a character who, as an Asian American, understands the beauty of wealth and the exploitative power in sexuality. The once-trophy boyfriend of a well-to-do white lover, the unnamed narrator, finds himself an object, no more than something to be thrown out when the relationship goes sour. As the narrative moves away from New York to the transnational space of Bangkok, Thailand, and Penang, Malaysia, the main character displays an erudite knowledge of the colonial ties that the Southeast Asian region has maintained with Great Britain as well as the politics of survival that many Southeast Asian individuals and governments have initiated in order to compete with the European powers economically. In this tenuous historical relationship between Southeast Asia and colonial Great Britain, the protagonist situates himself as an angry observer and scholar. He is particularly critical of Thai people for their complicity in the development of a decadent late capitalist economy and of the colonial powers for their destructive cultural influence on the Southeast Asian landscape. The textual complexity plays out in the protagonist's personal exploits. He regularly participates in sex tourism, which he conceives as a trade that arose in part due to the relationship between Great Britain and Thailand. While the narrator-character seems well aware of the reifying and exploitative consequences of the sex tourist trade, he nonetheless continues to hope that his particular relationship to a sex worker, Thong, will give rise to a fulfilling romantic relationship. When things do not work out between them at the conclusion of the novel, the narrator proclaims he is a citizen of the world and already imagines himself in other cities. Chua's text works as a cautionary critique of the politically cognizant subject who possesses both economic and cultural capital, but who cannot move sufficiently outside the relationship between consumers and commodities. The novel does not enact any closure; instead, it offers a replicating narrative of the process of sexual exploitation and hedonism that overpowers the efficacy of political and historical knowledge.

The narrative's nonlinear sequencing is perhaps one of the most difficult aspects of Chua's novel. Although the novel might at first read simply as a linear narrative, the drug-induced hazes of the protagonist (brought on by an eclectic cocktail of cocaine, alcohol, heroin, and sleeping pills) generate fractured episodes that include key flashbacks to events that contribute to the formation of character; as the narrator explains, "You were not born in a garden. But you replay the scenarios of creation and lost innocence over and over again" (Chua, *Gold by the Inch*, 1998, hereafter cited as *GI*, 14). One key stylistic element in Chua's text is his frequent use of the second-person viewpoint. The deployment of "you" to refer to the narrator-protagonist works to destabilize the narrative, provides a challenging tone to the text, and at the same time, suggests a strange interiority in the passages where he seems to be talking to himself. For example, the biblical reference to the "garden" in the passage above suggests what the character sees as his sexual deviancy and the carnal knowledge that came with exploring these "scenarios of creation and lost innocence." As a teenager traveling home by train, he is cruised by a fellow passenger, presumably an older white and married male. In this formative moment, when he finds himself engaging in sexual acts with a stranger in the space of the train restroom, the narrator discovers the intoxicating power of his queer sexuality. It is the narrator who commands the unknown man to enter the restroom and who initiates the particular sex acts that ensue. Later, when the narrator-protagonist desires a change in location, he is the one to suggest a motel room. The protagonist carries a strange mixture of power and subjection; he is offered money for his sexual services but eventually repudiates the offer. The narrator recalls: "You get off the train and he's right behind you as the train pulls away. Leaving you both there on the platform. I'll give you twenty. I'll give you thirty. OK, fifty. No. No way. I said, no. He is standing at the station as you walk into shuttered storefronts and gray dust. Mister: he could be dead now for all you know. The last words on his lips were numbers" (15). As the man propositions the narrator with monetary offers, the encounter moves into an ambiguous terrain of possible prostitution. In that moment, the narrator's body has become objectified and reified by the stranger's sexual desire. He is put under the potential power of this man's capital, the lure of his money. The narrator however, refuses to engage in the system, in such commodification of his body, and instead leaves the man to wallow in confusion. As the protagonist remarks that the man could be "dead now," he exhibits extreme detachment from the entire sexual encounter and recalls his past agency in that image of sexual discretion and denial.

In another flashback of "creation and lost innocence," the narrator recollect the stripping of a Rolls Royce by a group of mechanics, including his overbearing and abusive father. "They knowingly disassemble the machine until the only thing that remains is the wicked gleam of steel and oil. I inspect every piece as it is taken off. Needily. As if the engine itself held the secrets of my own desire. I want to see what's inside this great symbol of power and lust. I want to see what makes me burn" (GI, 23). The Rolls Royce's "wicked gleam of steel and oil" symbolizes the very insidious nature of the wealth that remains well out of the grasp of the narrator's family. Steel and oil, two of the earth's most important resources, become symbolic of a greater global affluence that the protagonist envies and desires. As the body of the Rolls Royce is dismantled, so begins the novel's unmasking of the relation between sexuality and power, money and objectification. In a strange, grotesque comparison, in the narrator's belief that he can find the "secrets" of his "own desire" in the very engine of the vehicle, queer desire is equated with capital and power. This flashback, voyeuristic in nature, literalizes the Rolls Royce as a body that is stripped not only for the protagonist to view, but also for the viewing of an entire group of mechanics. Feminist critic Eve Kosofsky Sedgwick notes of the homosocial, "the most natural thing in the world [is] that people of the same gender . . . should bond together also on the axis of sexual desire" (Epistemology, 1992, 87). Sedgwick's theory of the homosocial offers a triangulation between men and their objects of desire. As men "bond" in the ways by which they are simultaneously attracted to a particular body, individual, or object, they initiate very specific relationships with each other. In terms of Asian American history, Robert G. Lee notes the ways in which homosocial bonding led to the traffic of Chinese women into prostitution in the late nineteenth and early twentieth centuries as Chinese men sold young women off to crooked white politicians and officers.[3] In the case of Chua's novel, the power of the passage lies in its entangling of sexuality, monetary desire, and physical hunger, which are coded and intertwined in its very vocabulary. Although the narrator is seduced by the opulence of the Rolls Royce (a sort of queer desire in and of itself, loving that which is inorganic), the mechanics also "converge on the carcass like hungry animals" (*GI*, 87), physically drawn to the capital that the Rolls Royce possesses. In this instance, the axis of sexuality is rendered as queer and the body of the car is commodified.

In yet another flashback, the narrator remembers his deteriorating relationship with his Caucasian boyfriend, Jim, a well-to-do interior designer living in New York. As purveyors of all things beautiful, Jim takes them both on a trip to Paris during which the narrator concludes three essential aspects about their relationship. First, he realizes he "got a lot of free plane tickets" out of being Jim's "decorative companion" (*GI*, 55). Jim provides the material goods to permit both him and the narrator to live comfortably, travel the world, engage in constant cocaine usage, and buy expensive valuables like antiques. Their relationship was enabled by Jim's affluence. Second, the narrator realizes that he is simply a trophy boyfriend, valued for his looks more than anything else. As Jim fixes a value to the narrator-protagonist's exterior beauty, the narrator's body becomes both an object and commodity. For the narrator, his relationship with Jim remains mediated on one level in the exchange of his beauty for Jim's monetary support. The narrator notes of their relationship: "Ours took on a ghoulish objectivity. . . . The thing it became was an investment, and I was frustrated when I came to collect. The dividends were getting smaller. Maturity seemed farther away than ever before. It was depressing, watching all that money squandered up Jim's nose" (58). The relationship between Jim and the narrator-protagonist is clearly economically situated as it is described in relation to an "investment," "dividends," and "collection." In this particular passage, the relationship begins to lose its economic viability in the eyes of the narrator as both Jim's responsibility and finances dry up. If so much of their relationship depended on the exchange of the narrator's beauty for Jim's money, then what will happen when Jim no longer can maintain his side of the bargain?

Finally, the main character recognizes that being with Jim offers him the advantage of blending in, not standing out in a crowd. One day, while he is walking confidently alone on the streets of Paris, he finds himself accosted by the police: "Still, every edifice and corner announced [Paris] was mine. My shoulders fell back and my legs took the lead. I ventured out into the Metro with what could loosely be termed pride. It was the wrong fare. . . . I was surrounded by ten men in black paramilitary uniforms" (*GI*, 56). The protagonist's sense of security is shattered by the intrusion of the police who destroy any notion of his ownership of the Parisian cityscape. Instead, the main character is rendered as a foreigner and perhaps a criminal, ultimately someone who stands out in a negative way. That "ten men in black paramilitary uniforms" are needed to arrest one person exacerbates his feelings of deviancy and placelessness. He concludes "Jim gave me the appearance of belonging: to a place, to a time, to him" (57), but even as

Jim offers the protagonist a sense of "belonging," the narrator comes to realize that the relationship cannot be maintained.

Taken together, the scenes on the train, the stripping of the Rolls Royce, and the failed relationship between the narrator and Jim offer a foundational understanding of the narrator-protagonist in Chua's novel. In the instance with the old man in the train, he becomes the object of desire that then is taken as a commodity. He comes to realize the power of his own sexuality and beauty because of a man who will throw money at him just to engage him sexually. In the garage, he comes to understand the seduction of wealth, what it might afford and how inevitably wealth engenders desire. Finally, his relationship to Jim comes to cement the connections between queerness, commodification, and objectification. Not unlike the sexual encounter in the train, the narrator's relationship to Jim is based on the exchange of queer desire for money. In this exchange system, the protagonist is once again rendered as an object that can be bought. Even in this mutually exploitative situation, he has the power to leave, to deny love, to end the encounter. However, the cessation of the relationship brings with it uncertainty and unstable grounding. If belonging and value come at the price of being with a white lover, then with the loss of the lover, the narrator is reduced to a psychically displaced diasporic subject, removed from any sense of home. And with this lack of belonging, the narrator is also left economically deprived. It is this knowledge and these formative events that the narrator brings with him on his trip to Southeast Asia.

Gold by the Inch initiates its transnational movement with the story of its unnamed narrator (an Asian American of Malaysian-Thai descent living in New York) who travels to Bangkok at the behest of his brother, Luk, a successful architect. The narrative begins with a conspicuous and frenetic description of the cityscape of Bangkok: "The city as bitch, a sonorous lullaby of hungry flies. Garlands rotting at the feet of gods and sex tourists. A real piece of work. You and me sitting by the windows in Mahbunkrong dipping our straws in iced coffee and making crawling worms out of paper wrappers. The wind blowing off the river like a common suggestion" (*GI*, 5). This opening passage shifts between the protagonist's nostalgia for this homeland and his incisive critical observations of the changes that the city has undergone. Certainly there is a wistful quality to this passage in which the narrator finds himself drinking coffee with his prostitute-lover, but the intrusion of hot and humid weather and the increasingly commercialized landscape undermines such idyllic moments. Although the city is a "bitch" filled with "hungry flies," the sound these flies make is nonetheless "sonorous." The protagonist attempts to find moments of subtle beauty amid the decadent urbanscape. Sacred "gods" and the hedonistic "sex tourists" are yoked together in the image of "rotting garlands," testimony to the divided interests of the city.

The flies can be equated with the sex tourists themselves, both organisms desiring sustenance. The exclamation that Bangkok is a "real piece of work" expresses the narrator's amazement at the ways the city has been transformed into what the he conceives as a complicated nexus of desire, capitalism, and beauty. The constructed and commodified nature of the Mahbunkrong, a Bangkok mega-mall, is played directly against the natural majesty of the river with the "wind blowing off." This textual representation of Bangkok illustrates the complications of modernity in which the very nature of the city's existence depends on systems of monetary exchange and a location for deploying such systems (like malls). The city cannot be divorced from the very nature in and around it, from the "hungry flies" and "rotting garlands" to the "wind blowing off the river." Part of the narrator's attitude toward his environment is related to his particularity as an urban subject: he is a queer Asian American possessing capital who desires romance. Is it possible for him to find such love in this city? Even as the attractive hustler Thong sits across from him at the table, they make no conversation. Instead they are left "making crawling worms out of paper wrappers." Already the disconnection between the two is apparent, yet the narrator retains the hope that Thong will love him unconditionally. In the space of the mall, in contrast to the urban constructions that surround them, the protagonist finds himself inexorably drawn to Thong's natural beauty. In an apparent reversal, the main character now finds that he is the one purchasing a relationship rather than the one being pursued for purchase.

The ramifications of the failed relationship between Jim and the narrator in New York carry over in his current exploits in Bangkok through his critical disdain both for processes of commodification and his desires for capital. Thus, the narrator had discovered in himself the lure of wealth both as a child and in his relationship to Jim, but his attempts to articulate a higher moral ground cannot be maintained during his stay in Southeast Asia. In Bangkok, the narrator finds a location filled with commodities and commodified bodies, an inequality between classes, and a general lack of community. According to the narrator, "They have pills here that no one even knows the names of yet. You can buy Quaalude here also. Or something like it, anyway" (GI, 9). The proliferation of drugs in Bangkok correlates with the sex trade; many sex workers in bars and brothels remain high on "synthetic opiates" (10). Despite this critical view, the protagonist finds himself indulging in drugs as a form of escape. He begins to take on significant characteristics that he had observed in his ex-partner, Jim; he becomes an extensive drug user and, valuing the beauty of his new partner Thong, he purchases Thong's services. The backdrop to this relationship occurs in the decadent clubscape of Bangkok. One particular bar and brothel in the text, the Milk Bar, is "fitted with zebra skins and an American fifties retro theme. After midnight it fills up with the fresh faces of the nation's young elite. They may be wearing nothing flashier than jeans and a T-shirt, but from their arrived English to their discreetly confident gestures, they register their origins in the oldest and most respectable families in the nation" (10). The emblematic "zebra skins and American fifties retro theme" pushes this scene toward a global perspective; extra-national locations such as the United States and Africa are deployed as a way to market the bar. What is also interesting about this particular bar is that it is populated with transnational Thai elites, what Aihwa Ong (1999) has called the "flexible citizen," individuals who are tied to multiple nations, which contrasts against the relative immobility of the local go-go dancers. Class divides the consumers and these bar performers, who are "entwining themselves indifferently in each other's arms" (GI, 10). The acquisition of English registers as societal marker, conferring a lofty social status of the Thai elites. In this place of queer desire, the narrator works in a critique of Thai class, one that has bought into the inequalities rising out of late capitalism, and multinational and globalized economic systems. At the same time, the narrator's class advantage cannot be dismissed; he too speaks English and possesses the excess capital to indulge in nightly visits to bars and brothels.

Although it is clear that by purchasing Thong the narrator participates in the sex tourist industry, he is quick to attribute the historical rise of the industry to British colonial involvement. Thus, as reviewer Therese Murdza notes, the relationship between Thong and the protagonist "is set to a broad historical context" in which the main character "chronicles the politics of labor and wealth and the ugliness of one culture colonizing another" ("Review," 1998, 27). The narrator relates:

> "Remember that the dry season coincides with the sex tourism season here, dumb brown trash pouring in from the hills to keep their families alive during the drought. In the nineteenth century, prostitution expanded after the British pressured Thailand to grow rice for export. The small upcountry farmers had always grown rice.... But now there was a new hunger to feed.... Your great-grandparents became a resource. They learned to understand their bodies as prospects, dependent on an unquenchable commerce, dominated by foreign desires" (GI, 18).

The British and other European colonial powers jockeyed for a piece of Thailand during the eighteenth and nineteenth centuries, and the country was briefly ruled by Japan during World War II. Although the Thai peoples were never directly colonized, the tenuous relationship between Thailand and Great Britain clearly moved the Thais into a liminal space where national survival necessitated changes in their economy.

As Frantz Fanon noted of the colonial process, nations must be mindful of the ways in which the postcolonial regime can come to look not so different from the colonial system prior to revolution. In particular Fanon excoriates the middle class: "To them, nationalization quite simply means the transfer into native hands of those unfair advantages which are a legacy of the colonial period" (*Wretched*, 1963, 152). At root in this "transfer" of power, the indigenous middle-class inhabitants who, instead of generating a cohesive national structure, scramble for the power to cement their economic advantages. According to Fanon, the middle class, unintentionally perhaps, destructively replicates a system of colonial exploitation for its own economic benefit. Fanon's striking "postcolonial" prediction presages the continued presence of colonial power, albeit in an altered manner: "The national bourgeoisie will be greatly helped on its way toward decadence by the Western bourgeoisies, who come to it as tourists for the exotic, for big game hunting, and for casinos" (153). In this postcolonial context, world powers continue to dominate nations whose economies rest on catering to the most mobile members of global society: the passport holders, elite businessmen, the "tourists for the exotic." The general term "Western bourgeoisies" illustrates the multiple and multifaceted nature of this new colonialism. Although colonies were tied specifically to mother nations, the postcolonial country now finds itself variably dominated by multiple mother nations as a service provider.

Fanon's predictions cannot necessarily be mapped so closely to British involvement in Thailand. Thailand was never considered a viable British colony. In Chua's novel, however, the protagonist elaborates a critique of a social economic system where Thais adapt their culture to the commodification of bodies for foreign johns. The underlying motivation is access to capital and surplus profit. The narrator makes clear that a number of classes, not simply the middle class, are involved in the alteration of the Thai economic and cultural landscape. Just as the Thai government made concessions to the British to export more rice, the Thai laboring class also attempts to survive changes in the nation by employing their bodies as the site of production, that of an exotic sexuality to feed "foreign desires." The narrator implicates the Thai laboring class in the development of the sex tourist trade. The ambition to move beyond a subsistence economy and move into a surplus profit system means that they must exploit any possible market; in this instance, that market is sex tourism. The narrator's disdain for these farmers suggests a racist discourse when he calls them "dumb brown trash." Although the narrator purports to castigate both the Thai working class and British colonial powers, as the novel develops, he also participates in sex tourism. As critic Stephen O. Murray notes, "For all the rantings about the outrages of colonialism Chua and his narrator seem oddly ignorant of Chinese imperialism, Han Chinese arrogance, the resentments for Chinese arrogance and success felt by non-Chinese Southeast Asians, and the socio- or psycho-dynamics of his relations with symbols of white oppression" ("Representations," 2003, 130). In pointing out the narrator-protagonist's flawed viewpoint as he engages with the complex history of colonialism in Thailand, Murray seems to suggest that the narrator presents an overdetermined view of the European colonial powers, while eliding the historical faults of other Asian nations including China and Japan. It is in this contradictory and conflicted position of moral authority that narrator-protagonist grounds himself, a location that becomes increasingly untenable in the course of the narrative.

The process of identification and disidentification with Thai peoples constantly shifts and is complicated by the ways in which, in the narrative, native Thai individuals can mark the main character as a foreigner. In one encounter, where the protagonist gives money to a beggar girl, he admits: "I scrape my veins for the right words and then dive for my dictionary, because there are no words in my vocabulary for what I feel for her. I point to the word empathy and score the Thai word next to it with my fingernail" (GI, 34). In this instance, the narrator articulates his connection to this destitute figure as empathy, the comprehension of what she must go through to survive. Indeed, the protagonist's childhood upbringing in a small shack-like home in Penang, Malaysia, gives him insight into the life of the poor. However, at the same time, the difference in language forces him to "dive for [his] dictionary." Linguistic differences mark his distance from the girl. The scraping of his veins, the very attempt to find the words in the Southeast Asian blood flowing through his body, does not provide him with the language he seeks. Immediately after the girl becomes lost in a crowd, the narrator remarks, "I watch the girl amble into the crush of milling consumers outside the bar. Somehow, the poverty that spawned her seems even more remote than she is. We were growing, far above her tiny vanishing figure. Soon she would mean nothing. We were growing so fast and we needed respite from people like her, from the fried locusts and crumbling sidewalks outside the mall" (35). That the girl's poverty seems "even more remote" signals the divide between her life and the narrator's. While he exists on equal footing with the "milling consumers," he sees both himself and Thong "growing, far above" the beggar girl. Metaphorically, this growth in their bodies can be taken as the image of imposing figures in the stratified urbanscape, in which the ability to move into the air conditioned spaces of the mall signifies class privilege. The realization that he cannot permanently enhance or improve the quality of the girl's life leads him to escape into the air conditioned recesses of the mall and to a "respite from people like her." Once again the mall comes to symbolize the commodified nature of Bangkok, the very symbol of wealth that is placed in direct contrast to the poor, the "fried locusts" and "crumbling sidewalks."

As the protagonist identifies himself and Thong with an upper class in contrast to the beggar girl, he betrays a subtle idealism in his character—that somehow by being with Thong, he is changing Thong's life for the better. At one point, the narrator observes of their relationship, "Perfect lovers. Two identical clocks side by side ticking time perfect harmony" (*GI*, 29). Yet, the narrative also undercuts these romanticized moments, for the narrator knows the relationship is more complicated. In one instance, the narrator notes that he is "breaking rules, taking a prostitute on a date during the day. I'm not talking about taking him out to a bar and buying him drinks to loosen him up. This is different. I'm transgressing roles, crossing borders, that kind of thing. Of course I pay for the ticket" (21). The narrator's decision to bring Thong to a movie "during the day" indicates that he is not afraid to be seen with him anywhere; this relationship does not remain concealed in the nocturnal closet of clubs and bars. Such an outing hearkens to the gentle beginnings of a courtship with the narrator taking on the role of the provider. At the same time, the narrator is perfectly aware that while "transgressing roles," he is on a date with a "prostitute." His purchase of the ticket renders him not only the provider but also the customer. On this strange border between romance and prostitution, Thong and the protagonist vacillate between the intimacy of lovers and the distance between customer and hustler.

The complexities of this sort of relational limbo play out as Thong begins to open himself up to the narrator, revealing his tortured relationship with family, especially with his father. As the protagonist attempts to grapple with this newfound intimacy, he awkwardly throws "the wad of bills, each one blessed with His majesty's portrait, across the room at the mirror. [Thong] turns and frowns.—You should know better. You should show some respect" (*GI*, 28). There is double significance to Thong's exhortation that the narrator-protagonist "show some respect." In this scene, the narrator reveals his cultural ignorance of Thailand as he disrespectfully throws currency that bears the portraits of the Thai royal family, highly esteemed across all classes in Thailand. Moreover, this passage marks Thong's passage into the role of subject, endowed with his own desires, feelings, and insecurities. But as the narrator flagrantly pushes money at Thong, Thong comes to realize how he has been objectified as a commodity and finds his dignity assaulted. Thong thus seeks "respect" for himself and more largely, for the Thai royal family. In this moment, the relationship becomes its most exploitative as the protagonist fails to live up to the promise of being more than just another john. In fact, the scene bears signs of what Karl Marx had defined as commodity fetishism. As Michael T. Taussig elaborates, commodity fetishism "in a developed capitalist culture" occurs when "capital and workers' products are spoken of in terms that are used for people and animate beings. It is money as interest-bearing capital that lends itself most readily to this type of fetishism" ("Genesis," 1997, 139). In this instance, the worker's product, Thong's body, literally becomes the commodity as it is purchased by and for the exploits of the narrator-protagonist. In failing to be a good listener, the protagonist makes it abundantly clear that he perceives Thong as ultimately only a prostitute. Thong's warning that the narrator "should show some respect" epitomizes the very power Thong possesses in this relationship. Just as he is able to reiterate his humanity through this statement, Thong presents himself throughout the narrative as an agent imbued with charisma and force. It is the attractive pull, which Thong maintains over the narrator, that generates the obsession that fuels the final narrative moments. Finally, the inclusion of the "mirror" in this scene recalls the episode in the train where the man throws money at the protagonist in hopes of buying the sexual encounter; here the situation is reflected in reverse, as the narrator throws the wad of bills to compensate for Thong's services.

After the protagonist returns from visiting his family in Penang, Malaysia, he again seeks the companionship and services of Thong in Bangkok. The narrator attempts to affirm his own independence by setting up his own accommodations in Bangkok rather than sleeping at Thong's home: "You want him to know you can still have a life. You want him to show up at the bar and see you, a drink in your hand, a smile plastered on your face. You want him to be jealous. To know what ground he's standing on" (*GI*, 152). Even while the main character finds himself pulled further in his desire for Thong, he wants desperately to command a position of power, that it is Thong's desire that drives the relationship. This pretense only serves to demonstrate the extremity of a protagonist's tenuous position. Although hoping to see Thong again around the city, the narrator occupies his time by attempting to make "new friends. You and your new friends dump whole grams on the mirror and leisurely shape them into lines, sucking back gin and tonic" (159). In the disintegrating stages of their relationship, the main character escapes the pain of rejection through the use of drugs. The "mirror" here serves to recall the failed relationship between the narrator and his once-boyfriend Jim, who was unable to stop snorting cocaine. The narrator is placed in the position of the abject even as he continues to try to find ways to dominate his lover-prostitute by forcing Thong to spend time with him. In one particularly poignant instance, the main character intimates: "When you close your eyes it might be his chest you have your arms locked around. You won't let him go ever, you tease, but when you wake up your face is pushed into the mattress and the pillow is on the floor. When your eyes are open every noise belongs to him. The footsteps in the hall. A key turning in a lock. A motor idling. Your heart pounding in its coffin" (163). The narrator's obsessive desire renders the position of this transnational elite an unhappy one, filled with longing and emptiness. The narrator finds his very senses dominated by his need for Thong. As Thong is motivated and subjected to the power of capital and money, the narrator finds himself subjected to the power of Thong's indifference.

In the novel's conclusion, the protagonist recognizes that he cannot have Thong, even as a customer. "This is just a vacation for you isn't it" (*GI*, 201), Thong rails at him on the day their relationship ends. In the breakup scene, the narrator acknowledges that he is "just an American, darker than the rest, doing things in Thailand [he] can never do at home" (201). He finally admits that he cannot identify with Thong nor truly understand him, that he cannot come to a place where they could have anything more than a service relationship. The narrator is an American on a hedonistic journey during which time he can leave whenever he wants if things do not work out. He accepts the conclusive fact that he, too, has become an individual who is capable of commodifying and possessing others. For Thong, the situation is not quite the same. He is not on vacation and he prostitutes himself as a way of dealing with the difficulties in his life; the gulf between Thong and his father and the relative lack of options for a queer Thai individual to express his sexuality in the open has led to his hustling. The narrator cannot bridge this difference. In the end, the protagonist tells himself "the world is yours" (205) and books himself a plane flight to the United States where he resumes his dysfunctional relationship with Jim.

In a hotel room in Los Angeles, Jim and the narrator find themselves snorting coke together. When Jim says, "I love you because your body is expensive" (*GI*, 208), with this quick revelation the protagonist has moved back to the position of the object, his body again a commodity. As he reenters the national space of the United States, he disengages from the position of the exploiter and returns to Jim's side as a trophy boyfriend. The novel thus represents a queer Asian American character who engages in the objectification of Asian others as much as he himself is objectified. The formative moments of his queerness left him subjected to the power of wealth, which renders the body as a commodity. His experiences in Bangkok demonstrate his ambiguous stance toward capital. Even as he criticizes Bangkok for being overly commercialized, he nonetheless engages in sex tourism. In this way, the narrator embodies a fragmented subject. He is at once the queer Asian American male who has been objectified as a commodity in the United States, as well as a figure for the Western bourgeoisie who participates in sex tourism in Bangkok; he is the political pundit of colonialism who engages in spreading capitalist influence, and he is also the hopeless romantic, courting his beloved. His identity constantly shifts, unstable and uncertain.

The novel's intricate and complex formation of a transnational subject in a country located far outside the United States and its unyielding portrayal of a politically cognizant queer Asian American who engages in abject acts would seem to undercut and contradict any position of moral authority. In her article "Denationalization Reconsidered: Asian American Cultural Criticism at a Theoretical Crossroads," Sau-ling Wong voices concern for recent trends in transnational studies that tend to elide the importance of class-based critiques: "What is more, I wonder to what extent a class bias is coded into the privileging of travel and transnational mobility" (1995, 15). Indeed, Chua's novel cannot be understood without an exploration of transnationalism and class. Certainly, one problematic element in Chua's text is that mobility is afforded most obviously to the Asian American main character, who comes to Bangkok through the generosity of his brother's company and can purchase sex and indulge in cocaine. In this transnational city, the Asian American narrator-protagonist possesses a social cache that other Southeast Asian characters cannot claim. This fact is most evident in the distance between the young beggar girl whom the narrator encounters while in the marketplace with Thong.

At the same time, as class division collides with queer desire, complicated matrices of power form wherein those of different class backgrounds can still maintain positions of domination. According to Gordan Brent Ingram: "This decade, the last of the first century of prolonged urban activism by sexual minorities, is seeing an explosion of theories about queers in urban and rural space that involve a range of scales from the closet to the transnational region. And like most other environmental amenities in late capitalism, queer space is increasingly commodified" (*Queers in Space*, 1997, 40). In Chua's novel, the city of Bangkok must necessarily be seen as the combined site of queer desire and commodified bodies as a space where gay resorts, queer sexual tourism, and hustling occur. The reader is thus made aware that Thong does not necessarily come to prostitution out of pure financial necessity. The novel suggests that for Thong, the performance of gay prostitution comes from a complex set of relations in which he acts out queer desire in one of the only avenues afforded to Southeast Asians, in the commodified spaces of bars and brothels. As Peter A. Jackson notes of gay culture in Thailand, "it is the fact that commercial gay scenes in gay capitals such as Bangkok first emerged to provide services to their respective *local* gay markets that confers and degree of difference and cultural specificity to these cultures" ("Gay Capitals," 2003, 160). The emphasis on the word "local" demonstrates the importance of intranational relations that help to develop queer identity and culture.

In this sense, it would be impossible to read the sex tourist trade represented in *Gold by the Inch* as arising only from the influence of transnational elites such as the main character. Instead, the queer culture represented in the novel first serves the local area, a key element identified as certain bars and brothels that only cater to Thai nationals (*GI*, 10) and certain gay resorts that are primarily frequented by residents of Thailand rather than foreigners (20). Jackson's analysis contends that colonial influence could not be the sole progenitor of the commodified character of queer culture in Bangkok. Instead, Jackson argues that queer culture originated in the very marketplace of urban centers as "gay identities... are very readily commodified as sites of investment" ("Gay Capitals," 2003, 160). Although the protagonist in Chua's *Gold by the Inch* comes to find the increased urbanization and commercialization of Bangkok both stifling and unappealing, this very nature of the city allows the queer to form and flourish. As Jackson further expounds: "Despite the liberating potentials of homosexual autonomy that are made possibly by the city and the market, modern gay identity is only achieved at considerable cost, financial and moral. This cost can be quantified as the income required to sustain an aspirational middle-class consumerist lifestyle" (161). That is, according to Jackson, Bangkok queer culture is classed by its very nature. Not everyone can afford to be "gay" because being gay means having the capital to buy brand name clothing, attend gay resorts, and appear in the city's trendiest bars. In this respect, Thong's desire for extra spending money, even though his father is a sugar plantation owner, illustrates the commodified nature of Thai queer culture. For Thong to thrive in Bangkok's gay culture, a culture of excess, he needs excess capital. In this instance, he turns to hustling. Similarly, as a transnational entity with financial and spatial mobility, the narrator-protagonist is empowered in queer urban spaces that are themselves formed through "considerable cost," costs he fails to quite fully understand.

Viet Thanh Nguyen's *Race and Resistance: Literature and Politics in Asian America* asks Asian American Studies scholars to take on "an ethics of intellectual inquiry and political practice that rejects the idealization of both racial identity and political resistance" (2002, 14). For Nguyen, Asian American literary critics overemphasize the importance of the resistance narrative. He argues that in many foundational works of Asian American literature, a more intricate narrative of complicity and resistance troubles any sort of coherent notion of what it means to be Asian American. Lawrence Chua's novel presents this sort of challenge to Asian American Studies because the novel cannot be read as a simple resistance narrative. At the point in the narrative where the protagonist recognizes he does not wish to be treated as an object anymore and refuses to acknowledge that it is only Jim who legitimates his American identity, he returns to Bangkok. But, this is a journey that further troubles any discrete comprehension of his identity, especially as an Asian American. If anything, the narrator fails to find his place in Bangkok, as his relationship with Thong falters and the friends he makes are restricted to cocaine users. With nothing in Bangkok to ground him, one attractive recourse becomes his ex-boyfriend, Jim, whom he had earlier acknowledged as the person who gave him the "appearance of belonging" and beckons as a provider. Although knowledgeable about colonial history and self-aware of his lack of enfranchisement as a queer Asian American, the narrator is fully presented as corrupted by consuming desires, desires to consume the other and to be consumed himself. In this way, the ambivalence of the narrator also resists being categorized alongside representations of queer bodies in Asian American queer anthologies. Although anthologists avow the importance of visibility and political potential inherent in claiming and exhibiting the queer body, Chua's text provides a murky look at the ways in which the queer body also becomes complicit with problematic political trajectories.

Rachel Lee states that "Asian American critics do not simply resist globalization, but decry a particular form of global-Pacific studies—one that triumphantly heralds the entrepreneurial Asian transnational class, their alternative imagined communities mobilizes in dispersion but also formed through travel and ownership" ("Asian Americans," 1999, 250). In Lawrence Chua's *Gold by the Inch*, Asian American scholars and literary critics find a text that does not "triumphally herald" the transnational migration of the main character. The novel instead offers an invaluable, self-reflexive, and unyielding narrative that complicates the transnational landscape through the nexus of queer desire, the commodification of bodies, and class.

NOTES

1. I use the term *queer* to encompass the varying ranges of this identity grouping including but not limited to gays, lesbians, bisexual, transgender, and intersex.

2. Just some of the many fictional novel-length works to have cropped up in Southeast Asian American (including all of North America) writings concerning queerness and queer desire include: T. C. Huo's *Land of Smiles* (2000) and *A Thousand Wings* (1998); Lydia Kwa's *This Place Called Absence* (2000); R. Zamora Linmark's *Rolling the R's* (1995); Han Ong's *Fixer Chao* (2001). Other significant queer Asian American novels recently produced: Shyam Selvadurai's *Funny Boy* (1994) and *Cinnamon Gardens* (1999); Nina Revoyr's *Necessary Hunger* (1997) and *Southland* (2003); Ghalib Shiraz Dhalla's *Ode to Lata* (2002); Alexander Chee's *Edinburgh* (2001); and Catherine Liu's *Oriental Girls Desire Romance* (1997).

3. In Robert G. Lee's text, *Orientals: Asian Americans in Popular Culture* (2000).

Works Cited

Bao, Quang, and Yanagihara, Hanya, eds. *Take Out: Queer Writing from Asian Pacific America.* New York: Asian American Writers' Workshop, 2000.

Chee, Alexander. *Edinburgh.* New York: Welcome Rain Publishers, 2001.

Chua, Lawrence. *Gold by the Inch.* New York: Grove Press, 1998.

Chung, C., Kim, A., and Lemeshewsky, A. K. *Between the Lines: An Anthology by Pacific/Asian Lesbians of Santa Cruz, California.* Santa Cruz, CA: Dancing Bird Press, 1987.

Dhalla, Ghalib Shiraz. *Ode to Lata.* Los Angeles: Really Good Books, 2002.

Eng, David. *Racial Castration: Managing Masculinity in Asian America.* Durham, NC: Duke University Press, 2001.

Eng, David, and Fujikane, Candace. "Asian American Literature." *GLBTQ: An Encyclopedia of Gay, Lesbian, Bisexual, Transgender, and Queer Culture.* 2002. Retrieved from http://www.glbtq.com/literature/asian_am_lit,3.html.

Eng, David, and Hom, Alice Y., eds. *Q & A: Queer in Asian America.* Philadelphia: Temple University Press, 1998.

Fanon, Frantz. *The Wretched of the Earth.* New York: Grove Press, 1963.

Fung, Richard. "Looking for My Penis: The Eroticized Asian in Gay Video Porn," in *Q & A: Queer in Asian America.* David L. Eng and Alice Y. Hom, eds. (pp. 115–34). Philadelphia, Temple University Press, 1998.

Hagedorn, Jessica. *Dogeaters.* New York: Random House, 1990.

Huo, T. C. *A Thousand Wings.* New York: Dutton, 1998.

———. *Land of Smiles.* New York: Plume, 2000.

Ingram, Gordon Brent. *Queers in Space: Communities/Public Spaces/Sites of Resistance.* Seattle: Bay Press, 1997.

Jackson, Peter A. "Gay Capitals in Global Gay History: Cities, Local Markets, and the Origins of Bangkok's Same-Sex Cultures," in *Postcolonial Urbanism: Southeast Asian Cities and Global Processes.* Ryan Bishop, John Phillips, and Wei Wei Yeo, eds. (pp. 151–63). New York: Routledge, 2003.

Kwa, Lydia. *This Place Called Absence.* Winnipeg: Turnstone, 2000.

Lee, Rachel. "Asian American Cultural Production in Asia-Pacific Perspective." *Boundary 2* 26: 2 (1999): 231–54.

Lee, Robert G. *Orientals: Asian Americans in Popular Culture.* Philadelphia: Temple University Press, 2000.

Leong, Russell, ed. *Asian American Sexualities: Dimensions of the Gay and Lesbian Experience.* New York: Routledge, 1996.

Lim-Hing, Sharon, ed. *The Very Inside: An Anthology of Writing by Asian and Pacific Islander Lesbian and Bisexual Women.* Toronto, Ontario: Sister Vision Press, 1994.

Linmark, R. Zamora. *Rolling the R's.* New York: Kaya, 1995.

Liu, Catherine. *Oriental Girls Desire Romance.* New York: Kaya, 1997.

Murray, Stephen O. "Representations of Desires in Some Recent Gay Asian-American Writings." *Journal of Homosexuality,* 45: 1 (2003): 111–43.

Murdza, Therese. Review of *Gold by the Inch,* by Lawrence Chua. *Lambda Book Report* (June 1998): 27–28.

Nguyen, Viet Thanh. *Race and Resistance: Literature and Politics in Asian America.* London: Oxford University Press, 2002.

Ong, Aihwa. *Flexible Citizenship: The Cultural Logics of Transnationality.* Durham, NC: Duke University Press, 1999.

Ong, Han. *Fixer Chao.* New York: Farrar, Straus, and Giroux, 2001.

Parikh, Crystal. "'The Most Outrageous Masquerade': Queering Asian-American Masculinity." *Modern Fiction Studies,* 48: 4 (2002): 858–98.

Parmar, Pratibha. "That Moment of Emergence," in *Feminism and Film.* E. Ann Kaplan, ed. (pp. 375–83). London: Oxford University Press, 2000.

Quan, Shirley N. Review of *Gold by the Inch,* by Lawrence Chua. *Library Journal* (May 1998): 136.

Revoyr, Nina. *Necessary Roughness.* New York: Simon & Schuster, 1997.

———. *Southland.* New York: Akashic Books, 2003.

Sedgwick, Eve Kosofsky. *Epistemology of the Closet.* Berkeley, CA: University of California Press, 1992.

Selvadurai, Shyam. *Cinnamon Gardens.* New York: Hyperion, 1999.

———. *Funny Boy.* London: Jonathan Cape, 1994.

Takagi, Dana. "Maiden Voyage: Excursion into Sexuality and Identity Politics in Asian America," in *Contemporary Asian America: A Multidisciplinary Reader.* Min Zhou and James V. Gatewood, eds. (pp. 547–60). New York: New York University Press, 2000.

Tan, Cecilia. "For Queer Asian Writing, Individuality Defines Success." *Lambda Book Report,* 7: 10 (1999): 13.

Tan, Joel B., ed. *Queer Papi Porn: Gay Asian Erotica.* San Francisco: Cleis Press, 1998.

Taussig, Michael. "The Genesis of Capitalisms amongst a South American Peasantry: Devil's Labor and the Baptism of Money." *Comparative Studies in Society and History,* 19: 2 (1997): 130–55.

Wong, Sau-ling C. "Denationalization Reconsidered: Asian American Cultural Criticism at a Theoretical Crossroads." *Amerasia Journal,* 21: 1–2 (1995): 1–28.

5 Ethical Responsibility in Intersubjective Spaces

Reading *Jhumpa Lahiri's* Interpreter of Maladies *and "A Temporary Matter"*

Gita Rajan

Prologue

Jhumpa Lahiri won both the Pulitzer Prize for fiction and the Ernest Hemingway Foundation/PEN Award for 2000 for *Interpreter of Maladies*. South Asian writers are garnering praise on a global scale—most notably, V.S. Naipaul, who recently won the Nobel Prize and Amitav Ghosh, who was chosen but declined to accept the Commonwealth Writer's Award. Rohinton Mistry became a household name when Oprah Winfrey recommended his *A Fine Balance* on her show. The academy has for some time now been very familiar with the works of South Asian writers like Salman Rushdie, Michael Ondaatje, Bapsi Sidhwa, and Bharati Mukherjee. On the popular front, newcomers like Monica Ali (British Bangladeshi), Rukhsana Ahmed (British Pakistani), Shyam Selvadurai (Canadian Sri Lankan), Chitra Divakaruni (Indian American), Mohsin Hamid (Pakistani American), and Manil Suri and Amit Choudhuri (Indian) are being reviewed favorably in mainstream media like the *New York Times*; a welcome signal to ethnic writers today.[1] Such a literary landscape positions Lahiri in an interesting historicocultural spot, and allows her work to be read differently from earlier postcolonial or diasporic authors. She rode this wave of South Asian popularity, some academics whispered, by successfully maneuvering her work into the Pulitzer race. Others spoke of the Hemingway/PEN award as a happy marriage of Lahiri's work (debut novel) and her identity (ethnic-gendered body), which met the Foundation's prerequisites. Other recent Hemingway winners are Susan Power, Ha Jin, Chang-rae Lee, and Rosina Lippi—hyphenated Americans all. These American writers explore complex intersections of identity with such constructs as nation, gender, and race; thus Lahiri seemed a natural in this category.

Many were surprised that Lahiri, a woman in her twenties, had won the Pulitzer, the prestigious *American* award, for her very first book of short stories. Some remarked that the politics of global publishing, being what they are, and the fact that Arundhati Roy had won the Booker Prize indicated that it was time for the United States to play catch-up, which made Lahiri the appropriate (and felicitous) candidate for the Pulitzer. A tongue-in-cheek remark in *The Chronicle of Higher Education* captures this general mood of benevolent inclusion well: "in North America, South Asians represent rationality and spirituality—expected to meditate at dawn, hack code all day, and cook curry at dinner."[2] Such casual comments notwithstanding, readers seemed ambivalent about the magnitude of recognition that Lahiri has gained. Through such mostly uncharitable remarks many readers also dismissed her work and have critiqued, in informal spaces, the bestowing of grace upon this young writer.

Why did two acclaimed U.S. literary institutions bestow awards and rewards upon Jhumpa Lahiri? Granted, each one of the nine stories in *Interpreter of Maladies* is superbly crafted and delivered like carefully polished gems. But this is also true of innumerable other storytellers. Perhaps, the reason that Lahiri stands out is because she deploys two interconnected narrative strategies quite successfully. First, she crafts familiar, easily recognizable characters and situations, and second, she interrogates this cognizance by presenting them with uncomfortable, ethical issues. This chapter consequently explores how successful Lahiri's narrative strategies are in deploying these two steps by examining two of her short stories; the first, "Interpreter of Maladies" shows her grasp of ethical responsibility in the intersubjective space between strangers in chance encounters where the memory of *epistemic origin* (i.e., of India or as Indian) instigates a complex connectivity; and the second, "A Temporary Matter," which goes to the other side of the spectrum by examining her strategy of articulating codes of accountability between intimate, familial subjects located in the United States.

Lahiri's characters are predominantly South Asian, but she integrates them into the familiar life of U.S society. Arjun Appadurai's comment captures the idea of this ethos, even though he is not speaking of Lahiri's work. He writes:

> One of the principal shifts in global culture order, created by cinema, television, and video technology . . . has to do with the role of the imagination in social life. . . . In the past two decades, as the deterritorialization of persons, images, and ideas has taken on a new force, this weight has imperceptibly shifted. More persons throughout the world see their lives through the prisms of the possible lives offered by mass media in all their forms. (*Modernity at Large*, 1997, 53–54)

Lahiri executes neat, little scenes so that her othered characters exhibit emotions as they try to blend into generic American images depicted over time through various media, literature included. Lahiri then complicates this familiarity by having her characters face subtle, ethical dilemmas and nudges her readers into pondering her characters' choices. When her characters act in response to these challenges, their dealings appear as decent, perhaps even as predictable, options, which affirm reader expectations of the outcome as *just* and normative. This second narrative component, encrypted in the small dilemmas, answers a recent cry for ethical conduct in our world, a cry emanating from various disciplines, ranging from religion and literature[3] to medicine and business. Indeed, the coupling of ethics and literature has a long and complicated history, thus to claim that Lahiri's success is partially based upon her tackling ethical issues requires careful explanation. Ethics, considered in a traditional frame, refers to a variety of contractual obligations, ranging from moral principles and inviolable codes of right and wrong, to specific beliefs and sociocultural values. Ethics, understood in our contemporary, globalized frame, means conducting oneself responsibly in one's areas of interaction, wherein stated or subtle principles of justice undergirding one's actions are open to negotiations. Understood thus, ethics today spans that indeterminable space between communal responsibility and individual sovereignty with a spoken or silenced injunction to act *correctly*.[4]

Thus, one could make a case that what is refreshingly new in Lahiri's work is the radical dramatization of familiar events mapped over ethical situations that hark back to a brand of American pragmatism. She allows readers to glimpse her characters' overt and covert motives as they pause and reflect upon options on how to act while located at the crossroads of an ethical quandary. It seems appropriate to analyze Lahiri's stories by using Zygmunt Bauman's social science theories, with their pragmatic approach to one's ethical responsibilities vis-à-vis individual and communal accountability in a chaotic, randomly globalized world. Such a pragmatic framing of ethical imperatives enables Lahiri's stories to be read as vignettes of ethical, agentive moments. Bauman speaks of our potential to engage in responsible action in a fluid, imperfect world, enmeshed as we are in the messy grime of compromised and mediated realities of everyday life. He says:

> So let us celebrate the world unencumbered by imagined obligations and fake duties. With universal principles and absolute truths dissipated or kicked out of fashion, *it does not matter much* any more what personal principles and private truth one embraces. . . . Does it or does it not matter?—this is the question. And, it remains a question—perhaps the crucial, constitutive question of postmodern (late modern) life. One must say with considerable conviction that . . . *the demise of power assisted universals and absolutes has made the responsibilities of the actor more profound, and indeed more consequential than ever before.* One might say with still greater conviction,

that between the demise of universal absolutes and absolute universals on the one hand, and "everything goes" license on the other, there is a jarring *non sequitur.* (emphasis in original; *Life in Fragments*, 1995, 6)

Lahiri's stories are poised in this non sequitur, where her characters allow readers to share their commonsense notions of appropriate conduct as they seek plausible, possible resolutions to their problems. One can speculate that Lahiri's *Interpreter of Maladies* speaks simultaneously to Bauman's claim of agency, on the one hand, and to Appadurai's notion of simulacrum, on the other. Lahiri plots the thoughts and movements of her characters, putting them into motion as they ponder ethical issues, while infusing meaning into their actions (and the stories) by invoking familiar memories for her readers and bringing their sense of fair play to the fore.

GRAPHIC REPRESENTATION

Lahiri leads her characters and her readers in a carefully choreographed *pas de deux* by allowing her characters and her readers to glimpse small insights into human nature when experiencing familiar, everyday events in life. Her stories embody the very texture of average Americana, where often we are guided by codes that may be personalized, but are gathered from spaces of *collective memory* and common or populist models of wisdom. These nebulous spaces in popular culture suggest a course of action based on socially agreed-upon codes of *individual* honor and decency. Such a paradoxical and complicated combination of personal sensors and communitarian assumptions of *proper* action results in her characters' making difficult compromises, and leaves her readers feeling a little ambivalent about the outcome of the actions. Interestingly, this careful blend of directing action based upon an impulse toward right conduct with slightly opaque motives gives readers a sharp prick of poignant pleasure.

By contextualizing the unspoken rules of engagement in situations that make explicit the accountability factor in her characters' actions, Lahiri reveals the principles involved when forming relationships in society (i.e., the sense of responsibility grounded in reciprocity without compromising or oppressing any of the actors). Ironically though, right actions framed in a philosophical, abstract realm are often at odds when practicing them in the lived reality of America's multiracial society. Lahiri avoids this specific problem by not writing about race, since racial interactions in the United States are fraught with foundational moral problems. Instead, her characters focus reader attention upon the final meaning of the short stories in interactions between Indians and U.S. citizens as encounters between the new immigrant and old inhabitant, rather than between two races.[5]

Such a variegated but familiar (American) narrative frame allows Lahiri to skip over the complexities of racial differences. Her book may have been published in 2000, but most of the stories tell of a time gone by, a time when the melting pot metaphor of an idealized America was still very much imaginable, even quite believable. She thus uses an imaginary *culturescape*[6] of South Asianness and deploys what Appadurai argues, in another context, is the "central paradox of ethnic politics in today's world [wherein] primordia (whether of language or skin color or neighborhood or kinship) have become globalized" (*Modernity at Large*, 1997, 41). She deliberately bypasses this "central paradox" to mark ethnic (South Asian) differences as understandably familiar interactions between her minority subjects and majority cultures in the United States. By weaving together familiar events with carefully selected memories in the stories, Lahiri animates certain myths and images that are embedded in national, popular culture. Memory is used here not to elicit images of victimization or to signal loss. And, it is engaged differently from scholars who employ it in postcolonial studies (unrelenting nightmare of subjugation), or in traumatic contexts (to speak of slavery or the Holocaust that reveal horrendous cruelty), or to speak of amnesia induced by systematic violence and marginalization (the case of Native Americans). Further, memory in my analysis is also different from nostalgia, which connotes a longing for a romanticized place called *home*. Instead, memory in this framework signals a network of sepia-like images and ideas, to evoke forgotten or half-forgotten emotions that are partial and fluid and embedded unevenly at various levels in the collective locus of a nation.

The nine short stories in *Interpreter of Maladies* oscillate between events and scenes occurring in South Asia and America that describe everyday emotions of love, hate, jealousy, fear, anger, and disappointment as people go about their daily business. In spite of such a seeming banality, her stories are interesting because they allow readers to glimpse intricately chiseled filigrees of incidents. *Interpreter of Maladies*, one could say, is a sum of memorable incidents. Many of the stories present pleasant memories of South Asians in the United States, memories moreover that can be accessed by both immigrants and citizens as stereotypical in such encounters. Thus, Lahiri synchronizes numerous and varying images of South Asians as neighbors, colleagues, and friends that American readers have stored in the vast and irregular spaces of popular culture and gently controls the final meanings. She tackles the immigrant experience from the safe distance of an acceptable stereotype formulated around the 1960s when South Asians struggled and melted into America, because they were perceived as an ethnic and not as a *racial minority*.[7] That is to say, they were unmarked except as stereotypically quiet academics and professionals. She excavates such partially remembered stereotypes from the sites of popular culture as a discernable backdrop to position her characters as familiar (albeit ethnic) figures, while plotting their lives along orientalist lines. Such a marking, but a taming and domesticating of South Asianness, becomes readable much like subliminal messages that have been encoded in mass media over time. Then, she gently guides readers into recalling sights, sounds, smells, ideas, and images from other texts and contexts to complete the significance of the chain of events. In other words, Lahiri turns the axis on diaspora; to decipher her stories, she makes, not her characters, but her American readers recall memories of South Asia, for example, randomly mixed with other images of a world resembling glossy scenes from films such as *A Passage to India* or *The Jewel in the Crown*, descriptions from books such as the *Raj Quartet*. Readers are able to cull faint images from "cinema, television, and video technology" (Appadurai, *Modernity at Large*, 1997, 53) and supplement that with their own repository of memories and stereotypes to grasp the full import of her characters' actions. Her stories reorient, one could argue, Benedict Anderson's primary hypothesis of imagined communities of national citizens on to an *imagined community of readers* who (consciously or unconsciously) recollect impressions of South Asianness that are ensconced in their minds.[8] And, like Anderson's imagined community of citizens, her imagined community of readers is erratically formed, wherein readers' recollections of South Asia are fragmentary, uneven, drawn from collages; yet it is this unevenness that creates a pattern of meaning when Lahiri triggers certain memories.

This community of readers that I posit for Lahiri is different from those formulated in reader response theory. Lahiri's readers do not need special training or knowledge of literature because they are able to make meaning by relying upon a vast reservoir of incomplete images, partial ideas, quick impressions, presuppositions, and stereotypes, which circulate randomly in popular culture. It is through this reverse maneuver of an imagined community that she forces readers to contextualize the experiences of her characters and assess the ethical conduct of her characters' actions.[9] Here, Appadurai's general remarks on the impact of globalization shed light on Lahiri's specific strategies. He says that "disjunctive and unstable interplay of commerce, media, national policies, and consumer fantasies" breaks down stable markers of "ethnicity, [which were] once a genie contained in the bottles of some sort of locality (however large)" but are "now . . . a global force, forever slipping in and through the cracks between states and borders" (*Modernity at Large*, 1997, 41). Lahiri's ethnic characters too slip in and out of the "borders" of various media representations and her readers' imaginations, thus their actions need to be read in this liminality.

Exploring Memory, "Interpreter of Maladies"

The title story, "The Interpreter of Maladies," under the guise of narrating a troubled marriage, presents an ethical dilemma about responsible conduct between globalized citizens and local subjects played out in the epistemic zone of original memory (i.e., it becomes her ploy to examine the concept of trust between tenuously connected subjects)—Kapasi, an Indian and Mrs. Das, an Indian American. Such an intersubjective connection forms the ground for Lahiri to test the validity and durability of marriage as a social contract. The Dases, with their three children on vacation in India, journey to the Konarak Sun Temple with Kapasi, their tour guide. He speaks English and Gujarati; the latter, the reader is told, helps him communicate with the local doctor. He had prepared for a different kind of life, studied foreign languages because "he had dreamed of being an interpreter for diplomats and dignitaries, resolving conflicts between peoples and nations, settling disputes of which he alone could understand both sides" (IM, 52). But now he translates the affliction of patients who "came glassy-eyed and desperate, unable to sleep or breathe or urinate with ease, unable above all, to give words to pains" (66).

On the drive to the Sun Temple, Mrs. Das shows her boredom by consciously disassociating herself from the rest of her family while her husband seems only mildly aware of her discontent. When Kapasi tells them about his job, she says "'But so romantic'... dreamily, breaking her extended silence.... For the first time, her eyes met Mr. Kapasi's in the rearview mirror: pale, a bit small, their gaze fixed but drowsy" (IM, 50). She offers him some bubble gum and "as soon as Mr. Kapasi put the gum in his mouth a thick, sweet liquid burst onto his tongue" (50). Kapasi reads her tedium as availability and her gesture as a probable invitation to a liaison. Because of his visceral response, he fantasizes about receiving letters from her from New Jersey with pictures of their tryst in the Sun Temple. But, when they are alone, Mrs. Das abruptly blurts out that her husband did not father Bobby, and proceeds to challenge him with "'Are you surprised?'" (62).

Readers, aware of Kapasi's fantasy, wonder if she entrusts him with this intimate secret because she is capable of being unfaithful or if she sees him as a mere worker (i.e., a subordinate figure of no consequence). Kapasi too is unsure, and asks defensively, "'I beg your pardon Mrs. Das, why have you told me this information?'" to which she snaps, "'for God's sake, stop calling me Mrs. Das.... You probably have children my age'" (IM, 64). He is disappointed, even "disturbed to learn that she thought of him as a parent" (65), and, like the reader, is unable to position himself vis-à-vis Mrs. Das. Lahiri now directs readers' memories through three intricate, interlocked steps. The first is choreographed on Kapasi's expectations via a penetrating east-meets-west technique; the Indian guru figure encounters the Western Freud stereotype, where tradition bumps against modernity, forcing him and Mrs. Das to interact in the familiar social space of strangers confronting an uncomfortable truth. Bauman's explanation, made in a general context, of actions required in moments of ethical ambiguity is helpful in illuminating the unclear expectations of not only the characters, but of readers as well. He writes:

> The spoken demand (the articulated demand like the verbalized demand) has the modality of a rule. Like the rule it spells out what is to be done— and by commission or by omission—what must not or need not be done; obliquely it exonerates the rule-follower from not thinking beyond the spelled-out instruction, supplying him with the uncontentious probe of the duty fulfilled or "the obligation met," "the job well done." (*Life in Fragments*, 1995, 55)

Readers, like Mrs. Das, expect Kapasi, an Indian guide to the Sun Temple, to fulfill his stereotypical "obligation" (Bauman), go beyond sexual temptation, and give sage advice. But the reference to Kapasi as parent-father figure faced with Mrs. Das's "spoken demand" makes readers question what he will do, either by "commission or omission" (Bauman). "What must to be done" readers wonder, as they get distracted by a faint image of Freud, the cardinal therapist, forming in the background, when she retorts that she could easily be as old as one of his "children" (IM, 64). Kapasi acts neither guru-like—"he felt insulted that Mrs. Das should ask him to interpret her common, trivial secret" (66)—nor does he occupy a parent-Freudian place to explain away or assuage her guilt. Instead, he rationalizes his chagrin by resorting to the cliché, "honesty was the best policy" (66). Confident that his education would allow him to "preside over the discussion, as a mediator" (66), he "decided to begin with the most obvious question, to get to the heart of the matter, and so he asked, 'Is it really pain you feel Mrs. Das, or is it guilt?' . . . but as she glared at Mr. Kapasi some certain knowledge seemed to pass before her eyes, and she stopped. It crushed him; he knew at that moment that he was not even important enough to be properly insulted" (66). Readers pause in the act of making meaning here since the scene is fraught with conflicting images and expectations as the characters are out of step with one another. Unlike Dora, the dutiful daughter-figure in Freud's narrative, who hands over her subjectivity and her agency to the father-healer, Mrs. Das adroitly controls her femininity (and her transgression) by refusing to allow Kapasi to act outside of her perceived notion of his role or go beyond a response that she wants. By showing contempt for Kapasi, she inverts Freud's narrative and aborts the expected trajectory of the "interpreter of maladies" as both eastern guru and Western Freud. Kapasi, too, though rebuffed, disconcerts readers by exerting a diffused form of agency. He recoils from participating in Mrs. Das's explanations of sexual misadventure by offering safe advice, and he divests himself of the burden of the Freudian talking cure.

Lahiri uses this deliberate miscue to execute the second step in directing readers' memory. She draws out representations gathered from mass media. The Freudian talking cure is adapted and circulated, for example, through formulaic television shows in popular culture. Mrs. Das now resembles a housewife nursed on a steady diet of such daytime television shows, and enacts what is commonplace on such shows by casually (and abruptly) confessing her sexual transgression. She has internalized, as have countless other television viewers, the peculiarly participatory nature of this form of therapy. In other words, Mrs. Das, like so many television viewers, imagines that she straddles the participant/viewer locations, thereby confusing Kapasi and the reader about her role, which makes it difficult to interpret her casual admission. She is unprepared to accept Kapasi's implied suggestion that she take responsibility for her actions, and is angered by his inability to make irrelevant her transgression and to absolve her in the way that she has seen enacted on ,many popular television shows. By demanding "honesty" (IM, 66) and sovereign agency, however misguided, Kapasi relinquishes both his fantasy and his power over her. Thus, while Mrs. Das is partially recognizable as a talk-show viewer/participant, Lahiri satirizes that very recognition by refusing to provide a quick remedy or have this character and the story proceed in a predictable fashion. Similarly, Kapasi fails to act like a television host who can cure problems by the end of the encounter. Bauman's comment "'to be moral' does not mean 'to be good' but to exercise one's freedom of authorship . . . as a choice between good and evil" (*Life in Fragments*, 1995, 1) is useful here. Kapasi cannot absolve Mrs. Das of her transgression; she alone must be the agent, *the author* of that choice. Destabilizing reader expectations yet again at this point by collapsing the guru/Freud figures into laughably familiar, popular television images allows Lahiri to move to the third and final step in her intricate plan.

This third step in guiding memory subtly animates, in the minds of educated readers, the ethical question of right action between strangers in intersubjective contexts. Mrs. Das reminds one of an Adela Quested from E. M. Forster's novel, *A Passage to India* or David Lean's character from the film version. By narrating the story as Mrs. Das's journey to the Konarak Sun Temple, Lahiri allows her educated readers to recall some similarities between Mrs. Das and Adela's motif of self-discovery énroute to the Marabar Caves in Forster's text. But, she also brings to mind Adela's awareness of her sexual yearnings from Lean's filmic rendition. One memorable scene from Lean's film is mirrored but subverted in Lahiri's telling, where Adela's sexual desire peaks as she sees monkeys clamor in frenzied abandon upon the erotic Indian sculptures of female bodies in the temple ruins outside Chandrapore. In Lahiri's story, when monkeys threaten Bobby, Mrs. Das's maternal instincts overpower her discomfort over her sexual slip. By framing (but also slightly tilting) her story inside the textual and cinematic versions of *A Passage to India*, and by juxtaposing monkeys with secret sexual desires toward the end of her narrative, Lahiri carefully directs partially remembered (and processed) memories stored randomly in her readers' vast reservoirs to lead them to the final meaning. This final impact is felt when Lahiri carefully arranges randomly set cues beside specific suggestions and animates fragmentarily fused images of India as the land of self-discovery redolent with orientalized, sensual fantasies.

Kapasi's wish to interact with "honesty" (IM, 66) is useful in understanding how civil definitions of loyalty match up against moral underpinning of chastity in marriage as a social contract. Bauman writes, "to say that socially constructed and taught rules are secondary regarding the primal moral condition does not mean that evil comes from the distortion or incapacitation of original goodness by unwholesome social pressures or flawed social arrangements" (*Life in Fragments*, 1995, 2), which suggests that morality and goodness can neither be unilaterally equated nor fully dismissed as being vulnerable to contemporary sociocultural pressures. This implied difference between ethics as a negotiated, experiential reality, as opposed to morality as a desirable, but absolute tenet, sheds light on Kapasi's decision. His suggestion that the couple be honest and be held accountable in resolving this crisis shows his reticence to act unilaterally. The significance of "honesty" is that the husband must also share the responsibility for being inattentive to his role in the marriage. Kapasi does not assess the crisis as "good" or "evil," but rather as a situation that needs an *honest*, ethical intervention.

Kapasi's own "honesty" is seen at the end of the story when he rescues Bobby from the monkeys:

> Mr. Kapasi took his branch and shooed them away, hissing at the ones that remained, stomping his feet to scare them. The animals retreated slowly, with a measured gait, obedient but not intimidated. Mr. Kapasi gathered Bobby in his arms and brought him back to where his parents and siblings were standing. As he carried him, he was tempted to whisper a secret into the boy's ear. (IM, 68)

Unlike Adela, whose secret desires shatter constructed notions of self and allow Forster to signal the breakdown of empire in *A Passage to India*, Mrs. Das's transgression is safe with Kapasi. The passage motif in "Interpreter of Maladies" leads back, almost undisturbed, to the familiar home in New Jersey, because life for the Dases will go on as before. It is this moment of slippage that allows readers to witness the poignancy of a lost opportunity to right a wrong, for the monkeys "sat solemnly observing the scene below. Mr. Kapasi observed it too, knowing that this was the picture of the Das family he would preserve forever in his mind" (IM, 69).

In the final analysis, what makes this an ethical tale? What are the rules of engagement in intersubjective dialogues between members of a community, however fleeting that community formation may be? Did Mrs. Das hope that confessing her uncomfortable, yet pleasurably transgressive truth to a stranger would absolve her of her responsibility to her marriage or redefine her duty to her bastard child? These are questions that pertain to the ethical engagement of the characters. Mrs. Das wanted Kapasi to deal with the consequences, to take in Bauman's terms, "'responsibility for the responsibility'—that is the responsibility for deciding what practical steps the responsibility requires to be taken and what steps are not called for ('go beyond the call of duty')" (Bauman, 4). Kapasi realizes that the *correct or ethical thing to do* is to relinquish his fantasized desire for Mrs. Das, abstain from usurping power as the father figure with confused motives, and overcome his momentary (nasty) impulse to punish the child in an effort to get even with the mother. He discharges his responsibility with integrity by handing over agency to Mrs. Das to resolve her own dilemma. Kapasi's *ineffective* action defeats reader expectations yet again, making them ambivalent about his role, especially because the two characters seem at first to be heading toward a charged intimacy. Readers perhaps expect Kapasi to commit a social gaffe or make inappropriate advances toward Mrs. Das. Hence, this impasse in the ending is frustrating because nothing seems to be resolved. Yet Kapasi does act ethically; he lives up to his title of "interpreter of maladies" by deciphering Mrs. Das's problem as pathological boredom. He does not respond to her admission in terms of a moral taboo, but alerts the reader to the fine balance between individual responsibility and ethical choices in the bonds of marriage. In other words, Kapasi is the haunting figure who reminds us that individual responsibility must go beyond conventional morality or social orthodoxy. His ineffectual response makes the reader think about living life with ethical (maybe personal) standards of conduct, wherein every action is scrupulously contextualized and treated with "honesty" (66).

NOTICING MEMORY: "A TEMPORARY MATTER"

The inaugural story, "A Temporary Matter," is carefully nuanced and beautifully executed, which shows Lahiri's potential for scripting ethical interactions between a husband and wife, a relationship that is not only most personal and intimate, but one that is embroiled in a passionate, visceral give-and-take of life at its foundational level. This story moves delicately in the intersubjective space, between rights, duties, and accountability to loved ones, as it spotlights the individual actor's responsibilities. Shoba and Shukumar, a young Indian American couple born and raised in the United States and now living in Boston, are desperately trying to cope with Shoba's recent miscarriage. Shukumar feels guilty and helpless because it happened while he was "away at an academic conference in Baltimore" ("A Temporary Matter," hereafter cited as TM, 2). Although the scene of a marriage in trouble may be general enough, the specific detail of the husband as a doctoral candidate at MIT and explanations for cooking curries are noticeably stereotypical in positioning Indians as immigrants living the American dream.

The story is grounded on the scenario that the city is conducting electrical repairs, that residents will not have power after 8:00 P.M., but that it is a "temporary matter." The weight of this title phrase rests on specific connotations of power in the narrative. By pointing to the reality of a temporary power shutoff, Lahiri signals the temporariness of the emotional and social bonds, and then, uses this metaphor to speak of the dissolution of a marriage and the breakdown of tradition. It points to the husband's feebleness—his loss of power—that is dramatized when Shoba imbalances the sociocultural construction of masculinity by wresting full agency in the relationship. For example, Shukumar reflects on the fact that in spite of their tense relationship, they stay married because he has "learned not to mind the silences" (TM, 19). Although it has become customary to speak of women's silences in narratives, Lahiri experiments with hushing the husband.

Shoba recognizes that she has the power to smooth the situation, and suggests they play a game. She says, "I remember during power failures at my grandmother's house (in India) we all had to say something" (TM, 12), to which Shukumar responds, "I used to play that game in high school...when I got drunk" (13). By portraying the events in darkness, Lahiri ends this seemingly innocent and innocuous pastime in tragedy, and satirizes stereotypes of candle-lit dinners and romantic liaisons. She specifically uses this tragedy to address questions of ethical interaction by pointing to the confusion in the realm of public culture over the meaning of truth, its connection to conventions of morality, and its slippage into *right conduct*. The divergent attitudes that the husband and wife bring to the game in their intersubjective space are crucial in understanding the differential meanings of truth as revealed on a whim and in darkness against truth as an indicator of integrity in a relationship. This couple can speak the truth (either carelessly or with forethought) only in the absence of power (i.e., when both agree to play the game on par). For four nights they eat dinner by candlelight, telling each other inconsequential yet intimate secrets, which precipitates an ethical crisis.

Shukumar, beguiled by this play, asks after the repairs are completed, "Shouldn't we keep the lights off?" (TM, 20), to which Shoba replies:

> "I want you to see my face when I tell you this. . . . I've been looking for an apartment and I've found one." . . . It was nobody's fault, she continued. They'd been through enough. She needed some time alone. She had money saved up for a security deposit. The apartment was on Beacon Hill, so she could walk to work. She had signed the lease that night before coming home. (21)

Readers wonder if Shoba, in delayed shock after losing her baby, is lashing out and selfishly quitting the marriage, or if she is formulating her own conduct in figuring out her responsibility. She certainly sounds insensitive, cruel even, in announcing this break in banal or utilitarian terms of security deposits and signing leases. The answer lies between these two polar positions of selfishness and mature responsibility, and between momentous and banal comments of their game played in the dark. But, what evidence does the reader have that she is defining herself ethically vis-à-vis Shukumar? The narrator cues the reader that "somehow, without saying anything" their nightly, ritualistic game "had turned into this. Into an exchange of confessions—the little ways they'd hurt or disappointed each other, and themselves" (18). Even though the surface narrative points to romance, their underlying history of "hurts and disappointments" denies it, stating that they had "disappointed . . . themselves." Shoba is the stronger one while Shukumar is the more vulnerable, the more easily damaged partner (arguably, even the more thoughtless). He "wondered what Shoba would tell him in the dark. The worst possibilities had already run through his head. That she'd had an affair. That she didn't respect him for being thirty-five and still a student. That she blamed him for being in Baltimore the way her mother did" (16). Still, he consoles himself that these "things weren't true" (16), and continues to play the game, hoping to heal the widening fissure between them. But, when Shoba announces her decision to leave, he "stared at her. It was obvious that she'd rehearsed the lines. All this time she'd been looking for an apartment, testing the water pressure, asking a Realtor if heat and hot water were included in the rent. It sickened Shukumar, knowing that she had spent these past evenings preparing for a life without him. He was relieved and yet he was sickened" (21).

The situation is untenable for this couple because their marriage is not sustainable. Lahiri seeks to resolve the conflict between husband and wife in a credible and equitable manner, and relies on Shoba to take the lead. Bauman's comment, made in a different context (and also mentioned above), is pertinent here in understanding the scope and significance of ethical action. He writes:

> The spoken demand (the articulated demand, the verbalized demand) has the modality of a rule.... The spoken demand saves the actor a lot of trouble; whether coming in the form of a universal rule, or in the shape of a request from the partner of the encounter who invokes such a rule, it can be weighed according to the merit of the case.... In a rule-governed encounter, the actor is not confronted with another person... the true relationship is between the actor and the rule, while the other person, the cause or target of the action, is but a pawn moved around the chessboard of rights and duties. (*Life in Fragments*, 1995, 55)

Readers, like Shukumar, have heard Shoba's "spoken demand," have recognized he is but a "pawn moved around the chessboard of rights and duties." Shukumar, as the reader heard, is "sickened" but also "relieved" because the stress of the final break is lessened when Shoba points out that it "was nobody's fault" (TM, 21). Shoba has shouldered the responsibility for working out a solution in the dialogic, intersubjective space of their tense marriage, because she understands that "the true relationship is between the actor and the rule" (55).

This is a tricky place in the text where Lahiri's readers may become ambivalent. While one is saddened by the loss, it is uncomfortable to see the breakup of the marriage presented as a neat alternative. The candlelight dinners miscue the reader, just as they do Shukumar. However, since popular and academic culture sites are saturated with feminist interpretations of a woman's rights, it is probable, perhaps even possible, to read Shoba sympathetically. Lahiri now carefully channels that swelling tide of sympathy by presenting Shukumar as a weak, almost stereotypically effeminate character, incapable of resolving the situation.

Lahiri weaves together two stereotypes here. The first, built upon a tissue of popular discourse, sanctions Shoba's emancipation based upon widespread belief, which decrees that this is a land where women are free to make choices. The second stereotype banks upon the more academic (orientalist) *fabrication of Indian men as effeminate*. Lahiri deploys the first from the realm of ordinary experience and the other from a more rarefied one. She couples the popular with the slightly more academic forms to address the question of just and ethical actions, because she trusts her community of readers to grasp the crucial component of the story at either/both level(s). The ethical rule in marriage is to act with integrity toward the other partner. Marriage also implies an equal partnership, and thus far, Shukumar has proven to be the weaker partner. Common sense, aided by popular culture, allows readers to approve of Shoba's move because she deserves the chance to remake herself, with the hope that Shukumar will also, in common parlance, *move on.*

This quiet, albeit tenuous, interaction between the reader and the text is seen toward the very end of the story, when Shukumar tells Shoba deliberately, "'Our baby was a boy.... His fingers were curled shut, just like yours in the night'" (TM, 22), and then proceeds to stack dirty dishes in the sink. He remembers, "He had held him until a nurse knocked and took him away, and he had promised himself that day that he would never tell Shoba, because he still loved her then" (22). This is the only instance when readers are told that Shoba cries. Shukumar, readers recognize, wields a coward's weapon of selfishness (perhaps because of his pain), and gets even by hurting Shoba. He is indeed capable of moving on because he speaks of love in the past tense. Remembering those last moments when he held his dead son in his arms, he is ready to acknowledge the death of his love, marriage, and child. The narrative voice alerts the reader to the violence lurking under the surface of this bankrupt marriage. Thus, the vicious interruption by a weak husband, while swaying sympathy in the wife's favor, is also parodically pleasing because of the poignancy of an intimate situation gone hopelessly wrong.

Lahiri is committed, I posit, to exploring the ethics involved in sustainable relationships. She mirrors, at the level of popular culture, the experiential reality of so many young couples today. The death of a child and the demise of a marriage are traumatic, but are sadly routine occurrences in our society. If Shoba is to serve as the ethical agent, she must take steps to resolve the situation. She does act ethically and is unwilling to compromise her integrity by living a lie that has become her marriage. Rather than stay with Shukumar for the sake of upholding cultural traditions and the social institution of marriage, she frees him from a life of regrets and recriminations and herself from a life of reparations and justifications.

By inserting banal comments at crucial places in their nightly, ritualistic game, Lahiri emphasizes the need to act ethically at every stage in life. The couple's clichéd interactions balance the pathos of the final breakup, because life is made up of composite actions filled with inconsequential details, small deeds, wherein minor resolutions are mixed in with weighty issues, complex evaluations, and momentous decisions. The randomness and routineness of life—filled with joy and sorrow, the eventful and the ordinary—are inescapable realities. One thinks banal events can be kept at a distance when making major life decisions because one assumes that momentous choices are somehow separate from mundane reality. Lahiri shows that it is not always so. Bauman comments, "the true relationship is between the actor and the rule, while the other person, the cause or target of the action, is but a pawn moved around the chessboard of rights and duties" (*Life in Fragments*, 1995, 55), which shows how the individual is finally and fully responsible for his or her decisions and actions. Commonplace comments made by the couple become essential in understanding the rule-governed nature of their marriage. This is an average American family, one that has adapted to the exigencies of life conditions in the way that many of their friends and neighbors would have too. As Appadurai says, people today "no longer see their lives as mere outcomes of the givenness of things, but often as the ironic compromise between what they could imagine and what social life will permit" (*Modernity at Large*, 1997, 54). Shoba has the courage[10] to make the necessary compromise in her ethical choice, because the "responsibilities of the actor" have become "more profound" given the "jarring *non-sequitur*" (Bauman, *Life in Fragments*, 1995, 6) nature of our society.

Conclusion: Memory and Ethics

> Writing is a duty, suggests Lyotard, not the right—birthright, right of anoint-ment, or usurped right—of the intellectuals. The duty to express what oth-erwise would remain silent; and there in the twenty-four-hour-a-day din and commotion of electronic highways, among would-be, have-been and virtual realities that outshout each other in the vain struggle to document their own reality and out-real other realities, most of the voices stay silent permanently and without hope of ever being heard. The duty to make them audible is, though, a duty without authority.... The assumption of such duty means moving in the dark, taking risks—taking *responsibility* for the audibility of the numb. (emphasis in the original; Bauman, *Life in Fragments*, 1995, 241–242)

Is Jhumpa Lahiri doing her duty as a writer by "taking risks—taking re-sponsibility" and giving voice to ethics; a factor glibly invoked in our soci-ety but sometimes sidetracked or silenced by the increasing reality of con-spicuous consumption and globalization? The answer is a tentative "yes." Her stories gesture toward the different kinds of responsibilities each of us has by carefully evoking memories of people and places from con-temporary U.S. culture as experienced through a range of situations. She explores different facets of accountable action and just, reciprocal con-duct through familiar, interacting poles of intimate-communal, society-individual, national-transnational, cultural-crosscultural, and diasporic-cosmopolitan as relayed through commonplace emotions of love, fear, and anxiety. Such magic markers make reading fiction both meaningful and pleasurable. Lahiri, one could argue, is very much part of the "familiar imagination of [U.S.] social life" (Appadurai, *Modernity at Large*, 1997, 53), and consequently is enmeshed in the discursive practices of both popular and academic culture. Having lived and studied in the United States gives Lahiri the ability to draw upon *local* ideas, images, texts, and contexts to chart memories from readers' vast repertoire to deliver her unique, *global* message.

Like her readers, she has witnessed the gradual progression of story-telling from colonial to postcolonial and cosmopolitan modes (i.e., from Forster to Rushdie, and more importantly, to the contemporary, emerging focus on ethics in literature). As Bauman explained, a writer's "duty means moving in the dark" (*Life in Fragments*, 1995, 241); wherein Lahiri's ex-perimental focus may not always help readers get beyond a mild sense of curiosity about the characters' lives, but it does imprint a nagging sensa-tion that the reader carries long after putting the book itself down. This is the ethical component in Lahiri's work; in Bauman's words she performs the duty of "intellectuals . . . in the twenty-four-hour-a-day din and com-motion of electronic highways, among would be, have-been and virtual realities that outshout each other" (*Life in Fragments*, 1995, 241). Read-ers grasp the full import and compromised nature of value–laden terms such as truth, honor, commitment, and integrity as they get deployed and mediated in daily life. Ethical action is no longer located in the domain of absolute value dictated by abstract parameters because it has been pushed into the arena of personal responsibility, reciprocal accountabil-ity, and gradual efforts of global community building. In other words, Lahiri's work suggests that *democratic America* can set the standard for correct conduct by publicly acting in a *just* fashion.

NOTES

Acknowledgment: I thank Gurudev, Rohin Rajan, and Zygmunt Bauman for inspiring and encouraging me, and Annette Kolodny and Jonathan Hodge for their guidance. I am indebted to Shailja Sharma, Johanna X. K. Garvey, Rocio Davis, and Victor Rangel Ribeiro for patiently reading through drafts and suggesting revisions.

1. The subject of this chapter is the literary-cultural moment surrounding *In-terpreter of Maladies*, and does not extend to the publication of her second book, *The Namesake*, which capitalized upon her Pulitzer Prize fame in marketing both the book and the author.

2. "Inside a 'Model Minority': the Complicated Identity of South Asians," *The Chronicle of Higher Education* (June 23, 2000), 16, online version. Retrieved from <http://chronicle.com/free/v46/i42/42b00401.htm>

3. Some notable works in this arena in chronological order are, *The Ethics of Reading* (J. Hillis Miller, 1986), *The Quality of Life* (Nussbaum and Sen, 1992), *Living Contradictions: Controversies in Feminist Ethics* (Jaggar, 1994), *Renego-tiating Ethics in Literature, Philosophy, and Theory* (Adamson, 1999), *Shadows of Ethics: Criticism and the Just Society* (Harpham, 1999), *Codes of Conduct:*

Race, Ethics, and the Color of Character (Holloway, 1996), *Residues of Justice: Literature, Law, Philosophy* (Wai Chi Dimok, 1997), *Ethics after Idealism: Theory-Culture-Ethnicity-Reading* (Chow, 1998), *The Ethics of Deconstruction: Derrida and Levinas* (Critchley, 2000), and *Critical Ethics: Text, Theory and Responsibility* (Rainsford and Woods, 1999), which show both a sharpening of interest in examining ethical questions through or of literature, and how disciplines such as race and gender studies, philosophy, economics, or jurisprudence provide new instruments for analyses.

4. After various attempts to delink ethics from morality, the former still has an aura of the latter. Such sweeping generalizations notwithstanding, specifically within literature, ethics is often interpreted through aesthetic categories, such that the meaning of a work attempts to analyze the author's intuitive ability to represent some form of idealized (often Christian) truth.

5. Susan Koshy, in "Morphing Race into Ethnicity," argues that "Asian Americans produced, and were in turn produced by whiteness frameworks of the US legal system" because the national system of processing difference is fixed in the "black-white binary as the defining paradigm of racial formation" (154). She is not speaking of Lahiri.

6. Appadurai says we make meaning of our lives in this era of globalization via "an elementary framework" founded upon "five dimensions of global cultural flows that can be termed (a) *ethnoscapes*, (b) *mediascapes*, (c) *technoscapes*, (d) *financescapes*, and (e) *ideoscapes*. The suffix –*scapes* allows us to point to the fluid, irregular shapes of these landscapes, shapes that characterize international capital as deeply as they do international clothing styles" (33, emphasis in original; *Modernity at Large*, 1997, 33). I expand Appadurai's "scapes" to suggest a general field of meaning that is activated in popular culture in South Asian writing.

7. Susan Koshy notes that "South Asians renegotiated their classification . . . to be counted as whites" with the blessings of "a federal agency, the Census Bureau of 1970" ("Morphing," 2000, 158).

8. Benedict Anderson writes in *Imagined Communities* that the "nation is imagined as a community because, regardless of the actual inequality and exploitation that may prevail in each, the nation is always conceived as a deep, horizontal comradeship" (1991, 7), and that print culture (or print capitalism) united people as a nation by promoting a sense of community through the use of vernacular languages. By being able to communicate freely, people came to believe that they shared beliefs, experiences (i.e., a commonality that was not always on par, but was prevalent enough to form a cohesive, recognizable, larger community). This sense of community, though uneven and disparate, formed the modern nation. I adapt this hypothesis to the circulation and deployment of media ideas/images through memory, which serves as the basis of forming a community of readers.

9. Postcolonial critics use Anderson's "imagined community" to describe both commonality and angst in diasporic populations. I argue that Lahiri uses sites of memory that are forged upon readers' conscious/unconscious minds by various forms of media to guide them in understanding the sociocultural interactions of South Asians in the United States.

10. Bauman argues that "If ethics is about drawing the boundary of good while sitting on this side of the border, then morality as imagined in the ethically administered world must also be about the distinction between good (what you must do) and evil (what you must not do) and about staying put on the side of goodness. Whether an offshoot or sediment of ethics...or an alternative to the conventionality of ethical code...morality remains a reflection of the official portrait of ethics; painted after the likeness and in the image of an ethics self-confident (nay arrogant) enough to claim the ability to set apart good from wrong doing and to guide towards good while steering clear of the traps and ambushes of evil" (*Life in Fragments*, 1995, 60–61).

WORKS CITED

Anderson, Benedict. *Imagined Communities: Reflections on the Origin and Spread of Nationalism.* London: Verso, 1991.

Appadurai, Arjun. *Modernity at Large: Cultural Dimensions of Globalization.* Minneapolis: University of Minnesota, 1997.

Bauman, Zygmunt. *Life in Fragments: Essays in Postmodern Morality.* Oxford: Basil Blackwell, 1995.

Dimock, Wai Chi. *Residues of Justice: Literature, Law, and Philosophy.* Berkeley: University of California Press, 1999.

Forster, E. M. *A Passage to India.* London: Harvester Books, 1965

Harpham, Geoffrey Galt. *Shadows of Ethics: Criticism and the Just Society.* Durham, NC: Duke University Press, 1999.

Hillis Miller, J. *The Ethics of Reading: Kant, De Man, Eliot, Trollope, James, and Benjamin.* New York: Columbia University Press, 1989.

Holloway, Karla F. C. *Codes of Conduct: Race, Ethics and the Color of Our Character.* New Brunswick, NJ: Rutgers University Press, 1996.

Jaggar, Alison. M. (Ed.) *Living with Contradictions: Controversies in Feminist Social Ethics.* Boulder, CO: Westview Press, 1994.

Koshy, Susan. "Morphing Race into Ethnicity: Asian Americans and Critical Transformations of Whiteness." *Boundary 2,* 28 (1) 2000: pp. 153–94.

Lahiri, Jhumpa. *Interpreter of Maladies.* Boston: Houghton Mifflin, 2000.

Lean, David, Director. *A Passage to India,* film, 1984.

Nussbaum, Martha, and Amartya Sen. (Eds.) *The Quality of Life.* New York: Oxford University Press, 1993.

Rainsford, Dominic, and Tim Woods. (Eds.) *Critical Ethics: Text, Theory, and Responsibility.* New York: Palgrave Macmillan, 1999.

Waller, Bruce. *Consider Ethics: Theory, Readings, and Contemporary Issues.* New York: Longman, 2004.

6   Abjection, Masculinity, and Violence in Brian Roley's *American Son* and Han Ong's *Fixer Chao*

ELEANOR TY

HALF A CENTURY after gaining its independence from the United States, the Philippines are still very much in a neocolonial stage.[1] Epifanio San Juan, Jr., notes that "the Filipino has been produced by Others (Spaniards, Japanese, the *Amerikanos*), not mainly by her own will to be recognized" (*Articulations of Power*, 1992, 118). Filipinos are a transnational subaltern, used in many countries as cheap and temporary labor: the "'warm body export' of Filipino workers to the Middle East; Filipinas as 'mail-order brides,' ubiquitous prostitutes around enclaves formerly occupied by U.S. military bases; and 'hospitality girls' in Tokyo, Bangkok, Okinawa, and Taipei" (San Juan, *Philippine Temptation*, 1996, 79). The more than six million Filipinos scattered around the world earn on average "$3.5 billion a year for the Philippine government" (92), but at a great cost to Filipinos, especially to women and children.

Propelled by dire economic conditions in the Philippines and fed by the American dream of wealth and success, Filipinos migrate in large numbers and have become what Rhacel Parreñas (2001) calls "servants of globalization." By globalization, I refer to the movement of people, goods, and culture in the new global capitalism, which entails, as Arif Dirlik writes, the "transnationalization of production, . . . the decentering of capitalism nationally," the increasing importance of the transnational corporation, and the "fragmentation of the production process into subnational regions and localities" ("Global in the Local," 1996, 30). Negative effects of this migration and globalization include the separation of family members, perpetual states of exile and displacement, and self-hatred, which result from the neocolonial mentality of seeing oneself as other. What faces Filipino immigrants in their adopted countries is often not a life of ease, but difficulties due to prejudice, racism, and alienation. Two recent

Reprinted with permission from Eleanor Ty, "Abjection, Masculinity, and Violence in Brian Roley's *American Son* and Han Ong's *Fixer Chao*." *MELUS* 29.1 (Spring 2004): 119–36. © Copyright, MELUS, The Society for the Study of the Multi-Ethnic Literature of the United States, 2004.

novels by Filipino American writers, Brian Ascalon Roley's *American Son* (2001) and Han Ong's *Fixer Chao* (2001), document these problems and reveal the ways in which global capitalism takes its toll on the young.[2] Roley's and Ong's novels are told from the perspective of young adults whose familial and social lives have been changed by transnational migration, and who see themselves as failures because their everyday lives do not match up to the high expectations of the American dream. Fueled by Hollywood ideals of glamour and power, various characters in these novels suffer, and, in turn, lash out against others when they fall short of capitalist notions of success. Examples from these novels show the impact of global American culture on Filipinos and Filipino immigrants, problems in the construction of Filipino American ethnic subjectivity, and the violent effects of racial abjection on the body.

In general, these novels reveal a number of common negative effects of globalization on young Filipino Americans:

1. The overvalorization and desire for wealth, first-world products, and material goods. In these narratives, the children whose families are separated often compensate for their lack of familial bonds or dysfunctional family situation by coveting, buying, or in some cases, stealing goods. Transnational production does not just affect people's work and labor conditions, it also affects libidinal desire.

2. Overdetermined and unattainable ideals based on Hollywood models of masculinity and beauty. Because "the global distribution of power still tends to make the First World countries cultural 'transmitters' and to reduce most Third World countries to the status of 'receivers'" (Shohat and Stam, "Imperial Family," 1996, 147), the young protagonists in these novels identify with the American image of success. These images affect the way one perceives one's own body, and one's romantic and sexual relationships. When Filipino American men find themselves unable to live up to the seductive or forceful celebrity images they see in films and on television, they frequently resort to violence or aggression against those around them.

3. Emotional and psychic transnationalism. Diane L. Wolf argues that "second generation Filipino youth experience *emotional transnationalism* which situates them between different generational and locational point of reference—their parents', sometime also their grandparents', and their own—both the real and imagined" ("Family Secrets," 1997, 459). Children of first generation Filipino immigrants and Filipino American children belonging to the 1.5 generation group (individuals who immigrate at a young age) are brought up "accepting patriarchal family dynamics and the predominance of parental wishes over children's voices, resulting in internal struggles and an inability to

approach parents openly for fear of sanctions. Part of the struggle seems to stem from living and coping with multiple pressures and with the profound gap between family ideology and family practices" (473). While this phenomenon is common to many immigrant children, it is particularly acute for those youths who feel the pressures not only from their family in the adopted country, but who are also burdened with the responsibility that they are accountable in some ways to their family, friends, and relatives "back home."

In both *American Son* and *Fixer Chao*, Roley and Ong respectively explore the various effects of globalization on young Filipino American men growing up in contemporary America. The authors show the emotional and psychic struggles of the protagonists as they negotiate between the values of capitalist America and the self-sacrificing and self-abnegating attitudes of Filipino immigrants. Through the perspectives of the young men, we see the damaging effects of small but repeated acts of racism, and we witness the ways their masculine subjectivity has been interpellated by Hollywood representations. In both novels, the protagonists reveal how they become abject others of the dominant culture that desires and yet abhors them. What we witness is the youths' disappointment with a society that invites them to be part of the nation yet refuses to accord them the same privileges as white Americans. Through very different stories of growing up, Roley and Ong illustrate the complex ways in which cultural and racial marginalization, as well as a sense of failure from being unable to live up to their own and their parents' ideals, lead young Filipino Americans to aggression and criminal behavior.

CELEBRITY DOGS

Brian Roley's *American Son*, set in California in 1993, depicts much of the disenchantment of Filipino American youths, revealing the "underbelly of the modern immigrant experience" (backcover). Told from the point of view of Gabrielito Sullivan, a fifteen-year-old American boy born of a white father and a Filipino mother, the novel presents a stark, unsentimental portrait of a family torn between the allure and wealth of America, exemplified by the rich celebrities who live in West Los Angeles, and the traditional, Catholic, Filipino values, with their emphasis on filial piety, as voiced in the letters of Uncle Betino in the Philippines. Though Gabrielito (called Gabe), his mother, and brother, Tomas, emigrated to American almost ten years before, they, like many immigrants, have had to struggle economically, socially, and culturally to survive in the multiracial and multifarious city of Los Angeles. They have settled in the United States, but they have not been completely uprooted from their home country and assimilated into the new society, as one expects of immigrants who left their home over ten years ago. Instead, they are what Schiller, Basch, and Blanc term "transmigrants," immigrants "whose daily lives depend on multiple and constant interconnections across international borders and whose public identities are configured in relationship to more than one nation-state" ("Immigrant," 1995, 48). According to Schiller, Basch, and Blanc, several forces lead these immigrants to settle in countries that are "centers of global capitalism, but to live transnational lives" (50). The reasons include a deterioration of social and economic conditions "in both labor sending and labor receiving countries with no location a secure terrain of settlement" and "racism in both the U.S. and Europe," which "contributes to the economic and political insecurity of the newcomers and their descendents" (50).

Gabe, his brother, and his mother all experience dislocations that are similar to those experienced by other Filipinos who work at low-paying or dead-end jobs in various parts of the world. As Rhacel Parreñas has observed of migrant Filipina domestic workers, the dislocations include "partial citizenship, the pain of family separation, the experience of contradictory class mobility, and the feeling of social exclusion or non-belonging in the migrant community" (*Servants*, 2001, 12). Gabe has not seen his American father since the night he got drunk after returning from his station in Germany. After hitting the children and "making fun of Filipinos and her family," the father tells Tomas that he only married their mom because "he wanted someone meek and obedient, but had been fooled because she came with a nagging extended family" (*American Son*, hereafter cited as *AS*, 24). After his departure, the mother used to telephone her brother in the Philippines for advice on bringing up the boys. Gabe reports: "Our mother had long, distressed conversations on the telephone. . . . Sometimes she would sob. Other times she simply wrapped a strand of hair around her finger" (22). Uncle Betino's letters repeatedly urge the mother to send the boys back to the Philippines so that they can be educated to be good Filipino Catholics, so that "some of the Asian virtues of [the] family heritage" (201) can be instilled in them. These plans never materialize, however. To maintain her household in America, she works at one point "sixty hours at a department store's shoe section" and has a "second job looking after an invalid Jewish lady in the Hollywood Hills" (160). She is caught in a situation of transmigrancy, not able to assimilate into American white society because of her accent, her diffidence, her difficult economic situation, and yet she feels that she cannot go back to the Philippines where she complains of the heat and smelly showers, the insects, diseases, and relatives who make "tsismis about each other behind their backs" (33).

In the United States, the family is repeatedly reminded of their nonbe-longing and otherness. These scenes reveal the ways in which exclusionary practices delimit and mark the subjectivity of the ethnic other. Gabe and Tomas demonstrate two different ways of reacting to racist and discrimi-natory attitudes from the white majority. Initially, the brothers are divided into a dichotomy representing the good and the bad. Gabe is the obedient child, "the son who is quiet and no trouble" and who helps their "mother with chores around the house" (AS, 15). Tomas, the older brother, is the one who keeps the mother "up late with worry. He is the son who causes her embarrassment by showing up at family parties with his muscles cov-ered in gangster tattoos and his head shaved down to stubble and his eyes bloodshot from pot" (15). As a way of defending himself against ridicule and prejudice, Tomas tries to cover up his Asian identity. At first, Tomas tries to pass as a white surfer and attempts to dye his hair blond, though it turns red in the process. Then he began "hanging out with Mexicans, who are tougher" (30).[3] If anyone tried "calling him an Asian he beat them up, and he started taunting these Korean kids who could barely speak English" (30). Significantly, Tomas inscribes his desired Mexican identity onto his body: "his tattoos are mostly gang, Spanish, and old-lady Catholic," Gabe observes, "As he leans forward, the thin fabric of his shirt moves over his Virgin of Guadalupe tattoo that covers his back from his neck down to his pants" (17). The tattoos remake his Asian fea-tures, reconfiguring his body from the feminized Oriental into the more macho Chicano Latino body.[4] At the same time, the Virgin of Guadalupe tattoo places the teachings of his mother, the Catholic Church, the notions of sainthood and virginity in a new and potentially irreverent light. The markings on his body reveal the many ways in which contesting notions of racial identity are played out physically and corporeally on Tomas.

Seeing himself through the gaze of a dominant culture that sees him as servile, feminized, and different, Tomas is ashamed of being identi-fied as a Filipino American. To complete his public identity as Mexican, he pretends to understand Spanish when people speak it to him. How-ever, in his business, which consists of training attack dogs and selling them to "rich people and celebrities" (AS, 15), Tomas uses commands in German, telling his clients that the dogs have "pedigrees that go back to Germany, and that they descend from dogs the Nazis used" (20). Signif-icantly, only by aligning his dogs, and by extension, himself, with racist Nazis is Tomas able to claim power, legitimization, and recognition in contemporary U.S. high-class society. Moreover, he claims that "this is a Teutonic art that goes back to the Prussian war states" (20). That his lies are so easily accepted demonstrates the extent to which contemporary society relies upon racially and nationally based stereotypes. In contrast to the highly valued "Teutonic art," for both brothers, being Filipino

has demeaning associations, often linked to low-paying domestic occupations. Tomas tells his brother at one point, "If the client sees you standing
there like that he's gonna think you're my houseboy" (18). Similarly, when
Gabe runs away from home, he befriends a tow truck driver, who, though
kind to Gabe, makes derogatory remarks about the "fucking Mexicans,"
the "Cambodians, Vietnamese, Laotians," and those "mute Asians" who
"won't even learn to speak English" who are everywhere in Venice and
San Pedro (84). Gabe becomes embarrassed when the tow truck driver
later sees his mother and tells him that the dark-skinned woman at the
restaurant is their "maid" (116).

This scene, which occurs at the center of the novel, represents Gabe's
betrayal, an act almost as hurtful as Tomas's many acts of disobedience
and willfulness. The incident, though played out at the domestic level, is
significant as it is suggestive of larger cultural issues and national politics.
Gabe's mother represents the long-suffering Filipino who is abandoned
by her American husband and protector. She believes in the old world
traditional values of the Filipino—filial duty and obedience to the Catholic
Church and its priests. Yet as an immigrant and woman of color, she is
ineffectual in America and is left behind by her children. She is unable to
help her children improve their marginal status through legitimate means.
At one point in the novel, she goes with Gabe to a shopping Promenade.
Gabe notices that unlike Tomas, his mother always "steps out of other
people's paths" (AS, 179), and one man "in a yellow button-down shirt"
sees her but "acts as if he does not notice her, and she actually has to
squeeze beside a bench to let them pass" (179). At the makeup counter,
the beautiful tall, model-like redhead in a white doctor's coat chats with
another lady and ignores Gabe's mother as she waits at the counter to be
served. Only with Gabe's intervention does the saleslady take notice of his
mother, but, too shy at that point to make a scene, the mother pretends she
is "just looking" (183) and walks away. It is this kind of self-abnegation
and an inability to assert oneself that embarrass the boys and lead them
to react violently against those whom they perceive are treating them as
second-class citizens.

ASIAN AMERICAN MASCULINITY

Masculine identity has been problematic for the Asian American male
from the start (see Eng, 2001; Goellnicht, 1992; Wong, 1992). Historically, Asian males were subjected to exclusion laws, regarded as unassimil-
able (Takaki, 1989, chap. 3), and represented as threats to society because
of fears of disease, miscegenation, and sexual corruption (Lee, *Orientals*,
1999, 76). They were also feminized because of their work in laundries,
restaurants, and tailor shops. Today, many Asian American men still work

in poorly paid "feminized" service jobs. Cruise ships in the Caribbean and in Alaska employ Indonesian, Malaysian, and Filipino men and women as busboys, waiters and waitresses, and kitchen help. Filipino men work as houseboys, gardeners, orderlies, laborers, and cleaners in North America and in the Middle East. In popular media, Asian men are represented as hypersexual and dangerous, because they were unable to consummate their desires through legitimate relationships, or else they were seen as feminine. Young Asian boys and Asian women are exploited as prostitutes and sex workers in many parts of the world. As David Eng notes, in "marvellous narratives of penile privilege, the Westerner monopolizes the part of the 'top'; the Asian is invariably assigned the role of the 'bottom'" (*Racial Castration*, 2001, 1).

The particular situation of powerlessness for Asian American men is not unlike that of black men and the problems of black masculinity in America. As Kobena Mercer and Isaac Julien note, "Whereas prevailing definitions of masculinity imply power, control and authority, these attributes have been historically denied to black men since slavery" ("Race," 1988, 112). In order to "contest conditions of dependency and powerlessness which racism and racial oppression enforce," macho attitudes are developed. Macho is "a form of misdirected or 'negative' resistance, as it is shaped by the challenge to the hegemony of the socially dominant white male, yet it assumes a form which is in turn oppressive to black women, children and indeed, to black men themselves, as it can entail self-destructive acts and attitudes" (113). In Roley's novel, the difficulty of constructing a viable masculine subject for Tomas leads him to adopt a hypermasculine identity that manifests itself through violence and crime, as well as his identification with "tough" Mexicans. To make sure he is not teased as a weakling, as Asian, he takes on a macho identity, taunts others, and even beats his brother up whenever he is frustrated by Gabe's submissive attitude. The mother's pleas with Tomas do not stop him from a life of criminal activity, including breaking and entering, looting, assault, and robbery. Though Tomas and Gabe love her deeply, they respond with anger and outrage at their economic difficulties and her social helplessness. Their own place outside mainstream society and outside the capitalist system makes them resort to unlawful means in order to change the situation in their home. In the last part of the novel, Tomas brings Gabe along with him and they break into people's homes. While most of the items they steal are for reselling, some of them are used to elevate their mother's status. In one case, Tomas steals the brass sinks and faucets from an empty house and puts them into their mother's bathroom. He also replaces her couch and gets her a new bed. Breaking into a Hungarian lady's house in Brentwood Park, Tomas heads for the bedroom and tells Gabe, "Look for the pearls. Or anything with gold on it. Forget the silver stuff. It wouldn't look good on her brown skin" (AS, 147). Because success is typically represented as the possession of economic wealth, goods, and objects in America, as the man of the house, Tomas mistakenly tries to show his love for his mother by obtaining items that are featured in advertisements, glossy magazines, television, and film.

The problem of being in one of the centers of global capitalism, yet feeling excluded from full membership in it, is that one always feels inadequate and lacking. In capitalist societies such as North America, clothes, cars, jewelry, and other possessions often serve to compensate for one's sense of insufficiency. However, for the dispossessed, there are few legitimate ways to attain these goods. To borrow terms from studies on black masculinity, Tomas becomes a "hustler," not a prostitute like Han Ong's protagonist, but one who lives by dishonest means. As Mercer and Julien explain, "the figure of the hustler . . . is intelligible as a valid response to conditions of racism, poverty and exploitation, it does not challenge that system of oppression but rather accommodates itself to it: illegal means are used to attain the same normative ends or 'goals' of consumption associated with the patriarchal definition of the man's role as 'breadwinner'" ("Race," 1988, 114).

Roley's novel becomes doubly tragic because we witness not only Tomas becoming more and more involved in violent and criminal activities, but we also see the way Gabe, who initially was the obedient brother, slowly succumbs to the gratification of violence and the deadening of emotion. It seems to be the only way to respond to the situation of his family's economic immobility and his own sense of powerlessness. Toward the end of the novel, the two brothers go out and brutally beat up Ben, one of Gabe's schoolmates, the son of the rich woman who was threatening to collect $800 from their mother because their mother had accidentally bumped the woman's Land Cruiser in front of the school. As Gabe swings the tire iron across Ben's legs, Gabe thinks, "I feel a rush not of anxiety but of confidence. In a scary way I realize I like it. Strangely, that only makes my stomach worse" (AS, 215).

Ironically, it is only though violence that Gabe feels that he can become an "American son," that is, a citizen of the United States with authority and power. Because the narrative is told from Gabe's first-person limited point of view, we are not given any further explanations about his psychic state after his first act of aggression against another human being. In the closing scene, Tomas puts his hand on Gabe in a way that their American father used to do to both of them. The gesture is suggestive and supposed to be reassuring. Together, they have survived displacement, prejudice, and dispossession, but at a cost to their humanity. They, unlike their mother, can no longer be transmigrants, but in the process they have let go of the traditions and values she was trying to instill in them—respect for others, obedience to authority figures, and deference to the church and to the law. They have become American sons, not by being hardworking immigrants as their mother expected, but by becoming outlaws and urban cowboys.

ABJECT SUBJECTS

In a similar way, the protagonist of Han Ong's *Fixer Chao* gets himself into a "complicated, manufactured" life (*Fixer Chao*, hereafter cited as FS, 133) when he agrees to embark on a scheme of revenge for another. In Ong's novel, globalization, in particular, the movement of culture, people, and goods from the third world to the first world, is viewed with much irony and skepticism. *Fixer Chao* tells the story of a Filipino hustler, an ex-prostitute, William Narciso Paulinha, who is remade into Master William Chao, a revered Feng Shui expert from Hong Kong with the help of Shem C, "a disreputable, social climbing writer embittered by his lack of success" (inside cover). William Paulinha is lured deeper and deeper into a life of fraud and crime for many of the same reasons as Tomas and Gabe: racism and sense of self-abjection, the gap that he sees between the life of rich New Yorkers around him and his own hand-to-mouth existence. Like Tomas and Gabe, William is a Filipino who lives on the margins of society, never fully integrated into the U.S. culture because of a sense of rootlessness and class and racial differences.

Like Roley, Ong depicts social and economic inequities that have resulted from the global migration of Filipinos. Racial prejudice is a theme that is present, though muted, in the novel, as the book is largely a satire on the life of the privileged. As in Roley's novel, the characters in Ong's novel "view America through the fractured lens of its broken promises" (Freeman, "Review," 2002, par. 2). As John Freeman notes, "the nation invites them in, only to deny them the privileges of comfort in their own skins" (par. 2). When the novel begins, William tells us that in his twenties, he worked as a small-time prostitute in the Port Authority Bus Terminal. After that, William Paulinha drifted from clerical job to job without much drive or success, working as a typist, as a telephone receptionist, as a mail clerk, and a data entry clerk. Except for the clerical positions, the jobs in which William finds himself are directly linked to his identity as an Asian man in a predominantly white society. He is chosen by Shem to be the Feng Shui expert because of his Asian features. Shem thinks that he is Chinese, even though William is Filipino. In his younger days at the Port Authority Bus Terminal, race also played a part in his career. He had to "compete with frisky Puerto Ricans and athletic black boys for a cut of the overweight white businessman business" (FS, 12). His typical client was a "portly white gentleman, with a bald spot in the middle of his head . . . on [his] way home to the suburbs" (12). Young Asian, Latino, and African American boys serve to boost the egos of these businessmen and to enable them to reassert their position of dominance in U.S. society. As William says:

> They've had disastrous days and want to take out their frustration on someone. I'm perfect, a skinny colored kid, almost like the ones they see a lot of nowadays on TV, except shabbier. They're witnessing their time in the spotlight stolen by a whole crew of new, mystifying faces. Or so they think. And they want somebody to pay, be humiliated, physically put under them like restoring their natural position in the world. (12)

For these white businessmen, these young colored boys function as abject others, those who are like themselves, but have to be expelled. Abject figures are abhorred, yet they remain desirable. Julia Kristeva's definition of the abject includes those objects, persons, things that have to be ejected or excluded, "what disturbs identity, system, order. What does not respect borders, positions, rules. The in-between, the ambiguous, the composite" (*Powers*, 1982, 4). Because he is gay and Asian, William is doubly abjected and othered by his race and gender. His bodily differences function to reassure the white businessman of what the white male subject is not.

As David Leiwei Li argues, Asian Americans in the last half of the twentieth century, though no longer excluded by law, are still perceived to be not "competent enough to enjoy the subject status of citizens in a registered and recognized participation of American democracy" (*Imagining*, 1998, 6). Li notes, "the law cannot—even if it is willing to try—possibly adjudicate the psychocultural aspects of subject constitution; neither can it undo the historically saturated epistemological structures, and structures of feeling, which continue to undermine the claims of Asian American subjectivity" (11). In Roley's *American Son* and Ong's *Fixer Chao*, we see the repercussions of this inside/outside position on Filipino Americans who are "formal nationals and cultural aliens" (Li, *Imagining*, 1998, 12). Though as immigrants they are ostensibly part of U.S. society, there are many reminders of their status as subcitizens. These sometimes overt, sometimes subtle, repeated racist incidents and reminders of their otherness cause them to respond with violence and misdirected aggression to those around them.

As Master Chao, the Feng Shui expert, William uses what little knowledge he has of mystical harmony to help his clients. However, the first house he decides to deliberately sabotage is Cardie Kerchpoff's, a woman who complained endlessly about her Indian nanny at a party. Cardie states that "Third Worlders" do not understand "American nuances or Western nuances," and believes that her domestics should just take what she says with "divine truth" because they live in her house where she has "sovereign rights" (FS, 102). In the conversation, someone suggested that she should get "a Filipino. They make the best servants" (103). This comment enrages William so much that he could not help repeating it in his mind as he was fixing her house, and he could not help adding, "Why? . . . Because they [Filipinos] kneel by instinct and bend over like clockwork" (104). He then proceeds to "do everything wrong" (104) in her house so that harm would befall the arrogant Cardie. This damaging act starts a series of others that escalates into more serious acts of violence. Even though his reputation as a Feng Shui master earns him money, fame, and invitations to wealthy people's homes, William often identifies with the maids, doormen, and houseboys of the homes rather than with their white owners. He calls the doormen at the homes of rich people his "peers" (269). At one awards ceremony, he notices that "the doorman of that building kept regarding me quizzically, not certain why I wasn't carrying the Chinese food he was sure I'd come to deliver" (197). Like the adolescents in Roley's novel, he becomes disillusioned with a society that still bases its expectations and values on one's appearance, race, and ethnicity while claiming to be open and democratic.

What is significant about the way Ong deploys criticism about globalization and global capitalism is that he not only looks at the way transnational labor and people figure in the United States, but also gives a wry and humorous view of the way culture from the third world has been received, marketed, and commodified. In *Fixer Chao* the easiest clients to dupe are those, like Lindsay S. the poet, who are orientalists. Lindsay loves Oriental art and has a collection of beautiful Chinese scrolls, "teapots and teacups, Japanese swords, calligraphic ink sets, . . . hundreds of Buddhas of dazzling variety" (FS, 71). Lindsay believes that the "Chinese and the Japanese" have the "two greatest cultures in the world" (79). His appreciation of these cultures is shown mainly through the acquisition of objects and commodities from the East. The East becomes a large marketplace for people like Lindsay, a shopping paradise in order to enhance his own stature as consumer and collector. Hence, he willingly buys the services of Master Chao who is supposed to bring him the gift of Eastern harmony in his life.

Just as his young Asian body made him a suitable object of sexual desire for white businessmen at the Port Authority Bus Terminal, his seemingly asexual Asian masculine body now makes him an ideal Feng Shui master. In order to play his role as counselor, he has been made over with the help of Shem. William has a "handsome and conservative" (FS, 63) haircut, wears "kung fu shoes" (97), and in the fake magazine article about him, looks "Chinese . . . mysterious, gifted with powers" (87). He pretends to be "offhand, serene, gifted" (86), qualities that are often ascribed to inscrutable but clever Asians. Significantly, as a Feng Shui master, his queer sexuality is no longer visible to the rich New Yorkers.

Instead, he successfully mimics the handsome poses of pop stars, "whose aura was white rather than black, sexless and filled with wisdom" (87). Significantly, Ong points out the links between sexuality, race, and economic status here. While working as a homosexual prostitute, William saw himself as a "colored" kid, aligning himself with Latinos and African Americans. But in his upwardly mobile shift to become a member of the Manhattan elite, he affiliates himself with whites, and at the same time, becomes "sexless." Asian American queer sexuality disappears after the first third of the book, indicative of the way asexuality is still so easily written onto respectable Asian male bodies.

For people in developing countries, globalization and transnational trade have also created a skewed version of the West as a place of unlimited wealth, material goods, and promise. At one of the rare moments when William recollects his past, he tells his Filipino friend, Preciosa, that he came to America with his parents who "wanted a better life" (FS, 262). The images of this "better life" consist of luxury, "wall-to-wall carpeting," brand names like "General Electric, Sunbeam, Hoover, Proctor-Silex, Pfizer, Zenith" (263). He thinks, "They were all a short-hand for beauty, for quality, things that wouldn't break—as our appliances often did. That, for the longest time, had been my family's going definition of a better life: to own things that took a while to malfunction" (263). This dream, tied as it is to brand names, is a telling comment about the global impact of U.S. culture. People in the third world are interpellated by U.S. media and advertising so much that their desires are structured around these products. Hence, the worship of the United States and U.S. consumer culture starts before one even enters the country. Ironically, these products are now manufactured through transnational labor, so that what William's family covets is very likely produced using cheap laborers from his own country and from other countries in Asia and Mexico.

For William, his ten years in the United States have made him only too aware of the foolishness of those early dreams. In the bathroom of the Port Authority, "There had been a hyperactive automatic hand dryer which was a Proctor-Silex" (FS, 263). Recalling his family's reverence for the brand names before they came to the United States, William thinks he has finally understood the hidden meaning of Proctor-Silex, "as a shorthand for all the changes that are bound to happen in the process from wanting to get there to finally getting there, the process from dreaming the dream to eventually getting it—or some would say, killing it" (263). Wall-to-wall carpeting and the brand names do abound in the United States, but William and other Filipino Americans discover that they do not necessarily have the means to "walk on softness, coolness" (263), as they expected. Instead they find themselves cast as those who are expected to clean and maintain them for others to enjoy.

DESIRE AND WOMEN'S BODIES

Another Filipino character, Preciosa, experiences a similar trajectory of disillusionment in America. Preciosa had aspirations of becoming an actress, and she never tires of seeing Barbara Stanwyck and Bette Davis when she goes to the movies.[5] When Preciosa does land a job as an actress at Lincoln Center in New York, it is for a play called *Primitives*, where she appears, along with other dark-skinned men and women, wearing only a loincloth (FS, 42). Instead of being a sultry beautiful actress like Stanwyck and Davis, Preciosa is cast in a play about white missionaries going to Central America. In the play, Preciosa and the other "natives" only get to grunt and mumble gibberish. Her humiliation deepens when some of her Filipino friends come to see the play, witnessing her nakedness and loss of dignity. For those in the audience, "she was as good as what the title of the damn thing had promised them: a primitive!" (313). In the penultimate scene where she is supposed to be possessed by a pagan demon, the audience and her coactors mistake her anger for a convincing performance. Though not central to the main plot, Preciosa's story encapsulates many of the issues I have been raising regarding transmigrants. Like Tomas and Gabe's family in Roley's novel, and like William, Preciosa's dreams of a "better life" do not materialize in America. She only succeeds in occupations that the dominant culture in America expects her to be good at. Here she is cast in an undifferentiated pool of "native" women, passing easily for a primitive of Central America because to most white Americans, all dark skinned people look almost the same.

Her history presents an important critique of the way poor Filipino women's bodies are used in their own country and globally. Sent from the provinces to Manila to work as a maid in a Chinese household, she falls into the life of a prostitute for a while. After her escape from the brothel, she becomes a mail-order bride, choosing from all the letters sent to her to marry an old American man from Texas. Although he is kind to her, and she finds herself growing tender to him, she does remember having to kiss his "frog face with it wrinkly, perpetually sweaty skin dotted with all those carbuncles" (FS, 311). When she has to gratify his sexual appetites, "Preciosa all the while thought of the dark blue cover of her new passport, thought of the Philippines as of a dilapidated building on the wrong side of town passed by without a second glance from a dark-windowed, air-conditioned car. . . . Even if the sex was disgusting, it was still sex in Texas, U.S.A." (311). The U.S. passport functions as the imaginary object of desire. Though globalization gives Preciosa a better set of living conditions, it still means sexual servitude, this time in the United States instead of in the Philippines. Her youth and beauty are the only commodities that she can use, and it becomes her way of escaping and obtaining residency in America.

Immigration, however, does not necessarily mean a settled life in the United States. After her husband's death, Preciosa finds herself moving from one low-paying job to another. She thinks of some of the dreary prospects open to her as a Filipina: "frumpy nannies, matronly aides pushing wheelchair-bound wards on the streets, and nurses with the faces of servile dogs" (FS, 312). Her whole life in America is characterized by dislocation and displacement, as she never becomes fully integrated into the communities in which she finds herself. William remarks about her apartment:

> [E]ven while Preciosa had lived there, it had already had an air of vacancy, of transiency about it, an air that I now realized was a transfer from its owner, who, even before she had revealed the story of her peripatetic life, had already had the look of someone who would make of her present address a somewhere else, another in a long line of somewhere elses like the country she'd just vacated to get here, on and on as if carrying out the directive of some deficiency encoded into her genes, a hunger, some basic discontent. This, being one more definition of immigrant—torn between the competing pulls of the fiction of the promised land, on the one hand, and the fiction of the sustaining mother country, on the other. (FS, 325–326)

This transiency characterizes Preciosa's life, as it does William's and many other global migrants. To go back home, however, seems unthinkable. As William puts it, "returning to the Philippines . . . seemed like an admission of defeat. Could you imagine the glee of relatives who would point you out in family gatherings, then launch into a story about going to live in the fabled United States only to crawl back with your tail between your legs—kicked out, in effect?" (FS, 308). Underemployed in the United States but too ashamed to go back home, these Filipino Americans remain in the place of in-betweenness and transmigrancy, always living in an state of nonbelonging even though they emigrated years ago.

In these novels, Roley and Ong reveal the many ways in which globalization affects Filipino Americans economically, culturally, and psychically. The new "borderless" world has produced uneven results for workers and for those who own and manage corporations. For those laborers from sending countries who leave their home in search of a "better life," acceptance in the receiving countries has been mixed or half-hearted. The 1.5 generation children who grow up in these situations often resort to violence, fraud, and trickery in order to validate their sense of self, to gain acceptance into dominant culture, and to obtain what they perceive to be the rewards of those who pursue the American dream. It is not surprising that at the end of both these novels, the heroes are outlaws and exiles from society, distanced from their families. The children of this 1.5 generation, though burdened with the guilt and the ideological teachings of their parents, are unable to bear the hardships, the suffering, the humiliation of the first generation of Filipino immigrants. They, unlike their parents, want the fulfillment of the American dream of wealth and success, and they want it now. The novels by Roley and Ong show some of the desperate measures taken by these youths with thwarted dreams. Their *bildungen* (educations) do not conclude with a state of epiphany, but, like their lives, are choppy, episodic, and nightmarish. Instead of finding happiness through acceptance and assimilation, at best, they have only managed to survive the "rough draft" that has been their life (FS, 377).

Notes

1. As Ella Shohat and Robert Stam note, "neocolonial domination is enforced through deteriorating terms of trade and the 'austerity programs' by which the World Bank and the IMF, often with the self-serving complicity of Third World elites, impose rules that First World countries would themselves never tolerate" ("Imperial Family," 1996, 147).

2. Another novel that deals with these problems is Bino Realuyo's *The Umbrella Country*, which I studied in *The Politics of the Visible in Asian North American Narratives* (University of Toronto Press, 2004). Unlike Roley and Ong's works, Realuyo's is set in the Philippines. See Chapter 9 of *The Politics of the Visible in Asian North American Narratives*.

3. In his study of Filipino American youth gangs, Bangele Alsaybar notes that "urban type" Filipino American gangs, like the Santanas, "grew out of the inner city; its homeboys lived initially in predominantly Latino neighborhoods, thus getting exposed to Latino culture. It is not surprising, therefore, that Sanatans has borrowed heavily from the Latino *Cholo* tradition" ("Deconstructing," 1999, 126).

4. My comparison of the Asian and the Chicano body is based on cultural perceptions of them. In *Racial Castration*, David Eng analyzes the ways in which the "Asian American male is both materially and psychically feminized within the context of a larger U.S. cultural imaginary" (2001, 1). Hurtado, Gurin, and Peng note that first-generation Mexican immigrants "have to deal with stereotypes of the majority culture about them as manual laborers and about menial labor as 'Mexican work'" ("Social Identities," 1997, 264).

5. Preciosa's fascination for the films of this period is similar to the Filipino American protagonist in Bienvenido Santo's *The Man Who (Thought He) Looked Like Robert Taylor*. See my article (Ty, 2001) that deals with the negative effects of Hollywood on the Filipino subject.

WORKS CITED

Alsaybar, Bangele. "Deconstructing Deviance: Filipino American Youth Gangs, 'Party Culture,' and Ethnic Identity in Los Angeles." *Amerasia Journal*, 25: 1 (1999): 116–38.

Dirlik, Arif. "The Global in the Local," in *Global/Local: Cultural Production and the Transnational Imaginary*. Rob Wilson and Wimal Dissanayake, eds. (pp. 21–45). Durham, NC: Duke University Press, 1996.

Eng, David L. *Racial Castration: Managing Masculinity in Asian America*. Durham, NC: Duke University Press, 2001.

Freeman, John. Review of *Fixer Chao* by Han Ong. *Post Gazette*. Sunday, May 6, 2002. Retrieved February 3, 2003, from www.post-gazette.com/books/reviews/20010506review765.asp.

Goellnicht, Donald C. "Tang Ao in America: Male Subject Positions in *China Men*," in *Reading the Literatures of Asian America*. Shirley Geok-lin Lim and Amy Ling, eds. (pp. 191–212). Philadelphia: Temple University Press, 1992.

Hurtado, Aida, Gurin, Patricia, and Peng, Timothy. "Social Identities—A Framework for Studying the Adaptations of Immigrants and Ethnics: The Adaptations of Mexicans in the United States," in *New American Destinies: A Reader in Contemporary Asian and Latino Immigration*. Darrell Y. Hamamoto and Rodolfo D. Torres, eds. (pp. 243–67). New York: Routledge, 1997.

Kristeva, Julia. *Powers of Horror: An Essay on Abjection*. Trans. Leon S. Roudiez. New York: Columbia University Press, 1982.

Lee, Robert G. *Orientals: Asian Americans in Popular Culture*. Philadelphia: Temple University Press, 1999.

Li, David Leiwei. *Imagining the Nation: Asian American Literature and Cultural Consent*. Stanford, CA: Stanford University Press, 1998.

Mercer, Kobena, and Julien, Isaac. "Race, Sexual Politics and Black Masculinity: A Dossier," in *Male Order: Unwrapping Masculinity*. Rowena Chapman and Jonathan Rutherford, eds. (pp. 97–164). London: Lawrence and Wishart, 1988.

Ong, Han. *Fixer Chao*. New York: Farrar, Straus, Giroux, 2001.

Parreñas, Rhacel Salazar. *Servants of Globalization: Women, Migration and Domestic Work*. Stanford, CA: Stanford University Press, 2001.

Realuyo, Bino. *The Umbrella Country*. New York: Ballantine, 1999.

Roley, Brian Ascalon. *American Son*. New York: W. W. Norton, 2001.

San Juan, Jr., Epifanio. *Articulations of Power in Ethnic and Racial Studies in the United States*. Atlantic Highlands, NJ: Humanities Press, 1992.

———. *The Philippine Temptation: Dialectics of U.S. Literary Relations*. Philadelphia: Temple University Press, 1996.

Schiller, Nina Glick, Basch, Linda, and Szanton Blanc, Cristina. "From Immigrant to Transmigrant: Theorizing Transnational Migration." *Anthropological Quarterly*, 68: 1 (January 1995): 48–63.

Shohat, Ella, and Stam, Robert. "From the Imperial Family to the Transnational Imaginary: Media Spectatorship in the Age of Globalization," in *Global/Local: Cultural Production and the Transnational Imaginary*. Rob Wilson and

Wimal Dissanayake, eds. (pp. 145–70). Durham, NC: Duke University Press, 1996.

Takaki, Ronald. *Strangers from a Different Shore: A History of Asian Americans.* Boston: Little, Brown and Company, 1989.

Ty, Eleanor. "A Filipino Prufrock in an Alien Land: Bienvenido Santo's *The Man Who (Thought He) Looked Like Robert Taylor. Lit: Literature Interpretation Theory.* Ed. Karen Chow. Special issue, *Asian American Literature and Culture,* Part II. 12: 3 (2001): 267–83.

———. *The Politics of the Visible in Asian North American Narratives.* Toronto: University of Toronto Press, 2004.

Wolf, Diane L. "Family Secrets: Transnational Struggles Among Children of Filipino Immigrants." *Sociological Perspectives,* 40: 3 (1997): 457–82.

Wong, Sau-ling. "Ethnicizing Gender: An Exploration of Sexuality as Sign in Chinese Immigrant Literature," in *Reading the Literatures of Asian America.* Shirley Geok-lin Lim and Amy Ling, eds. (pp. 111–29). Philadelphia: Temple University Press, 1992.

II. MEMOIR/
AUTOBIOGRAPHY

7   Begin Here

A Critical Introduction to the Asian American Childhood

Rocío G. Davis

ASIAN AMERICAN autobiographies of childhood challenge the construction and performative potential of the national experience, particularly in the experiential categories of epistemology and phenomenology. The progressive development of the autobiographical form and the politics of identity formation in this century have made writers and critics increasingly conscious of the play of the autobiographical act itself, "in which the materials of the past are shaped by memory and imagination to serve the needs of present consciousness. Autobiography in our time is increasingly understood as both an act of memory and an art of the imagination" (Eakin, *Fictions*, 1985, 5–6). This understanding has important implications for ethnic life writing, which challenges and widens traditional autobiography by negotiating narrative techniques, experimenting with genre, and raising increasingly complex questions about self-representation and the process of signification. In this chapter, I trace a crucial transition in the autobiographical subgenre defined as the "Childhood" by Richard N. Coe, and address its increasingly creative and subversive appropriation by Asian American writers.[1] I examine the artistic project of Asian American writers—from Yan Phou Lee to Ilhan New and Loung Ung and Kien Nguyen—who choose to deploy narratives of their childhood years in their representation of their individual processes of self-identification and negotiation of cultural or national affiliation.

The title of this chapter gestures toward the critical process enacted in these revisionary texts. Coe explains that "[c]hildhood revisited is childhood *re-created*, and re-created in terms of art" (*When the Grass*, 1984, 84). The statement "Begin Here" is significant on both thematic and discursive levels. It echoes what Paul John Eakin considers "the fundamental rhythms of identity formation" as "the writing of autobiography emerges as a second acquisition of language, a second coming into being of self, a self-conscious self-consciousness," becoming a "theater of self-expression, self-knowledge, and self-recovery" (*Fictions*, 1985, 18, 3).

Further, the genre problematizes the simultaneous awakening of temporal and spatial consciousness; "here," as much as "now," becomes constitutive of the subject's itinerary of selfhood. It also suggests that, for immigrant children, for example, being in a new place implies a "rebeginning," which functions as "a framework for understanding" (Ricou, *Magic*, 1987, 36). Recapturing early memories or events that lead the child to contemplate him- or herself as an individual heightens the performative aspects of a genre that enacts the manner in which personal circumstances and cultural contingencies function in the process of self-awareness and self-inscription.

Specifically, my concern in this chapter is the manner in which Asian American writers rewrite the inherited scripts of the Childhood, as defined in Coe's seminal study *When the Grass Was Taller: Autobiography and the Experience of Childhood* (1984), a text that has been crucial in identifying and classifying this subgenre.[2] He describes the genre as

> *an extended piece of writing, a conscious deliberately executed literary ar-*
> *tifact, usually in prose* (and thus intimately related to the novel) *but not*
> *excluding occasional experiments in verse, in which the most substantial*
> *portion of the material is directly autobiographical, and whose structure*
> *reflects step by step the development of the writer's self; beginning of-*
> *ten, but not invariably, with the first light of consciousness, and conclud-*
> *ing, quite specifically, with the attainment of a precise degree of maturity.*
> (emphasis in the original, 8–9)

The Childhood enacts the step-by-step construction of a preadult self, beginning as near the beginning as possible and ending at a point of total awareness of self as an entity and, especially, as a writer, who will produce as evidence of his or her mature poet-identity, *this* Childhood. In the field of Asian American writing, I have identified over twenty autobiographies that center primarily and fundamentally on the author's childhood, validating the imperative to examine the paradigms that Coe sets out, expanding and rearticulating them in order to address the specificities of the Asian American experience and articulation of childhood.

Because of the indeterminate place of ethnic subjects in American inscriptions of history, Asian American writers who deploy the Childhood are expanding the possibilities of an established genre to limn particular forms of belonging and knowledge. As Asian American writers negotiate aesthetically what Paul Smith has called "positions of subjectivity" (*Discerning*, 1988, xxxv), these Childhoods become experimental and revisionary narratives, which challenge textual authority and prescriptive paradigms.[3] Indeed, to engage Asian American narratives effectively, we must move beyond an analytical model of merely reading the surface of texts for potential meanings and attend to the cultural and generic codes addressed by the authors to unravel what the texts execute within the contexts of larger questions of cultural and political mobilization. Genre definition and the manipulation of generic dispositions direct the act of writing and readers' reception of the ideological issues and concerns embedded in the narrative. This affirmation implies that a reconstruction of the Childhood is necessarily inflected by the relationship between creative writing and immigrant or ethnic configurations of subjectivity and national affiliation. Writers sensitive to how differences in cultural contexts and paradigms create specific responses revise established genres to destabilize ideology and conventional strategies of meaning in order to enact distinct sociocultural situations. Readers who encounter these revisionary texts are thus obliged to reexamine their expectations and critical perspectives.

Criticism is only now arriving at a point where the problematic and shifting conclusions of many ethnic autobiographies, specifically those by nonwhite subjects, may be addressed fruitfully. Contemporary cultural and diasporic studies, as well as ethnic literary theory, have sought to redress the presumptive predominance of Euro-American critical paradigms. Betty Bergland's (1994) and William Boelhower's (1991) works on ethnic and immigrant autobiographies may be productively deployed in this context. Their contrapuntal scholarship limns the corrective agenda of ethnic studies to demystify Euro-American theory's exclusivism, particularly its universalizing and prescriptive prerogative that sets the white male as normative subject, and successful integration into mainstream society as the prescribed conclusion. Bergland's exploration of postmodern autobiography successfully contextualizes ethnic life writing within American literature, and suggests innovative approaches to this multiply positioned genre. She argues that autobiographies of ethnic groups in the United States "provide a key and meaningful site for examining the politics of culture and identity past and present. Collectively, representations of diverse histories, memories, and identities challenge any simplistic, unified, or dualistic map of the American society" ("Representing Ethnicity," 1994, 70). This strategy interrogates the tradition of American autobiography, which tends to posit the trajectory of successful socialization of its subject, usually a white male, in his process of identification with the norms of society. Oftentimes the "necessary" socialization is not completed at the end of these autobiographies, and its lack of closure tends to be problematic, questioning, in turn, the very notion of the subject's "Americanness." Importantly, the nature of the speaking subject remains a critical arena for continued discussions on life writing because the subjects represented in these autobiographies are constructed ethnically and positioned historically in changing worlds and shifting discourses.

Boelhower's approach to ethnic autobiography draws upon poststructuralism and semiotics. He argues that the fundamental issue in ethnic life writing becomes the occasion of ethnic subjects' appropriation of the primary American mode of self-representation that entitles them to tell their own histories, name themselves, and depict alternative versions of U.S. culture and society. He points out that "the speciality of ethnic autobiographical signification, its unique semiotic jeu, largely consists in consciously re-elaborating or simply re-writing the received behavioral script of the rhetorically well-defined American self" ("Ethnic Autobiography," 1991, 125). Insofar as ethnicity is an intrinsic component of identity and self-representation in U.S. society, the discourse of ethnic life writing becomes a powerful mode of cultural criticism. Ethnicity itself is not a stable category and must be reinvented, reinterpreted, and rewritten in each generation by each individual of each ethnicity. The processual character of ethnic identification and representation leads the ethnic autobiographer to be more "at ease among the chaos of signs" than most people, which suggests to Boelhower that ethnic autobiography might be "the most suitable vehicle for new and exquisitely modern versions of the American self" and "a lens for interpreting the complex structural tensions" (139) of America's narrative of itself. Furthermore, when ethnic subjects write autobiography, they control the representation of the American subject, instead of allowing themselves to be passively represented by the received scripts of the dominant culture.

As they gesture toward new perceptions of cultural contexts and choices, ethnic American autobiographies challenge the generic scripts prescribed by Euro-American autobiography. Specifically, Coe highlights a concept that acts as a cognitive device, which he calls "myths of childhood," a trope that defines recurrent preoccupations and obsessions that seem to operate as symbolic embodiments of experiences and acquire the status of myth in its modern, post-Jungian sense ("Reminiscences," 1984, 2). As a product of a racial or a cultural subconscious, a myth of childhood incarnates anxieties, or drives, or urges too deeply buried to be clearly and rationally apprehended by the individual but which, when analyzed, demonstrate a positive and deterministic relationship between the social, cultural, and religious environments surrounding the child and the subsequent creative recall of those experiences.[4] By analyzing these myths, Coe suggests, we can trace a path "from the merely contingent to the genuinely significant in any particular recall of the child-self" ("Portrait," 1981, 129).[5] The myth of what Coe calls the "Third-World child" is that "of the white presence"; and the North American child, whose autobiographical writing foreground community (130). This formulation becomes problematic in the case of the Asian American Childhood and requires critical reexamination.

Performing the translation of Coe's Euro-American focus to negotiate Asian American exercises in life writing is a complex process. The
transaction between formal and cultural modes produces texts that consistently challenge inherited ideas of autobiographical structure and content. Importantly, the nuanced approaches of these narratives clearly
serve a significant didactic purpose, as Traise Yamamoto explains, as
they implicitly gesture "toward the shift . . . from uncritical, naïve notions
of the American ideals of democracy and respect for the individual to
a perspicacious awareness of the failures and limits of those ideals"
(*Masking*, 1999, 125). The increasingly dialogic nature of life writing
reflects a multivoiced cultural situation that allows the subject to control and exploit the tensions between personal and communal discourse
within the text and signify on a discursive level. Issues of ethnic representation therefore become central to the autobiographical strategies
employed by these writers and the manner in which each text performs
the writer's process of self-awareness. The autobiographer is not merely
"an actor who follows ideological scripts, but also an agent who reads
them in order to insert him/herself into them—or not" (Smith, *Discerning*, 1988, xxxiv–xxxv). The engagement with the act of narrative
evolves into a strategy that blends subjectivity and history, in an attempt
to stress individual sensibility, challenge contextual authority, or claim
agency.[6]

Acknowledging the traditional privileging of white androcentric autobiographical scripts in American theory highlights the subversive potential
of Asian American Childhoods. These writers transform the constituent
characteristics of the Childhood through two complementary processes.[7]
In the first place, I wish to challenge and rearticulate Coe's proposal of the
"myth of childhood" for Asian American writers. I argue that the Asian
American myth of childhood is, rather than merely the white presence or
community, the idea and definition of *America itself*, which involves the
negotiation of white hegemony. This renewed formulation accommodates
those Childhoods set outside the United States. The concept of America,
and its corresponding dream, often becomes constitutive of the Asian
child's perception of sociocultural and spatial location: the subject who
inscribes the childhood—the Asian American adult—critically deploys the
process of Americanization in the act of writing itself. Second, a complex
mesh of three processes, which stem from a rearticulation of Coe's "myth
of childhood" and acknowledge the intertext but that signify differently
on a discursive level, include: (1) a revised process of subjectivity, which
involves differentiation rather than identification with the mainstream,
situating the subject in multiple discourses; (2) renewed approaches to
national and ethnic affiliation, which include overt connections to the diaspora, and the complex working of racial discrimination and separation

in America; and (3) truncated or unsuccessful socialization, rather than the successful socialization typical of the Euro-American model.

Processes of Subjectivity

In general, autobiography centers on development and change in the subject's life, narrating the events, choices, and transformations constitutive to the self's evolution. Asian American Childhoods enact subjectivity through a complicated mesh of dispositions, associations, and perceptions that are represented through a singular selection and ordering of the accounts of events and persons who have played important roles in their distinct processes of selfhood. In these Childhoods, subjectivity and self-representation intersect or dialogue with narrative construction and textuality. The constructedness of the text highlights the writers' consciousness of the processes of meaning and memory, subjectivity, and representation. As Sau-ling Wong notes: "From an intraethnic point of view, the writing of autobiography may be valued as a means of preserving memories of a vanishing way of life, and hence of celebrating cultural continuity and identity; in an interethnic perspective, however, the element of *display*, whether intentional or not, is unavoidable" ("Autobiography," 1992, 264). Furthermore, because issues of subjectivity and representation are central to the autobiographical strategies of these writers and the manner in which the text inscribes the writer in her or his own process of self-identification, we have to consider the highly metafictional component of life writing, where what the reader ultimately witnesses is the process that leads to the writing of the memoir.

The two earliest known Asian American Childhoods posit a model of subjectivity that obliterates the individual to focus on cultural concerns, specifically the need to describe Asian culture to American society. Yan Phou Lee's *When I Was a Boy in China* (1887) and Ilhan New's *When I Was a Boy in Korea* (1928) were part of a series of twenty-one books published by the Lothrop, Lee, and Shepard Publishing Company. The chapter titles of Lee's text outline his primary concern: "The House and Household," "Chinese Cookery," "Games and Pastimes," "Schools and School Life," "Religions," "Chinese Holidays," and so forth. New's autobiography begins with the boy's memory of begging his father for more roasted chestnuts, but then quickly departs from the personal to describe the market system, Korean education, clothing, language, holidays, and sports, among others. The text ends with the description of a wedding, which signals the end of boyhood. By presenting these primarily anthropological accounts of boyhood in Asian countries, New and Lee fall into the category of "ambassadors of goodwill," defined by Elaine Kim as writers who sought to explain the East to the West in positive terms, in an attempt to plead for tolerance, challenge stereotypes, and alter the negative view Americans had of Asians (*Literature*, 1982, 24–25).[8] The concern is cultural and political, rather than personal, and the lack of personal references suggests a collective rather than an individual voice.[9] These narratives, commissioned within the tradition of autobiographies of Childhood, offer interesting readings on the early Asian American subject positionality, and the nature of the American prerequisite for writing about Asians.

After Lee and New, Asian American autobiographers of childhood began to explore more critically their processes of change and the nuances of subjectivity.[10] As such, later texts foreground their protagonist's struggle with the alternatively divergent and intersecting markers of personal and cultural identity. Jade Snow Wong, in *Fifth Chinese Daughter*, notes: "she was now conscious that 'foreign' American ways were not only generally and vaguely different from their Chinese ways, but that they were specifically different, and the specific differences would involve a choice of action" (1945, 21). To an extent, Wong follows the pattern set by Lee and New, as she adopts what Sau-ling Wong defines as the "stance of the cultural guide" found among Chinese-born and American-born autobiographers, "conscious of their role as cultural interpreters who can obtain a measure of recognition from whites for the insider's insight they can offer" ("Autobiography," 1992, 262, 264). Narratologically, Jade Snow's use of the third person to refer to herself stresses the distance that she, as an adult writer, takes from her subject: herself as a child and as a developing subject positioning herself in the ethnic script of America.[11] In this text, Wong highlights what will become a recurrent theme in immigrant Childhoods—the conflict between the ways of the country of the parents and the American ways the child grows up knowing. When she informs her parents that she is going to see a movie with a boy, the clash between her father's patriarchal stance and her American "unfilial theory" (*Fifth Chinese Daughter*, 1989, 128) climaxes: "'This is America, not China.... You must give me the freedom to find some answers for myself'" (129). But the father challenges her obsession with individual freedom with a reminder of her racial and cultural origins, and her tenuous position as an outsider: "Your skin is yellow, your features are forever Chinese.... Do not try to force foreign ideas into my home" (130). The Asian American child's need to identify with the American ethos of individual freedom—which includes the liberty to choose his or her cultural affiliation—becomes part of the itinerary of subjectivity. Further, apart from familial demands, the child must negotiate acceptance in school and the peer community, a quest that often involves the acquisition of language.

Specifically, language becomes a contested site for identity formation, and the presence of two languages in a child's life often creates an arena of conflict. Some texts deal with this issue in the simplified terms of a binary opposition between the child's desire to assimilate and the parents' attachment to the heritage culture. Nonetheless, a critically informed close reading might suggest that the nuances of such a problematic is highly subversive. In most Asian American Childhoods, the question of language obsesses the child or his or her parents, who read the acquisition of English to the detriment of the original language as a manner of moving away. The children grasp at English as a matter of survival in school and the neighborhood community. Many of the texts also suggest that the loss of the heritage language is fundamental to the process of Americanization, something the children seek. Heinz Insu Fenkl's *Memories of My Ghost Brother* (1996) focuses on a biracial child's struggle with English as his passport into his American father's world of privilege and possibility.[12] Though his emotional connection is to Korean, which represents his mother's world, he wants to please his father, and longs for all that America promises. Language choice is a barrier between father and son: the father teaches the boy that English signifies education; what the child receives at home and in the streets is the language of ignorance and poverty. Thus the "home" language and the "white school's" language elucidate the binary oppositions the child must negotiate, which imply a series of beliefs, family relationships, manners, and behaviors.[13] Richard Kim's engagement with the issue of language in *Lost Names: Scenes from a Korean Boyhood* (1970) is particularly illuminating. Kim narrates the consequences of Japanese occupation of Korea and focuses, significantly, on the imposition of the Japanese language, which entailed the replacement of Korean names with Japanese ones. Interestingly, Kim does not inscribe a single Korean word in the narrative—no proper names are used or familial terms of endearment or names of food, which are described rather than identified—to textually illustrate the loss of a language. He therefore enacts the consequences of language prohibition in his narrative and demonstrates how the process of subjectivity involves a negotiation with language.

The family structure plays a pivotal role in most of these narratives, as does the community. Texts such as Wong's *Fifth Chinese Daughter* (1989) and Wayson Choy's *Paper Shadows* (1999), for example, foreground the role of the Chinatown community as part of the protagonist's itinerary of self-awareness. Notably, texts that center on the Japanese internment experience stress the experience of the group: Jeanne Wakatsuki Houston and James Houston's *Farewell to Manzanar* (1995), Monica Sone's *Nisei Daughter* (1991), George Takei's *To The Stars* (1997), and Yoshiko Uchida's *The Invisible Thread* (1991) necessarily privilege the role of the Japanese American community because of the imperative to survive in a country that had turned against them. The processes of subjectivity articulated by these writers stress the importance of belonging to a group and preserving group identity, while simultaneously gesturing toward membership in mainstream society. Houston and Houston focus on their family's trauma, Sone centers on the nisei's growing awareness of their identity in relation to both their issei parents and their native lands, while Uchida examines her doubled feeling of loyalty for Japan and America. Significantly, by focusing on community, we see how these writers' positions and, more importantly, their creative strategies for agency, arise from their negotiation with shifting ethnic affiliations. Rather than serving as simply a new alternative designation, however, Bhabha's "terrain" is the space, "unrepresentable in itself," in which racial self-articulation is disconnected from "primordial unity or fixity" (*Location*, 1994, 37). The protagonists of the texts mentioned each undergo highly individual itineraries of cultural denial and affiliation, represented by a pivotal "in-between" space. These spaces are what Boelhower describes as "extra-territorial cultural zones within the political boundaries of the nation" ("Ethnic Autobiography," 1991, 129): literally, Chinatown for Wong and Choy, and the internment camp for Houston and Houston, Uchida, Takei, and Sone, and, figuratively, the less definable liminal position they occupy as ethnic subjects. Negotiating these American spaces is part of the narrators' awareness of their positions and roles as ethnic subjects caught in American historical and social construction. These places also become alternative spaces for self-discovery and self-assertion, and illuminate processes of subjectivity in the context of twentieth-century American history.

NATIONAL AND ETHNIC IDENTIFICATION AND AFFILIATION

These revisionary models of transnational and transcultural position and affiliation have nuanced reductivist ideas of otherness and the process of othering. I suggest that Asian American Childhoods can exemplify that new "intermittent time and interstitial space" (Bhabha, *Location*, 1994, 312) in literary studies. Many of these writers engage increasingly complex ways of understanding and articulating migrant and ethnic identity by choosing a transnational position, one that is neither purely assimilationist nor oppositional. Writing the self and locating the ethnic body in America leads to the more challenging strategy of normative self-fashioning in ethnic zones, as acted out by the child, the emblematic symbol of America and its most-beloved literary character. As such, the performance of the Asian American child or the Asian child who will become the Asian American adult complicates issues in the discourse of nationalism and affiliation. In this context, Boelhower's ("Ethnic Autobiography," 1993) approach to ethnic autobiography stresses historical contexts as well as the socially constructed dimensions of the cultural discourses adopted by immigrants and their children, specifically the macrotext of immigrant autobiography, which revolves around the contrapositioning of the Old World and the New World, and the idea of the American Dream imbedded in dominant cultural discourses. When the spaces represented in the text are located outside the United States, the implications for national and cultural allegiances become more complex.

A significant number of Asian American Childhoods are set in Asia and end with departure from the homeland or arrival in the United States. The journey acquires symbolic import—it refers to a physical journey as much as to a journey toward self-formation, leading to questions of liminality and mythology. Younghill Kang's *The Grass Roof* (1966), Kim's *Lost Names* (1970), Loung Ung's *First They Killed My Father* (2000), Kazuko Kuramoto's *Manchurian Legacy* (1999), Chen's *Colors of the Mountain* (2001), Fenkl's *Memories of My Ghost Brother* (1996), and Kien Nguyen's *The Unwanted* (2001) all end with a disruptive point that authorizes multilayered interpretations. First they validate a non-American childhood setting for the Asian American subject. This particular aspect expands and subverts the hegemonic prescription of the location of the childhood experience of the (Asian) American subject: narrating non-U.S.-set experiences reconfigures America's image of its children, or at least, of its citizens' pasts. Second, these Childhoods, in particular, reinscribe the myth of America by forging a palimpsestic itinerary of location and affiliation. If, as Coe asserts, the writing of the Childhood is the writer's attempt to find an order or pattern, then setting the childhood away from the United States and stressing a pre-American life is consequential because it complicates the traditional fixed representation of the American child's awareness of position. Third, and most importantly, it posits Americanization as a process, rather than as a fixed disposition or merely an inherited patrimony. Asian American Childhoods set outside North America articulate itineraries of affiliation in a way that the Euro-American texts Coe reads do not, as they stress trajectories and transitivity rather than static or endowed identification. Kuramoto's text, for example, which recollects a colonial Japanese childhood in Manchuria, shifts between the construction of spaces whose historical status modifies in accordance with political circumstances and the repeated renegotiation of selfhood that this process limns. Her eventual moving to the United States requires, thus, another paradigm shift in concepts of occupation, on the level of permanence and possession. Biraciality, in the case of Claire Accomando (*Love and Rutabaga*, 1993), Fenkl (*Memories of My Ghost Brother*, 1996), Norman Reyes (*Child of Two Worlds*, 1996), and Nguyen (*The Unwanted*, 2001), complicates this itinerary, as their one American parent necessarily nuances their perception of themselves in France, Korea, Vietnam, and the Philippines, respectively, as well as their notion of and access to the American Dream. Significantly, these texts also permit us to examine the combined effect of class and race in a manner that is alien to the social construction of the United States. For Accomando and Reyes, biraciality is not viewed negatively, and even proffers them privilege. For Fenkl and Nguyen, biraciality is a treacherous space between affiliations, one that influences the mode of their interaction with their peers. In different ways, these children demonstrate a distinctive ambivalence in their inscriptions of their homelands, perhaps because of the adult writers' consciousness of the transitional role of that place and the culture it nurtures.

Often, the desire to participate in society is defeated by marginalization, a history of racial discrimination, heightening the child's sense of indeterminacy in a nation from whose history he or she has been written out and from whose present children like him or her appear to be excluded. Interestingly, much of the difficulty for many of these Asian American children lies in the gap between their perceptions of themselves and their encounter with the gaze of the mainstream white observer. Asian American children's features consistently identify them as mere denizens, rather than the citizens they often are proud to be. A major feature of Asian American literature is the concern with either developing or recovering an appropriate identifying relationship between self and place because it is precisely within the parameters of place and its separateness that the process of subjectivity can be conducted (Davis, *Transcultural*, 2001, 130). Bhabha's optimism regarding what he calls "interstitial spaces," because they "initiate new signs of identity, and innovate sites of collaboration, and contestation, in the act of defining the idea of society itself" (*Location*, 1994, 1–2), becomes vulnerable to revision in this context. Detailed depictions of the streets and cities that the children function in often limn their acute sense of marginalization from those specific places that, ironically, they know so well. Laurence Yep, in *The Lost Garden*, narrates his perception of the dramatic change in his neighborhood, from a predominantly Chinese one to African American when Yep was seven, turning him into "an outsider in what had once been my own home turf" (1991, 37), a sociological alteration that made him aware of ethnicity as a social marker. As such, many narrators of their Childhoods undergo highly individual itineraries of cultural denial and affiliation, represented by a pivotal "in-between" space. These spaces correspond to Boelhower's definition of "extra-territorial cultural zones within the political boundaries of the nation" ("Ethnic Autobiography," 1991, 129). Two places, in particular, can be addressed critically in this context: Chinatown and the Japanese American internment camps.[14]

In Childhoods such as Wong's *Fifth Chinese Daughter* and Wayson Choy's *Paper Shadows*, representations of Chinatown as a cultural space for the enactment of ethnicity inflect the process through which place becomes the site where originary national culture is reconstituted and transmitted. The word *Chinatown* itself is laden with sociohistoric connotations, and a realm of complex, dynamic valences lies beyond the name. To most of the Chinese population of any given large U.S. or Canadian city, Chinatown connotes *habitation*, permanent home, a locus of familiarity, security, and nurturance. To the tourists seeking exciting but ultimately safe cultural encounters, however, Chinatown means *spectacle*, a diverting, exotic sideshow (Wong, "Ethnic Subject," 1994, 253). These autobiographies reinvest multiple meaning and possibility into a sociospatially segregated Asian American cultural space. In theory, the Chinatown structure suggests home and family, yet these narratives use the child's voice to disclose alternative approaches to Chinatown, signaling a critical junction in the workings of both Asian American subjectivity and the organizations of kinship and collectivity within the community. Wong and Choy suggest that we have to reconceptualize the connection between place and subject, expanding the boundaries of this location of origin for many Chinese Americans. These engagements with Chinatown rearticulate the very notion of space, belonging, and heritage for Chinese Americans as Chinatown is represented as both a seemingly static place that habitants must struggle to escape from, while at the same time it produces and is marked by particular forms of travel and transitivity (Davis, "Backdaire," 2001, 85).

Sone's *Nisei Daughter*, Houston and Houston's *Farewell to Manzanar*, Takei's *To the Stars*, and Uchida's *The Invisible Thread* juxtapose the narrators' perceptions of themselves as American children with that of America's classification of them as foreigners. This phenomenological divergence leads to the physical construction of an interstitial place that embodies America's government-sanctioned racism. The shifting paradigms of Uchida's vision of herself, which she repeatedly compares or contrasts with those of the people around her, address the complicated process of affiliation for the Asian American child in the process of acquiring self-esteem and acknowledging her positionality. Her relationships with her peers are represented positively, although she recognizes that her own insecurity might have prevented her from developing more relationships: "I was careful to close myself up to insure against being hurt" (Uchida, *Invisible Thread*, 1991, 55). In the chapter titled, "Unhappy Days," Uchida describes her growing awareness of ethnic division in California and the racism against Asians. A reference to an episode when a photographer, taking a picture of the Girl Reserves for the local paper, tries to "ease [her] out of the picture" (55), gestures significantly to the official portrait of itself that mainstream American desired at the time, which denied the presence of Asians. Uchida's perception of the nature of the American gaze becomes even more acute as she recounts the story of their internment: to the government, they were "aliens and nonaliens" (69); to the army they were simply "prisoners" (73), a word she stretches ironically as she defines their new situation: from law-abiding citizens, the Japanese Americans had been converted into "prisoners of our own country" (74). Her child-hood questions as to her identity begin to reverberate significantly: "How could America—my own country—have done this to us?" (79).

SOCIALIZATION

Patricia Chu, writing on the Asian American bildungsroman, explains that "Asian American subjectivities in these texts are characterized by the emergence of a critical ethnic intelligence that deploys and interrogates traditional narratives of Americanization" (*Assimilating Asians*, 2000, 6–7). In this context, Asian American Childhoods perform a necessary task: by recontextualizing the forms and themes of traditional American autobiography, they enact alternative modes of being and identifying as American, through itineraries marked by separation and difference, rather than by integration. Sau-ling Wong points out that one of the most thor-oughly naturalized scripts in the United States is the idea of cultural conflicts as the inevitable result of immigration: the forward-looking, freedom-loving American-born child, acting out what amounts to an im-mutable law of physics, contends with the tradition-bound, tyrannical foreign-born parents. The canonical denouement of the drama is assim-ilation; the child, after waging an appropriate struggle not only against the deputies of unreason but against his or her own incomprehension, finally puts aside outdated ethnic differences and wins his or her place in the larger society of free agents ("Autobiography," 1992, 277).

The stereotypical notion of socialization predicated upon assimilation must be reexamined. This strategy interrogates the tradition of American autobiography, and, in particular, its paradigm of the trajectory of success-ful socialization of its subject. Oftentimes the "necessary" socialization is not completed at the end of these autobiographies, and its lack of closure tends to be problematic, questioning, in turn, the very notion of the sub-ject's "Americanness." The experiences that mark each individual child's itinerary of socialization begin with personal experiences that are later reconfigured and inflected in the larger context of social obligation and interaction. As with mainstream American children, the experiences that may be classified as traumatic cloud a number of these Childhoods to dif-fering degrees. Disability (blindness in Ved Mehta's *Vedi*), mental illness (anorexia nervosa in Aimee Liu's *Solitaire*), abuse (Adeline Mah's *Falling*

Leaves), and war (Ung, Reyes, Nguyen, Accomando, and Kuramoto) necessarily shape the way the autobiographical subject acts in society and,
importantly, enacts the Childhood.

Specifically, for instance, Coe notes the experience of loss of religious
faith as a pivotal experience in Euro-American Childhoods, but has little
concern for the impingement of early political or social ideas. He explains
that "the exception to this is to be found when the political history of a
country or of a culture is so consistently tragic that it penetrates, as it
were, the communal subconscious—in which case, once again, it acquires
the status of "Myth" ("Childhood," 1984, 7–8). Political issues and experiences configure Asian American autobiographies of childhood epis-
temologically and phenomenologically. In these texts, the private world
of the child is often invaded by public events. War in Asian countries
figures predominantly and, though American children have not experienced a war in their own land since the Civil War, internment of the
Japanese Americans as a result of the bombing of Pearl Harbor, for example, recurs. The Japanese colonization of China and Korea permeates
the experiences of Kim and Kuramoto; the communist takeover and governments in Vietnam, Cambodia, and China are at the heart of Nguyen's,
Ung's, and Chen's narratives, respectively. These three texts conclude with
immigration. Life in the United States is not described, except, in the case
of Ung and Nguyen, in a brief epilogue.[15] The itinerary of adaptation,
the gap between the experience of the child who leaves the Asian country
and the writer in the act of writing, is not satisfactorily filled. The writers choose to leave the reader with the moment of dislocation, stressing
the juncture of transformativity, and choose not to recount the narrative
of socialization. Concluding the narrative at this point illustrates discursively a point of rebeginning, a gap between a familiar world, where one
belongs, and a state of liminality. It might also subversively indicate a
cyclical movement: those who may have suffered forms of rejection in
their own countries might be condemned to repeat them. Importantly,
and in opposition to Coe's prescriptive view of the text concluding at a
pivotal point of maturity, formulated in terms of temporality, these Asian
American Childhoods stress the import of the subject's movement through
space. As such, rather than the individuated and spatially localized subject of the Euro-American Childhood, which privileges qualities such as
wholeness and resolution, these Asian American texts propose a renewed
configuration of subjectivity, where children exist in a state of cultural
simultaneity, multiplicity, and dislocation. For this subject, poised on the
verge of travel, resolution is deferred, perhaps indefinitely.

In narratives that describe the child's process of learning about and
attempts to integrate into American society, issues of racism, awareness
of difference, and the desire to belong persist. The question of naming

becomes highly symbolic in this context. In a diverse society, names become signifiers of more than merely individual or familial identity, but gestures toward membership in a particular racial, ethnic, or cultural group. As Daniel Nakashima notes, the combination of words that constitute the personal name can become a contested site for the negotiation of the private and the public selves: "What one calls oneself, personally as well as ethnically, is thus a site of political struggle, where conventional racial classifications can be transgressed, accepted, or ignored" ("Rose," 2000, 113). For many of these autobiographers, the names they were given at birth reflect their cultural heritage or their bicultural positions. Jade Snow Wong's name links her to her siblings; Monica Sone's full name is Kazuko Monica, the Japanese name meaning "peace" and the English name from Saint Monica, the mother of Saint Augustine, though she is called Kazuko at home. Fenkl is called "Insu" by his Korean mother and "Heinz" by his German American father. The child does not identify himself as "Heinz" until he begins to go to American school, where he is not allowed to use his Korean name or speak in Korean. The names he uses on different occasions, therefore, correspond to spaces he occupies. For immigrant children, a name change can be more traumatic. M. Elaine Mar, in *Paper Daughter*, content to be "Mar Man Yee," is informed by her aunt that she needs an American name "to fit in" (1999, 61). The child panics: "Mother won't be able to say my name if it's American...I don't know English either. How will I know my name?" (61). The child construes the name change as a shift away from selfhood. When they choose the name, the child struggles to pronounce it— "Eee-laine"; "I repeated the sound. So that's who I was. My life cleaved in two" (62). Naming, and being denoted by a name, for these Asian American subjects, is their primary mode of representation in American society. When the name is rejected as too foreign, it alienates the child from his or her peers; but a name shift for the sake of adaptation often has more insidious consequences on the child's evolving sense of self-in-place.

But the Asian American child's process of socialization is not invariably negative. Indeed, several of these Childhoods end precisely with a version of successful socialization, turning to art as a manner of healing the difficult trajectory of the past. Uchida's story ends as she begins her career as a teacher, and she states explicitly her metanarrative purpose in inscribing her memoir. In the epilogue, she analyzes the creative impulse and acknowledges that her writing is her attempt to pass on a legacy of ethnic appreciation to the Sansei—the third generation Japanese Americans—"to give them the kinds of books I'd never had as a child. The time was right, for now the world too, was changing" (*Invisible Thread*, 1991, 131). Yep and Takei both narrate how they use their awareness of their difference in their artistic pursuits: "In writing about alienated people and aliens in my science fiction, I was writing about myself as a Chinese American" (Yep, *Lost Garden*, 1991, 104). Takei also explains that his experience in the internment camps and subsequent involvement with political and social issues nuance his visionary portrayal of Mr. Sulu in *Star Trek*. At the end of his narrative, after serving actively as a soldier in the U.S. Army in the Pacific in World War II, Reyes solves his problem of bicultural affiliation, as he realizes that "I could no longer hear the inner question that had walked with me all through my boyhood and teen years: am I Filipino or American? The question was irrelevant now; the 'or' between us had been replaced by an 'and.' We had just been through a Filipino *and* American war against a common enemy" (*Child of Two Worlds*, 1996, 285). But even the ostensibly successful stories are not unproblematically formulated, and we are required to discern the particular nature of the success and the price the subject has had to pay for it. Mar goes to Harvard, in fulfillment of her Chinese parents' dream, but she construes this success story as a metaphorical repetition of her family's story: "Like my grandfather, I'd immigrated with no way to send for my family" (*Paper Daughter*, 1999, 292). As Bergland notes, ethnic autobiographies "serve as instruments of collective opposition to progressive power and document the effects of long-term struggle on ethnic lives and communities ("Representing Ethnicity," 1994, 87). We can therefore read these representations of autobiographical subjects as gestures toward a renewed resistance to prescriptive norms of social conformity and prevailing discourses on the paradigms of the genre.

Bergland affirms that "[w]hat is at stake in ethnic autobiography is the possibility of ethnic groups telling their own stories, naming themselves—in short, presenting their own histories, identities, and representations of truth and memory" ("Representing Ethnicity," 1994, 77–78). The approach I introduce and endorse in this chapter, one that reads Asian American autobiographies of childhood in terms of how they subvert traditional modes of autobiographical self-authentication, gestures significantly toward an understanding of the unique problem of a canonical search for forms of self-representation through language in ethnic texts. Using Coe's definition of the Childhood as a model, this necessary translation deploys ethnic criticism and creative writing to extend the paradigm, and read the texts attentive to a wider aesthetic as well as personal and social implications. By writing these experiences, the writers symbolically control them—and become the protagonists of their self-representation. The highly metafictional character of many of these accounts attests to this claim: Uchida's didactic purpose, Yep's admission that his fictional characters were born from his own experiences, Reyes's acknowledgment that his literary exercise allowed him to think through his own process of ambivalent affiliation, Houston's text as an act of catharsis, and so forth. Importantly, the control the writers exert

manifests itself, not only in the fact of narrating, but in the manipulation of narrative strategies that signify discursively. Wong's use of third
person, Fenkl's double-voiced perspective, Houston's collaborative autobiography, Yep's and Uchida's engagement with children's literature,
Kim's aesthetically controlled representation of the erasure of language,
among others, show the writers as attentive to the expressive possibilities
of actively negotiating generic and narrative configuration. Indeed, their
conclusions sustain Bergland's and Boelhower's description of the processual character of ethnic autobiographies, which stresses multilayered
positioning and problematizes uncritical inscriptions of identification as
Americans

NOTES

1. This chapter is a précis of a full-length book in progress that proposes a
critical definition and analysis of the Asian American Childhood. In that longer
study, I expand and nuance the theoretical questions and critical readings of the
texts that here are, for reasons of length, referred to briefly. I will use the term
"Childhood," with a capital C, in the manner Coe does, to refer to the autobiographical subgenre.

2. In this book, as in subsequent articles that elaborate on specific issues, Coe
presents a review of over six hundred accounts of childhood written in six major
European languages over the past 150 years. The existence of a multiplicity of texts
justifies Coe's decision to define it as an autonomous subgenre of autobiography,
with its own internal rules and strategies. The study is admirably comprehensive,
if we ignore his limited references to texts written by ethnic American writers or
writers of the postcolonial world. Coe limits his mention of ethnic Childhoods
to those written by Maya Angelou, Alfred Kazin, Maxine Hong Kingston, Joy
Kogawa (though he notes that this is not really an autobiography and only shares
some characteristics of the genre), N. Scott Momaday, Philip Roth, and Jade Snow
Wong. Nonetheless, I argue that *The Woman Warrior* is not strictly a Childhood,
because of Kingston's complex use of biography in her life writing exercise and
her collagic construction. For that reason, I do not include her in my catalogue of
Asian American Childhoods, although her work limns many of the characteristics
of the genre.

3. Donald Goellnicht supports this idea when he claims that "one of the
most powerful and productive aspects of life-writing by marginalized peoples is
its ability to challenge, destabilize, and subvert traditional generic conventions"
("Blurring," 1997, 344). The issue of rewriting established genres is one I have
explored on other occasions, notably in my book, *Transcultural Reinventions:
Asian American and Asian Canadian Short Story Cycles*.

4. "When they rise to the surface," Coe explains, "they do so in the form
of themes, or symbols, or images which recur in the works of writers or artists
having contact with one another in space or time. . . . There is strong evidence to
suggest that the myths reveal an alternative, and profound relationship: not one
of determinism, but rather one of symbiosis" ("Reminiscences," 1984, 2–3).

5. Coe analyzes in detail the specific myths of national Childhoods that he identifies: the idea of education for the English child, language for the French, the recall of the mother in the case of Russian Childhoods, and so forth ("Portrait," 1981, 130).

6. As Yamamoto explains in the context of Japanese American women's narratives, "[w]hat is at stake here is not simply the question of whether the autobiographical form, as though it had a life of its own, empowers or disempowers its practitioners. At issue are crucial acts of discursive agency and the (re)appropriation of representational power, both of which are directly related to whether one reads these autobiographies as the introspective impulses of self-contemplation" (*Masking*, 1999, 106–107).

7. In diverse ways, these texts dialogue with Coe's description of the archetypal experiences of childhood: school, the need for secrets, solitude, and the figure of the absent or weak father and the dominant mother (*Grass*, 1984, 147–157). Nonetheless, I will center, for this chapter, on the elements that challenge or expand Coe's paradigms.

8. Norman Reyes, in *Child of Two Worlds* (1996), enacts a similar strategy. As he ostensibly meditates on his biraciality and struggles to decide whether he really is Filipino or American, he introduces the reader to Filipino history, customs, and traditions. Reyes's binary classification of racial/cultural affiliation is quite problematic and simplified, and will be addressed in more detail in my full-length study of Asian American Childhoods.

9. Interestingly, both texts contain numerous photographs—mostly archival prints of typical scenes, candy vendors, a traditional family, and so on—but only the frontispiece of each depicts the authors themselves.

10. In the pluralistic American society, as Bergland suggests, we must critically examine the notion of "the humanist and essentialist self at the center of the autobiography and recognize the multiply situated subject in autobiography, socially and historically shaped. In such a context, ethnic autobiographies provide a meaningful site for exploring multiple subjectivities with implications for the larger culture" ("Postmodernism," 1994, 134).

11. Coe asserts that the truth of this form of life writing "would be better served by using a third-person narrative, thus forcing the reader into a conscious awareness of the *differences* between himself and that alien other whose truth he is attempting to assess" (*Grass*, 1984, 82).

12. Fenkl's (*Memories*, 1996) text hovers between autobiography and fiction. In this chapter, I will heed the autobiographical pact the author enacts and consider it a Childhood.

13. The struggle for English is also crucial for Da Chen in *Colors of the Mountain*. Here, English becomes the way out of communist China where it represents the American dream of success and opportunity.

14. Loung Ung's *First They Killed My Father* also privileges the space of the children's camp in Cambodia, and, later, the refugee camp as in-between spaces, where identity and affiliation are negotiated. Because of the limits of this chapter, I cannot engage the specificities of that text.

15. Fenkl (*Memories*, 1996), for instance, operates an interesting narrative strategy that juxtaposes the voices of the child-in-Korea with the adult-in-America.

By alternating normally formatted chapters with italicized ones, he attends to the double-voiced discourse of the translated and relocated subject.

Works Cited

Accomando, Claire Hsu. *Love and Rutabaga*. New York: St. Martin's Press, 1993.

Bergland, Betty. "Postmodernism and the Autobiographical Subject: Reconstructing the 'Other'," in *Autobiography and Postmodernism*. Kathleen Ashley, Leigh Gilmore, Gerald Peters, eds. (pp. 130–166). Amherst: University of Massachusetts Press, 1994.

Bergland, Betty Ann. "Representing Ethnicity in Autobiography: Narratives of Opposition." *Yearbook of English Studies*, 24 (1994): 67–93.

Bhabha, Homi K. *The Location of Culture*. London and New York: Routledge, 1994.

Boelhower, William. "The Making of Ethnic Autobiography in the United States," in *American Autobiography: Retrospect and Prospect*. Paul John Eakin, ed. (pp. 123–41). Madison: University of Wisconsin Press, 1991.

Chen, Da. *Colors of the Mountain*. New York: Anchor Books, 2001.

Coe, Richard N. "Portrait of the Artist as a Young Australian: Childhood, Literature and Myth." *Southerly*, 41 (1981): 126–82.

Coe, Richard N. "Reminiscences of Childhood: An Approach to a Comparative Mythology." *Proceedings of the Leeds Philosophical and Literary Society*, 19: 6 (1984): 1–95.

Coe, Richard N. *When the Grass Was Taller: Autobiography and the Experience of Childhood*. New Haven, CT: Yale University Press, 1984.

Choy, Wayson. *Paper Shadows: A Chinatown Childhood*. Toronto: Viking, 1999.

Chu, Patricia P. *Assimilating Asians: Gendered Strategies of Authorship in Asian America*. Durham, NC and London: Duke University Press, 2000.

Davis, Rocío G. "'Backdaire': Chinatown as Cultural Site in Fae Myenne Ng's *Bone* and Wayson Choy's *The Jade Peony*." *Aborder: North American Literature and Culture at the End of the Century*. Special issue of the *Revista de Canaria de Estudios Ingleses*, 43 (2001): 83–99.

Davis, Rocío G. *Transcultural Reinventions: Asian American and Asian Canadian Short Story Cycles*. Toronto: TSAR, 2001.

Eakin, Paul John. *Fictions in Autobiography: Studies in the Art of Self-Invention*. Princeton, NJ: Princeton University Press, 1985.

Fenkl, Heinz Insu. *Memories of My Ghost Brother*. New York: Dutton, 1996.

Goellnicht, Donald C. "Blurring Boundaries: Asian American Literature as Theory," in *An Interethnic Companion to Asian American Literature*. King-Kok Cheung, ed. (pp. 338–65). New York: Cambridge University Press, 1997.

Houston, Jeanne Wakatsuki, and Houston, James. *Farewell to Manzanar*. Original publication 1973. New York: Bantam, 1995.

Kang, Younghill. *The Grass Roof*. Original publication 1931. Chicago: Follett, 1966.

Kim, Elaine H. *Asian American Literature: An Introduction to the Writings and Their Social Context*. Philadelphia: Temple University Press, 1982.

Kim, Richard. *Lost Names: Scenes from a Korean Boyhood*. New York: Praeger, 1970.

Kuramoto, Kazuko. *Manchurian Legacy*. East Lansing: Michigan State University Press, 1999.

Lee, Yan Phou. *When I Was a Boy in China*. Boston: Lothrop, Lee, and Shepard, 1887.

Liu, Aimee. *Solitaire*. New York: Harper and Row, 1979.

Mah, Adeline Yeh. *Falling Leaves: The True Story of an Unwanted Chinese Daughter*. New York: John Wiley and Sons, 1998.

Mar, M. Elaine. *Paper Daughter*. New York: HarperCollins, 1999.

Mehta, Ved. *Vedi*. New York: Norton, 1982.

Nakashima, Daniel A. "A Rose by Any Other Name: Names, Multiracial/Multiethnic People, and the Politics of Identity," in *The Sum of Our Parts: Mixed-Heritage Asian Americans*. Teresa Williams-León and Cynthia Nakashima, eds. (pp. 111–119). Philadelphia: Temple University Press, 2000.

New, Ilhan. *When I Was a Boy in Korea*. Boston: Lothrop, Lee, and Shepard, 1928.

Nguyen, Kien. *The Unwanted*. New York: Little, Brown, 2001.

Pascal, Roy. *Design and Truth in Autobiography*. Cambridge: Harvard University Press, 1960.

Reyes, Norman. *Child of Two Worlds: An Autobiography of a Filipino-American, or Vice Versa*. Colorado Springs, CO: Three Continents Press, 1995. Reprinted Pasig City: Anvil Publications, 1996.

Ricou, Laurie. *Everyday Magic: Child Languages in Canadian Literature*. Vancouver: University of British Columbia Press, 1987.

Smith, Paul. *Discerning the Subject*. Minneapolis: University of Minneapolis Press, 1988.

Sone, Monica. *Nisei Daughter*. 1953. Seattle: University of Washington Press, 1991.

Takei, George. *To the Stars: The Autobiography of George Takei, Star Trek's Mr. Sulu*. New York: Pocket Books, 1997.

Uchida, Yoshiko. *The Invisible Thread*. New York: Simon and Schuster, 1991.

Ung, Loung. *First They Killed My Father: A Daughter of Cambodia Remembers*. New York: HarperCollins, 2000.

Wong, Jade Snow. *Fifth Chinese Daughter*. Original publication1945. Seattle: University of Washington Press, 1989.

Wong, Sau-ling Cynthia. "Autobiography as Guided Chinatown Tour? Maxine Hong Kingston's *The Woman Warrior* and the Chinese-American Autobiographical Controversy," in *Multicultural Autobiography: American Lives*. James Robert Payne, ed. (pp. 248–79). Knoxville: University of Tennessee Press, 1992.

Wong, Sau-ling Cynthia. "Ethnic Subject, Ethnic Sign, and the Difficulty of Rehabilitative Representation: Chinatown in Some Works of Chinese American Fiction." *Yearbook of English Studies*, 24 (1994): 251–62.

Yamamoto, Traise. *Masking Selves, Making Subjects: Japanese American Women, Identity, and the Body*. Berkeley: University of California Press, 1999.

Yep, Laurence. *The Lost Garden*. New York: Simon and Schuster, 1991.

8 The Poetics of Liminality and Misidentification

Winnifred Eaton's Me *and Maxine Hong Kingston's* The Woman Warrior

KATHERINE HYUNMI LEE

IN 1915, CENTURY MAGAZINE serialized the anonymously authored *Me: A Book of Remembrance*, and the story and its author were
soon caught in a whirlwind of controversy. Although the autobiography
focused principally on the author's artistic maturation, readers found
her romantic escapades much more engaging. With dramatic flair ("I
was love's passionate pilgrim"), the heroine describes her ill-fated
affair with a wealthy married man, an unwelcome kiss from a black
Jamaican politician, a lecherous doctor's advances, and her simultaneous
engagement to three men, as she is too kind and inexperienced to refuse
their proposals (Eaton, *Me*, 1997, 346). The *Toronto Star* reported that
"while shocking the sensibilities of many of the old subscribers," *Me*'s
racy subject matter "increased [*Century*]'s circulation considerably";
publicity also fueled sales as New York City subway advertisements and
billboards asked, "Who is the author of *Me*?" ("Famous" [clipping];
Birchall, *Onoto Watanna*, 2001, 116).[1] Reviewers responded to both
Me's sensational content ("if all is true therein, the orthodox will find
comfort in that the book ends with the heroine at prayer"; Clipping,
Star, 1915) and to the question of the author's identity ("the author
of 'Me' is probably much more clever and fascinating than during the
impulsive maidenhood of which she writes"; Clipping, *Times*, 1915).
The speculation ended when a *New York Times Book Review* article
("Is Onoto Watanna Author of the Anonymous Novel *Me*?") deduced
the author's nationality, and ultimately her identity, from various clues
(including a scene featuring the heroine kissing a man's sleeve, which the
writer claimed was a Japanese custom) (qtd. in Birchall 116).[2]

Katherine Hyunmi Lee's "The Poetics of Liminality and Mis-Identification: Winnifred
Eaton's *Me* and Maxine Hong Kingston's *The Woman Warrior*" originally was published in
Studies in the Literary Imagination, vol. 37: 1, pp. 17–33. © Copyright (2004), Department
of English, Georgia State University. Reprinted by permission.

Although the article satisfactorily resolved the mystery for readers, it served another, more important purpose by safeguarding the actual identity of the author, as "Onoto Watanna" itself was a pseudonym for the more pedestrian and distinctly Western-sounding Winnifred Eaton. The Canadian-born Eaton, whose father was British and mother Chinese, assumed a Japanese authorial persona in order to bypass late-nineteenth-century North American Sinophobia and exploit the Japonisme fad, dissociating herself from stereotypes of the Chinese as debased and inassimilable and appealing to the seemingly more benevolent stereotypes of the Japanese as exotic yet civilized. A prolific author whose fiction and non-fiction appeared in magazines such as *Ladies' Home Journal* and *Redbook*, her principal success stemmed from the popularity of Watanna's "Japanese" romance novels and short stories, most of which were published between 1898 and 1922, and featured picturesque settings, naïve and childlike Japanese heroines, and the occasional act of hari-kari.

A significant departure from the Japanese novels, *Me* is nonetheless a narrative befitting its chameleonic author. In addition to depicting Eaton's romantic exploits, the account details the crucial year in which the seventeen-year-old leaves her familial Canadian home to pursue a writing career and charts her travels to Jamaica, Richmond, Chicago, and New York. Although the plot trajectory essentially follows the events of Eaton's life, many other details are fictionalized, especially those related to the author's racial identity. Eaton refers to herself throughout *Me* as "Nora Ascough" and avoids mentioning her mother's Chinese heritage in a rather unconvincing attempt to "pass" as white (as evidenced by the *New York Times Book Review* "exposé").[3] Further conflating fact and fiction is *Me*'s evocation of various literary genres, including the bildungsroman, the fairy tale, and not surprisingly, the romance novel. Her dependence upon other genres and predilection for melodramatic phrasing ("[fate] was a black, monstrous thing, a thief in the dark that hid to entrap me") often propel the autobiography into implausibility and reflect Eaton's treatment of her identity as merely another device that could be manipulated, fabricated, and exploited (*Me*, 346).

Present-day critics generally characterize the text and its author as little more than literary novelties. Amy Ling wryly notes that the "boundary between fact and fiction is not at all clear" (*Between*, 1990, 32) in *Me*, while James Doyle derides Eaton for "perpetuat[ing] an artificial and ethnically false legend about herself" ("Sui Sin," 1994, 55). Caroline Sin limits Eaton's literary legacy to the creation of a "lucrative market for a particular kind of Orientalist exotica written by Asian or Eurasian Americans," exemplified today by authors such as Amy Tan ("Review," 1999, 180). Within the current scholarly schema, then, Eaton is remembered as an author whose works, including *Me*, perpetuated rather than subverted racist stereotypes and ideologies, especially in light of the Asian American literary tradition that has since developed. As Tomo Hattori says, "There is not much at first glance that recommends [*Me*] for canonization as Asian American literature, women's literature, or literature" ("Model," 1999, 236).

The text that is considered the seminal Asian American autobiography, Maxine Hong Kingston's *The Woman Warrior*, indeed seems to be *Me*'s ideological opposite. A serious treatise of racial and gender identity formation and a radical departure from the traditionally linear autobiography narrative structure, *The Woman Warrior* is hailed by critics as an exemplar of Asian American literature's subversive nature, as well as an emblematic feminist bildung in which, as Ling and Elaine Kim describe, "Kingston transforms her victim's state of cut frenum into a victor's state of full-throated song" (Ling, *Between*, 1990, 130) in her attempt to "find a uniquely Chinese American voice to serve as a weapon for her life" (Kim, *Asian*, 1982, 207). By contrast, *Me* appears to be a simple hoax, an often fictional autobiography written by a Chinese North American woman "passing" as white, and an example of one author's "false consciousness" regarding issues of identity, gender, and race.[4]

I argue, however, that there are ways to examine *Me* as an Asian American autobiography without divesting these literary categories of meaning. Feminist critics have revised traditional autobiographical studies by refusing to privilege a poetics of "truth" that centers around an autonomous autobiographical "I," instead emphasizing selfhood as a communal and cultural process. Thus, rather than obscuring or embellishing the autobiography's truthfulness, *The Woman Warrior*'s distinct blend of fact and fiction reveals the dizzying array of cultural narratives that bombard the young Maxine.[5]

I similarly view *Me*'s mediation between Nora's story and the storytelling conventions she employs as illustrating the cultural orientations that inform her personal and artistic maturation. When situated within a feminist framework, then, Eaton's autobiography presents thematic concerns that anticipate those of Kingston's work, especially the complex engagement between women autobiographers and dominant social and literary forces.

More significantly, *Me* brings into sharp relief aspects of *The Woman Warrior* that feminist and Asian American scholars have been reluctant to discuss, namely, those associated with dominant cultural complicity rather than resistance. The impulse to construct "Asian American woman" as a politically cohesive and subversive identity stems from a sincere and impassioned desire to effect social change, but it misguidedly elides any dissonance that might exist. As Judith Butler contends, "[a]lthough the political discourses that mobilize identity categories tend to cultivate identifications in the service of a political goal, it may be that the persistence of *dis*identification is equally crucial to the rearticulation of democratic contestation" (emphasis added; *Bodies*, 1993, 4). Adapting Butler's argument, I suggest that the mutual theme of *mis*identification in *Me* and *The Woman Warrior* undermines critical celebrations of subversion and cohesion, and that the two autobiographies instead represent identity as a perpetual negotiation between rebellion and concession, commensurability and disavowal. After a brief analysis of feminist revisions of autobiographical studies, I will situate both texts as examples of Asian American literature that destabilize rather than define the category "Asian American woman."

THE FICTION OF NONFICTION

"Life is always like a sketch. No, 'sketch' is not quite the word, because a sketch is an outline of something, the groundwork for a picture, whereas the sketch that is our life is a sketch for nothing, an outline with no picture" (Kundera, *The Unbearable Lightness of Being*, 1984, 8). Literary scholars have traditionally argued that the goal of autobiographies (that is, canonical texts such as Benjamin Franklin's) is to represent identity development as a process by which the subject becomes liberated from and ultimately transcends his or her social surroundings. James Olney states that autobiography ideally reveals "consciousness, pure and simple, consciousness referring to no objects outside itself, to no events, and to no other lives; we can understand [autobiography] as participation in an absolute existence far transcending the shifting, changing unrealities of mundane life" (qtd. in Benstock, "Authorizing," 1997, 1138). The autobiographical narrator tells his or her story not because of his or her "mundane life," but in spite of it. According to this approach, identity is neither a product of cultural and historical forces, nor a communal or process-oriented entity, but rather, unified (or in Olney's words, "absolute"); in other words, autobiography is only worthy of study or "successful" when it represents the achievement of metaphysical selfhood.

Feminist scholars have problematized this traditional reading by arguing that a totalized identity is an alibi that can only be perpetuated by those with the luxury of ignoring their "mundane" lives and the ability to transcend their social location—namely, white male authors.[6] In fact, Anne McClintock argues that the notion of the autobiographer-as-transcendent implicitly stems from and perpetuates a Western mythos of individuality and progress: "In the history of the West, autobiography is the genre most closely associated with the idea of the potency of self-identity, metonymically expressed in the signature: the emblem of a unique, unrepeatable and autonomous identity created at a stroke of the metaphysical pen(is)"

(*Imperial*, 1995, 313). Feminist theorists assert that the social transcendence characteristic of male autobiography and privileged within autobiographical studies is simply not possible for those whom, as Simone de Beauvoir has famously stated, are granted only immanence by dominant culture.

Women's autobiography is thus marked by contestation, as authors struggle toward representation without the models of transcendence available to male authors. Claiming that fragmented, multiple, and collective consciousnesses are constitutive of a woman's authorial identity, scholars such as Sidonie Smith argue that those who belong to marginalized groups present autobiographical subjects who are "severally situated within diverse, sometimes congruous, often competing, even contradictory discursive levels" (*Subjectivity*, 1993, 21). In other words, rather than view autobiography as a narrative through which the self springs fully formed, feminist theorists have redefined the genre as one that encompasses negotiation and contradiction, in which the self, by dint of its ties to social forces, cannot (and does not necessarily desire to) achieve transcendence.

Another underexamined aspect in autobiography studies is the integration of fictional elements such as plot structure and conventions of other literary genres. Traditionally, the autobiography simultaneously depends on and attempts to elide its fictional influences, insofar as the imposition of narrative order on one's "true" *story* cannot help but evoke and invoke other genres. According to Shari Benstock, "autobiography reveals the impossibility of its own dream. What begins on the presumption of self-knowledge ends in the creation of a fiction that covers over the premises of its construction" ("Authorizing," 1997, 1138). The representation of a metaphysical, transcendent self can only be achieved through a seemingly seamless integration of exactly that which autobiography claims to oppose: fiction. Again, feminist theorists have been among the most prominent in calling attention to this relationship, contending that the autobiography is inherently intertextual and that women's autobiographies tend to make this intertextuality explicit. One subtext of women's autobiography is what Smith calls a negotiation among "the complex imbroglios of cultural fictions that surround the autobiographer," rather than a representation of a "pure" consciousness ("Filiality," 1997, 1117).

These two aspects of feminist revisions of autobiographical studies—identity as fragmented and the genre's intertextuality—have prompted scholars to focus on narratives such as *The Woman Warrior*, Audre Lorde's *Zami* (1982), and Harriet Jacobs's *Incidents in the Life of a Slave Girl* (1861), which demonstrate that the process of racial and gender identification, especially for women of color, resists the linearity, transcendence, and coherence found in traditional autobiographies. Furthermore, these texts also negotiate with the "complex imbroglio" of other narratives, alternately critiquing dominant culture's investment in certain kinds of narratives (*Zami*'s critical assessment of the traditional autobiography), revising these narratives to address social issues (Jacobs's use of the sentimental novel), relying upon narratives outside the purview of dominant culture (Maxine's mother's "talk-story"), or sometimes engaging all three actions simultaneously.

It is hardly surprising then, that *The Woman Warrior* resides as a particular favorite among feminist scholars. Yet in spite of the feminist revitalization of the autobiography as a politically charged and multifaceted genre, the general interpretation of Kingston's text as representing a "victory" against dominant culture ironically substitutes transcendence with subversion. For example, Smith's interpretation of *The Woman Warrior*, like those from Ling and Kim cited earlier, invokes the language of transcendence and individualism even as it critiques traditional autobiographies: "Using the autobiography to create identity, [Kingston] breaks down the hegemony of formal 'autobiography' and breaks out of the silence that has bound her culturally to discover a resonant voice of her own" ("Filiality," 1997, 1117). Smith's view of Kingston as "creating" and "discovering" her own voice seems vulnerable to McClintock's earlier criticism of the autobiography as privileging "a unique, unrepeatable and autonomous identity," and problematically resembles Olney's view of the autobiographical consciousness.

This disproportionate critical emphasis on Maxine's metamorphosis from victim to victor and her reclamation of a "uniquely Chinese American voice" casts "Asian American woman" as a discrete identity category that one can recuperate or recover, and troublingly equates "authenticity" with political subversion. As Hattori argues, the effort to establish "an ethnic singularity that can provide a bounded sense of coherence and 'truth'" results in a compulsory sameness that ironically reinstates overdetermined identity categories and renders Asian Americanness into "a sublime and socially futile object" ("Model," 1999, 229). I am not arguing here that feminist interpretations of *The Woman Warrior* as a subversive text are unfounded; Kingston's narrative undeniably disrupts dominant ideologies regarding race, gender, and nation. My discomfort stems from the fact that the valorization of subversion masks the circulation of contradictory discourses that scholars claim are embedded in autobiographies. In other words, if autobiographies are *constitutively* contradictory, then they cannot *only* be subversive.

In the next section I will examine the mediation between fact and fiction that feminist theorists identify as one of the characteristics of autobiography. In *Me*, this mediation allows us to see how dominant ideology intervenes into the psychic processes of identification for the racial Other, and transforms the autobiography, ostensibly a narrative charting the journey of identification, into a narrative charting the journey of misidentification. *The Woman Warrior* similarly mediates between fact and fiction and depicts the tension produced by identification and misidentification, but intensifies this tension by depicting the dual (and sometimes dueling) interventions of both Chinese and American cultures in the psyche of the autobiographer.

Maxine's attempt to initially identify with Chinese tradition bears a striking resemblance to Nora's identification with dominant culture; their respective misidentifications resist facile assignations of subversion and concession and underscore the contestatory nature of Asian Americanness.

Neither Princess Nor Warrior: The Fairy Tale and the Fa Mu Lan Myth

As previously discussed, the inevitable integration of other genres within an autobiography generally appears seamless to the reader and perhaps even to the autobiographer. Both *Me* and *The Woman Warrior* avoid the pretense of seeming "empirically" or "objectively" truthful, however, and explicitly invoke other literary genres. This invocation illustrates the fictional impulses inherent in the autobiographical genre, and more importantly, reveals a more urgent task: the autobiographer's negotiation with other cultural narratives as a means of situating the self.

However, rather than ameliorate this negotiation, the usage of other genres prompts a crisis of identity for both Nora and Maxine, as they attempt to define themselves using the stories they have heard as children, but fail in doing so. Nora uses a Western genre, the fairy tale, to narrate her story, only to discover that its racist, sexist, and elitist conventions further marginalize her, even as she attempts to "pass" as white. Similarly, Maxine's fantasies of herself as the famed military heroine Fa Mu Lan cause tremendous psychic grief when she realizes that she is incapable of voicing and defending herself both within her own familial household and society at large. Her status as an ersatz Fa Mu Lan and Nora's inability to become a fairy tale princess result in tortured relationships with their projected ideals, situating Maxine and Nora in the liminal state of almost-but-not-quite; Anne Cheng calls this a "double malady," or "[t]he condition of having to incorporate and encrypt both an impossible ideal and a denigrated self" (*Melancholy*, 2001, 72). In other words, the girls' engagement with their respective fictional narratives compels their desire to identify with these heroines and simultaneously denies them the possibility of complete identification.

In *Me*, Nora's initial usage of fairy tale language and figures seems appropriate in reflecting her youth and naïveté; fairy tales also buffer her from the realities of her impoverished family, a "hungry, crushing brood" (*Me*, 6). Her vision of a fairy tale existence involves romantic adventure and escape, and she alludes to dreams in which she is "the heroine in a hundred princely romances" (9). By contrast, she describes her mother as a "creature from whose life all romance had been squeezed by the torturing experience of bearing sixteen children," and implicitly rejects her as a role model because she is partially responsible for Nora's poverty-stricken life (3). In discussing her own position within the family, Nora portrays herself in Cinderella-esque terms, oppressed by the work necessitated by her siblings, a "noisy, tormenting brood for whom it had been my particular task to care!" (6). Thus the fairy tale plot trajectory, in which the hero rescues the heroine and resolves both her romantic and financial anxieties, causes resentment toward her family and deeply informs her ambitions and perceptions of society at large.

Although Nora enthusiastically turns to fairy tales as a form of child-hood therapy, she also unwittingly absorbs the genre's patriarchal and racist subtexts. Racially, the fairy tale landscape is one in which all its inhabitants are, of course, snow white. Nora's discussion of her familial history illustrates the genre's compulsory whiteness and her internaliza-tion of whiteness as privilege, both socially and economically. She proudly proclaims her father's British heritage and says little of her mother's back-ground, except when it merges with her father's: "the greatness of my father's people had been a sort of fairy-story with us all, and we knew that it was his marriage with mama that had cut him off from his kindred" (*Me*, 26). Linda Trinh Moser insightfully observes that "the narrative im-plicates racism as one of the causes behind the Ascough family's low eco-nomic status," yet Nora's uncritical assessment of the "greatness" of her British relatives indicates that she views her mother's Chinese heritage, rather than racism, as the catalyst for the "unhappy ending" and her poverty ("Afterword," 1997, 364). The racial landscape of the fairy tale world thus causes Nora to implicitly link racial otherness with poverty.

The sexual economy of the fairy tale genre is distressing, to say the least: within this world, a woman's worth and moral integrity are directly proportional to her attractiveness, women contend against one another in fierce competition, and above all else, the heroine must depend upon her Prince Charming to provide material security. Nora turns time and again to the various men in her life as "rescuers": she relies upon a young reporter, Verley Marchmont, to write her pieces for the *Lantern*; she ap-peals to Manning's interest in her as a means to leave Jamaica; and she uses Hamilton's money to secure her escape from Manning. Her friend Lolly criticizes her for blindly romanticizing these men: "She said I was a hero-worshipper, and made idols of unworthy clay and endowed them with impossible attributes and virtues. She said girls like me never really loved a man at all. We loved an image we created" (*Me*, 217). Yet for most of *Me*, Nora considers Lolly's advice to be a cynical intrusion into her fantasies that blur the line between romance and material wealth: "I did want pretty things (what young girl does not?), I hated my work, and I loved [Hamilton], and wanted above all things on earth to please him" (244). Lolly's perceptive criticism and Nora's own admission of her desires demonstrate not only her investment in the fairy tale, but her lack of awareness about how deeply entrenched she really is in its belief systems. If the racial politics of the fairy tale connect racial otherness with poverty in Nora's mind, then the genre's sexual politics privilege traditional forms of femininity; thus the "ideal" world promoted by the fairy tale is one in which whiteness, wealth, femininity, and romance are inextricably linked.[7]

But as *Me* progresses, the fairy tale's conventions become less applicable to Nora's life and more difficult for her to sustain in the narrative. What's interesting (and disturbing) is that Nora's initial success as an author is prompted by her use of nonconventional narratives. She finds artistic inspiration in that which she has most rejected—her mother's stories: "one day I wrote a little story of my mother's land. I had never been there, and yet I wrote easily of that quaint, far country" (*Me*, 125). While her description of China as "quaint" illustrates her internalization of the dominant viewpoint, she nonetheless describes herself as having a connection with at least part of her Chinese heritage. In fact, she later tells Hamilton that she has "'an instinctive feeling about that country,'" and declares, "'I feel as if I knew everything about that land, and when I sit down to write—why, things just come pouring to me, and I can write about *anything* then'" (176). Nora claims to feel the most empowered as an author when she writes about China, yet she ironically insists on using a culturally sanctioned genre to inform her own story. This irony underscores Cheng's contention that "the education of racism is an education of desire"; in this instance, Nora's *desire* to construct a specific kind of social identity has, in fact, *become* her identity (19).

Ultimately, her desire for a "happily ever after" ending is shattered when she finds out Hamilton is married, but another, equally important dream persists—fame and material success: "Dreams, too, came of the days when I would be famous and rich....My poems would be on every one's tongue, my books in every home" (*Me*, 153). Moser argues that Nora subverts the fairy tale by "sever[ing] the link between love and material gain...[d]eflating unrealistic expectations of a Cinderella match" (362). Although Nora makes an important distinction between romance and material success, she nonetheless substitutes romance with finance. She transfers her investment in one dominant narrative to another, shifting from the romantically oriented fairy tale to its modern American equivalent, the economically informed Horatio Alger story, and her "happily ever after" ending becomes predicated upon the achievement of material success.

Yet wealth and fame do not become the panacea to her romantic failures, nor do they situate her as a female Horatio Alger. Even though Eaton's friend Jean Webster informs us in *Me*'s introduction that "[t]he author has written a number of books that have had a wide circulation. The aspirations of the little girl of seventeen have been realized!", disrupting this fairy tale ending is the perspective of the older Nora, the narrator. The older Nora concedes that the conventional happy ending of attaining material wealth is an unsatisfactory one: "I can say of my novels that they are strangely like myself, unfulfilled promises" (*Me*, 319). Her description of herself as "unfulfilled" implies that something remains absent, incomplete, and undercuts Webster's neatly drawn conclusion; thus while *Me* charts Nora's maturation and the achievement of her authorial identity, this concession undermines the entire narrative and its generic influences. In the end, *Me* demonstrates ambivalence toward dominant narrative forms as both influential and incompatible, and implies that a socially prescribed narrative that privileges whiteness and patriarchal values is incapable of addressing the experiences of those it marginalizes.

The solution to Nora's sense of dissatisfaction would naturally seem to be for her to reject Western narratives altogether and instead rely upon alternatives, such as her mother's Chinese stories. In fact, the older Nora implies that her sister (who we assume is Edith Eaton/Sui Sin Far) more fully realized her artistic potential, in part because Edith refused to be governed by Western narrative models: "I thought of other sisters ... the eldest, *a girl with more real talent than I*. . . . She is dead now, that dear big sister of mine, and a monument marks her grave in commemoration of work she did for my mother's country" (emphasis added; *Me*, 194). Nora's misidentification with Western narratives and her negotiation between artistic expression and material success are themes that still concern current Asian American literary critics and authors, including Kingston.

Indeed, unlike *Me*, *The Woman Warrior* integrates a number of alternative narratives, including stories that either take place in China or stem from Chinese folkloric tradition. Yet as *The Woman Warrior* unfolds, Maxine develops an equally ambivalent relationship toward Asian narratives, demonstrating that those stories that seem the most empowering might in fact be the most disabling.

Of the five sections that comprise *The Woman Warrior*, the one critics have most frequently discussed is the second, "White Tigers." In it, Maxine recounts one of the childhood tales her mother has repeatedly "talk-storied," the legend of Fa Mu Lan. The legend traces Fa Mu Lan's training with a mystical elderly couple and her rise as a masterful "female avenger" who disguises herself as a male and leads her army into battle against corrupt enemies. She is able to move easily between exhibiting masculine (though not masculinist) behavior in front of her troops and privately choosing marriage and motherhood (she secretly marries and gives birth while encamped). After vanquishing her foes and liberating her village from a tyrannical baron, she returns to her family and happily begins her role as a civilian. In contrast to the fairy tale, the Fa Mu Lan myth promotes several feminist themes, including the woman's body as a site of empowerment, the performative nature of gender, and a critique of militaristic patriarchy; the narrative also subverts the dominance of Western narratives by representing a Chinese woman as a model of strength and utilizing a Chinese story as a source for racial and gender identification.

Given its compelling subject matter, this narrative greatly influences Maxine's worldview, as does the fairy tale with Nora's. But while the fairy tale indoctrinates Nora into a patriarchal Western value system, the Fa Mu Lan legend introduces Maxine to feminist values: "When we Chinese girls listened to the adults talk-story, we learned that we failed if we grew up to be but wives or slaves. We could be heroines, swordswomen" (*The Warrior Woman*, hereafter cited as *WW*, 18). Maxine completely emulates Fa Mu Lan, claiming that "I would have to grow up a warrior woman," and attempts to reenact the legend by battling a new breed of barons: "[f]rom the fairy tales, I've learned exactly who the enemy are. I easily recognize them—business-suited in their modern American executive guise" (20, 48). Instead of battling power-hungry tyrants in ancient China, then, Maxine sees herself pitted against institutionalized racism in contemporary America.

Yet as she grows older, the Fa Mu Lan story becomes increasingly disempowering, and Maxine admits that "[m]y American life has been such a disappointment" in contrast to the legend (*WW*, 45). Although the story celebrates a woman's independence and portrays her potential as limitless, the patriarchal values Maxine encounters within her family and community undermine the feminist lessons she has absorbed. She cannot reconcile the tale with the Chinese culture that produced it, noting that sexism is constitutive of the language itself: "There is a Chinese word for the female *I*—which is 'slave.' Break the women with their own tongues!" (47). Although she rails against her family's devaluation of girls, she cannot make herself be heard: "'I'm not a bad girl,' I would scream.... I might as well have said, 'I'm not a girl'" (46). Marginalized in America because she is Chinese and marginalized by the Chinese community because she is a woman, she becomes increasingly dislocated, claiming that "I could not figure out what was my village" (48). She thus loses her sense of identity because she no longer knows how to fight or whom she is defending.

Even more bewildering to Maxine is the fact that the Fa Mu Lan tale fails to resonate with the stories she hears about her family still in China. After the communist revolution, Maxine's family loses its fortune and her relatives are tortured, executed, or financially (and one would presume, psychically) ruined. Her uncle is executed for trying to trap birds in a tree for food, which the communists view as a "selfish" act. Maxine cannot reconcile these new stories with the ones from her childhood: "It is confusing that my family was not the poor to be championed. They were executed like the barons in the stories, when they were not barons" (WW, 51). Within the moral framework of the Fa Mu Lan legend, villains are easily identifiable and receive their due, the heroine emerges victorious, and justice prevails. But Maxine has increasing trouble applying this framework to the complexities of her family's story and to the complexities of American and Chinese societies. She still attempts to configure herself as a new Fa Mu Lan, but realizes that the battles she must fight are more extensive, wide-ranging, and untenable than any Fa Mu Lan herself faced: "Nobody in history has conquered and united both North America and Asia" (49).

At the end of "White Tigers" Maxine nonetheless makes one important though tenuous connection to Fa Mu Lan through the depiction of their bodies as sites of cultural inscriptions. In the legend, Fa Mu Lan's parents tattoo her back with a list of the injustices the baron has committed. When Maxine (imagining herself as Fa Mu Lan) finally encounters the baron, who thinks she is a man, she dramatically removes her shirt to reveal her tattoos: "'You've done this,' I said, and ripped off my shirt to show him my back. 'You are responsible for this.' When I saw his startled eyes at my breasts, I slashed him across the face and on the second stroke cut off his head" (WW, 44). Fa Mu Lan's body becomes doubly significant as a record of and tool against patriarchal oppression, and her tattoos are literal representations of the ways in which dominant culture has historically attempted to control women's bodies. Leigh Gilmore characterizes this scene as one of transformation: "the body as a text of revenge instead becomes the female body that must be avenged," as Fa Mu Lan sheds her male disguise in order to perform her final, and most important, act of justice (*Autobiographics*, 1994, 182).[8] The baron, a metonymic representative of patriarchy, can only react in a sexist and objectifying fashion to her unveiling ("his startled eyes at my breasts"), and his violent demise signifies the end of subjugation both for Fa Mu Lan's village and for women in general.

Again attempting to adapt the legend to her own identity, Maxine claims that as an author, she is a type of woman warrior whose body is similarly inscribed by dominant culture and her battle against it: "What we have in common are the words at our backs. . . . And I have so many words—'chink' words and 'gook' words too—that they do not fit on my skin" (WW, 53). Smith views this final connection as a resolution to the previous incompatibility between Maxine and Fa Mu Lan. She argues that Maxine conquers the confusion wrought by legend by substituting a sword for a pen: "Kingston manages to shatter the complacencies of cultural myths, problematic heroines, and the illusory autobiographical possibilities they sanction"; in other words, Maxine exorcises Fa Mu Lan's overpowering influence by authoring her own story ("Filiality," 1997, 1125). Yet I interpret Maxine's observation as expressing ambivalence, rather than (or perhaps alongside) triumph. Although she draws a connection between herself and Fa Mu Lan, she also makes an important distinction: by claiming that she has "so many words," Maxine describes not just the power of the words that she wields but the power that words wield over her. Their overabundance and the inclusion of racist epithets leads the reader to wonder if words do not fit on her "skin" because she is caught in so many contradictory discourses that they coexist without resolution.

The ambiguous ending of the "White Tigers" section implies that, like Nora, Maxine also senses that something remains unfinished, unfulfilled. Cheng insightfully sums up the cause of this irresolution as an illustration of the contradiction and fragmentation that feminist scholars have previously discussed: "the Fa Mu Lan myth is told as much for its negation as for its promise. . . . Instead of a wish fulfillment, the tale of the Woman Warrior gives the narrator an identification *through* difference, disappointment, and failure" (*Melancholy*, 2001, 101). Similarly, Nora's attempts to identify with dominant culture consistently fall short; instead of the expected autobiographical resolution, the achievement of a unified and totalized identity, she is instead left with ambiguity, contradiction, and ambivalence.

When read alongside one another, *Me* and *The Woman Warrior* depict the inadequacy of both Western and Asian narratives to address Asian American identity, and the strangely liminal position Asian Americans are assigned, as not-quite-Asian and not-quite-American. They also undermine the traditional feminist and Asian American critical views of the identification process as a dialectical phenomenon whereby one reaches a state of "authenticity," by representing it as constitutively encompassing negotiation and misidentification; that is, to identify with someone or something necessarily requires the elision of those things that mark difference. In Nora's and Maxine's cases, these elisions simultaneously facilitate identification (insofar as they provide narrative models) and problematize identification because of the unbridgeable gap between the "impossible ideal" and the "denigrated body," and the racial and sexual economies that consistently marginalize Nora and Maxine.

Thus *Me* is an Asian American autobiography not because it neatly "fits" into these categories, but because it disrupts them. If Asian American identity is a continual process of seeking rather than achieving a cohesive identity, then Eaton's textual attempts to "pass" as white and the resultant narrative contradictions illustrate the process of occupying the place of the racially abject in a culture that privileges whiteness. But the general critical assessment of *Me* and *The Woman Warrior* reveals a hesitance on the part of scholars to acknowledge the contradictions inherent in the process of identification, perhaps one of the ongoing legacies of identity politics-based criticisms.

The political and communal urgency that drives Asian American and feminist literary criticism has perhaps led to convenient celebrations of subversion that belie the complexity of *The Woman Warrior* and conversely prompted facile dismissals of *Me*. My intention here is neither to discount the enormous contributions of Asian American and feminist literary scholarship, nor to fetishize victimization; rather, I suggest that insofar as identity is itself incomplete and never fully realized, then exclusively seeking or privileging subversion provides an incomplete critical apparatus. Literary scholars need to explore what it means to talk about subversion of marginalized identities with a willingness to engage in the same kinds of difficult explorations as Eaton and Kingston.

Notes

1. According to Birchall, Eaton's granddaughter, the original source of information on *Me*'s New York City publicity campaign is Doris Rooney's article, "Souvenir from the Past," *Field, Horse and Rodeo* (June 1963): 45–47.

2. Birchall provides a very thorough and amusing discussion of the article itself and speculates that the anonymous writer most likely knew Eaton, though it is not clear whether the author knew that "Onoto Watanna" was a fabricated persona.

3. *Me*'s narrative does make two temporal alterations: first, the plot compresses the five years between her stay in Jamaica and her arrival in New York into one year. According to Birchall, Eaton probably journeyed to Jamaica in February 1896, where she served as a reporter for the Canadian-run *Gall's News Letter* for five months, and did not reach Chicago until May 1897. Although the exact nature of her movements in the interim are unknown, Birchall speculates from *Me* and from the many profiles that featured the young Onoto Watanna that she may have stayed in "Boston, the South, Cincinnati, or New York," or a combination of these places. See Birchall, *Onoto Watanna: The Story of Winnifred Eaton*, 2001, 30, 42. Another temporally related discrepancy is the protagonist's age: Eaton was actually twenty, not seventeen, when she left for Jamaica. Although this difference in age is marginal, it was apparently one that she readily promoted for the rest of her life. Birchall suggests that this gesture was common among American women writers (including Willa Cather), and that by making herself younger, Eaton could

seem even more "precocious"; she may also have altered her age in order to evade scrutiny into her past and her childhood, thereby protecting her Onoto Watanna persona. In fact, Eaton's obituary in a Calgary newspaper clipping in the Reeve Collection lists her year of birth as 1879 instead of 1875 (the actual year she was born), and the Reeve Collection itself lists 1879 as her birth date. According to Birchall, Eaton never told her children about her actual age, and the birth year engraved on her tombstone is 1879; more incredibly, she made her children unwitting accomplices by taking two years off their ages as well, a fact they did not discover until well into adulthood!

4. Eaton was Canadian, and therefore one of the founders of the Asian Canadian literary tradition. However, the majority of her works were published while she was living in the United States, and *Me* itself deals mainly with Eaton's initial experiences in the United States, so she is firmly established in the Asian American literary tradition as well.

5. I am using "Maxine" and "Nora" to refer to the autobiographical personas, and Kingston and Eaton to refer to the authors themselves.

6. Poststructuralist scholars have also questioned the seemingly unproblematic relationship between identity and language implicit in analyses such as Olney's. Benstock argues that insofar as identity is formed through language, it is always already compromised: "[f]enced in by language, the speaking subject is primordially divided" ("Authorizing," 1997, 1143). Michael Bernard-Donals adds that the metonymic conveyance of events distances readers even as it attempts to illustrate these events: "[metonymy forces] the reader to pay attention not to that which appears familiar—the different aspects of the same—but to the impossible relation between all the attributes of the object or event and the singular, palpable sense of the object or event itself" ("Beyond," 2001, 1309).

7. For more about the gender and racial politics of fairy tales, see Harischandra, "Fairy Tales," 2001.

8. It must be noted, however, that Gilmore (*Autobiographics*, 1994) argues that *The Woman Warrior* shows us that Maxine's achievement of unified sense of identity can never be completed.

WORKS CITED

Benstock, Shari. "Authorizing the Autobiographical," in *Feminisms: An Anthology of Literary Theory and Criticism*. Robyn R. Warhol and Diane Price Herndl, eds. (pp. 1138–54). New Brunswick, NJ: Rutgers University Press, 1997.

Bernard-Donals, Michael. "Beyond the Question of Authenticity: Witness and Testimony in the *Fragments* Controversy." *PMLA* 116: 3 (October 2001): 1302–15.

Birchall, Diana. *Onoto Watanna: The Story of Winnifred Eaton*. Urbana: University of Illinois Press, 2001.

Butler, Judith. *Bodies that Matter: On the Discursive Limits of "Sex."* New York: Routledge, 1993.

Cheng, Anne Anlin. *The Melancholy of Race: Psychoanalysis, Assimilation, and Hidden Grief*. New York: Oxford University Press, 2001.

Clipping. *Kansas City Star*, August 28, 1915. Winnifred Eaton Reeve Fonds, Special Collections, University of Calgary Library.

Clipping. *Los Angeles Times*, August 29, 1915. Winnifred Eaton Reeve Fonds, Special Collections, University of Calgary Library.

Doyle, James. "Sui Sin Far/Onoto Watanna: Two Early Chinese-Canadian Authors." *Canadian Literature*, 140 (Spring 1994): 50–58.

Eaton, Winnifred. *Me: A Book of Remembrance*. New York: Century, 1915. Reprinted. Jackson: University of Mississippi Press, 1997.

———. *Me: A Book of Remembrance*. New York: Century, 1915. Reprinted with Afterword by Linda Trinh Moser. Jackson: University of Mississippi Press, 1997.

———. *Me: A Book of Remembrance*. New York: Century, 1915. Reprinted with Introduction by Jean Webster. Jackson: University of Mississippi Press, 1997.

"Famous Canadian Novelist Visits Toronto To-day." *Toronto Star*. Undated Clipping. Winnifred Eaton Reeve Fonds, Special Collections, University of Calgary Library.

Gilmore, Leigh. *Autobiographics: A Feminist Theory of Women's Self-Representation*. Ithaca, NY: Cornell University Press, 1994.

Harischandra, Neshantha. "Fairy Tales and the Concept of Femininity." *Nivedini: A Sri Lankan Feminist Journal*, 9: 1 (June 2001): 58–87.

Hattori, Tomo. "Model Minority Discourse and Asian American Jouis-Sense." *Differences: A Journal of Feminist Cultural Studies*, 11: 2 (Summer 1999): 228–47.

"Is Onoto Watanna Author of the Anonymous Novel *Me*?" *New York Times Book Review*, October 10, 1915, 869.

Jacobs, Harriet. *Incidents in the Life of a Slave Girl. Written by Herself*. [1861.] New York: Signet, 2000.

Kim, Elaine. *Asian American Literature: An Introduction to the Writings and Their Social Context*. Philadelphia: Temple University Press, 1982.

Kingston, Maxine Hong. *The Woman Warrior*. New York: Vintage, 1989.

Kundera, Milan. *The Unbearable Lightness of Being*. New York: Harper, 1984.

Ling, Amy. *Between Worlds: Women Writers of Chinese Ancestry*. New York: Pergamon, 1990.

Lorde, Audre. *Zami: A New Spelling of My Name*. New York: Persephone, 1982.

McClintock, Anne. *Imperial Leather: Race, Gender and Sexuality in the Colonial Contest*. New York: Routledge, 1995.

Rooney, Doris. "Souvenir from the Past." *Field, Horse and Rodeo* (June 1963): 45–47.

Sin, Caroline. Review of *Me: A Book of Remembrance*. *MELUS*, 24: 4 (1999): 180.

Smith, Sidonie. "Maxine Hong Kingston's *The Woman Warrior*: Filiality and Woman's Autobiographical Storytelling," in *Feminisms: An Anthology of Literary Theory and Criticism*. Robyn R. Warhol and Diane Price Herndl, eds. (pp. 1117–37). New Brunswick, NJ: Rutgers University Press, 1997.

———. *Subjectivity, Identity, and the Body: Women's Autobiographical Practices in the Twentieth Century*. Bloomington: Indiana University Press, 1993.

9 Nation, Immigrant, Text
Theresa Hak Kyung Cha's Dictee

SRIMATI MUKHERJEE

IN 1982, THERESA HAK KYUNG CHA was assaulted, raped, and killed by a security guard in the basement of a New York City building.[1] Thus ended a career of promise at age thirty-one. In an uncanny instance of life imitating art, this incident drew Cha close to Yu Guan Soon, a Korean political activist, killed at age sixteen, in *Dictee*.[2] Although such a connection was, no doubt, unforeseen by Cha, other parallels between Soon and the ethnic woman writer exist in *Dictee*. In this chapter, I explore the interface of imperiled female nationalists in Korea during the Japanese occupation of 1910–1945 and the immigrant identity presented in the text, which seems similarly threatened by imminent erasure. I read Cha's work as one that displaces the trauma of immigration and ethnicity and relocates it in the trauma of Korean nationalist struggles. Thus, this chapter addresses the unvoiced or an identifiable absence in *Dictee* that I also connect to the historical space of woman reiteratively represented by Cha as whiteness or blankness. Yet, concurrently, the clustered images of resilience in Korean female nationalists, the authorial aligning of women with columns, and the responsibility placed on the female immigrant writer in the United States for voicing the trauma of dislocation situate woman as the site of resistance against political, masculinist, and cultural oppression.

In the section of *Dictee* titled "Clio: History," Cha focuses on the figure of Yu Guan Soon, a sixteen-year-old Korean female revolutionary who is taken captive, stabbed in the chest, interrogated, and incarcerated. Historical authenticity for Cha's Yu Guan Soon is provided, for instance, by Kumari Jayawardena in her book *Feminism and Nationalism in the Third World* (1986).[3] In the section of her book devoted to resistance movements in Korea, Jayawardena addresses the establishment of the Ewha Haktang, the first school for women in Korea, founded in 1886 by Mary Fitch Scranton. Jayawardena notes the school's crucial role in nationalistic movements against the Japanese:

> Ewha students...played a prominent role in the agitation organized by the March First Movement in 1919 against Japanese occupation. On this day when an Independence ceremony was held and the Korean flag raised,

women marched at the head of demonstrations and processions and many were wounded or killed. One of the most prominent of these protestors was Yu Kwang-Sun, a secondary student at Ewha. She was arrested and imprisoned for a short time after demonstrating in Seoul. When all schools were closed by the Japanese, she returned to her home town in Ch'ung-Ch'ong province and, assisted by her brother and other friends, organized similar demonstrations. Her parents were killed in the course of these struggles; she herself was arrested and died in 1920, aged 16, after long months of torture. (*Feminism*, 1986, 222)[4]

In *Dictee*, Cha details how Guan Soon's precursive role as leader of a resistant group of fellow students and her active revolutionary work are gendered. She writes, "There is already a nationally organized movement, who do not accept her seriousness, her place as a young woman, and they attempt to dissuade her" (*Dictee*, 30). In this regard, Elaine H. Kim reminds us of Korea, "In general, the state treats female devotion to the nation with ambivalence unless it is expressed through the filter of the family" ("Poised, " 1994, 15). Undeterred, Guan Soon continues to demonstrate her dedication to the nationalistic cause until she is taken captive and physically tortured by the Japanese. Imperiled and brutalized, Soon figures as an embodiment of the debased woman and the endangered nation. She, however, is resolute in maintaining her stance of nonrevelatory silence against the Japanese.[5] I argue that Guan Soon's ravaged and imperiled body in Korea is analogous to the ethnic identity of the immigrant progressively repressed and threatened by the forces of mainstream culture in the United States. The author does not hesitate to imply that the immigrant herself can also become complicit in this process of assimilation. And Cha's reinscribing of Soon's resistance is an authorial attempt to underscore, through analogy, both the trauma of immigration and the resilience needed to subvert homogenization and voice the ethnic self.

The pertinent question to be answered then is how does Cha, as both postcolonial and Asian American writer, connect the colonial context of Japanese occupation in Korea with the neocolonial[6] context of the United States in which she perceives the immigrant's ethnic identity to be endangered? In order to answer this question, I will first discuss a few instances of Cha's representation of the immigrant.

In *Dictee*, Cha foregrounds early the "difference" of the immigrant, bringing into question issues of identity and unqualified claims to the United States.[7] In her agonized query:

From A Far
What nationality
or what kindred and relation

what stray ejection misplaced
Tertium Quid neither one thing nor the other
What transplant to dispel upon (*Dictee*, 20)

"Stray ejection misplaced" and "transplant to dispel upon" suggest not only displacement but a more extended lack of grounding, while "Tertium Quid neither one thing nor the other" clearly underlines the fact that a divided or hybrid identity is not enticing to Cha. Her disaffection for this pluralistic identity (although *Dictee* is, no doubt, about multiple subjectivities) is also implicit in her reiteration of the singleness of Yu Guan Soon's parentage, "She is born of one mother and one father" (*Dictee*, 25).

The notion of a hybrid or, more accurately, submerged identity also figures in the section in which one of Cha's personae addresses the acquisition of an American passport: "Somewhere someone has taken my identity and replaced it with their photograph. The other one. Their signature their seals. Their own image" (*Dictee*, 56). In a much earlier section of *Dictee*, Cha also uses the concept of the image, although that particular reference is to the image of the divine: "God who has made me in His own likeness. In His Own Image in His Own Resemblance, in His Own Copy, In His Own Counterfeit Presentment... in His Cast.... Acquiesce, to the correspondence.... Theirs. Into Their tongue, the counterscript, my confession in Theirs" (17–18). Cha, of course, extends the notion of divine likeness to include ideas of "Copy," "Cast," and, more suggestively, "Counterfeit Presentment." If one couples these expressions with the notion of a Korean identity substituted by "Their own image" in the section on the acquiring of an American passport, then "Image" has connotations not just of divine resemblance, but of mechanical imitation, a mimicry of the mainstream culture in the United States, and a surrender to its demands for assimilation. The words "Theirs. Into Their tongue, the counterscript, my confession in Theirs" further accentuate, for the reader, that this section of *Dictee* is hardly only about the ritual of the Catholic confession, but about cultural assimilation not viewed fondly by Cha.

The trace of that Korean identity, however, is indelible, and the doubleness of an ethnic self threatened by extinction and yet nonerasable is intriguingly matched by a double page of script in which vestiges of words are visible through their deletions.[8] In fact, *Dictee* presents to the reader a consuming sense of national identification through its multiple narratives of exile. One such narrative is that of the character addressed as "Mother" in the text, who is born in Manchuria despite being of Korean origin, whose parents have chosen voluntary exile rather than witness the Japanese colonization of Korea. It is ironic, however, that the Japanese are once more in control after invading Manchuria in 1931.[9] The most visible and felt sign of this control is the imposition of Japanese as the mandatory language. In this context in which Korean immigrants are once again under Japanese domination, Cha addresses the character "Mother": "you speak the tongue the mandatory language like the others. It is not your own. Even if it is not you know you must.... The tongue that is forbidden is your own mother tongue. You speak in the dark. In the secret. The one that is yours. Mother tongue is your refuge. It is being home. Being who you are" (*Dictee*, 45). Here deprivation of national language is also the denuding of national identity, an identity that has to be reconstructed and consolidated in secrecy.

This reconstruction is a continuously imperiled but perpetually ongoing process because, as Cha says of the Mother, "your MAH-UHM, spirit has not left. Never shall have and never shall will.... It is burned into your ever-present memory. Memory less. Because it is not in the past. It cannot be" (*Dictee*, 45). In a multilayered and nuanced text such as *Dictee*, it is not only the Korean Mother exiled in Manchuria who must negotiate the threat of an undercutting of national identity; it is also the immigrant in the United States. In fact, at a later point in the text, Cha pluralizes the exilic predicament: "Our destination is fixed on the perpetual motion of search. Fixed in its perpetual exile" (81).

To recapitulate briefly, in Cha's representation of the immigrant in *Dictee*, dislocation, hybridity, and the notion of an endangered Korean identity are reiteratively foregrounded. Yet the trauma resultant from a perception of these issues is compounded by a memory, which is also "Memory less" because it is persistently in the immediate present, a memory that frequently situates the predominant persona of *Dictee* in the Korean context. This subjectivity, then, is a split or, more precisely, fractured one, physically placed in the United States, sensible of a gradual loss of ethnic identity, and yet consumed by a sense of the presence of Korea.

It is in this notion of fracture that I would like to locate the most suggestive connection Cha makes between Korean female revolutionary Yu Guan Soon's colonial context and the Asian American immigrant's context that Cha perceives as neocolonial. Apart from the resisting body of Guan Soon and its brutalization, Cha provides other instances of the massacre of Korean nationalist volunteers by the Japanese. In one instance, she writes, when shooting down thirty volunteers was not enough, "'two other volunteers who had been captured were brought out and were decapitated by one of the officers'" (*Dictee*, 31–32). In generalized reference to incidents such as these and in more specific reference to the ravaged body of Guan Soon, Cha writes:

> The decapitated forms. Worn. Marred, recording a past, of previous forms. The present form face to face reveals the missing, the absent. Would-be-said remnant, memory. But the remnant is the whole.
>
> The memory is the entire. The longing in the face of the lost. Maintains the missing.... Some are without. (38)

In my reading, Cha connects the decapitated Korean volunteers, the "marred" body of Yu Guan Soon, with the fractured subjectivity of the immigrant whose present is, and must be, constructed by an awareness of the "missing, the absent." Earlier in this chapter I compared the imperilment of Yu Guan Soon by the Japanese colonizers (the same who decapitate the Korean volunteers) to the endangering of the immigrant's ethnic identity in the United States. The analogy, however, is not completely without redeeming features. Yu Guan Soon's body is ravaged, and the mutilated Korean nationalists are missing body parts, yet it is their martyrdom for the patriotic cause that immortalizes them in the Korean national psyche. The Korean immigrant in the United States has lost a nation, yet it is this sense of dispossession and her awareness of her imperiled ethnicity that largely structure her identity and motivate her to voice her difference. Hence, even though "some are without," "the memory is the entire. The longing in the face of the lost. Maintains the missing."

In a text of such complexity as *Dictee*, however, the implicit connection between Korean nationalists and the immigrant in the United States is one of several strands in the weave. What of the general situating of women and the responsibility placed on the female immigrant writer in the work? In regard to each of these areas, I will address two broadly identifiable strains. In terms of reading woman, Cha often links her historical role to a whiteness, blankness, or absence, presenting her as defined by the male. (It is not surprising that white is the color traditionally associated with death and mourning in Korea.) Two instances of such representation will suffice at this point: "Still the apprenticeship of the wife to her husband. He leaves the room. She falls to the floor" (*Dictee*, 104) or "Gratuity is her body her spirit. Her non-body her non-entity. His privilege possession his claim. Infallible is his ownership. Imbues with mockery at her refusal of him, but her very being that dares to name herself as if she possesses a will. Her own" (112). Just as the latter of these quotations from the text closes with an intimation of the woman on the verge of self-definition, so also other sections of *Dictee*, such as "She opens the cloth again. White. Whitest of beige. In the whiteness, subtle hues outlining phoenix from below phoenix from above facing each other in the weave barely appearing" (113), juxtapose notions of whiteness or blankness with nascent possibilities of delineation or regeneration.

This second strain in Cha's representation of woman, the strain that hints at woman's potential for self-definition, emerges far more forcefully in her depiction of women as activists. Whenever Cha shifts her focus from woman in the domestic sphere to woman in the sociopolitical, she foregrounds her as intransigent and empowered. Let me briefly revert to Jayawardena before I proceed further with this point. Jayawardena notes that following the failure of the Korean nationalist movement to obtain

independence in 1919, "resistance against Japanese occupation continued sporadically, . . . and women participated in these struggles" (*Feminism*, 1986, 224). She addresses women's attempts "to resist on several
fronts":

> First through education they challenged Confucian orthodoxy and tried to
> modernize society. The need for female education was increasingly accepted
> in the 1920s. . . . Second, Korean women continued to be active in the demo-
> cratic anti-Japanese struggle. . . . Third, was the participation of women in
> the socialist movement. A new agitational base developed among women
> workers who were harshly exploited in industries and other enterprises
> owned by the Japanese. They set up the Chosan Women's Cooperative So-
> ciety which had a socialist orientation and was mainly concerned with the
> problems of working women. (224)

Dictee corroborates, through photographs and other forms of signification, Jayawardena's points on the activism of Korean women. However, before I return to the issue of Cha's representation of women as activists, I would like to refer to one other critic who sounds a premonitory
note regarding the gendering of militant or activist endeavors. Gayatri
Chakravorty Spivak, in an analysis of a Bengali short story on bonded
labor by Mahasveta Devi, warns us: "if one considers recent historical
examples, one is obliged to suggest that, even if, in the crisis of the armed
or peaceful struggle, women seem to emerge as comrades, with the return of the everyday, and in the pores of the struggle, the old codings of
the gendered body, sometimes slightly altered, seem to fall into place"
("Woman," 1992, 102).

It is precisely the sort of coding Spivak addresses in her essay that Cha
attempts to subvert in *Dictee* through repeated grouping of women with
columns, both linguistically and pictorially. In a photograph in *Dictee*
(a text that uses the pictorial extensively), women figure as part of a
rallying, protesting mass against a background of erect columns (122).
Although not specified, it is fair to say that the women are agitating for
a political cause. Shu-mei Shih clarifies that these are supporters of "the
independence marchers of March 1, 1919" ("Nationalism," 1997, 151).
This photograph of women as articulate and empowered is positioned
in deliberate contrast to "In the whiteness / no distinction her body in-
variable no dissonance / synonymous her body all the time de composes
/ eclipses to be come yours" (*Dictee*, 118), lines on the page of script
that immediately precede it. Although these lines might connote the traditional historical role of women, the martyrdom of the Korean female
revolutionary for the nationalist cause, the assimilation of the (female) immigrant into the majority culture, Cha provides a contrapuntal thrust by
frequently associating women with columns or upright land formations.

The cover photograph (of an Egyptian ruin) of *Dictee*, for instance, contrasts vertical and horizontal planes by depicting mound-like formations that rise from the land. Toward the end of the text, another photograph presents a similar juxtaposition of the vertical and horizontal; in this photograph, upright formations (undecipherable whether they are battered tree trunks or headless statues—possibly another representation of the effects of war on landscape) are foregrounded on an undulating land surface (*Dictee*, 166). The facing page begins a narrative of a woman and a young girl in a third-world context, the former raising water from a well and the latter actually a child on "her way home from the neighboring village to take back remedies for her mother who was very ill" (169). Shih alerts us to the fact that here, Cha uses the "Korean myth of princess Pali . . . [which] tells of the princess's search for remedies for her ill mother and her acquisition of nine pockets of medicines from the well-keeper" ("Nationalism, 1997, 156). In *Dictee*, the woman gives water to the exhausted child, provides "special remedies for her mother" (*Dictee*, 169), and sends her on her way, more rejuvenated than before. The time of year is specified in this section as summer, and the enduring of these female figures, despite the intensity of the heat and the circumstances of their labors, and particularly one's sustaining of the other, clearly aligns them with the erect tree trunks / statues in the photograph mentioned earlier. In fact, I am tempted to suggest that since both that and the cover photograph of *Dictee* present upright formations, by analogical extension, the cover also signifies the enduring of women.[10] And by implicitly connecting photographs of the land to the endurance of women, Cha once again reminds the reader of the Korean female nationalist who unhesitatingly gives her body so that her land may be reclaimed from the Japanese.

Through such systematic aligning of women with columns and upright formations and through focusing on the resistance of Yu Guan Soon, Cha positions women as "superobject[s]" (Spivak, "Preface," 1981, 388) against diverse manifestations of oppression.[11] Yet, in *Dictee*, patriarchal and political oppression are more than historical realities; they are voiced analogues that accentuate the silence at the heart of the text—the silence surrounding the slow loss of ethnic identity. From the beginning of *Dictee* to the end, it is the female immigrant writer who is given the responsibility of breaking the silence. It is she who must scatter the words like seeds, must voice and individualize the predicament of the immigrant, and must ultimately engender revitalization against the ominous possibility of erasure.

As with the two strands in her presentation of women, so also two strands are discernible in Cha's presentation of the female immigrant writer. One involves what Cha perceives as an enjoinder to covertness or silence. I will cite two instances from *Dictee* to indicate how the author views covertness or muteness as a necessary concomitant for the immigrant writer. The first instance—"she writes hidden the essential words must be pretended invented she try on different images essential invisible" (*Dictee*, 15)—suggests dissembling and a predicament in which the writer's original identity (if any such one thing exists) must be invisible in as much as that is possible. The second instance—"veiled voice under breath murmuration / render mute strike dumb voiceless tongueless" (127)—urges the reader to question why Cha, if she is mainly addressing Korean nationalism, would focus on an inability to articulate publicly a forced movement toward silence when the Korean protest against Japanese occupation has already been articulated, both politically and in written records thereafter. It is clear, then, that *Dictee* is not just about the Korean nationalist struggle, but uses that context as a metaphor for and as a site on which to displace what Cha perceives as the difficulties of ethnicity in the United States.

The issue of displacement, more specifically in relation to time, is, in fact, addressed directly in *Dictee*: "The present redeeming itself through the grace of oblivion. How could she justify it. Without the visibility of the present. She says to herself she could displace real time. She says to herself she could display it before and become its voyeur" (*Dictee*, 140). The first part of this quotation clearly indicates the speaker's desire to obliterate the present. Yet, the difficulties of the present must be articulated, and rendering this time period completely invisible will not do. The speaker of *Dictee* in this section, thus, displaces "real time" that she passes through in the United States on to the context of colonized Korea and recounts nationalistic struggles against oppression in which she did not and could not have participated. The word "voyeur," of course, suggests this absence of direct participation, but becomes significant for two reasons, in this instance connoting both the expected pleasure associated with voyeurism and the less expected pain. The speaker derives pleasure from identifying with resistance movements in an earlier historical period, with implications, at other points in the text, that she desires similar resistance in the present.[12] However, her voyeurism is simultaneously aligned with pain because the speaker feels compelled to escape the present. Unable to withstand the trauma of existing in a culture and timeframe in which her difference is not truly comprehended, the speaker wishes to look in on the present only from the outside, through the lens of the past as it were.

Despite such movements toward displacement, dissembling, and silence, once again, as with her double-stranded representation of women, we can locate a counterstrain in Cha's conceptualization of the immigrant woman writer. Through this second strain, she urges, repeatedly, a breaking of the silence and a voicing of the immigrant/ethnic predicament in the

United States. In some ways, she views this articulation as an exposure, when the artist is no longer in conformity with the mainstream. Several passages in *Dictee* convey, not without considerable force, this notion of exposure and stripping oneself bare. I will use two such passages here to substantiate my point. The first is one that Cha attributes to Sappho, but which has never been found in Sappho's extant works.[13] It reads, "May I write words more *naked* than flesh, stronger than bone, more resilient than sinew, sensitive than nerve" (emphasis added; n.p.). The second follows shortly thereafter: "She takes. She takes the pause. Slowly. From the thick. The thickness. From weighted motion upwards. Slowed. To deliberation even when it passes upward through her mouth again. The delivery. She takes it. Slow. The invoking. All the time now. All the time there is. Always. And all times. The pause. Uttering. Hers now. Hers *bare*. The utter" (emphasis added; *Dictee*, 5).[14] In *Dictee*, it is not difficult to draw a connection (although situational differences, no doubt, exist) between this verbal or written revelation and the imperiled body of the female Korean freedom fighter taken captive by Japanese colonizers. The offering up of the self, by voicing and differentiating the predicament and problems of immigrants, metaphorically connects the writer to revolutionary Yu Guan Soon.

In fact, several passages in *Dictee* imply a connection between speech/writing and nationalistic gestures against colonization because of which the body is endangered or decimated. The lines "Something of the ink that resembles the stain from the interior emptied onto emptied into emptied upon this boundary this surface. More. Others. When possible ever possible to puncture to scratch to imprint" (*Dictee*, 65), indicate not only this link between the spilling of blood and writing[15] but suggest also a progressively extended endeavor to work against homogenization, break through the codes laid down by the majority culture, and individualize oneself.

A more subtle reference to the link between the freedom fighter and the immigrant writer can be found in:

void to the left void to the right, void the
words the silences.
I heard the signs. Remnants. Missing.
The mute signs. Never the same.
Absent. (*Dictee*, 69)

In this section from *Dictee*, "[r]emnants," "[m]issing," and "[a]bsent" foreground, once again, for the reader either the mutilated or the lifeless body of a colonized subject such as Yu Guan Soon, one who imperils and obliterates the physical self for nationalistic causes. The passage, however, also traces the predicament of the immigrant writer who, in Cha's conceptualization of her, maintains a condition of silence, as suggested through "void to the left void to the right, void the / words" and "[a]bsent," or is merely capable of partial, and perhaps cautious, articulation, as implied through "[r]emnants." Thus, this section conflates notions of fractured (colonized) body and fragmented (immigrant) speech/writing[16] as also decimation and silence, but becomes particularly resonant because of "void the / . . . silences" and "I heard the signs. . . . / The mute signs." Even as the ethnic woman writer always understands that a part of the self is under erasure, is persistently on the verge of being lost, because not everything can be articulated unreservedly, her endeavor, perhaps precisely because of this possibility of slippage, is to "void the/ . . . silences" and articulate, although this voicing might entail a different endangering of the self within the mainstream. That she also hears "the signs. . . . / The mute signs" positions her as receiver of signals from a silent minority whose experiences, losses, and hopes she must voice.[17]

Of several responsibilities Cha assigns to the immigrant woman writer, in *Dictee*, I would like to address only one in the last section of this chapter, and that is the individualization of the predicament of the Korean immigrant to the United States. Once again, Cha draws on the context of the Japanese colonization of Korea:

> To the other nations who are not witnesses, who are not subject to the same oppressions, they cannot know. . . . Not physical enough. Not to the very flesh and bone, to the core, to the mark, to the point where it is necessary to intervene, even if to invent anew, expressions, for *this* experience, for this *outcome*, that does not cease to continue.
> To the others, these accounts are about (one more) distant land, . . . without any discernable [*sic*] features in the narrative, (all the same) distant like any other. (*Dictee*, 32–33)

An almost exact sentiment, as regards an uninvolved audience's misreading of or apathy to catastrophic experience, is expressed by Cathy Caruth in her significant work on trauma and its place in narrative and history. In her discussion of Alain Resnais's film *Hiroshima mon amour*, Caruth refers to the impact of the bombing of Hiroshima in an international context, "Just as the French understand the event of Hiroshima as the end of their own war, so the perception of Hiroshima itself, from the perspective of an international history, turns the very actuality of catastrophe into the anonymous narrative of peace" (*Unclaimed*, 1996, 29). Whether the target is Korea or Hiroshima, both Cha and Caruth appear to be opposed to such ominous misreadings of or obliviousness to catastrophe. Thus, Cha, or the immigrant woman writer in *Dictee*, must "invent anew, expressions, for *this* experience, for this *outcome*, that does not cease to continue."

The Korean American woman writer must transform "these accounts [which] are about (one more) distant land, like (any other) distant land, without any discernable [*sic*] features in the narrative" (*Dictee*, 33) by, ironically, investing them with the tangibility of the pain endured by freedom fighters such as Yu Guan Soon. Her narratives must strike "the other nations who are not witnesses, who are not subject to the same oppressions...to the very flesh and bone, to the core, to the mark" (32) by detailing, graphically, the denial of nationhood to the Koreans and the usurpation of their natural/national rights.[18] As a postcolonial and ethnic American writer, Cha's movement, clearly, seems to be toward individualization and differentiation rather than homogenization of immigrants and, what I will call a process of cultural leveling.

In nations largely unaffected by catastrophe or trauma resultant from colonial oppression, Cha seems to censure the role of the media, which successfully affects this cultural leveling: "This document is transmitted through, by the same means, the same channel without distinction the content is delivered in the same style: the word. The image. To appeal to the masses to congeal the information to make bland, mundane....The response is precoded to perform predictably however passively possible. Neutralized to achieve the no-response, to make absorb, to submit to the uni-directional correspondence" (*Dictee*, 33). In these "other nations" (32), on account of processing by media, the majority of the population receives and absorbs "the information" stripped of the intensity of its pain.[19] But despite such attempts at leveling, neutralizing, or canceling out the audience's possible perception of traumatic experience, the memory or reality of such experience is stark for many Korean immigrants to these nations.

The above notion facilitates a second possible reading of the double page of script in *Dictee* (40–41) in which traces of words are visible through their deletions.[20] Earlier I suggested that these pages might connote the ethnic self threatened by possible obliteration and yet non-erasable. The pages, however, could also signify that despite efforts at leveling or erasure by media in uninvolved nations, the script narrating trauma, the truth about colonial oppression remains alive in the minds of Korean immigrants to these countries. In this regard, Homi K. Bhabha's formulation of the distinction between cultural diversity and cultural difference becomes particularly significant:

Cultural diversity is the recognition of pre-given cultural "contents" and customs; held in a time-frame of relativism it gives rise to anodyne liberal notions of multiculturalism, cultural exchange, or the culture of humanity. Cultural diversity is also the representation of a radical rhetoric of the separation of totalised cultures that live unsullied by the intertextuality of their historical locations, safe in the Utopianism of a mythic memory of a unique collective identity.

Through the concept of cultural difference I want to draw attention to the common ground and lost territory of contemporary critical debates. For they all recognize that the problem of the cultural emerges only at the significatory boundaries of cultures, where meanings and values are (mis)read, or signs are misappropriated. "Culture" only emerges as a problem, or a problematic, at the point at which there is a "loss" of meaning in the contestation and articulation of everyday life, between classes, genders, races, nations. ("Commitment," 1989, 127)

In *Dictee*, Cha suggests that the memory (personal or racial) of Korean nationalist struggles against Japanese colonization is an integral part of the "everyday life" (Bhabha, "Commitment," 1989, 127) of several Korean immigrants to the United States. However, this significance of the memory of trauma is "(mis) read . . . [and] there is a 'loss' of meaning in the contestation and articulation of everyday life, between . . . races [and] nations" (127) because the mainstream population in the United States remains apathetic to the trauma inherent in the struggles of the colonized, and the processing of information by media, "to achieve the no-response" (*Dictee*, 33), perpetuates this apathy.[21]

The Korean American woman writer, in *Dictee*, must work against this continuing movement toward erasure and obliviousness. Just as the Korean immigrant's awareness of her imperiled ethnicity motivates her to voice her difference in the United States, just as the woman's perception of masculinist oppression pushes her to the verge of self-definition, so also the Korean American woman writer must present the narratives of colonial oppression and trauma, which are sharply delineated in the memory of Korean immigrants, from the Korean perspective. She has to "extract each fragment by each fragment from the word from the image another word another image the reply that will not repeat history in oblivion" (*Dictee*, 33). She must retrieve these narratives from a condition of marginality in the United States, from their subjection to mainstream media, which processes them for minimal impact, and she must foreground "another word another image the reply that will not repeat history in oblivion."[22]

Elaine H. Kim affirms that Cha, indeed, does just that, "And by bringing Korea and Koreans into view after the damage done by Japanese colonization has been glossed over by history, she creates a space for justice as well as for difference" ("Korean," 1997, 175). Kim further reminds us of the continuing need for such foregrounding in the light of more recent historical tragedies. In her preface to *Writing Self Writing Nation: A Collection of Essays on* Dictee *by Theresa Hak Kyung Cha* (1994), she addresses "the *sa-i-ku* crisis, the rebellion-riot during which the livelihoods of thousands of Korean immigrants in Koreatown and South Central

Los Angeles were destroyed" (x). She notes that this April 1992 event brought Korean Americans "by force into the Asian American legacy of 'becoming American' through violent disenfranchisement" (x). "The Los Angeles tragedy reminds us that the issues Cha raises in *Dictée* are still salient. What happened to Korean Americans during *sa-i-ku* grows out of the same lack of Korean-centered history and critical discourse that impelled us to put this book together in the first place" (x).

As discussed earlier, in *Dictee*, Cha gives the woman writer the responsibility of writing the narrative from the Korean perspective. Through such a gesture of unreservedly voicing the other narrative, the narrative from the Korean perspective, the Korean American woman writer will not only prevent erasure, but will also bring into sharper focus the constituents in the identity of the Korean immigrant to the United States. In a discussion of women's autobiographical writing, Julia Watson and Sidonie Smith address the role of such a minority woman writer in a first-world context:

> Western eyes see the colonized as an amorphous, generalized collectivity. The colonized "other" disappears into an anonymous, opaque collectivity of undifferentiated bodies. (xvii)
>
> For the marginalized woman, autobiographical language may serve as a coinage that purchases entry into the social and discursive economy. To enter into language is to press back against total inscription in dominating structures, against the disarticulation of that spectral other that [Rey] Chow calls the "dominated object." . . . Deploying autobiographical practices that go against the grain, she may constitute an "I" that becomes a place of creative and, by implication, political intervention. ("De/Colonization," 1992, xix)

Although not explicitly autobiographical, *Dictee* does contain autobiographical elements; moreover, the text is polyphonic, at times speaking in the voice of the Korean revolutionary, at times in the voice of the Korean immigrant, and at times in the voice of the minority American writer. Cha writes not only a personal autobiography but a collective one as well.[23]

Thus, "[d]eploying autobiographical practices that go against the grain, [Cha] constitute[s] an 'I' [or a 'We'] that becomes a place of creative and, by implication, political intervention" (Watson and Smith, "De/Colonization," 1992, xix). Without a doubt, she works against American mainstream media's attempts at cultural leveling and eliciting the homogenized response ("the no-response") as she foregrounds and individualizes the predicament of the Korean immigrant. Toward the end of *Dictee*, "preparation is made for communion when the inhabitation should occur, of this body, by the other body, the larger body" (*Dictee*, 161). Almost like a prayer, the Korean American woman writer offers up

the hope for comprehension "of this body," this text, this collective autobiography by "the larger body," the mainstream audience in the United
States.[24]

Notes

Acknowledgments: I would like to thank Shirley Geok-Lin Lim for her faith
in this chapter. I am grateful to Carolyn Karcher and Jane Tompkins for helpful
commentary on previous drafts. Thanks are also due to Kathy Uno and Sook Kim
for helping me understand Korean history and culture better.

1. The guard, "[Joey] Sanza was convicted of Cha's rape and murder in 1987,
the second trial for the case. After slaying Cha and dumping her body in a parking
lot, he fled to Florida, where he was arrested on December 18, 1982.... His first
conviction in Cha's case was overturned by the Appellate Division of [the] State
Supreme Court in Manhattan, on the grounds that three of his rape victims from
Florida should not have been asked to testify against him." This information is
provided by Kristina Chew in her essay "The Losses of Theresa Hak Kyung Cha's
Dictee," in Srimati Mukherjee, ed., *Writing Dispossession, Writing Desire: Asian
American Women Writers*, unpublished manuscript to be submitted shortly for
consideration to university presses.

2. Theresa Hak Kyung Cha, *Dictee* (Berkeley: Third Woman, 1995). All subsequent references to the text will be from this edition. The book was originally
published by Tanam Press in 1982.

3. See Jayawardena for a comprehensive discussion of women's changing roles
in Korean history and more particularly, for their role in the anti-Japanese Korean
nationalist movement.

4. Jayawardena draws an interesting connection between the Korean context
and other concurrent nationalist movements in Asia. She notes that the "Korean
events influenced other Asian nationalist movements. Commenting on the 1919
struggle, Nehru in a letter to his daughter wrote: 'The suppression of the Koreans
by the Japanese is a very sad and dark chapter in history. You will be interested
to know that young Korean girls... played a prominent part in the struggle'"
(*Feminism*, 1986, 222).

5. In *Dictee*, Korean history is also inserted pictorially; through the incorporation of a photograph of three blindfolded figures with arms outstretched facing
uniformed military men (war or resistance movement left unspecified), Cha again
presents the concept of the self under threat of erasure. See *Dictee*, 39.

6. I use the term "neocolonial" not as Jenny Sharpe, for instance, does in
footnote 17 of her essay "Figures of Colonial Resistance"—"a system of political
independence and economic dependency" (142)—but to imply a sociopolitical
climate within a given country in which immigrant/ethnic groups (and particularly
those of color) are "otherized" by the majority culture and frequently made to
feel they need to conform to the values of that culture.

7. In this regard, it is useful to note that Cha was born in Pusan, Korea,
in 1951, and her family migrated to the United States in 1962, when Cha was
eleven years old. They first lived in Hawaii and then moved to San Francisco. This

and more detailed biographical information on Cha can be found in a narrative chronology by Moira Roth, in Elaine H. Kim and Norma Alarcón, eds., *Writing Self Writing Nation: A Collection of Essays on* Dictee *by Theresa Hak Kyung Cha*.

8. See *Dictee*, 40–41.

9. In her narrative chronology of Cha, Moira Roth points out that Cha's parents had been raised in Manchuria and came to Korea in the 1940s ("Theresa," 1994, 151).

10. One final instance of Cha's associating women with columns may be found on page 93 of *Dictee*, which presents a haunting photograph of a lone woman, with crutches, standing by the columns of an arcade. The crutches underscore, again, women's endurance despite odds.

11. In her critical introduction to this short story, "Draupadi," by Mahasweta Devi, Spivak discusses how ravaged, battered, or raped women, despite being weapon-less, can challenge the oppressor in various ways. In such circumstances, they are no longer objects, but "terrifying superobject[s]."

12. See, for instance, *Dictee*, 87, "SHE opposes Her. / SHE against her. / More than that. Refuses to become discard / decomposed oblivion." Refer also to lines such as "*her* fraction *her* invalid that inhabits that rise / voluntarily like flint / pure hazard dead substance to fire" (88) that conflate the insurgence of Korean nationalists with the struggles/resistance of minority groups in the United States. Even if not stated explicitly, in my reading, lines such as "Arrest the machine that purports to employ democracy but rather causes the successive refraction of *her* none other than her own" (89), following shortly after, take the audience beyond the context of a colonized or, later, divided Korea to that of a nation such as the United States in which schisms between the mainstream and ethnic groups abound.

13. See Kristina Chew's essay, particularly endnote 29. See also endnote 3 in Shelley Sunn Wong's "Unnaming the Same: Theresa Hak Kyung Cha's *Dictée*," in Kim and Alarcón.

14. The reiterative use of "[h]ers" is also to be noted here. Cha clearly makes a distinction between *her* "utter" (*Dictee*, 5) and "[s]he would take on their punctuation. She waits to service this. Theirs" (4). The movement toward individualization of the ethnic writer's voice is a primary one throughout *Dictee* and stands in contradistinction to mimicking the majority culture or being assimilated into it. I addressed these points on ethnic identity and resisting cultural assimilation earlier in this chapter. In this regard, see Kristina Chew's essay on how Cha takes liberties with the linguistic exercise of the *dictée* ("Losses," 6–7). See also Elaine H. Kim's "Korean American Literature" (1997, 175). For an in-depth and stimulating discussion of how, in *Dictee*, Cha uses "dictation as a model for other processes through which cultural and ideological systems transform individuals into subjects" see Lisa Lowe's "Unfaithful to the Original: The Subject of *Dictée*" (1994, 43). Lowe advises that this should remind "us to read *Dictée* in terms of the differentiated layers of colonial and imperial languages within and against which it is written" (43).

15. For a discussion of the connection between blood and ink in relation to inside and outside in *Dictee*, see Elaine H. Kim's "Poised on the In-between: A Korean American's Reflections on Theresa Hak Kyung Cha's *Dictée*" (1994,

18, 23). See also Shu-Mei Shih's "Nationalism and Korean American Women's Writing" (1997, 153–154).

16. Lisa Lowe addresses this connection between the colonized, mutilated body and fragmented speech in her essay, with a particular focus on the image of the tongue in *Dictee*, to explicate the issues of "linguistic colonialism" and the use of dominant languages for "voicing an oppositional utterance" ("Unfaithful," 1994, 47). One of the elements of this "oppositional utterance," as the "colonized subject" moves through and beyond those "forced fluencies" in the dominant languages, is "composing coherence through fragmentation" (47). In this regard, see also Eun Kyung Min's "Reading the Figure of Dictation in Theresa Hak Kyung Cha's *Dictée*" (1998, 313). Min also addresses issues of resistance in Cha's writing and notes that Cha evokes "a model of creative writing as the unlearning of language, the very antithesis of dictation" (313).

Lowe's point leads me to address briefly how Cha's style reflects her positionality as a writer within the mainstream culture. In *Dictee*, Cha's style works through partially blank or blank pages, the pictorial, displacement (as discussed earlier), and general suggestiveness. It is not just an attempt to create "coherence through fragmentation" but also coherence through absences. I argue that, sadly, this typifies the predicament of many ethnic writers working within the parameters of a dominant culture, when much has to be left implicit. See, for instance, bell hooks, *Talking Back: Thinking Feminist, Thinking Black* (1989) for a similar observation.

Although a more extended discussion of Cha's style is beyond the scope of this chapter, other interesting analyses are found, for instance, in Elisabeth A. Frost's "'In Another Tongue': Body, Image, Text in Theresa Hak Kyung Cha's *Dictée*" (2002, 182) and Timothy Yu's "Form and Identity in Language Poetry and Asian American Poetry" (2000, 443–444). Frost addresses, among other things, postmodernist and poststructuralist aspects of Cha's style while Yu speaks briefly of Cha as a poet whose work might show the "possible complementarity of Asian American and Language poetics."

17. Here and in the following sections of this chapter, when I refer to Korean immigrants, I am thinking of first generation Korean immigrants to the United States who came immediately before or in the early years of the Japanese colonization of Korea. For a comprehensive account of their involvement in the Korean nationalist cause and the Korean independence movement, see Ronald Takaki, *Strangers from a Different Shore* (1990, 270–293).

18. For a fairly extended discussion of this usurpation, see *Dictee*, 28–32.

19. See Lisa Lowe for a discussion of what constitutes liberal pluralism in the United States and the role communications media play in this system: "In the United States, pluralism admits the existence of differences, yet requires conformity to a public culture that tends to subordinate alternative cultures—not only racial and ethnic cultures, but gay and lesbian cultures, and working class culture, as well. The state apparatuses—schooling, communications media, the legal system, as well as apparatuses of citizenship—which assimilate immigrant individuals into citizenship, are integral to the constitution of a state in which their racial and ethnic differences are sublated and silenced" ("Unfaithful," 1994, 53).

20. The fact that these pages address the continuing significance of lives that have been abruptly cut short is particularly suggestive.

21. Elaine H. Kim writes, for instance, "Although hundreds of thousands of Korean peasants were pressed into forced labor in Japanese mines and factories in the 1930s and 1940s, few Westerners know that many Hiroshima and Nagasaki atomic bomb victims were Korean conscripts in Japanese munitions plants and other war industries" ("Poised," 1994, 10).

22. Giovanna Covi makes a similar observation in her discussion of Jamaica Kincaid's *Lucy*: "The untelling of the stories of marginality recovers marginality as a condition of the center, as a displacement involving the invention of new forms of subjectivities and implying the continuous renewal of critical work" ("Jamaica," 1996, 62).

Further, in "Reading Asian American Poetry," Juliana Chang makes the re-markable point that in *Dictee*, "Cha recovers violence that is often 'covered up' in official discourse by enacting and embodying violence in the very form of her sentence structure . . . . Cha links the material production of language to blood and saliva, bodily fluids that signify a transgressive break in borders. In this analogy, language has the potential to break through the conventional surface of the 'no-response' . . . , to stimulate or demand, through its own transgressions, a response to violence" ("Reading," 1996, 94).

On a different note, see Anne Anlin Cheng's "Memory and Anti-Documentary Desire in Theresa Hak Kyung Cha's *Dictée*" for a discussion of the "impossibility of the task" of "recording history," "mediated representation" (1998, 122), and how *Dictee* "problematizes the very nature of a 'cultural rescue mission'" (123).

23. In this regard also, see Watson and Smith: "Attention to the politics of identity can also become a source of hybrid forms . . . , and what others in this vol-ume explore as counterhegemonic narratives: ideographic selfhood, ethnography, collective self-storytelling" ("De/Colonization," 1992, xxi).

24. My discussions in earlier sections of this chapter should make it evident to the reader that here, Cha uses Holy Communion, the rite of the Catholic Mass (with which she could have been familiar both because of French Catholic missionary influence in Korea and because she attended Catholic school in the United States) for her own purposes.

Works Cited

Bhabha, Homi K. "The Commitment to Theory," in *Questions of Third Cinema*. Jim Pines and Paul Willemen, eds. (pp. 111–32). London: British Film Institute, 1989.

Caruth, Cathy. *Unclaimed Experience: Trauma, Narrative, and History*. Balti-more: Johns Hopkins University Press, 1996.

Cha, Theresa Hak Kyung. *Dictee*. Berkeley: Third Woman, 1995.

Chang, Juliana. "Reading Asian American Poetry." *MELUS*, 21 (1996): 81–98.

Cheng, Anne Anlin. "Memory and Anti-Documentary Desire in Theresa Hak Kyung Cha's *Dictée*." *MELUS*, 23 (1998): 119–33.

Chew, Kristina. "The Losses of Theresa Hak Kyung Cha's *Dictee*," in *Writing Dispossession, Writing Desire: Asian American Women Writers*. Srimati Mukherjee, ed. Unpublished anthology.

Covi, Giovanna. "Jamaica Kincaid's Prismatic Self and the Decolonialisation of Language and Thought," in *Framing the Word: Gender and Genre in Caribbean Women's Writing*. Joan Anim-Addo, ed. (pp. 37–67). London: Whiting, 1996.

Frost, Elisabeth A. "'In Another Tongue': Body, Image, Text in Theresa Hak Kyung Cha's *Dictée*," in *We Who Love to Be Astonished: Experimental Women's Writing and Performance Poetics*. Laura Hinton and Cynthia Hogue, eds. (pp. 181–92). Tuscaloosa: University of Alabama Press, 2002.

hooks, bell. *Talking Back: Thinking Feminist, Thinking Black*. Boston: South End, 1989.

Jayawardena, Kumari. *Feminism and Nationalism in the Third World*. London: Zed, 1986.

Kim, Elaine H. "Korean American Literature," in *An Interethnic Companion to Asian American Literature*. King-Kok Cheung, ed. (pp. 156–91). New York: City University Press, 1997.

———. "Poised on the In-between: A Korean American's Reflections on Theresa Hak Kyung Cha's *Dictée*," in *Writing Self Writing Nation: A Collection of Essays on* Dictee *by Theresa Hak Kyung Cha*. Elaine H. Kim and Norma Alarcón, eds. (pp. 3–30). Berkeley: Third Woman, 1994.

———. "Preface," in *Writing Self Writing Nation: A Collection of Essays on* Dictee *by Theresa Hak Kyung Cha*. Elaine H. Kim and Norma Alarcón, eds. (pp. ix–xi). Berkeley: Third Woman, 1994.

Lowe, Lisa. "Unfaithful to the Original: The Subject of *Dictée*," in *Writing Self Writing Nation: A Collection of Essays on* Dictee *by Theresa Hak Kyung Cha*. Elaine H. Kim and Norma Alarcón, eds. (pp. 35–69). Berkeley: Third Woman, 1994.

Min, Eun Kyung. "Reading the Figure of Dictation in Theresa Hak Kyung Cha's *Dictée*," in *Other Sisterhoods: Literary Theory and U.S. Women of Color*. Sandra Kumamoto Stanley, ed. (pp. 309–24). Urbana: University of Illinois Press, 1998.

Roth, Moira. "Theresa Hak Kyung Cha 1951–1982: A Narrative Chronology," in *Writing Self Writing Nation: A Collection of Essays on* Dictee *by Theresa Hak Kyung Cha*. Elaine H. Kim and Norma Alarcón, eds. (pp. 151–60). Berkeley: Third Woman, 1994.

Sharpe, Jenny. "Figures of Colonial Resistance." *Modern Fiction Studies*, 35 (1989): 137–55.

Shih, Shu-Mei. "Nationalism and Korean American Women's Writing: Theresa Hak Kyung Cha's *Dictee*," in *Speaking the Other Self: American Women Writers*. Jeanne Campbell Reesman, ed. (pp. 144–62). Athens: University of Georgia Press, 1997.

Spivak, Gayatri Chakravorty. "Preface to 'Draupadi,' by Mahasveta Devi." *Critical Inquiry*, 8: 2 (1981): 381–402.

————. "Woman in Difference: Mahasweta Devi's 'Douloti the Bountiful,'" in *Nationalisms and Sexualities*. Andrew Parker, Mary Russo, Doris Sommer, Patricia Yeager, eds. (pp. 96–117). New York: Routledge, 1992.

Takaki, Ronald. *Strangers from a Different Shore: A History of Asian Americans*. New York: Penguin, 1990.

Watson, Julia, and Sidonie Smith. "Introduction: De/Colonization and the Politics of Discourse in Women's Autobiographical Practices," in *De/Colonizing the Subject: The Politics of Gender in Women's Autobiography*. Julia Watson and Sidonie Smith, eds. (pp. xiii–xxxi). Minneapolis: University of Minnesota Press, 1992.

Wong, Shelley Sunn. "Unnaming the Same: Theresa Hak Kyung Cha's *Dictée*," in *Writing Self Writing Nation: A Collection of Essays on* Dictee *by Theresa Hak Kyung Cha*. Elaine H. Kim and Norma Alarcón, eds. (pp. 103–40). Berkeley: Third Woman, 1994.

Yu, Timothy. "Form and Identity in Language Poetry and Asian American Poetry." *Contemporary Literature*, 41 (2000): 422–61.

III. POETRY

10 Kimiko Hahn's "Interlingual Poetics" in *Mosquito and Ant*

ROBERT GROTJOHN

ZHOU XIAOJING places Kimiko Hahn in a group of Asian American women poets that includes Marylin Chin, Cathy Song, and Trinh T. Minh-ha. Zhou identifies these poets as "experimental" for a "poetic hybridity" built on "explor[ing] the possibilities of subversion and invention by drawing from both Asian and Western cultural and literary discourse" ("Breaking," 1998, 200), and on "invent[ing] new poetic forms and styles" (205). Traise Yamamoto considers a similar meeting of "cultural and literary discourse" in Hahn's poetry when she examines the complexities of Hahn's "trope of translation," observing how Hahn "explor[es] the problematics and possibilities of translation understood as a mode of cultural transmission" (*Masking*, 1998, 241). In the crossing over of languages and cultures, Hahn shows what Juliana Chang calls "[a]n interlingual poetics." According to Chang, such a poetics "would change the shape and sounds of dominant languages like English by pushing the language to its limits and breaking it open or apart. The interpenetration of languages acknowledged and performed by interlingualism allows us to re-imagine these languages and cultures not as discrete entities, but as radically relational" ("Reading," 1996, 93). Chang further observes that "poetic discourse performs critique . . . through the construction of alternative forms and structures that simultaneously reveal and disrupt more socially dominant structures" (94), an observation that fits Hahn's poetry well.

Chang's imagination of an "interlingual poetics" offers a way of reading Hahn's work throughout her career, and can be especially helpful in considering her 1999 collection, *Mosquito and Ant*. Hahn's various "trope[s] of translation" lead to "invention and subversion," or to various sorts of transgression, a term I prefer because of its etymological kinship with "translation," both indicating a crossing of boundaries,[1] and because the etymological connection parallels the trope of etymological translation from Chinese radicals, which I will emphasize below. Hahn's transgressions build from her "interlingual poetics" that creates the "trope[s] of translation," and, in doing so, "reveal[s] and disrupt[s]"

—particularly disrupts—"more socially dominant structures." Those disrupted structures include the conventions of unified lyric expression, an "orientalism" in which Asia is embedded in Western discourse, and a masculine "dominant" structure in which women are embedded in male discourse. Hahn's disruptions/transgressions of the latter two parallel and build on one another, as she creates, sometimes fragmentarily, dominance over the conventionally dominant: Asian discourse creates Western, and feminine discourse defines and constrains the masculine. Rather than attempt to isolate artificially these three transgressions/disruptions, I ask that you keep them in mind as always contingent as you read this chapter.

Mosquito and Ant begins as translation of a transgressive discourse: the title translates a description of *nu shu* script, which Hahn defines as "a nearly extinct secret script used by Chinese women to correspond with one another" (*Mosquito and Ant,* hereafter cited as MA, 101).[2] A "translation" of *nu shu* sisterhood to the present serves as a structural device throughout the volume, as the connecting motif for many of the poems is a correspondence with an intimate female friend identified by the initial "L." This translation crosses over to multiple connections with other forms of women's writing, one of which is the juxtaposition of the actual ancient women's language with the theoretical proposition of such a language in Hahn's allusions to, epigraphs from, and quotations of French feminists associated with *écriture feminine.* She also blends homage to Japanese women writers of the Heian period, who have been a significant influence throughout Hahn's career.[3] She further layers those feminine/feminist translations by using Chinese characters, one of which heads each of the collection's four sections, three of poetry and one of notes.

Hahn constructs several interrelated narratives behind the poems, a key narrative in the first two sections being an extramarital flirtation, the story of which is pieced together in fragments from the correspondence with L. In that flirtation, the poems "disrupt...dominant structures" in a way similar to that presented by Eileen Tabios, when, in discussing Hahn's use of French feminist sources as "triggering" devices for poems in *Mosquito and Ant,* she quotes Sandra Gilbert's summary of a story told by Catherine Clément in "The Guilty One," an essay to which Hahn refers: "Clément tells a tale of a woman in the Mezzogiorno who can be cured of imaginary spider bites only by doing a ceremonial dance.... At the end of the episode, she transcends 'the divine bite' and 'leave[s] risk behind.... to settle down again under a roof, in a house, in the family circle of kinship and marriage...the men's world.' But she has had her interlude of orgasmic freedom" (Tabios, "Expressing," 1998, 25).

Throughout the first two sections, Hahn engages in something like an "interlude of orgasmic freedom" in the flirtation that transgresses the dominant social structure of marriage. In the third section, however, her persona returns to "the family circle of kinship and marriage," but with a difference that translates the circle as matrilineal, a maternal return, and so no longer '"the men's world."'

Because Hahn makes it clear that her poems have constructed speakers (Tabios, "Expressing," 1998, 30, 59), that she does not read them herself as unmediated personal revelation, I read the poems not as primarily personal lyrics of private expression, although that clearly relates to the origin of the poems. I am more interested in the public reading, the interactions with the reader, than in seeing these poems as representative ethnic autobiography; therefore, even though I will use "Hahn" for efficiency, I intend that use to indicate the personae of the poems. One might read the poems as individual, independent, though problematic, lyric expressions, and I will also to a certain extent, but the volume also has multiple crossovers between poems; therefore, I frequently will read across the volume, through the intra- and intertextual combinations and echoes in the poems. I will return to several passages and reread them as I develop my argument. My crossover reading and rereading reflects the epigraph to "Morning Light" (*MA*, 19–21), a quotation from Irigaray— "*But this* one *does not exist*" (19)—and the ways "one-ness" dissolves to offer a problematized "self" that is, ultimately, not a problem.

Hahn emphasizes the reader's responsibility when she tells Tabios, while discussing lines she has deleted from "Responding to Light," that she was "doing the work of the reader" in those lines. "The writer needs to trust the reader," she asserts (Tabios, "Expressing," 1998, 52). She discusses deleting an entire stanza because it was "redundant and boring," but also because "it was *not fun*" (61). One should not dismiss the "*fun*" of reading the poems, and I have tried to keep it in mind in this chapter.

Some of the *fun* surfaces in the title poem when Hahn foregrounds poetic language as she challenges a male reader's translative capacity at the same time as she suggests a necessary translative attempt when she questions whether "a straight man can read such lines" (*MA*, 30). The play on "lines" refers most obviously to Hahn's own poems, but it also suggests the physical appearance of Chinese *nu shu* script, the "lines" or strokes out of which the script is constructed.[4] Of course, since *nu shu* is a secret *women's* script, men *cannot* (or at least could not) read it.[5] Furthermore, the play between "straight" and "lines" suggests the old saw about the distance between two points: "straight" lines are, of course, the shortest distance between the points. In fact, the preceding section of the poem develops this play when Hahn states that "the shortest distance between two points" is "tenacity not seduction" (*MA*, 29), disrupting the straight meaning of the old saw. Neither tenacity nor seduction seems necessarily straightforward. If lines move like the mosquito and the ant, they are circuitous, not straight. Neither Hahn nor I would be the first to note that conventional patriarchal discourse is linear and hierarchical, while transgressive women's discourse may be more devious.

The concreteness, even physicality, of language indicated by suggesting the "lines" of *nu shu* script appears again when Hahn "Imagine[s] words with a dimension" ("'Guard the Jade Pass,'" MA, 55). Or again, along with the context of ancestral Asian women writers, when she writes of their Chinese "words weighted in object" ("Orchid Root," 57). Those "weighted" words suggest the pictographic etymology of the characters with which the Chinese women poets write; those characters are "words with a dimension" in their imagery, unlike the flat phonetic script of English. She refers directly to the pictographic elements of Chinese writing when, later in "Orchid Root," she simply refers to "the grass radicals" (59).

Radicals are, of course, basic components of Chinese characters, or *kanji*, and Hahn's reference to radicals, along with her references to the physical dimensions of a language that suggest written Chinese, add to her uses of *nu shu* another layer of "interlingual poetics." The scripted embeddedness of various of the 214 radicals in Chinese written language parallels and suggests the transgressive "embedding" of the Western in the Eastern and the male in female discourse. Her own "radical method" is important because it builds an East/West dialogue in the poems not just through themes but in the forms of the language, making the meeting points adhere to the structure of the words. Hahn asserts, "'Wordplay is an important element in my writing'" (quoted in Tabios, "Expressing," 1998, 39), and she introduces cross-linguistic structural embedding of Asia in America (and vice versa) through her wordplay.

Cross-linguistic wordplay gives structure to the collection, as Hahn heads each of the four sections with a Chinese character. She does not translate the characters, so she requires a reader to participate in the act of translation and places the poems in a context set by a non-English language. The characters are, in order, 言 (*yán*: "speech" or "to speak"), 女 (*nü*: "woman"), 心 (*xīn*: "heart"), and 雨 (*yǔ*: "rain"). One might expect that the first and second characters would refer, in reverse order, to the women's language of *nu shu*; however, Hahn transgresses that expectation and complicates translation by using a language-signifying character different from the one used for *nu shu*. She uses 言, while the character for *shū* is 書: "writing" or "to write."

言 is comprised of two other characters. The boxlike shape on the bottom is the radical for "mouth." The series of lines above the mouth are an abbreviation of the character for "crime" or "offense"; thus, 言 can be translated as a "crime of the mouth" (Harbaugh, *Chinese*, 1998, 191), and, indeed, the volume disrupts or speaks of a crime against a decorous feminine poetic. Within the apparently innocuous character for "speech," Hahn already embeds a transgressive poetic direction.

Hahn does not always appear to write from a transgressive, or "criminal," position, however, particularly as she writes of her husband. As in the few extant *nu shu* writings, Hahn complains about marriage (Silber, "Daughter," 1994, 49). In "Orchid Root," for instance, Hahn refers to women writing complaints about gender relations to one another, as they exchange poems in which they "protest the man's inattention" (*MA*, 58). Although she does not specify this as a complaint about her spouse, her "protest" echoes several preceding poems in which Hahn complains to L. about "inattention" from her husband.

Hahn creates "Jam" as one of those epistolary complaints mentioned in "Orchid Root." In "Jam," it at first appears, contrary to my earlier claim, that the speaker herself is excluded from and defined outside of masculine discourse, as represented by "the News" that the husband "turns on" several times in the poem instead of attending to the speaker (*MA*, 32). The husband reading the news and complaining about interruption occurs in other poems as well ("Morning Light," 20; "Note on Thematic Redundancy in Women's Verse, No. One," 27).

In "The Tumbler," the poem that immediately follows "Jam," Hahn updates the letters passed between *nu shu* sisters to a phone call and at the same time includes the poem itself as one of the epistles between modern *nu shu* sisters. As in the traditional *nu shu* communication, Hahn uses the image of "female as plant or flower" (Silber, "Daughter," 1994, 54) when L. tells the speaker that she is "giving to others / the tendrils [she] should be giving [her]self" (*MA*, 33).

I have noted that Hahn "disrupt[s] . . . dominant structures," but "Jam" and "The Tumbler" do not seem very disruptive or "criminal" in their speaking, at least not from what I have noted thus far. In "Jam," Hahn seems barely to make an impression on the husband, much less "disrupt" his attention from his reading and television-watching. Hahn seems to be the one most disrupted—she seems distanced from her physical as well as mental or emotional self, a distance indicated when Hahn reports L.'s observation that she "count[s] on him / to retrieve [her] own body." Her comment that she "miss[es]" her "self" anticipates the disruption of self indicated by the "tendrils" that she is "giving to others" but "should be giving [her]self." Ultimately, retrieving her own body becomes essential as a metaphor in her transgressive radical reconstructions of self, as I will discuss below, but she seems distanced from that self in these poems. That distance seems to make these two poems "not *fun*."

In "Jam," the fun lies in the manipulations of language that embed some ironic humor in the apparently dismissive actions of the husband, humor that dismisses his actions as ultimately not very attractively male.

That humor turns on the word "turns" when, in the second section, she ends a line with the anticipation of something potentially orgasmic and exciting when "he turns on." That anticipation leads to a definite anti-climax, when, as Hahn continues past the line break, he "turns on / the News" instead of helping his wife "retrieve" her body. The fourth section emphasizes this lack of excitement in two repetitions of the verb "turns on." The first does not create any anticipation because it is buried in the middle of a line and lacks even the brief anticipatory pause of a line break. The second, which again occurs at the end of a line, has lost most of its possible anticipation because, by now, the anticlimactic turn on has been habitualized through repetition. Finally, when she turns "on" to "in," as her husband "turns in" after watching the television news, reading the newspaper and a spy thriller, the lack of intimacy is emphasized by the suggestion of sleep trumping romance. Of course, the "in" also indicates a turn *in*ward, away from Hahn, toward self-absorption. If she has de-pended on him to retrieve her body, she will be rather disappointed. The husband seems almost stupidly uncomprehending of his lack of intimacy when he responds with a bewildered "What?" to Hahn's apparently ro-mantic memory of walks by the seashore.

In the development of the embedded narrative of the flirtatious poten-tial "orgasmic interlude," it is not surprising that "Jam," with its com-plaints about the husband's inattention, is immediately followed by "The Tumbler," which introduces Hahn's extramarital flirtation. In the first section of "Jam," Hahn responds to her husband's suspicions with the as-surance that he need not worry if he keeps on "supplying / the jam" (MA, 30). Hahn's bluesy *double entendre* suggests that the husband's alternative suspicion and inattention will land him in a jam, and not the sweet kind to which Hahn refers. When Hahn turns to the extramarital flirtation, she might not seem to get herself outside of masculine constructions—this construction being one of desire rather than of disregard. However, the epistolary discourse makes the other man as well as the husband the spoken of; both men are contained within the letters to L. The two men are always the topic of the discourse, embedded without active participa-tion in it, included as object but excluded as speaking or writing subject. Although L. is addressed in the second person multiple times, a point of view that implies close communication, only one of the poems is ad-dressed in the second person to a male, and that poem is complicated by its translative positioning, as I will discuss below. Furthermore, the husband is almost never named in the first two sections of the book; he is usually referred to simply by third-person pronouns, and twice as just "the husband" (MA, 51, 75).

The embedding of the masculine begins in "Wax," the first poem of the first section—the first "crime of the mouth"—before either the husband or the other man is introduced. Hahn uses relatively decorous language to describe her own youthful inability to understand her "lithe" and "tremulous beauty" in lines of fairly regular length and rhythm. "[L]ithe" and "tremulous" show decorous diction; the soft sounds of the lines seem vaguely and pleasantly nostalgic, as the reveries of someone in her forties might very well be. These lines reflect a desire to recapture younger days with more developed self-knowledge—"If I only knew then . . ." The sound and diction change abruptly in the next three lines, which are not "tremulous" at all when she recalls her desire "to fuck [her] professor" (*MA*, 17). "[F]uck" transgresses the preceding diction, contrasting sharply with the softly sounding "lithe" and "tremulous"; it might be jarring, even offensive to some readers. It also prepares the way for the almost "orgasmic interlude" sketched in the flirtation narrative.

The nostalgic desire and Hahn's construction of the male as generically embedded object in her discourse gain focus a few lines later, as she initiates her contemporary *nu shu* correspondence to L. in desiring one of those passionate "initial encounters" that will bring her "Pulse" to "the boiling point" (*MA*, 18). She constructs an unnamed and as yet apparently only imagined almost lover (she does not imagine sex in her encounter) as the object of her desire. The desired other is not even necessarily a man, is as yet only an idea; the idea precedes the appearance of any particular other man in the volume, so that the particular man becomes categorized before his actuality. This suggests a sort of generic man, so that the man who later appears is more significant for the completion of Hahn's desire rather than for himself. The earlier nostalgia reappears in Hahn's recollection of encounters that she cannot retrieve because they are past. For one long married, blood-boiling "*initial* encounters" *should* be a thing of the past, at least in conventional constructions of the marital tie, so expressing desire for extramarital romance might be construed as a "crime of the mouth." However, it might also capture the truth of one's forties, prime time for a midlife crisis no matter what one's gender.

Hahn subtitles "Wax" "*Initial Correspondence to L . . .*" (*MA*, 17). "*Initial*" most obviously refers to this as the first of her letters to a contemporary *nu shu* sister, but it also self-reflexively and jokingly refers to Hahn's communication with an initial, "L." Furthermore, the "correspondence," while it refers to the poem's epistolary rhetoric, also suggests some level of identification, or sameness, with her friend L. In fact, this fits nicely with the contemporization of *nu shu* custom, since, as Cathy Silber points out, *nu shu* sisters were often identified as "sames."[6]

The "initial correspondence" in the subtitle is echoed by the "initial encounter" Hahn desires later in the poem. When a particular guy fulfills her flirtatious desire in other poems, beginning with "The Tumbler," he is also identified by an initial, so that the "encounters" with him are always, in Hahn's setup for the pun, "encounters" with an "initial." Hahn emphasizes the generic nature of this flirtatious "initial" in a later poem when she seems to long for the particular man, "*his* mouth," but revises that longing to one for "*any* initial encounter" (emphasis added; "Radiator," MA, 61).

Hahn's desire, even when tied to a specific man, maintains the generic male status of the opening poem in the section because this *is* an "*initial* encounter," and it remains generic because of the particular initial Hahn selects to identify the man: "X." "X." is the generic signifier of the unknown; it could be anything, or, in this case, anyone. From this reading of the initial, it is not especially important whether Hahn may have a particular man in mind; the "confessional" nature of these poems becomes beside the point. In "Pine," the man does get a name in the advice Hahn receives from L., but even that name is so generic as to render it unindividualized: "*John*" (MA, 36). Even if there is a real "John" for Hahn, the name as representation within this women's writing becomes an abstraction, transcending the personal. This man becomes, at least primarily for a reader, a construction embedded in the discourse.

Hahn reports to L. her attraction for X. and X.'s pursuit of her through the first two sections of the book, always speaking of X. in the distancing third person until the final poem of the second section. This poem is the only one addressed directly, and apparently very intimately, to a man in the second person. Although Hahn does not indicate that the poem is imagined as a direct address to X. in particular, since Hahn has been building the ghost narrative of the potential affair with X. for most of the volume, a reader will have X. in mind when reading the poem. She expresses explicitly sexual desire of her body for his in this second-person address; "her inner thighs," for instance, yearn for his "hips" (MA, 81).

The poem "Komachi to Shōshō on the Ninety-ninth Night" builds from a legend about Ono no Komachi, the famous woman poet of the Heian period, a legend who has been depicted in the Noh play by Kwanami Kiyotsuga, "*Sotaba Komachi*" ("Komachi on the Gravepost").[7] Shōshō desired to become Komachi's lover (the parallel with X. and Hahn is clear); she promised to fulfill his desires if he could keep vigil outside her residence for one hundred consecutive nights. Unfortunately, he was caught in a snowstorm and died on the ninety-ninth night, so his ardor was never rewarded. In the poem, then, when Hahn's Komachi expresses in some detail her desire for sexual union with Shōshō, the implications of the Japanese story suggest that Hahn's flirtations with X. ultimately do not result in the "crime" of infidelity, but she does commit a "crime" against the male ego. The poem uses a conventionalized cultural story, so that, again, the male who is addressed becomes not a particular man but any man who fits a standard plot. When Hahn finally reaches the apparent intimacy of second-person communication with the man she desires, when he becomes an apparently particular "you" rather than the generic "X.," the intertextual implications actually signify a distance between Hahn and X.

The allusion to Komachi and Shōshō is, in fact, "predicted" earlier, in "Radiator," when Hahn claims her relationship with X. will end with "the predicted blizzard" (MA, 61). Since Shōshō meets his demise in a blizzard, this passage suggests that the flirtation with X. will not move to its potential sexual end. Since "Radiator" predicts the end of the relationship and suggests this affair remains on the level of abstraction or imagination rather than actual consummation, it is appropriate that the last direct mention of X., which occurs in "Croissant," is followed by a return "home" (68).

Immediately after the reference to her return home, Hahn returns to feminine discourse and correspondence, or likeness, in a pun she finds embedded in earlier references to the "Immortal Sisters" ("'Guard the Jade Pass,'" MA, 55–56; "Mosquito and Ant," 28–30), who were legendary Chinese adepts of the Tao (see Cleary, *Immortal*, 1989). She writes of how she and her daughters "fall in love with" a female photographer who has come to take her picture, and qualifies that loving with the phrase "immoral sisters" (MA, 68). In disentangling the "immoral" pun from "immortal," Hahn returns to a "home" that echoes the illicit implication of her earlier "crimes of the mouth." Along with the corresponding implications, she seems to translate the way of reading Chinese characters to English, since many Chinese characters have other characters embedded in them, just as "immoral" is embedded in "immortal." Hahn makes English read like Chinese, just as she has asked a reader to see her contemporary sisterhood as like the *nu shu* sisterhood. In her interlingual embedding, a sort of sinological English, Hahn makes the languages "radically relational" in a way not anticipated by Chang's use of the phrase: she makes the puns in English read like they are composed of the internal radicals that make up most Chinese characters.

The "radical" echo of "crimes of the mouth" in the "immortal"/ "immoral" pun is reflected with humor—the "*fun*" she invests in her poetry—when, between the last reference to X. and Hahn's "flight home," she recalls a conversation with her oldest daughter, who asked about sex with a man. Hahn tells her that the details of heterosexual intercourse, details that they agree are "silly and slimy" (MA, 68). This sounds like a crime against seriousness in the comedy it makes of male desire, and it is predicted by an earlier "radical" pun that, like the "immortal"/"immoral" pun, juxtaposes humor and gravity by the shift of one letter when she says her "desire to merge" is "*cosmic*" and responds to that with the single summary word "COMIC" ("Zinc," 42).

She uses the same technique as yet another means of embedding men into her women's discourse. She pulls out the "*he*" from other words twice: "You say it's the *he* in *heat*" ("Pine," MA, 36); "the *he* residing in the *she*" ("Garnet," 52). The first disembedded "*he*" occurs in one of the epistolary poems to L., so that the male is contained by the sisterly discourse on at least two levels, within the correspondence and within the single word. That containment reflects the initial abstract desire that precedes any particular man in "Wax," since the "*heat*" without any particular man precedes and perhaps produces the particular "*he*." The second disembedding, of "*he*" from "*she*," also suggests the masculine as a construction of this women's discourse.

In a reversal of conventional assumptions of patriarchal heritage in discourse, the male is defined by a "feminine" discourse that is itself constructed as at least a partial inheritance from Asian influences—written Chinese, *nu shu* sisterhood, the immortal sisters, Ono no Komachi. In the confines of this volume, and, by implication, in a tradition of women writing, men take on the historically feminine role as objects of but not significant participants in the discourse. This female-defined aesthetic gets further historical antecedent in "The Downpour," when Hahn considers Sei Shōnagon, another important woman writer of the Heian period; Hahn writes of how "women, prohibited from learning Chinese, wrote in the vernacular, in the language of their islands" (*MA*, 44). Two paragraphs later, she continues her lesson in literary history, telling the reader, "The language invigorated the literature, made the bloodless literature flush, and was so dominated by women, their sensibility became the aesthetic. Some men wrote in the female persona. And men of any worth became tainted by their radiant influence" (44–45). The pressure of being prohibited from the dominant (though derivative) discourse is the very thing that led to the reinvigoration of the literature when Heian women chose other means of discourse, much as the *nu shu* sisters created their own language because they were restricted from learning to write Chinese characters. Hahn's metaphor of the women writers "mak[ing] the bloodless literature flush" recalls Hahn's own earlier pulse pounding in "Wax," and it is a pulse pounding that stems from feminine influence. Just as she has celebrated the "crimes" of her women's discourse, she overturns a primary negative understanding of being "tainted." Following her reference to a "flush," "tainted" indicates a coloring of what had been monotonously pale, or "bloodless."

The "radiant influence" ascribed to Heian women poets echoes "Radiator," the title of the poem that predicts the end of Hahn's flirtation with X., but, more importantly, it also suggests a metaphor for how the male in *Mosquito and Ant* is constructed out of the writing woman's desire, and I mean "out of" in two ways—the male is created by and eliminated from the feminine correspondence at the same time, which I think is emphasized in "Orchid Root" when, after the women exchange their poems that "protest the man's inattention," "they fall in love" (*MA*, 58) with one another, apparently through their writing, the act of creating their own discourse, much as the photographer's art caused Hahn and her daughters to fall in love with her. The lesbian suggestiveness of the stanza recalls the indefinite gender of the imagined love interest in "Wax," and it is troped in the action of "honeysuckle" as it creeps across boundaries of "one garden" to another. The honeysuckle, in moving out of bounds, becomes transgressive, criminal, immoral, and leads to connections between women—Hahn's friends, her daughters, her mother and grandmother—which in turn lead to a return to the "self" that seemed to have gone missing in "Jam" and "The Tumbler." Those connections and inspirations imaged by the climbing honeysuckle return again to the *nu shu* "tropes of female as plant or flower" (Silber, "Daughter," 1994, 54).

The male "inattention" depicted earlier in "Jam," when the husband "turns on" to "the News," is in fact followed by a crossing over to sisterhood. In the final stanza of the poem, Hahn recounts reading about "Immortal Sisters"; as she reads, her "blood quickens" (MA, 32). In the lesbian suggestiveness of "blood quicken[ing]," these lines from "Jam" radiate into "Orchid Root" as that quickening is a response to connections between women and reflects the almost sexual excitement of a "Pulse at the boiling point" that Hahn recalls from "initial encounters" in "Wax." Even in that earlier poem, Hahn refused to limit the possibility of this boiling pulse to a heterosexual encounter. The quickening through language, as Hahn reads about the Immortal Sisters, also echoes in "The Downpour" when, as I noted above, Hahn honors the Heian women writers who "made the bloodless literature flush."

The connection with a feminine tradition, a reciprocity of sameness like *nu shu* sisterhood, often operates through sexually suggestive imagery of the heart, as in the boiling pulse and quickening blood. That physical imagery offers a restitution of the physical loss of self indicated in "Jam" when L. pointed out how Hahn depended on "him / to retrieve [her] own body." When Hahn feels her blood quicken at the end of the poem, she offers a retrieval of her body for her self; instead of "miss[ing her]self," she finds it in the physical feeling of her pulse speeding up. She has returned to that physical self, at least a bit, through the imagination of the Immortal Sisterhood, a connection to a female genealogy rather than as a response to male desire. She embodies Asian women's writing as she writes a connection to physical reactions that cross over to an explicit eroticism that echoes Irigaray's call: "Let us try to situate ourselves within that female genealogy so that we can win and hold on to our identity" (quoted in Tabios, "Expressing," 1998, 47). That sort of body-centered retrieval of self, while hinted at by the end of "Jam," is incomplete there.

Hahn completes her physical retrieval of self in a later poem when she echoes and rectifies the language of loss introduced in "Jam." In recalling a metaphor I pointed out earlier, Hahn gives her "tendrils" to herself in

"The Lunar Calendar She Pins to the Door" as she attempts self recovery by "coming alone" (MA, 70). In "Jam," Hahn wrote, "I miss my self"; here, she seems hopeful that she can "stop *forgetting [her]self.*" Instead of "count[ing] on him / to retrieve [her] own body," she hopes here to stop searching for someone else "to locate [her] own body." She retrieves her own body for herself in the autoeroticism that develops the imagery of the heart when she describes hearing the sound of her own heart beating; she does not require a man, neither her husband nor X., to find her self. Finding the self has been equated with the retrieval of the body throughout the volume, and explicitly in "Jam"; thus, the autoeroticism of "coming alone" represents that return to self. The return is again connected to women's correspondence in the reference to what seems like a comment from L., who remarks positively on Hahn's self-constructed independence. She has retrieved herself and has had that retrieval confirmed by another woman.

In fact, the only depicted "orgasmic interludes" are autoerotic, another one of which occurs in "Responding to Light." Irigaray has an explicit importance to that poem, and she appears in the title through translation: Hahn points out that she used "Light" in part because it is the English translation for Irigaray's given name, "Luce" (Tabios, "Expressing," 1998, 57). In light of this poem being a response to Irigaray's essay "Body against Body: In Relation to the Mother," it is helpful to consider Irigaray's statement that "[W]e need ... to discover our sexual identity, the specialness of our desires, of our autoeroticism, our narcissism, our heterosexuality, our homosexuality. In this context it is important to remind ourselves that, since the first body we as women had to relate to was a woman's body and our first love is love of the mother, women always have an ancient and primary relationship to what is called homosexuality" (Irigaray, "Body," 49). Hahn's autoeroticism and lesbian suggestion seem to affirm Irigaray's statement. In the fifth section of the poem, Hahn connects mothers and daughters through the body, as she has reconnected with herself through the body, with an epigraph from Irigaray that connects "*our body, her body, the body of her daughter*" (MA 79).

In the body of the poem, she continues connecting: as "she tastes" and "touches herself," she also "is tasting the mother and daughter" and, in so doing, feels the "pulse that penetrates like an echo" (MA, 79). Hahn constructs this return to her own body as a return to the maternal body, as simultaneously mother and daughter, with a return or "echo" of the "pulse" that has pounded throughout the volume. The layering and intermingling of mothers and daughters through physical sensation carry over from "Tissue," a poem that includes bodily connection even in its title. After Hahn writes in that poem of yearning for the protections and sensations of a long-gone childhood, she addresses her mother directly: "I forgot your heartbeat," she writes, but remembers it in listening to her own "daughter's tiny chest" (*MA*, 72). The cluster of pulse/heart imagery returns to the Chinese characters and comes to completion in the third section, with its heading of 心 (*xīn*: "heart") and its commitment to the maternal connection (as daughter, then as mother) as the "radical" that resonates from one "character" (or poem) to another. The two longer poems that make up the third section, the final section of poems, are "Becoming the Mother" (*MA*, 85–88) and "Sewing without Mother" (89–98), the only two titles in the volume that refer to "Mother." However, in "The Razor" (13), the prefatory poem that precedes the 言 (*yán*: "to speak") section, Hahn depicts a moment with her father at the temple, crying and saying a sutra for her deceased mother, who is a significant presence in all of her poetry, and whose sudden death in a traffic accident has been important since it was a central motif in *The Unbearable Heart* (1995), her third individual collection. Hahn frames the entire collection with poems about her mother, so that all the poems are embedded within her maternal genealogy. After "Razor," the mother does not appear again as a major focus until "Responding to Light." The importance of the latter poem is suggested by the return to the mother, by its length (one of the longer poems in the book), and by its placement just before "Komachi to Shōshō on the Ninety-ninth Night," the poem that implies the end of the unconsummated flirtation.

The two long poems of the third section focus on the maternal return home '"to settle down again under a roof, in a house, in the family circle of kinship and marriage...the men's world,'" as depicted by Clément (Clément, "Guilty," 1986, 22). As I noted earlier, however, this return, while it is to home and "the family circle," is not a return to "the men's world." In fact, it is just the opposite: Hahn's husband becomes again embedded in this maternal world when, "for a dozen years," he "had nearly become the mother" ("Becoming the Mother," *MA*, 86). That becoming is not unproblematic, but it reincorporates the husband into the discourse as a named identity, which he had almost never been throughout the rest of the collection. It reincorporates him, however, in a twist of correspondence through the *nu shu* motif and through Hahn's reconnection to a maternal genealogy. Her husband's name becomes the last word in the last poem of the volume, and he is blended into the "circle of kinship" when Hahn writes an observed similarity between her husband and their daughter, but that relationship is contained within an address to her deceased mother, who, in being addressed, is imagined as an "immortal sister," I suppose: "Mother, Rei's feet are narrow and long like Ted's" (98).

The importance of *Mosquito and Ant* lies in Hahn's developments of what Shirley Geok-lin Lim calls the "linguistic" level of an Asian American

"ethnopoetics" ("Reconstructing," 1987, 54–55). When Lim first identified the linguistic level, she observed that the "survival of first language
expressions" reflects "certain values, concepts, and cultural traits" extant
"in the original language itself" (54). As Lim observed it, the linguistic
level functions in the content meaning, either denotative or connotative,
of the original language expressions. Hahn uses that level, but she also
uses Asian linguistic constructions as a kind of "deep structure," by which
I mean that Asian linguistic structures, particularly the "radical" structure based in the etymology of *kanji*, offer a formal underpinning for
the volume's fundamental construction. Hahn's poetics in *Mosquito and
Ant* depends on the way language is built as much as on what it means.
This seems to me an extremely valuable innovation, one that other writers
also engage in recent works such as Carolyn Lei-Lanilau's *Ono-Ono Girl's
Hula* (1997), Myung Mi Kim's *Dura* (1998) and*Commons* (2002), and
Marilyn Chin's *Rhapsody in Plain Yellow* (2002).[8] I think that Hahn's is
a particularly successful effort, and, along with those of the other writers,
her effort points toward a growing structural sophistication in the flour-
ishing of an Asian American ethnopoetics. Her powerfully transgressive
women's discourse grows from the historical antecedent of Asian women
writing, and it is rooted in the structures of those antecedents.[9]

NOTES

1. The etymology of "translate" is from "transfer"—to carry (*latus* past par-
ticiple of *ferre*, to carry) across (*trans-*); "trans-gress"—to step (*gradi*) across
(*trans-*).

2. For further information on *nu shu*, see Liu, Metz and Tobin, Silber, and the
film *Nu Shu: A Hidden Language of Women in China*.

3. Her other individual collections are: *Airpocket* (Brooklyn: Hanging Loose
Press, 1989), *The Artist's Daughter* (New York: W. W. Norton, 2002), *Earshot*
(Brooklyn: Hanging Loose Press, 1992), *The Unbearable Heart* (New York: KAYA
Production, 1995), and *Volatile* (Brooklyn: Hanging Loose Press, 1999).

4. See Metz and Tobin for examples of *nu shu* script.

5. Unfortunately, few women can read the script any longer, either, as most of
the texts were destroyed during the Cultural Revolution. One hopes that recent
efforts will help the script to recover.

6. Silber notes that these sisters were supposed to be "of the same age. . . . They
came from families of similar social and economic standing, preferably with the
same number and sex distribution of elder and younger siblings, in the same birth
order. Ideally, the two girls had the same height and the same size feet, and one
was no prettier than the other" ("Daughter," 1994, 50–51). Although this degree
of sameness is not revealed as part of the relationship between Hahn and L.,
there are other parallels between the two: they ask each other for advice about
romantic others, and they at least discuss exchanging clothes with each other, a

sort of exchange common to *nu shu* sisters, which was the reason for them to be the same size (51).

7. Besides the version translated by Tyler and directly attributed to Kwanami in the Works Cited, the play has been translated by Ezra Pound from Ernest Fenollosa's notes. (Pound, Ezra, and Ernest Fenellosa, ed. and trans. *"Noh" or Accomplishment: A Study of the Classical Stage in Japan*. London: MacMillan, 1916.) and by Arthur Waley (Waley, Arthur, ed. and trans. *The No Plays of Japan*. New York: Alfred A. Knopf, 1922.)

8. These writers use the original language as "deep structure" in ways different from Hahn, especially Kim, with her challenging, disruptive experimentalism.

9. Hahn's formal homage to the prose-poem *zuihitsu* of Sei Shōnagon's *Pillow Book* offers further fruitful explorations of this structural rooting, but space prohibits that exploration in this chapter.

WORKS CITED

Chang, Juliana. "Reading Asian-American Poetry." *MELUS*, 21: 1 (Spring 1996): 81–98.

Chin, Marilyn. *Rhapsody in Plain Yellow*. New York: Norton, 2002.

Cleary, Thomas, ed. and trans. *Immortal Sisters: Secrets of Taoist Women*. Boston: Shambala, 1989.

Clément, Catherine. "The Guilty One," in *The Newly Born Woman* (original publication 1975). Hélène Cixous and Catherine Clément. Trans. Betsy Wing. (pp. 1–61). Minneapolis: University of Minnesota Press, 1986.

Gilbert, Sandra. "Introduction," in *The Newly Born Woman* (original publication 1975). Hélène Cixous and Catherine Clément. Trans. Betsy Wing. (pp. ix–xviii). Minneapolis: University of Minnesota Press, 1986.

Hahn, Kimiko. *Mosquito and Ant: Poems*. New York: W. W. Norton, 1999.

———. *The Unbearable Heart*. New York: KAYA Production, 1995.

Harbaugh, Rick. *Chinese Characters: A Genealogy and Dictionary*. Claremont: Zhongwen.com Publishing, 1998.

Irigaray, Luce. "Body against Body: In Relation to the Mother" in *Sexes and Geneologies*. Trans. Gillian C. Gill. (pp. 7–21). New York: Columbia University Press, 1993.

Kim, Myung Mi. *Commons*. Berkeley: University of California Press, 2002.

———. *Dura*. Los Angeles: Sun and Moon, 1998.

Kwanami Kiyotsuga. "Sotaba Komachi," in *From Granny Mountains: A Second Cycle of Noh Plays*. Trans. Royall Tyler. Cornell East Asia Series no. 18. (pp. 105–15). Ithaca, NY: Cornell University East Asia Program, 1978.

Lei-Lanilau, Carolyn. *Ono Ono Girl's Hula*. Madison: University of Wisconsin Press, 1997.

Lim, Shirley Geok-lin. "Reconstructing Asian-American Poetry: A Case for Ethnopoetics." *MELUS*, 14: 2 (Summer 1987): 51–63.

Liu, Fei-wen. "The Confrontation between Fidelity and Fertility: *Nüshu, Nüge*, and Peasant Women's Conceptions of Widowhood in Jianyong County, Hunan Province, China." *Journal of Asian Studies*, 60: 4 (November 2001): 1051–84.

Metz, Pamela K., and Jacqueline L. Tobin. *The Tao of Women*. Atlanta, GA: Humanics, 1995.

Nu Shu: A Hidden Language of Women in China (film). Directed by Yue-Qing Yang. East-West Film Enterprise Ltd. New York: Women Make Movies, 1999.

Sei Shōnagon. *The Pillow Book of Sei Shōnagon*. Trans. Ivan Morris. New York: Penguin, 1967.

Silber, Cathy. "From Daughter to Daughter-in-law in the Women's Script of Southern Hunan," in *Engendering China: Women, Culture and the State*. C. K. Gilmartin, Gail Hershatter, Lisa Rofel, Tyrene White, eds. Harvard Contemporary China Series, 10 (pp. 47–68). Cambridge, Mass: Harvard University Press, 1994.

Tabios, Eileen. "Expressing Self and Desire, Even If One Must Writhe," in *Black Lightning: Poetry in Progress* Eileen Tabios, ed. (pp. 23–68). New York: Asian American Writers Workshop, 1998.

Yamamoto, Traise. *Masking Selves, Making Subjects: Japanese American Women, Identity, and the Body*. Berkeley: University of California Press, 1999.

Zhou Xiaojing. "Breaking from Tradition: Experimental Poems by Four Contemporary Asian American Women Poets." *Revista Canaria de Estudios Ingleses*, 37 (1998): 199–218.

11 "Composed of Many Lengths of Bone"

Myung Mi Kim's Reimagination of Image and Epic

JOSEPHINE NOCK-HEE PARK

MYUNG MI KIM'S difficult poetry is preoccupied with the open wound of history, particularly in the intertwining stories of Korea and the United States. Kim's experimental poetry engages with these two nations and the wide ocean in between; it shows us the ways in which her voice is shaped by both historical and personal convergences between Korea and America and the distance between them. What is striking about Kim's work is her use of modernist poetic tradition in order to express her particular obsession with crossed histories and destinies. I read Kim against Ezra Pound's high modernist legacy, and Kim's redeployment of these aesthetic tools shows us new, strategic uses of this literary past. Specifically, Kim's work returns to Pound's Image, reimagining this modernist poetic renewal, which had been shaped by fantasies of the ideogram. Pound's poetic innovations recreated both lyric and epic poetry; short, piercing lyrics and *The Cantos* stands as a pole in his legacy. Myung Mi Kim, too, interrogates the American long poem in her complicated epic *Dura*; she engages with both ends of this modernist inheritance in fashioning her poetry. Ultimately, I contend that Kim's complicated refigurations of this legacy work to implicate American involvement in the Far East, from orientalist hallucinations to the tragedy of the Korean War.

Kim's daring aesthetics follow from the groundbreaking work of Theresa Hak Kyung Cha's *Dictée*—an innovative and experimental text that self-consciously returns to the epic tradition. In contrast to the multiple screens, translations, and the figure of the "diseuse" who stands at the borders of the opposing spaces in Cha's work, however, Kim instead focuses on the concrete existence of the immigrant. Unlike Cha's sweeping and beautiful text, Kim's fractured and shattering poetry shows us more quotidian concerns: the patient process of naturalization, the forms to be filled out. Kim's poems examine this condition intimately, showing us the broken pieces that comprise the drama of this existence as they appear, amid everyday actions and in sudden, small bursts of feeling. Elaine Kim discusses this lineage from Cha to Kim in her essay "Korean

American Literature," and she describes Kim's first collection, *Under Flag*, as poems that "explore the immigrant's loss of homeland and the Korean American's encounters with racism and the experiences of lost language" (176).[1] Myung Mi Kim shows us this immigrant sensibility in word plays that register the movement between Asia and the United States. One of the joys of reading Kim's poetry is the desire to look up a known word because it suddenly sounds so different in the context she has made for it; to make uncertain our own competence in the language is not only a demonstration of the experience of the immigrant but an aesthetic renewal of the language along the lines of the great American innovators.[2]

DIASPORIC VOICE

Under Flag's opening poem, "And Sing We," imagines voice as tidal movement:

> What would the sea be, if we were near it
>
> Voice
>
> It catches its underside and drags it back (13)

The lines suggest that the voice figured as movement can approximate the sea, and the poem goes on to give us an example of this tidal word play:

> Depletion replete with barraging
> Slurred and taken over
> Diaspora. (13)

The sound values of "Depletion replete" not only ring together; in conjunction with the barrage, the line evokes the movement of waves as they successively empty out and fill with crashing surf. We can imagine the slurring as the waters mingle and are taken over again to repeat the motion. The single word of the third line, "Diaspora," adds another level of comparison to the initial one between voice and wave; Kim lays this tidal motion onto diasporic movement, explicitly mapping the action of the words of the poem onto the immigrant experience.

The final line of "And Sing We" closes on the figure in transit: "Mostly, we crossed bridges we did not see being built" (15). The poem has constructed an intricate web of memories, in Korea and the United States, and at its end, we return to the initial comparison of voice to ocean; what emerges by the end of the poem is the Pacific, the water traversed that stands between childhood in Korea and a later, American existence. This final line adds another dimension to what has now become both the movement of words and letters and people: unseen bridges, already built by the time we know to cross them. This bridge across the Pacific has been multiply built and rebuilt, and it is heavily overdetermined by those who have already traversed it in both directions long before the individual in this poem walks its length. Kim's work continually returns to the elaborate and special connections between Korea and the United States, and later poems in the collection explicitly return to the Korean War as the site for examining the painful intertwining of these two realms.

Kim reimagines the complicated interactions among Koreans in America and Americans in Korea, using a dazzling array of technical tools to convey these different understandings. Elaine Kim discusses a crucial moment in which these two experiences overlap in her reading of a later poem in *Under Flag*, "Food, Shelter, Clothing." She cites a crucial passage in the poem:

> They had oared to cross the ocean
> And where had they come to
> These bearers of a homeland
> Those landing amphibious (under cover of night)
> In a gangplank thud and amplification take
> Spot of ground. (22)

Elaine Kim discusses this moment:

> Kim draws an ironic parallel between the Korean immigrants' "landing amphibious (under cover of night)" and the U.S. military landing in Korea.
>
> Unlike the U.S. invaders, however, the immigrants walk a "gangplank," taking up only a "little space" in the vastness of the United States, a limited and restricted "spot of ground" where they will live tyrannized by fear of "smear" and attack. Korea becomes the "homeland" when they leave home. ("Korean American Literature," (1997, 176)

Elaine Kim reads the Korean example as an indictment of destructive U.S. action. I think that this "ironic parallel" between Korean and U.S. action stands at the heart of Myung Mi Kim's poetic technique. She consistently lays one experience onto the other, creating a palimpsest in which Korea and America are seen together, simultaneously. Her art insists that it is impossible to think of modern Korea without this American term, just as it is impossible for the individuals in these poems to be in America without thinking back, across the ocean, to Korea.

These two sites must be understood together because they are part of the same universe: one is the bridge built that the other has to cross. Ultimately, the action of the immigrant cannot be separated from the military and political forces behind it because her migration is a result of these actions. Kim shows us the ghostly imprints these opposing experiences make on each other because the connection exists, painfully, in the history of Korea: her work shows us the bridges that we could not see being built.

IMAGISM *UNDER FLAG*

Under Flag's title poem, "Under Flag," shows us the battlefield of the Korean War, a battlefield comprised of not only weaponry and soldiers but of "Chonui, a typical Korean town" in which elders "would have been sitting in the warmest part of the house with comforters draped around their shoulders peeling tangerines" (16). The conditional construction of this image is followed by a clear assertion: "Of an uncle with shrapnel burrowing into shinbone for thirty years" (16). The speculation of the former event and the certainty of the latter memory reflect the speaker's position to the events: "Not to have seen it yet inheriting it" (17). This vision of war depicts a kind of collective or cultural memory, and Kim repeatedly returns to this inheritance in her work.

The notion of an ethnic inheritance is balanced against a different American experience, however. In the section that immediately follows the admission of not having seen it, Kim describes the experience of U.S. soldiers: "After dawn the next morning, firing his machine gun, Corporal Leonard H. was shot and instantly killed while stopping the Reds' last attempts to overrun and take the hilltop" (*Under Flag*, hereafter cited as UF, 17). This scene provides a dramatic counterpart to the elders: the inside of the house against the open hilltop, victims against soldiers, old against young, Korean against American. Yet these diametrically opposing scenes have been forced to share the same world. We realize that, despite these differences, the poem is describing a shared experience, and both sets must face a list of proper nouns of weapons that explode in succession: "Lockheed F-04 Starfire/Lockheed F-803/Bell H-13 Sioux / Bell H-13 Ds" (17). And as Kim writes, "More kept coming. More fell" (18).

At this point the poem reprises its opening line, "Is distance" (UF, 18). The first time around, the poem qualifies this statement with "If she knows it" (16): the central figure is positioned after the fact of distance. We may imagine the inverse of the first sentence, "Distance is," but setting the blank before the copula lends a finality to the distance; unlike the possibility of finishing the sentence, to place anything into the space before "Is distance" forces it into distance. Distance, then, simply cannot be attenuated. After the doubled list of military weapons, the poem repeats the opening line, but with a slight difference: "Is distance. If she could know it." The opening "knows" moves us into the different scenarios Kim describes, but the second invocation opens a new scenario the speaker envisages with a kind of desire: "If she could know it." What follows this revised line is a third aspect of this war, beyond victims and soldiers: "Citizens to the street marching / Their demands lettered in blood" (18). The poem evinces a desire to have participated in "the crowd's ambition."

"Under Flag" goes on to ask "And how long practice how long drill to subvert what borders are" (UF, 18), and this lingering question brings us into the present because the border between north and south traumatically persists. We may imagine that the poem could have ended here, in the same way that the divided nation is unable to become whole; but the poem continues by evoking family relationships that must "go unsaid" and returns us to the battle even as the figures on the field grow smaller in the distance, become "figures dwindling in size" (19). The poem expresses its protesting voice by recording both its distance from the Korean War and the wounds that persist despite the years. Although the passages explicitly about the war are cast in the past tense, much of the poem is written into the present; indeed, the speaker can "know" the "crowd's ambition" because such crowds still congregate and make their demands. As Kim tells us, "The eye won't be appeased" (19) and the emphatic present tense of the contraction reminds us that the way we see is indelibly marked by war, even as the figures gradually recede from view. A lost figure of a schoolchild propels us into the future tense:

> His name stitched on his school uniform, flame
> Flame around what will fall as ash
> Kerosene soaked skin housing what will burn. (19)

Distance does not make the flames any less scorching; their intensity pushes them before us.

"Under Flag" finally closes with an image:

> Faces spread in a field
>
> On the breeze what might be azaleas in full bloom
>
> Composed of many lengths of bone (UF, 19)

The poem shows us the effects of years under "Sun, an affliction hitting white" and returns us to the battlefield. Even if the poem has cast the battle itself into the past, the battlefield cannot be left behind and the poem returns to it to find a place of uneasy rest. The Korean War settled with the divide, even after the losses of both Korean civilians and U.S. soldiers, and what is striking about this final image is that the faces in this field could be Korean or American.

This closing image echoes Pound's most famous Imagist poem:

> In a Station of the Metro
>
> The apparition of these faces in the crowd;
>
> petals on a wet, black bough ("In a Station of the Metro," [1913], 1286).

Pound presents us with an "apparition," and this image has been fashioned with techniques learned from his study of Chinese writing. In his monumental study *The Pound Era*, Hugh Kenner asks, "is the surest way to a fructive western idea the misunderstanding of an eastern one?" (1997, 230), and Pound's serendipitous discovery of Chinese poetry provides the impetus for his revolution in American poetry. In Ernest Fenollosa's papers, bequeathed to Pound by his widow, Pound discovers meditations on precise seeing, visible etymologies, and the poetic nature of the ideogram; these assertions provide Pound with the necessary evidence for his Imagist doctrine.[3] According to Fenollosa, Chinese writing bypasses the arbitrariness of the literary sign that cripples Western writing; in this logic, the ideogram is a uniquely true instance of language. And, crucially for Pound, accurate poetry, too, can demonstrate a one-to-one correspondence between the thing seen and the marks put together to designate it on the page. In 1913, Pound defines the Image: "An 'Image' is that which presents an intellectual and emotional complex in an instant of time" (*Literary*, "A Retrospect," 1935, 4). The Image, then, can function in the manner of Pound's belief in the ideogram.

"In a Station of the Metro" encapsulates Pound's idea of the Image. Instead of describing the crowd, Pound shows us their faces in the flash of Imagism's "instant of time." The poem has been carefully crafted: we note the doubling patterns of the second line posed against the tripling gait of the first, the hardness with which "Petals" is stressed, the near-rhyme that seals this small poem into its lapidary and complete figuration. Pound tells us, "the image is the word beyond formulated language" (*Memoir*, 1970, 88), and the Chinese character provides the model for the embodiment for this "word beyond formulated language." The art of the ideogram, with its precise strokes, stands as Pound's ideal.

The beauty of the faces figured as petals in Pound's poem resonates with Kim's image, but the contrast between life and death establishes an inexorable difference. Kim's image is the afterimage of Pound's: these faces have been reduced to their bones; they are like flowers because they dot the field. The collision of the subway with the natural image in Pound's poem has been recast onto an altogether different level; if Pound's juxtaposition surprised with its urban setting, Kim's is startling in its deceptively pastoral quality. The flowerlike faces in the field and the bones that comprise them have returned to nature. What is missing is the modern engine that created the image—and by virtue of its significant absence, Kim leads us directly to it. The negative space of this image is the machinery of war, and it is Kim's innovation to use the tools of Imagism to direct us to what is no longer visible. In this, she turns Imagism away from the image and toward the past, to the event of war.

Kim's image startles because it uses the precise art of the modernists, borrowed from Far Eastern poetry, and retrains it on the Asian stage of war. Imagist technique, famous for its evocation of presence and emotion, is here borrowed in the service of rendering something that happened in the past immediate in its emotional impact. Kim turns the Imagist innovation back on itself, taking it back to its origins in Asia, and through this imagined return she renews the innovation of the beginning of the century into a tool for a late-twentieth-century plight. If we return to the beginning of "Under Flag," we see that the poem opens with the motion of "Casting and again casting" and the present tense of the figures of evacuees in this opening, in the "Rigor of those who carry households on their backs" (UF, 16). I suggest that it is possible to cast this particular line even further: the "singular wave" of these evacuees is part of a larger movement of many singular waves that make their way to American shores. The poem gestures toward the different flows of displaced people whose link to another time and place shapes their relation to America. And if "Casting and again casting" is further stretched to mean casting and *re*casting, in this line the poem may already be signaling the labor of reenvisioning and refashioning modernist poetry that closes it. Recasting the American poetic lineage allows the poet both to register her difference and even dissent and to add herself to the line.

For Kim, the active manipulation of the stylistic traces of what had been an American poetic renewal provides a means of addressing American involvement in the world beyond its borders. In assigning the Image to the traces of the Korean War, she forces the American orientalist poetic renewal to confront the neocolonial maneuvers of American intervention in the Far East. What finally emerges from this confrontation is the fact of American manipulation. Yet we must also see that, in recasting Imagism, she finds a supremely lyrical way to close a difficult poem. The closing image in "Under Flag" results in a strangely still moment, fraught with desolation and a chilling loveliness.

Epic Duration

Kim's long poem, *Dura*, comprised of seven titled sections, is a refashioning of the American long poem as initiated by Walt Whitman. In his study of the American epic, James E. Miller describes the major tenets of this poetry that Whitman inaugurates: this new epic is characterized by freer forms, an emphasis on interior action, the casting of the self of the poet as hero, and it is set in a continuous present in which new myths are actively sought and created (Miller, *American*, 1979, 34–36). Pound takes up this inheritance and uses it in his ideological epic, and in a later poem in *Under Flag*, "Demarcations," Kim alludes to *The Cantos*, the arduous work that stands at the other end from Pound's Imagist legacy. In his modernist epic, Pound takes on the mantle of American bard, installing his idiosyncratic voice as the guiding force in the text. Pound's instantiation of the American bard expresses, arguably, the end of the possibility of this figure; *The*

Cantos explicitly addresses the possibilities of the American epic and the difficulties of the bardic position in the modern world.[4]

The closing lines of "Demarcation," in its depiction of the Korean divide, returns us to *The Cantos*:

> As compass locates relocates cuts fresh figures
> As silence to mate(d) world
> Not founded by mother or father
> Spun into coherence (cohere)
> Cohere who can say (UF, 38)

The particular tragedy of Korea lies in its continued and singular division, and the poems in *Under Flag* never attempt to resolve its paired figures into something more harmonious. The arbitrary line of the thirty-eighth parallel "cuts fresh figures," two new figures in the world. This rupture creates what Kim suggests could be considered a mated pair (in a mated world, aligned with the dyad of the United States and Soviet Union in the cold war), but one that disfigures the notion of a couple. Further, the idea of a country "Not founded by mother or father" underscores the unnaturalness of the division, one that issues from a larger power struggle between superpowers. The dismissal of coherence in the final lines of "Demarcations" provides an ending while describing a continuing separation.

This question of coherence takes us to Pound's failed coherence at the end of *The Cantos*: "I cannot make it cohere" (Canto CXVI). Kim invokes Pound's voice of epic failure, but in her hands what emerges is the fact of this division having been "Spun into coherence." The trouble is that the incoherence of the division has become obscured, and Kim indicts those who would cover over this fact. Unlike *The Cantos*, it is not that she cannot make it cohere, but that in historical and present fact it simply does not. Pound's fantasy of the world providing models for a coherent state that drives *The Cantos* does not quite fall apart, but he laments that the poem does; in contrast, the world Kim witnesses remains arbitrarily divided and she implicates attempts at spinning this fact into coherence.

Following Pound's epic innovation, Theresa Hak Kyung Cha revisits the American long poem: *Dictée* brings Korean history into the continuous present of epic because Korea's fractured past exists in the present of the "diseuse," the complicated heroine of the text. Cha's experiments create a crucial foundation for the poets who follow her work because she reimagines the form in dazzling ways; the free flow between history and myth in Cha's art is the cornerstone of her reinvention of the American long poem. Myung Mi Kim follows this lineage, and in the wake of the American bard, I believe that the means the modernists took in order to find a uniquely American voice have become useful tools for describing a complicated relationship to America. Indeed, minority poets are uniquely positioned to take up this particular inheritance; Kim's active manipulation of the vestiges of the bard in fact make this lineage new for the end of the century.

It is with *Dura* that Kim deliberately takes up the tradition of the American long poem as reformulated by Cha. The title of the poem itself is a tribute to the labors of *Dictée*'s diseuse; the title word itself returns us to a crucial opening in *Dictée*: "She makes complete her duration" (28). We must remember that this line describes the diseuse in her readiness to be a voice for others; this completion results from the expansion of the diseuse in order to take on these others. Although Kim does not use the array of languages that Cha does within her text, this title sends us into different languages: "dura" is the French passé simple for "to last" in the third person singular. This conjugated verb does not pinpoint a subject, though the fact of the passé simple not only makes it a completed action but lends the verb a written quality. Perhaps this definitive past tense in French signals the fact of Kim's predecessor, Cha and *Dictée* itself. We may imagine that *Dura* not only refers to the state of the diseuse during the ritual, but suggests as well the entirety of *Dictée* as a completed project that lasted but is now completed; *Dura* takes the whole of *Dictée* as its first premise.

In addition, "dura" can be a complete sentence in Spanish, and in Spanish, the conjugated verb is in the present tense; this word can be translated as the sentence "It lasts." Hence, if we switch into Spanish, we can see that though Cha's ritual has been completed, Kim's project is very much in the present of its duration. Indeed, there is a sense of the future in the sentence "It lasts"—we may imagine the extension of this project of duration as well. There is another possibility in Spanish, however: "dura" is also the adjective "hard," and its ending makes this a modifier for a feminine noun. This adjectival and gendered sense of "dura" suggests a revision of Cha's gendered diseuse in Kim's text: the quality of hardness that had been assigned to the stones in *Dictée* may here be applied to the heroine herself. These readings into different languages provide multiple approaches to this single word yet keep the word itself opaque. Kim's poetry has harder edges;[5] the kinds of connective tissue that Cha so elegantly formulates in her mythic invocations have fallen away in Kim's work because Kim's project exposes seams at every opportunity and refuses coherence, even the kind of fragile understanding of the single boundary that Cha arrives at by *Dictée*'s end. This is a rather different speaker, one whose focus is not so much to allow others but who is herself a sharpened tool that can engrave her words into stone.

WEST AND EAST AND BACK AGAIN

The opening section of the poem, "Cosmography," elaborates the universe of the text. This section opens with a sense of a primordial and prelinguistic ocean, "The beginnings of things" (*Dura* 9), and goes on to show us the slow dawning of land and language through an individual figure: "I see . . . and look about"(ellipses in original, 11). This gradual observation of the world is interspersed with sudden, staccato visions ("Parchment bark skin," 11), which demonstrate the sudden epiphanies that happen with discovery. The "I" of this poem cannot separate learning to see the world from learning to write it, and we can see her handwriting in the text as she translates four words—"a short lyric poem or, the founder of a family," "an ancestral tablet," "a new world," and "dried radish leaves"—into Korean. These four words have a mysterious connection in English; the first three phrases describe origins, but the fourth is a puzzling addition. Yet the inclusion of this final word is understandable if one hears the Korean: the sound of "a new world," shin-sae-gae, sounds like "dried radish leaves," shi-rae-ghee. In fact, the first two words in the list rhyme in Korean, and the third and fourth describe a more complicated aural connection; we can see that the Korean words drive the movement in this list. In *Dictée*, Hangul has a kind of ghostly presence; by contrast, Hangul is an integral part of the establishment of *Dura*'s cosmography, and Korean supplies a kind of ordering logic to the text. "Cosmography" closes with an invocation:

> Sound as it comes. Alkali. Snag snag sang.
> Usher liberty. (18)

The emphasis on sound as a chemical base for the reactive forces in the text is followed by a quick demonstration, from "snag" to "sang," and the closing line, "Usher liberty," stands as an invocation for the six sections to come.

"Cosmography" elaborates gradual discovery, and Kim includes the titles of the last three sections of the poem in this opening section: "Thirty and Five Books," "Progress in Learning," and "Hummingbird." What has not been explicitly figured in this opening cosmography of the text, however, are the three sections between this opening "Cosmography" and "Thirty and Five Books": "Measure," "Labor," and "Charts." In a more detailed fashion than the broader opening strokes of "Cosmography," these middle sections lay the groundwork for the "I," which fully emerges with the "Thirty and Five Books" section. *Dura*'s universe is divided into East and West, and these sections describe the basis for the movements between these realms.

"Measure" opens with an epigraph from *The Travels of Marco Polo* and the section imagines this foundational journey eastward. This epigraph, however, is balanced with that of a fourteenth-century Korean poem: "All of you whose boats are leaky/heed the warning and take care" (*Dura*, 21). The section as a whole takes up this dialogue, imagining Polo's voyage out against the experience of those living in the fantastic region Polo seeks to discover. The page embeds the experience of the Asian native into that of the traveler bound for the East:

Motion on the seas

Larded ships

   : Gather soil and water

   : Morning risen evening fallen mushroom

So writ the purpose

Voyage laid bare (*Dura*, 23)

Against the backdrop of the ocean, the lines after the colons show us the actions of those who work the Eastern land. Although the use of the colons may suggest that there is some equivalence between the experience of the voyagers and the lives of those who live in the East, the poem will go on to proliferate the lines that describe the voyagers' experience and the space after the colon will gradually fall silent. After "A way is open(ed), a hole is made" (27), we are given only the colon (":") surrounded by empty space, and the last page of the section shows us a series of alternating lines and stranded colons. It is important, however, that this mark—in its stubborn and repeated appearance—persists even in the face of this onslaught.

The next section, "Labors," describes the opposite movement, from East to West: "Due west directly west" (*Dura*, 32). Those who make this voyage encounter hard work, a labor that comes to define this New World:

Its second member /ric/ meaning "powerful"
First member /am/, "labor," endurance of toil (34)

The component parts of "America" show us two very different kinds of "members" in this Western land: those who are powerful, and those who toil. Kim suggests different ways of considering these two levels, as "Two cycles of growth":

First rank and chiasma
A bearing. Affix. (*Dura*, 35)

Perhaps we may be affixed to a certain bearing, a particular position, but the inclusion of "chiasma" suggests richer possibilities of cross-connection.

This notion of crossing between different positions is carefully developed in the third section of *Dura*'s groundwork, "Chart." This difficult and powerful section creates a complicated music comprised of two separate strands, kept distinct in their consistent placement on the page. On each left-hand page, we are given seven lines of phrases that describe the condition of the immigrant and her evocation of a Korean past. The first of these lines, "Collect the years' duration," reminds us again of Cha's diseuse, and the observations that follow along these left-hand pages are memories of hardship in Korea from within the expanse of "An America as big as it is" (*Dura*, 42). These passages describe the effects of occupation and war, like the bitter explanation that a mother "doesn't have legs" (48). These pages conclude with a succinct and powerful statement from the immigrant in America: "To be precisely from nowhere" (50).

Along the right-hand pages, however, we are shown compact collisions that graphically demonstrate the immigrant condition:

Purpose lost
Sure belief lost
Ritual feign
Hostile warrant
Burning stylus
Manacle pole
Dispel embrace
Native place (*Dura*, 39)

The word "dispel" takes us back to *Dictée*; Cha used this term to describe the act of writing, notably in a description of giving blood figured as ink. Kim engages with Cha's diseuse, reimagining her for this epic. This version, however, does not take on others and speak for them in the manner of *Dictée*. Instead, Kim imagines the confinement of this figure ("Manacle pole"), a diseuse with her belief lost and her ritual feigned.

Further, this burning pen describes a condition in which words can cross and collide. The first two lines encourage a chiasmic action on the part of the reader: "Purpose" can cross over to the "lost" on the next line, and vice versa with "Sure belief." Similarly, the last two lines suggest a chiasmic reading: "Dispel" with "place"; "Native" with "embrace." And the displacement of this "native embrace" describes the isolation of *Dura*, in which the words themselves create drama and tension in their position. There is no simple rule for reading these passages, and Kim uses all manner of sound plays to collide the two terms of each line, but lines that can be crossed like "Human density/River condition" (47) show us the imbrication of the human condition within the natural condition of the river. Further, lines like "Heir inculcate/Apparent corona" (49) suggest reading straight down, connecting "Heir" to "apparent." This downward drive sets up the dramatic closing couplet of these right-hand-page lines: "Jutting shaped/Baffle flung" (49). The double "t" of "Jutting" lends its consonantal force to the word directly below, converting "Baffle" into "Battle." To be able to consider simultaneously "Baffle" and "Battle" is one of the fruits of Kim's complicated word plays; she trains our eyes and ears to make adventurous overlapping and crossing moves in our reading.

Kim uses the phrase "Crude fugue" (*Dura*, 45) in one of these compact lines, and we can extend this phrase to describe the whole of the section. The different forms of the right- and left-hand pages alternate, and, like a musical fugue, one strand opens the section, with the other lagging slightly behind and finally closing the piece. The themes in the two lines are interconnected, but as one touches the other, sounds suddenly resonate together. Indeed, it is only at the second or third glance that we realize how systematically the two halves are plotted—it is a single emotional drive that moves both strands, and the two variations create a complex and extending musical line that stretches out the momentary emotion of the lyric poem into a longer and dramatic act of clarifying emotion.

Hero's Journey

After the careful establishment of East and West in the first four sections of *Dura*, "Thirty and Five Books," the longest section, shows us the journey of the immigrant. The section opens with an admission: "Never having been here when the sun rose" (53), an initial moment in the past, but we move rapidly through this unknown past, arriving at the point of "Deployments to the assigned parallel" (54), the nation divided. This is a compressed history of Korea, and upon this establishment of the DMZ we meet something like a protagonist: "Unrecognized she went about the city" (54). This line, taken from Odysseus's movements through the Phaiakian city while shrouded by Athena's powers, describes Odysseus's last stopping place before his return to Ithaka. As a guest in Alkinoos's palace Odysseus tells his greatest tales, and with the assistance of his host he is sent on his way home fully stocked and rested. Clearly, this is a journey in the epic sense of the word; and in referring to this moment in *The Odyssey*, Kim pinpoints both the heights of Odysseus's skill as a storyteller and the beginning of Odysseus's actual journey home. Kim deliberately calls upon the epic voyage and refigures it for the "she" of the female immigrant whose path is a direct one from Korea to the United States. Further, in alluding to this moment in *The Odyssey* Kim suggests that the move from Korea to the United States is a kind of homecoming. This is more than an "ironic parallel": perhaps this suggestion of the Korean going to the United States to claim her household may implicate the shaping force of U.S. foreign policy in Korea; it is a kind of homecoming to the neocolonial center.

The first few pages of this section provide us with markers that place us in Korea: "Various kinds of rice in the manner of living in that country" (*Dura*, 55), "Little in the way of progress. Firesticks bundled" (59), "Primitive tabulation of need" (60). This enduring agricultural existence is subject to violence from without:

> First assembled fire. Far off estimation the sun offers.
>
> Operate machinery and the line. Bark branch phrase interrupted.
>
> Distended beyond assembly and parts.
>
> Describe the success of the random bomb. Black rain had its mark. (61)

"Bark branch" is a phrase literally interrupted, broken by military intervention, and this dispassionate mention of an exploding bomb is followed, on the next page, with a playground scene previously hinted at in "Charts":

> Speed of water drop. Speed of cease-fire. Playground
> when the planes close in. The hands of the boy and girl
> are firm hands. Fume, vapor, forge of metal aimed. Each
> child's hand in the mother's hands. No heads, fugitive
> heads. Eyes turned lid. Blood mat hair. Each their
> hands (held). (62)

This compact description shows us the speed of the event, the horror of the simultaneous separation, and fusing together of bodies as a result of the smoking metal.

The next page shows us the migration:

> In so locating a time of geography before the compass.
> Do not ask again where are we.
> [...]
> Population gathered to population. More uninhabited
> space in America than in elsewhere. (63)

In the confusion of the journey, we can hear the voice of the adult admonishing the child for asking "Where are we?" In setting off for this new land, this family takes a course long ventured, "before the compass": the geography of the ocean between East and West remains the same. America is remarkable for its space, but the tendency of "Population gathered to population" signals the troubles that are to come in this place of uninhabited spaces.

AMERICAN SPACE

Immediately after the statement of arrival in America, *Dura* shows us the L.A. riots:

> He was wearing a white T-shirt and jeans
> Beat the fresh burning
>> The boy in the newspaper wore a dark shirt
> Flakes of fire ripen fire
>> It could not be my son
> Agate of insistence
>> Contents of the boy's pocket—a dime and a pen
> Percussive
>> In the *LA Times* the picture was in color
> Body moving in circle be fire
>> What looked black in the Korean newspaper was
> my son's blood (64–65)

This passage describes a literalization of Cha's conflation of blood and ink in *Dictée*; here, the bloodied shirt is rendered in black ink in the newspaper, and this giving of blood supplies words for the newspaper. This blood does not have an expressive function; it is only the result of violence. Kim frames this episode within the hard facts of economics: "Express the value of A over B. Dominant relation as that of owners of commodities" (*Dura*, 71). The factionalism within what had been imagined as "uninhabited space" results in another scene of smoking ruins.

Kim shows us different ethnic groups as variables in a painful and persistent equation:

> _____ arrived in America. Bare to trouble and
> foresworn. Aliens aboard three ships off the coast.
> _____ and _____ clash. Police move in.
>
> What is nearest is destroyed. (*Dura*, 67)

This passage presents *Dura*'s most blunt portrait of America. Like a document to be filled out, these blanks demonstrate the process of becoming American: after one set has arrived, more aliens hover just off the coast. And we are not led to imagine that these recent arrivals in America will ever fully shed their alien status. Kim makes this clear for even those who have inhabited America's space for generations:

> Torch and fire. Translate: 38th parallel. Translate:
> the first shipload of African slaves was landed at
>> Jamestown (68)

The ship off the coast carries not only the next wave of immigrants, but suggests the ships of African slaves; these longtime inhabitants, too, retain a sense of their alien status in America. This rewritten translation exercise describes an unrelenting pattern, showing us that translating the Korean experience into America is an echo of the African American one.

The equivalence of the groups that can be filled in for the two blanks of the repeated American story is here demonstrated for the two groups implicated in the L.A. riots, and both parties have arrived on these shores as a result of American intervention: for Koreans, the arbitrary assignment of the thirty-eighth parallel which the United States effected, dividing the nation in two and allowing the subsequent establishment of a puppet regime in the south; for African Americans, the commissioned slave ships. Kim goes on to imagine other possible groups that could fill the blank spaces:

> Bodies in propulsion. Guatemalan, Korean, African-American
> sixteen year olds working check-out lanes. Hard and noisy
> enunciation.
>
> A banter English gathers carriers.
>
> What is nearest is destroyed. (*Dura*, 73)

The figuration of "A banter English" amassing speakers turns the concept of naturalization on its head: instead of aliens folding themselves into America and English, a spoken English gathers and carries along these aliens. This is the extent of naturalization: a shared, spoken banter that brings together its speakers.

The passage closes with a line heard twice in this section, "What is nearest is destroyed." This is the conclusion drawn from examining America, and this repeated statement resonates with similar lines in *The Cantos*:

> What thou lovest well remains,
>> the rest is dross
> What thou lov'st well shall not be reft from thee
> What thou lov'st well is thy true heritage (Canto VXXXI)

Pound wrote these lines during his incarceration in Pisa, and their bittersweet recognition has been heralded as the point of greatest beauty in his epic. This allusion reminds us of the previous mention of the failure of coherence in *Under Flag*; in both cases, Kim mentions Pound at a moment of crisis in the notion of naturalization. She rewrites the modernist epic in order to question the American experience. In the face of the riots, however, the heroic self of Kim's epic arrives at a very different conclusion: Pound's "true heritage" is, for Kim, the Korean American son, and the fact of his death shows how readily what is nearest can "be reft from thee." This guarantee of destruction stands as a kind of truth of America on the order of the blank spaces of the two replaceable parties that clash.

This depiction of the riots closes with a series of proposals:

> Propose: constant translation. Propose: the
> application of the compass to navigation. Propose: from
> a settlement, a capital grows. Propose: foray, expansion.
> Propose: as relates to an America. Propose: as relates
> to immigrant. Propose: knowledge becomes the parlance
> of the state. Propose: sound combinations. Propose:
> nameless days. (*Dura* 78)

This frank discussion of the project at hand reminds us of the coda in "Cosmography": both sections close by mentioning the importance of sound, from the earlier "Sound as it comes" to this proposal for "sound combinations." This exhortation to "constant translation" itself translates "as relates to an America" as that which "relates to immigrant" because the story of the immigrant is the American story; as we have seen in the blank spaces in the American story, there is always a ship off the coast.

Kim explicitly shows us how the cosmography of the text "relates to immigrant" in a two-paged chronology, numbered from 6.1 to 35.0:

6.1   How expressed
[...]
9.8   One of the first words understood in English: stupid

10.9   Diamondback on Oklahoma red dirt
[...]
14.8   Lightning struck roof father spinning on ice
            and killed what happened in what order
[...]
28.3   A million marching in the streets
[...]
32.10   Given birth 5:05AM
[...]
35.0   If seventy is the sum of our years (*Dura*, 79–80)

The events described thus far in "Thirty and Five Books" have been devoted to showing two lands, Korea and America. This chronology refocuses the figure at the center of this text, she who "walked about the city": this is a chronology of Kim's life, a kind of autobiography. These personal memories inscribe her into the center of "Thirty and Five Books," and we see that her life is at the heart of this text in the title of this section, which rewrites her thirty-five years into books. In imagining *Dura* as a rewriting of the modernist epic, we see that the poet has herself entered the poem; she no longer exists above the action as the bard, the overriding voice of the epic.

This long section closes with a brief evocation of the final myth of *Dictée*, in which a young girl is given ten pockets of medicine for her ailing mother:

> Inside the hand-stitched pouch. Pebbles. A clean wind.
>
> Having arrived here. Trace of timber in a gravelly loam,
> possibly part of a collapsed fence.
>
> Affection to touch dirt.
>
> All harmonics sound. (*Dictée*, 85)

Kim imagines what was in the pockets of medicine in Cha's text, and this final arrival not into a house but its traces rewrites the moment of the child at the screened door in *Dictée*, about to enter home and cure her mother. In this case, the structure has fallen, but the closing lines provide a calming end to this lengthy examination of the immigrant experience. Although these lines do not somehow cover over the loss of "What is nearest is destroyed," they close on a note of affection. We touch the dirt after the destruction and cannot help but notice the sound of harmony— this is a recasting of the ringing bells that close *Dictée*, but this time the sound issues from the earth itself.

Constant Translation

"Progress in Learning" shows us the slow work of making progress and creating something like a home. This labor is arranged on the page in two diagonally placed and differently sized sets of lines. The smaller lines in the upper corner constantly remind us of the difficult realities and contexts of this hard-fought progress: these lines remark on the "accidents of places" (*Dura*, 89), suggest the relation between land and immigrant as something like that between "Host and swarm" (92) and finally caution us that "The same force could destroy all things alike" (93). Against this necessary voice, the other set of lines exhorts us to "Be the hostel in the light" (92) and even suggests that the work of our hands could be "Shaped like relation suggested like progress" (93). In "Cosmography," the line "Progress in learning" appears in the context of raising children, and what follows is a moment in which one can enjoy the fruits of the hard work of learning: "If one thing is seen and seen clearly and the effort to see it/Hummingbird in foxglove whir" (14). The hummingbird stands as a kind of test for seeing correctly, and the final section of the poem elaborates this vision.

"Hummingbird," the final section of *Dura*, opens with a translation exam, comprised of sentences that state homilies of agricultural life. This command to translate is reminiscent of *Dictée*, and after these twelve sentences, the poem seems to move us through the translation exam, starting with "Fill in the name" (*Dura*, 98). Any possible guidance or instruction is difficult to follow, however, because the lines are broken up with brackets inserted at random, grouping together different possible combinations of words beyond the line breaks and spaces. The passage meditates on these "Twelve calls and responses" but returns again and again to the figure of a hummingbird; the banality of the exercise is set aside, and the poet instead observes the hummingbird:

> All these letters including those classed as unnecessary
> or not genuine are formed by the sound of any voice
>
> O hummingbird, swift trill
>
> Open a page What does it look like (102)

The intervention of the hummingbird breaks into the dictated lines and refocuses our attention to the appearance of the page. Further, we are diverted from the task of translation into different contemplations of how words could be used more effectively: "Letter, syllable, and word model plurality/Studious need might useful arts explore" (*Dura*, 105). The translation exam has been set aside and Kim instead takes on the task of transforming translation itself into a useful art, an art that could assist "studious need"; *Dura* reforms the task of translation into a necessary art.

The poem goes on to suggest different events—working in a store, a brief courtroom scene—but gradually moves out of the difficult, bracketed phrases to contemplate the hummingbird:

> wright's deer vetch
> scarlet pimpernel
> filaree
> thistle
> monkey flower
> cow's parsnip
> scotch broom
> horse chestnut
> Hummingbird on lavender (*Dura*, 107)

This list describes a series of flowers with small blossoms that may entice the hummingbird, a catalog of flowers that delineates the possible journey of the hummingbird. This is the hummingbird's cosmography; the poem tells us that "Hummingbird happens as a sound first" (106), and from this sound we move on to careful observations, which ultimately result in mapping out the path of the hummingbird. Kim's epic maps the complicated movements of sound, paying particular attention to the transformative forces of the gulfs that must be bridged between the different points along the path. The epic finally ends with redefinitions of the critical concepts it engaged:

> *Place*, such expression as, *in fury*
> *Time*, for instance, *yesterday, at evening*, as in *purpose lost*
>
> *State* is, for instance, *having armor on, having shoes on*
>
> *Attitude* is, for instance, *is-lying, is-sitting, wayfarer*
>
> *Activity* is, for example, *burning, cutting*
>
> *Experiment* is each scroll of white pages joined together (*Dura*, 108)

These are the translations the poem has effected: each abstract concept is redrawn in terms of a single experience, an individual act. The end of what began writ large as cosmography closes on a new understanding of the individual condition, and this individual sense of each term closes on the poet herself, in her experiment.

The figure of the hummingbird finally brings together the minute observation of its image and of the points in its pathway, initiated by focusing on the sound of its hum. "Under Flag" took on the Image and locked its precise vision onto the Korean War; by *Dura*'s end, Kim brings together the American lyric and epic, image and journey. This play within an American tradition, however, is undergirded by the handwritten Hangul, which fills in the blanks in the epic cosmography—a precursor to the blanks to be filled in Kim's portrait of the American experience. Kim's work interrogates American action in Korea and Korean American experience in America, and her use of the modernist inheritance brings to the fore an American story, one that infiltrates the Far East and propels the constant arrival of new individuals to its shores, the ones who will fill in the blanks.

Notes

1. This lineage from Theresa Hak Kyung Cha to Myung Mi Kim is also discussed by Shu-mei Shih in "Nationalism and Korean Women's Writing: Theresa Hak Kyung Cha's *Dictée*," Juliana Spahr in *Everybody's Autonomy: Connective Reading and Collective Identity*, and Laura Hyun Yi Kang in *Compositional Subjects: Enfiguring Asian/American Women*. These readings tend to understand Kim

as a contestatory voice who uses the surface of words in order to register her difference. My analysis differs in linking Kim's art back to American modernist poetic
innovations.

2. I follow Kim in using "America" for the United States at certain moments
because of the connection to an American literary genealogy that this inquiry
foregrounds.

3. As elaborated in Pound's edited version of Fenollosa's essay, "The Chinese
Written Character as a Medium for Poetry." Interestingly, Pound effects his revolution in American verse through lessons learned from the Orient—and I think the
mediating term of the Orient reflects his own distance from America, the home
he has fled.

4. I read Pound's bardic intentions in his 1909 essay "What I Feel About Walt
Whitman," in which Pound evinces a desire to achieve Whitman's stature in ac-
cessing "the sap and fibre of America" (*Selected Prose*, 1973, 145).

5. Similarly, Kim's poetry privileges the consonants in Hangul over Cha's fascination with its vowels (as seen in Cha's video work); Kim's work repeatedly returns
to the hard sounds of the Korean alphabet, as evidenced in her poem "Primer," a
series of meditations on each of the consonants in Hangul (*The Bounty*, 1996).

Works Cited

Cha, Theresa Hak Kyung. *Dictée*. Berkeley, CA: Third Woman Press, 1995, 1982.

Fenollosa, Ernest. *The Chinese Written Character as a Medium for Poetry*. Ezra
Pound, ed. [1920]. San Francisco: City Lights, 1986.

Kang, Laura Hyun Yi. *Compositional Subjects: Enfiguring Asian/American
Women*. Durham, NC: Duke University Press, 2002.

Kenner, Hugh. *The Pound Era*. Berkeley: University of California Press, 1971.

Kim, Elaine H. "Korean American Literature," in *An Interethnic Companion to
Asian American Literature*. King-Kok Cheung, ed. (pp. 156–91). Cambridge:
Cambridge University Press, 1997.

Kim, Myung Mi. *The Bounty*. Minneapolis: Chax Press, 1996.

———. *Dura*. Los Angeles: Sun and Moon Press, 1998.

———. *Under Flag*. Berkeley, CA: Kelsey St. Press, 1991.

Miller, James E., Jr. *The American Quest for a Supreme Fiction: Whitman's Legacy
in the Personal Epic*. Chicago: University of Chicago Press, 1979.

Pound, Ezra. *A Memoir of Gaudier-Brzeska*. New York: New Directions, 1970,
1914.

———. "In a Station of the Metro," in *The Norton Anthology of American Literature*. Volume 2, 6th Edition. Nina Baym, ed. (p. 1286). New York: Norton,
2002.

———. *Literary Essays of Ezra Pound*. T. S. Eliot, ed. New York: New
Directions, 1935.

———. *Selected Prose of Ezra Pound*. William Cookson, ed. New York: New
Directions, 1973.

Shih, Shu-mei. "Nationalism and Korean Women's Writing: Theresa Hak Kyung Cha's *Dictée*," in *Speaking the Other Self: American Women Writers*. Jeanne Campbell Reesman, ed. (pp. 144–62). Athens: University of Georgia Press, 1997.

Spahr, Juliana. *Everybody's Autonomy: Connective Reading and Collective Identity*. Tuscaloosa: University of Alabama Press, 2001.

12 A Way in the World of an Asian American Existence

Agha Shahid Ali's Transimmigrant Spacing of North America and India and Kashmir

MAIMUNA DALI ISLAM

KASHMIRI-AMERICAN poet Agha Shahid Ali, on May, 5, 2000, while undergoing treatment for brain cancer, told his friend Amitav Ghosh, the noted Indian writer, that his battle with cancer was coming to an end. Among the rustles of spring and of new beginnings, Ali told his friend that the news from his latest brain scan was not good at all, and that, basically, the doctors were going to stop all his medicines—the chemotherapy and so on. "They give me a year or less," Ali poignantly encapsulated his situation to his friend (Ghosh, "Ghat," 2002, 35). When Ghosh asked Ali what his plans were for the rest of his time on earth, Ali responded, interestingly enough, with the statement, "I would like to go back to Kashmir and die" (35). Ali's sentiment is striking because in his desire for a final resting space, he specified Kashmir as his home, choosing in his hyphenated Kashmiri-American existence a hierarchical preference for the country that he had left decades ago. Ali's preference in Ghosh's interview is significant because, throughout his career as a poet and as an academic in the United States, Ali considered both Kashmir and the United States to be his home, and he proudly emphasized the fact that he belonged comfortably and equally in both countries. Rejecting the patterns of homelessness or rootlessness found in discourses by transnational immigrants, Ali often emphasized, in interviews and essays, that he always felt rooted in both India and the United States, a sentiment captured well in a parenthetical, but paradoxically emphasized, aside in the essay "The Rebel's Silhouette," where Ali describes himself as "a bilingual, bicultural (but never rootless) being" (1995, 79). In the essay, Ali does acknowledge that his poetry can sometimes give readers the idea that, in his departure from India, like other postcolonial writers, he has been left feeling unanchored from a homeland. For example, Ali cited a poem of his own called "Dear Editor," from his 1992 collection of poems, *Belovéd Witness*. In the poem, especially in the last line, Ali states explicitly that he deals with words from mixed cultures and that mix of cultures leaves him feeling rootless. The last line of that poem exemplifies typical transnational themes of displacement and of diaspora, and the poem appears to demonstrate that Ali's mix of cultures has actually left him without an India or an America to call home. Ali insists, however, that despite what the poem may appear to say, he has never felt uprooted or disconnected from his homeland, and that while his life has been binary and hyphenated,[1] it has "[c]ertainly not" been "[r]ootless" ("Rebel's Silhouette," 1995, 78). Ali explains that that particular poem was a form of discourse, and that he was simply discoursing about the "inherent dominative modes" of prevailing postcolonial theories that dictated that "one should not write in English because it was not an Indian language" (78). Thus for Ali, the poem is his response to academic readings of his work, and to literary theory that defines—or tries to define—how a transnational person can or cannot and does or does not use a second language to define the experiences of one's mother tongue. Thus, it is not that he felt uprooted from his homeland but, rather, that his use of English as a medium of discourse made him feel as though he had to be. Significantly, Ali insisted that the problem lay in the assumptions underlying the "inherent dominative mode" of postcolonial studies and in their assertions that English (as a language) for postcolonial natives is and has to be "alien" (78). For Ali, both English and Hindi (and Urdu) and both the United States and India (and Kashmir) always lay firmly within his grasp, and despite his movements and time away from each country, Ali never felt that he had given up India in order to live in the United States. Instead, both languages and both countries became home. It is this truly binary existence of Ali's that Amitav Ghosh finds remarkable, and he states that for Ali, "America and India were the two poles of his life, and he was at home in both a way that was utterly easeful and unproblematic" ("Ghat," 2002, 34).

If we are to take Ali's protestations seriously, then from this vantage point, Ali was a poet who was simultaneously Kashmiri and American, and who linguistically and conceptually had never left Kashmir or had never left the United States. Although a poet's identity does not necessarily define the identity of the poet's persona in his or her works, I do find that Ali's poetry lacks the distinct qualities of either diasporic, exilic, or transnational writing—all of which are anchored by the common premise of homelessness, or a loss of a home. Instead, Ali was a poet who truly celebrated his hyphenated existence by equally embracing and using both North America and India as muses for his poetry. The end result is poetry that traverses nations and histories with ease, and in the spirit of genuine multinationalism. It is poetry that is multicultural in the truest sense of the word, but is not in the sense of it being an amorphous cultural stew, boundaryless and devoid of any specific national signifiers. What makes

Ali a challenging poet is the fact that he etched with equally vibrant colors his Indian and his American identities, never relegating to any one identity the sepia-tinged nostalgia of a lost home. Unlike a lot of postcolonial writers, Ali was never out-of-place in this world, and his India never became an imaginary homeland.

Several critics, however, define Ali as a postcolonial and diasporic writer. Lavina Shankar and Rajini Srikanth point out that immigrant writings (minority and ethnic literature) in the United States are generally set against "the backdrop of the U.S. sociopolitical landscape" ("South Asian," 2000, 371), while "postcolonial exilic, expatriated Asians in America, or... South Asians' writing frequently exhibits a tendency to render the United States not as the central stage on which the action of their texts unfold, but as only one site of relevance amidst a number of possible locations worldwide" (371). Shankar and Srikanth find that South Asians in North America exhibit what Shirley Geok-lin Lim has defined as the "exilic" sensibility or experience, where one's existence in the land to which one has immigrated is signified "by continued bonds to the lost homeland" (qtd. in "South Asian," 2000, 374). Thus, the exilic poet is diasporic, straddling two worlds, while never quite belonging to any one place. As Benzi Zhang defines it, diasporans are like "stranded 'migratory birds'—they are strangers from elsewhere who, without a sense of belonging, never feel at home in a new country yet unable to return to their homeland" ("Identity," 2000, 126), and diasporans have to mediate constantly between "home-ness and homeless-ness" (126). Jahan Ramazani, in his analysis of South Asian writers, argues that postcolonial poets have been "unhoused by travel, modernity, colonialism, etc." (Hybrid, 2001, 12) and are instead "[h]oused in houselessness" (13).[2] In a brief commentary on Ali's poem "Postcard from Kashmir" from the collection The Half-Inch Himalayas, Ramazani finds that "Ali dramatizes the postcolonial and diasporic condition that Homi Bhabha ... terms 'unhomeliness'—that is the condition of extraterritorial and cross-cultural initiations" (Hybrid, 2001, 12). Shankar and Srikanth also briefly discuss Ali's poems from the collection A Nostalgist's Map of America, and they find Ali to be an "exilic poet-persona . . . [who] re-presents the desperate loneliness and alienation of the postcolonial immigrant who, as a result of colonization can no longer live in the native homeland, and yet despondently searches for new communities" ("South Asian," 2000, 379). The critics, thus, place Ali firmly within the boundaries of transnational literature where the poet's depiction of the United States in his poetry acts simply as a backdrop to India, where "real living, meaning existence, takes place off the [American] turnpike—away from the frenetic motion that is America—and [instead] in India" (378), and the focus of Ali's artistic quest remains on recapturing or attempting to recapture his lost homeland of Kashmir. Ali's Kashmir is given a privileged position, and in contrast to Ali's own sentiments (supported by writers such as Ghosh), the critics categorize Ali as one yearning for a home to which he cannot return.[3]

Although Ali's poetry has some distinct markers of transnational literature—that is, there are yearnings for and re-creations of a Kashmir that are infused with memories of a past that are seemingly lost, as evidenced through poem titles such as "A Lost Memory of Delhi," "In Memory of Begum Akhtar," and "I Dream It Is Afternoon When I Return to Delhi" (*The Half-Inch Himalayas*)—the poems actually capture an India that is present, palpable, and coexistent with the North American landscape of the poet's current life, and the consequent poetry captures dual existences that are both independent of each other as well as complementary to each other—it is a poetry that I would define as transimmigrant[4] writing, that is, it is a literature that demonstrates an anchoring in two distinct cultures, two distinct homes, that exist and coexist independent of each other. I emphasize the issue of independent homes because so much of one's ethnicity or nationality in postcolonial or transnational literature is defined by the transgressions of boundaries or by the hyphen in a hyphenated identity, and the consequent posttransgression-of-boundary identity heralds the presencing of a new hybrid space that cannot or does not have any authentic features of the homeland—and the homeland can be the place that one has left or it can be the place that is nonrepresentational because it is now an imaginary construction of the past—or of the land to which one has immigrated (since this land is not one's own). The hybrid space is one of restlessness and of motion, and is a transnational space beyond any one culture. In his opening to *The Location of Culture*, Homi Bhabha states: "It is the trope of our times to locate the question of culture in the realm of the *beyond* . . . [and] [t]he 'beyond' is neither a new horizon, nor a leaving behind of the past . . . in the fin de siecle, we find ourselves in the moment of transit where space and time cross to produce complex figures of difference and identity. For there is a sense of disorientation, a disturbance of direction, in the 'beyond': an exploratory, restless movement" (1994, 1). In his analysis, Bhabha finds that the demography of the new internationalism is the "history of postcolonial migration . . . the poetics of exile, the grim prose of political and economic refugees" (5), and in this demographic space, "the boundary becomes a place from which something begins its presencing" (5). And it is the space of intervention emerging in the cultural interstices that "introduces creative invention into existence . . . [a] recreation of self in the world of travel, the resettlement of the borderline community of migration" (9). Bhabha's articulation of the hybrid space is a powerful phenomenological approach to understanding the boundaries of one's existence or the presencing of one's identity. However, I am hesitant to place Ali in Bhabha's "Third Space" because it is an "alien territory" (38) and an "'inter'—the cutting edge of translation and negotiation, the *in-between* space—that carries the burden of the meaning of culture" (38).[5] I am also hesitant to place Ali in the space of cultural hybridity of U.S. ethnic studies, where "hybridity" has become synonymous with the pluralistic, multiethnic, and multicultural world of literary studies.[6] I emphasize that Ali's poetry is neither a "mixing of cultures" nor a hybridized-interstitial representation of his Kashmiri and American identities, since I find that such a hybridity signifies a dilution of the national markers in the hyphenated identity equation, resulting consequently in a "melting pot" stew that effaces all distinguishing aspects of one's diverse cultural background.[7] Furthermore, in transnational studies, the binary aspects of one's hyphenated existence are set at polar opposites to each other, that is, to be American is to not be Kashmiri, and to be Kashmiri is to not be American, or that by being one, the other must be elided—in a Michael Ondaatjian sort-of-way from *Running in the Family*, where the presence of Canada—the festivities of a party, the "[s]treet lights bounc[ing] off the snow" (*Running in the Family*, 1982, 21), and the brittle Lake Ontario lake wind howling over "frozen cars hunched like sheep" (21)—is superseded by a dream of Asia, by a Sri Lankan "[d]awn through a garden," and by "the floors of red cement polished smooth, cool against bare feet" (17). Even though Ondaatje had lived in Canada for decades by the time he wrote about his return to Sri Lanka, Ondaatje's Canada has an incidental presence (it could have been any Western country), and its sole purpose is to give Ondaatje a space from which to run back to his childhood home. I find that Ali's poetry, instead, houses him, if you will, firmly and comfortably in both the United States and in India, and he represents both nations as legitimate anchors to his existence. This is demonstrated in and through his poetry, in a unique transimmigrant space that is situated within the narrative and textual space of poetry.

A comparative study of Ali's early collections of poetry, *Bone Sculpture* (1972) and *In Memory of Begum Akhtar* (1979), both of which contain poetry written before Ali moved to the United States in 1975, as well as of the later collections, *The Half-Inch Himalayas* (1987) and *A Nostalgist's Map of America* (1991), written after Ali had been living in the United States for more than a decade, shows virtually no consecutive difference in Ali's treatment of India. Also, in contrast to other critics' categorization of Ali's poetry as embodying the postcolonial "exilic poet-persona," who is desperately lonely and forever searching for a home, Ali's poetry embodies a poet persona who never lost India because it remains entirely within his grasp. This is evident in his earliest poetry, at which point he had not yet left India for the United States. For example, in "Painting a Kashmir

Landscape," from the 1979 collection, Ali states:

> I took the peaks by the neck,
> my hands holding the silver crayon:
> Snow covered the naked Harmukh.
>
> I walked by the Dal ...
>
> My colors could hold nothing:
> As I caught the reflections, one
> by one,
> the sunset ran through my fingers. (*In Memory of Begum Akhtar*, 14)

Here, though Kashmir is being represented through various layers of mimesis (that is, this is a poem about painting Kashmir), and though the paint colors appear to seep through Ali's fingers, thereby refusing Ali the ability to capture Kashmir, it is still a Kashmir that is palpably present and, thus, representational because it is a landscape that can be held, taken, and shifted like sand through one's fingers, and, more importantly, there is a poet who is present in the landscape, walking by the lake, breathing in the colors and hues of the landscape. India features similarly vibrantly and Kashmir continues to be a living entity in Ali's poetry in collections published after he had been living in America for more than a decade. Ali's poem "Postcard from Kashmir," published in 1987, ten years after "Painting a Kashmir Landscape" is a good representative example. In the poem, the poet, who was by then already residing in the United States, reflects on the process of capturing his homeland:

> Kashmir shrinks into my mailbox
> my home a neat four by six inches
> [...]
> This is home. And this the closest
> I'll ever be to home. When I return,
> the colors won't be so brilliant,
> the Jhelum's waters so clean,
> so ultramarine
> [...]
> And my memory will be a little
> out of focus, in it
> a giant negative, black
> and white, still undeveloped. (*Half-Inch*, 1)

Although Ali talks about his homeland as a simulacrum of the original (it is a postcard), and though the poet is not present in India (he states, "this [the postcard] is the closest / I'll ever be to home"), in his present time, Kashmir still exists. The poet's statement, "This *is* home," is a definitive assertion about a place that exists. Moreover, the author's awareness that home, memories of home, and representations of home are and will always be mutable, heightens, in a paradoxical fashion, the immutability of the original place and time—that is, an original must exist against which later representations are undeveloped or overexposed. Thus, even though the colors over the pristine lakes of Srinagar may be muddied and the sunlight less incandescent, the reality is that there is a place that *can* be captured in a snapshot, which remains pristine and aquamarine.

One of the reasons why Ali's hyphenated identity may be difficult to fit into prevailing concepts of postcolonial transnationalism is his background. Ali was born in New Delhi and he grew up Srinagar, Kashmir. From the age of twelve to fifteen, Ali lived in the United States, in Indiana, where his father was working on a doctorate degree. Ali returned to Kashmir and then to New Delhi for his college years. By the time Ali moved to the United States for his Ph.D. and M.F.A., all three places of his childhood had taken a powerful hold on him. Ali's identifications with three different homes is supported by Amitav Ghosh who believes that "it was that early experience [of living in different countries], I suspect, that allowed Shahid to take America so completely in his stride when he arrived as a graduate student years later" ("Ghat," 2002, 34). Moreover, though Ali's family lived in Srinagar, they also owned a flat in New Delhi, where they spent their winter months (35). Thus, Ali, unlike a lot of immigrants, lived his early life in homes in Kashmir, India, and the United States, without ever having to choose one country over another, and I agree with Ghosh's assertions about the reasons contributing to Ali's easeful triple home life, a situation aided, I would argue, by the unique experience of being a foreign student in the United States. During Ali's studies toward his masters and doctoral degrees, he was a foreign student in the United States. Unlike immigrants or expatriates, foreign students enter and remain in the United States in an unusual nonimmigrant space that is highly structured and, even, surreal. The foreign student's F-1 visa status encourages, and even requires, that the student exist entirely within the confines of a visa-granting college (foreign students cannot legally work off-campus and are not eligible for any federal or state loans or benefits), and, thus, for a period of years (depending on the number of degrees), the students' time in the states is both finite, that is, their time in the country is determined by the length of study articulated clearly in the visa, and impermanent, that is, the course of study will come to an end. The F-1, nonimmigrant status in the states provides a unique ethereal space in which to exist where, though one has physically left a homeland, it is one to which one can (a lot of students return home regularly during the summer or winter holidays) and must return to (once the visa runs out or unless one switches to an H1-B *immigrant* and, thus, a nonstudent status visa). There cannot be, then, any diasporic loss of homeland because by leaving, foreign students have actually heightened the homeland's presence because one's ability to come to the United States in the first place is determined by the student's ability to return. As a matter of fact, at U.S. consulates, in order to get approval for visas, students have to demonstrate that they *intend* to return to their home after their course of study, and students typically use evidence of family assets, family ties, and finances to demonstrate that they can and will want to return home after getting a degree in the United States.[8]

Consequently, I would argue that the literature by writers who have entered and remained in the United States as "foreign students" can be analyzed differently from the literature by those who are—what I would call—immediate immigrants, those who come to the United States with the sole purpose of remaining in the country permanently (as opposed to those who switch to immigrant status after years of stay). Immigrants and exiles—those immediate immigrants (those who cannot return, irrespective of how they enter the country)—have to consciously bid farewell to their original homeland in order to reside in their adopted land. Transimmigrants, on the other hand, have years, and sometimes decades, before they have to consciously feel that their original home has been lost, if ever at all. It is evident that Ali frequently (as much as once a year) traveled and returned to his parents in Kashmir and in New Delhi, during his studies and during his academic positions in the United States—returns that allowed him to clearly delineate between his life in India (which clearly continued to exist and evolve) and his life in the United States (which also continued to exist and evolve). Thus, his customary summer visits to India also allowed him to demarcate two homes into his life.[9] As a result, for Ali the landscape of the United States retains as much a hold on and significance in his poetry as does the landscape of India, and both cultures remain palpably and equally present in his works.[10]

This binary existence is demonstrated particularly in Ali's collection *A Nostalgist's Map of America*. In this powerfully evoked homage to the North American landscape, Ali does not write *about* the United States, he instead writes *as* a North American—as a member of a vanished tribe of the Hohokam's of the Sonora desert, as a Penitente and a nomad of the Sangre de Cristos of New Mexico, and as a wandering tribesman of the Catalinas and the Superstition Mountains. In the collection, Ali captures with exquisite love and appreciation, as well as a sense of urgency, the landscape of Pennsylvania, Arizona, and New Mexico. Ali does not just write *about* the vanishing traces of the tribes of the Southwestern deserts, instead he *becomes* their echoing voices as he speaks their existence into the present time. In the poem "Beyond the Ash Rains," Ali talks about *his* history in the desert and how *he* has lived among the vanished tribes of

Native Americans, two and three thousand years ago (*A Nostalgist's Map of America*, hereafter cited as NMA, 23). Furthermore, Ali's presence in that past, in the past of the vanished Hohokam tribe, is so visceral that in the poem "Leaving Sonora," during a flight take-off while leaving Tucson, Ali actually sees the blue lights of the runway fade into diamondlike sparkle of lights from a faded past, from a faded outline of a vanished Native American village from centuries ago (29). In the collection, Ali's North American landscape is not filtered through the eyes of an outsider (a Kashmiri-Indian). Instead, the poet captures a land and a culture that are wholly and completely his own as he navigates through a suburb of Pennsylvania with trees that resonate with colors of gems—emeralds and diamonds—and as he fishes skies of the desert (85). Most significantly, Ali navigates not only through—and, consequently, appropriates as his own—the literal landscape of the United States, but he also traverses and comes alive in the literary landscape of North America. In the title poem "A Nostalgist's Map of America," Ali, while traveling through a town in Pennsylvania, transforms the concrete aspects of his surroundings (the streets, the road signs, and the houses) into literary renditions from Emily Dickinson's poem, "A Route of Evanescence." Ali constructs his present surroundings out of imaginative markers from Emily Dickinson's poetry as he pretends that the town he is in is Evanescence because, after all, for Ali, there just has to be an Evanescence—a space of poetry—in Pennsylvania (35). In his creation of this particular Evanescence, Ali uses words from Emily Dickenson's original poem. Thus, in Ali's poem—a poem that captures the death of a lover and that exists as an elegy—the metaphorical landscape of death and the literal landscape of Pennsylvania become the poetic landscape of one of the America's most noted writers. Ali's exquisite pain can only be rendered through Dickenson's pain. Borrowing lines and words from Dickenson's poem, Ali ends "A Nostalgist's Map of America" with overwhelming images of sounds from Dickenson: The sounds of hummingbirds, of blood rushing through routes of veins, and of an electric, red rush of the cochineal (37). Thus in Ali's poetry, North America is not just a series of representations springing from the vision of an outsider or from that of a traveler or a tourist passing through the land. Instead, for Ali, the space is a collective construction of its national as well as its mundane monuments, its history, and its literature—all aspects that Ali makes his own by traveling through its mountains, lakes, and cities, by becoming and speaking the land's language of the extinct tribes, and by reimagining and reconstructing his surroundings from the imaginings of the country's celebrated poet. Ali's detailed and multifaceted representation weaves through the historical, cultural, and literary legacies of the United States, and Ali speaks as one who not only *knows* the land's myriad narratives, but as one who can speak from *within* its narratives, and also as one who by *speaking* establishes another narrative that is as legitimate as those he borrows and remakes. In this collection, Ali's evocation of Georgia O'Keefe's paintings particularly exemplifies Ali's ability to speak from within the culture.

Ali's poem "In Search of Evanescence," is an imitation of Emily Dickinson's typical style; that is, it is a poem with short staccato phrases and lines separated by numerous hyphens, and with eccentric accentuations of words through random capitalizations. Furthermore, the content of the poem is also an imitation of quintessential road-trip narratives, with Ali as a passenger watching and delighting in the passing landscape outside (NMA, 53–55). Interestingly, Ali not only speaks from within these recognizable constructs, he further represents the landscape within this Dickinsonian-style poem with images inspired by Georgia O'Keefe's paintings. Thus Ali becomes an O'Keefe-ian painter painting the Southwestern desert *through* an Emily Dickinson poem. Ali becomes a character and painter in O'Keefe's landscape by becoming a solitary passenger in a train, at a ghost-station, in a desolate desert, at night (53). Ali's layering of narratives is ultimately encapsulated toward the end of the poem, when the poet passes through the Southwest desert of O'Keefe-ian pink and green mountains, with a red sky, black Mesa, ghost-ranch cliffs, and vast nights of lightning and stars (55). Ali says that the paintings capture the landscapes that we all own—that *he* owns—and he claims that O'Keefe painted the landscape for us all—and for him. This America that Ali maps in his collection is unequivocally his own.

Furthermore, Ali's depicts the syncretic nature of his dual Kashmiri-American identity by bringing Kashmir and India *into* this vividly rendered American landscape. Thus, unlike traditionally nostalgic immigrant narratives where one remembers and pines for a lost homeland that is separate and distinct from one's present place, Ali's India resides comfortably in and with his American counterpart. For example, in the poem "In Search of Evanescence," a poem about Ali's search for Emily Dickinson's fictional city, Ali does not just have remembrances of his India. Instead, Ali's India actually exists alongside the familiar landscape of Midwest United States. He states that while traveling on Route 80, in Ohio, he came across an exit for Calcutta, and he realizes that his India always exists, just off the turnpikes of America (NMA, 41); that is, Ali's India *exists* as an actual place that is right off the exit in Ohio. Ali's India is not constructed from a tapestry of nostalgic memories of a lost home, but is instead represented as a viable and, also significantly, accessible reality— that is, Ali need only take the exit and he would be in India. The space, therefore, allows for both North America and India to coexist simultaneously. Therefore, in the midst of paying the toll in this Midwestern city, Ali actually hears—rather than has a memory or flashback of—India as percussions of the sun on tamarind leaves (42) and as the voices of vendors and bargaining women in Indian bazaars (42)—all this while he drives in Ohio.

Additionally, just as Ali had used American literary traditions, such as Dickinson and O'Keefe, to inform his rendition of the Southwestern deserts and the vanished Native American tribe, Ali also uses his Islamic heritage, and its literary traditions, to further depict this landscape. The final section of the collection is devoted entirely to re-creation of the eleventh-century Persian love narrative, *Layla and Majnoon*. This final section is titled "From Another Desert," and in it Ali uses his intense identification with the North American desert landscape to retell the tragic story of Majnoon's love for Layla, focusing primarily on the final scene of the narrative where Majnoon, overcome with madness, wanders the Arabian desert for decades. It is noteworthy that Ali would choose to re-create this particular story because this love narrative has had a significant literary impact upon the literature of the Indian subcontinent, and though he does mention in a footnote that the story of Layla and Majnoon has been reenvisioned and re-created throughout centuries in Urdu and Persian literatures, it is important to further note that this Persian story (and its various renditions such as *Khusrao and Shirin*) significantly affected literature of fifteenth- and sixteenth-century North India, resulting in the creation of a new Indian literary genre known as the *prem-kahanis*.[11] Thus, Ali's use of this narrative is important because *Layla and Majnoon* is a recognizable literary symbol of the Islamic presence in northern India. More importantly, just as Ali had imagined a North American landscape into existence through the American historical and literary lenses, he also reimagines his America through the literary lens of another desert that comes from his Indian heritage, a desert in which Majnoon weeps for his loved one. Though the section remains removed from the rest of the poems in the collection, Ali's stylistic choice of speaking through and to Majnoon—who is the hero of this traditional Sufi story about the impermanence and transience of earthly love, with Layla being representative of Allah's love—is reminiscent of other poems in the collection, where Ali speaks through, as, or to the decimated or vanished tribes of America. Ali's identification with the myriad cultures, literal—Native American, Persian, and Indian—as well as literary—Emily Dickinson, Georgia O'Keefe, and Sufi love-narratives—transforms *A Nostalgist's Map of America* into a palimpsestic bricolage of North American, Indian, and Indic-Islamic literary traditions—all accentuating each other and all coexisting in the fertile landscape of a poet who is at home everywhere.

It would remiss of me to ignore the fact that most critics who comment on Ali refer to the overwhelming loss evident in his poetry. There is absolutely no denying that a lot of Ali's poetry is filled with images of death and loss, and it is this pervasive theme of death in his poetry that is used by critics as proof that Ali is an exiled or lost being. Lawrence Needham, in a powerful analysis of the theme of loss in Ali's poetry, describes Ali as a "triple exile" ("Sorrows," 1992, 64) and as, primarily, a poet of absence and of loss (72). Needham argues that it is because of Ali's triple-exile background—the fact that Ali was born in New Delhi, grew up in Srinagar, and then was educated and became a resident for each half of his adult life in India and in the United States—that Ali is particularly tuned to the language of loss (64). Needham argues that, in the midst of loss and eroding faith in God, Ali turned to not only Urdu poetry and ghazals, but that through poetry, the poet found a "location between cultures, recognize[d] the political implications of that position, and register[ed] the lived consequences of alienation" (67). Needham, like other critics, sees Ali's use of poetry as a medium to ease his alienation from India as a result of his immigration to the United States.

There is no denying that being a Shia Muslim from a predominantly Sunni Kashmir, as well as from a predominantly Hindu India, and then, also, from a predominantly Caucasian North America could have made Ali feel exiled from these communities. Needham's argument would imply that Ali suffered not from just a loss of home, but that he never had a home to begin with. The assumption behind Needham's assertion seems to be that one must belong to a majority community in order to have a sense of belonging to a nation. However, the mere fact that Ali is a Kashmiri-Indian-Shia-Muslim does not necessarily place him in the position of an exile, an outsider, or a victim, nor does it leave him in the role of one who has lost his homeland metaphorically or literally.[12] Moreover, identifying Ali as an exile in India because of his Shia background[13] also undermines the legitimacy of the Shia presence, especially in northern India, established as early as the tenth century. Furthermore, unlike the spread of Islam under the caliphs, Islam established itself in the Indian subcontinent as part of a Turkic-Persian-Arab expansion movement, and it was, thus, already a syncretic amalgam of various languages and sects. Additionally, various rulers during the reign of the Delhi Sultanates (1206-1526) used Sufi holy men, who advocated a mixture of Sunni and Shia beliefs, in order to unify India under their rule. This religious mixture allowed for the thorough establishment of the more philosophical and theoretical aspects of Shia Islam, the influence and presence of which are, therefore, deeply ingrained in the arts, architecture, literature, and culture of India.[14] I realize that I am venturing into a controversial minefield of creating historiographic authenticity, and I also realize that the postcolonial exile and alienation that the critics are referring to are specific to the religious and regional carving up of the subcontinent after 1947, but, regardless, I do not think Ali's presence (even his nonpresence because of his immigration to the United States) in Kashmir can metaphorically, let alone literally, be effaced by virtue of his movement elsewhere.

It is important to note that Ali's collection *The Country without a Post Office* does represent a poet attempting to return, in a seemingly nostalgic fashion, to Kashmir, a feat that he is able to achieve only as a disembodied voice and as a phantom, ghostlike presence. However, the ghostlike presence is not because Ali was suddenly cognizant of the fact that he had lost his homeland and that a return was, thus, not possible. Instead, the collection's context of the sanguinary reality of the Kashmiris' contemporary struggle for secession from India allows for Ali's presence to be one of fragmentation and one fraught with self-guilt. The collection is set against the backdrop of the 1996 Kashmiri uprising and struggle for self-determinacy, and the dislocation in this collection emanates from the actual destruction and violence occurring in Ali's land. Therefore, I would argue that Ali's inability to return to Kashmir is literally impossible *at that point of time* because of the turmoil in Kashmir, not the result of being exiled. There is a strong presence of death in Ali's poetry (and death is read by critics as a motif of loss of a homeland, in the case of postcolonial writers). There is no denying the pervasive and omnipresent theme of loss and of death in Ali's poetry, a theme that, I would argue, is not the result of any exilic, transnational, or diasporic sensibilities in Ali, but is rather the result of Ali's own intense preoccupation with the phenomenological aspect of death, especially of his own death. This metaphysical awareness of one's own mortality is fueled by Ali's acutely realized binary existence, and Ali's coexistence in two distinct nations allows him to more fully appreciate and represent the transience and the ephemerality of life.

There is no denying the intense theme of loss that pervades Ali's poetry, however, I would argue that it is Ali's intense *placing* of himself in both countries that allows this loss to exist. Ali's identification with the historical as well as the present times of Kashmir, India, and the United States serves to heighten his sense of transience of life—of all life. We all must die, and we are always dying, as evidenced in Ali's poem "Snow on the Desert." In the poem Ali talks about how each ray of sunshine is seven minutes old and, thus, every present second of life has already become the past (*MNA*, 100). Whether it is the vanished tribes of the Sonora desert or the vanished cries of elephants of Mihiragula,[15] the pervading motif in Ali's poetry is the inevitable aspect of life itself: that it must come to end. In life, however, there is home, and Ali's poetry captures the life that still speaks through the past voices of American-Indian-Islamic-Kashmiri histories and literature.

And, it is in his death that Ali's final transimmigrant poem is truly written. Ali never did return to Kashmir, and he is instead buried in Massachusetts, near Amherst, in his other Kashmiri home.

NOTES

1. In their essay "South Asian American Literature: 'Off the Turnpike' of Asian-America," Lavina Shankar and Rajini Srikanth assert that Ali also referred to himself as a "Kashmiri-American-Kashmiri." They argue that the triptych appellation "cleverly . . . suggests that America takes him back to Kashmir" and that "'America' is not the end-point of his identity, not the destination of his being" (378). In my research, I found that Ali was generally referred to as the "Kashmiri-American."

2. Jahan Ramazani's book *The Hybrid Muse* is a much needed thorough analysis of postcolonial *poetry*. The field of postcolonial studies has been dominated by examinations of prose narratives and of novels. Ramazani attributes this lack of critical attention to poetry to the relative density and lack of transparency of the medium, and also to the fact that poetry as a genre, unlike other genres, has often been identified with a national spirit. In the current postcolonial and "World Literature" discourses, the transnational aspect of the poet is rarely highlighted and instead "[c]riticism and anthologies tend to focus on national or regional group of writers, such as West Indian poets, African poets, Indian poets" (4).

3. Ramazani, Shankar, and Srikanth all cite colonialism as a reason for Ali's inability to return to Kashmir. Ramazani does make a point of qualifying that the colonial factors are those of the European as well as those of "internalized colonialism of more recent governments" (*Hybrid*, 2001, 12), thereby possibly acknowledging both India's and Pakistan's duplicity in creating an inhabitable situation in Kashmir.

4. My term "transimmigrant" literature may seem similar to Benzi Zhang's concept of "transrelation," which defines the spacing (not the space) of the hyphen. According to Zhang, transrelation, which is a "back-and-forth movement that transrelates and works through different historical temporalities and cultural locations" ("Identity," 2000, 129) allows for the articulation of hyphenated identities. However, Zhang's concept of transrelation is strikingly similar to Homi Bhabha's concept of the "Third-Space," where the space is still defined by the presence of boundaries.

5. I do appreciate Homi Bhabha's poststructuralist approach to the concepts of the "Third Space" and of hybridity, and the fact that culture resides in the elliptical space or *difference* of language/enunciation/the process of iteration. Even if it sounds like a poststructuralist joke—"it's all words, words, words" (*Location*, 1994, 59)—when analyzing a poet like Ali, who focused on and loved the form of poetry as much as he did, it is impossible to ignore the ultimate transnational-transimmigrant space of words.

6. Bruce Simon in "Hybridity in America: Reading Conde, Mukherjee, and Hawthorne" summarizes the various studies on the genealogy of the word and concept of hybridity, and its colonial/racist heritage. Simon questions what it may mean to "translate hybridity from its colonial context [,] [and] to redeploy a term with such a checkered past" (2000, 419)—and he concludes that to answer such questions requires us not to treat hybridity as a melting pot or multiculturalism or acculturation or diversity, and so forth, but instead to treat hybridity as an invitation to consider cultural politics. I think that all culturally loaded terms and

concepts should make us question ways in which we approach cultural studies. However, the overwhelming force and presence of the United States' dominant culture can possibly disallow the unique politics of multifaceted identity to exist in the "hybridity."

7. Benzi Zhang presents articulate arguments against the use of "hybridity," and he finds that it blurs the "dynamic internal politics in the articulation of identity" ("Identity," 2000, 129).

8. For more information on the status of and expectations regarding foreign students in the United States, see Bureau of Consular Affairs, U.S. Department of State, December 26, 2004, http://travel.state.gov/ and R. Dewan, U.S. Immigration and Naturalization Law; Foreign Students, December 27, 2004, www.studyoverseas.com/america/usaed/visa.htm.

9. I am thankful to Dr. Iqbal Agha, one of the trustees of the Agha Shahid Ali Literary Trust, for confirming that Agha Shahid Ali was indeed a foreign student in the United States during his study toward both his M.F.A. and Ph.D. degrees ("Request," 2004).

10. In my analysis here, I am focusing on Ali's poetry up until and preceding *The Country without a Post Office*, a collection that shows a marked shift in Ali's depiction of Kashmir.

11. *Prem-kahanis* as love tales are narratives of spiritual quests where the protagonist's search for his beloved serves as a metaphor for a journey toward spiritual maturity. These romances were composed from the fourteenth century onward by Sufi poets in the Allahabad-Benares region, Bihar, and Bengal, where the poets were patrons of the regional sultan. *Prem-kahanis* as a genre follows the conventions of the romance narratives from Persia, with *Layla and Majnoon* being a very famous and an immediately recognizable narrative from the Middle East. Medieval Persian court poetry combined courtly ethic, conduct, and loyalty with love. For more information on *prem-kahanis*, consult Julie Scott Merisami's book *Medieval Persian Court Poetry* (1987), Aditya Behl's dissertation "Rasa and Romance" (1995), and Shantanu Phukan's dissertation "Through a Persian Prism: Hindi and *Padmavat* in the Mughal Imagination" (2000).

12. As a matter of fact, in some ways, to categorize a tenured U.S. academic who could, and often did, return to Kashmir as an exile, a homeless, or an unhoused person seems particularly offensive in light of the plight of millions of Palestinians—the only people in this supposedly postcolonial era currently living under colonial and occupied rule (I am ignoring U.S. occupation of Iraq for now)—who are the only truly exiled people who genuinely have no option of returning to their homeland (under any peace plan or road map brokered so far). Radhakrishnan in his essay "Postcoloniality and the Boundaries of Identity" makes a similar point when he states: "For the rest of the world both to enjoy nationalism and at the same time to spout a deconstructive rhetoric about nationalism in the face of the Palestinian homelessness is downright perfidious and unconscionable" (1993, 757).

13. Ali's mother was from a well-known Sufi family in Uttar Pradesh.

14. For information on Sufi and Islamic presence in east and north India, I have found the following two books to be quite informative: Richard Eaton's *The Rise of Islam and the Bengal Frontier, 1204–1760* (1993) and Abdul Karim's *History of*

Bengal, Mughal Period (1995). For brief, yet incisive and comprehensive information about the rise and establishment of Islam in India, read Bruce B. Lawrence's essay "The Eastward Journey of Muslim Kingship: Islam in South and Southeast Asia" (1999) and Ira M. Lapidus's "Sultanates and Gunpowder Empires: The Middle East" (1999). For information on Sufi influences on Indian literatures, consult "Rasa and Romance" by Aditya Behl and "Through a Persian Prism: Hindi and *Padmavat* in the Mughal Imagination" by Shantanu Phukan, and "Introduction" to *Madhumalati: An Indian Sufi Romance*, edited by Behl and Weightman (2000).

15. This reference to the elephants of Mihiragula crying as they were pushed off the cliffs of Pir Panjal cliffs in Kashmir is the context for the first poem "Lennox Hill" from Ali's last collection, *Rooms Are Never Finished* (2003).

WORKS CITED

Ali, Agha Shahid. *The Beloved Witness: Selected Poems*. New York: Viking, 1992.

———. *Bone Sculpture*. Calcutta: Writer Workshop Books, 1972.

———. *The Country without a Post Office*. New York: W. W. Norton, 1998.

———. *The Half-Inch Himalayas*. Middleton: Wesleyan University Press, 1987.

———. *In Memory of Begum Akhtar*. Calcutta: Writer Workshop Books, 1979.

———. *A Nostalgist's Map of America*. New York: W. W. Norton, 1991.

———. "The Rebel's Silhouette: Translating Faiz Ahmed Faiz," in *Between Languages and Culture: Translating Cross-Cultural Texts*. Anuradha Dingwaney and Carol Maier, eds. (pp. 75–90). Pittsburgh: University of Pittsburgh Press, 1995.

———. *Rooms Are Never Finished*. New York: W. W. Norton, 2003.

Agha, Iqbal. "Re: Request for Info about the Agha Shahid Ali Literary Trust." E-mail to the Trustee. December 20, 2004.

Behl, Aditya. "Rasa and Romance." Dissertation, University of Chicago, 1995.

Behl, Aditya, and Weightman, Simon, eds. *Madhumalati: An Indian Sufi Romance*. Oxford: Oxford University Press, 2000.

Bhabha, Homi K. *The Location of Culture*. New York: Routledge, 1994.

Eaton, Richard. *The Rise of Islam and the Bengal Frontier, 1204–1760*. Berkeley: University of California Press, 1993.

Ghosh, Amitav. "The Ghat of the Only World: Agha Ali in Brooklyn." *Nation*, February 11, 2002, 31–36.

Karim, Abdul. *History of Bengal, Mughal Period*. Rajshahi: Institute of Bangladesh Studies, 1995.

Lapidus, Ira M. "Sultanates and Gunpowder Empires: The Middle East" in *The Oxford History of Islam*. John L. Esposito, ed. (pp. 347–93). New York: Oxford University Press, 1999.

Lawrence, Bruce B. "The Eastward Journey of Muslim Kingship: Islam in South and Southeast Asia" in *The Oxford History of Islam*. John L. Esposito, ed. (pp. 395-431). New York: Oxford University Press, 1999.

Merisami, Julie Scott. *Medieval Persian Court Poetry*. Princeton, NJ: Princeton University Press, 1987.

Needham, Lawrence. "The Sorrows of Broken Time: Agha Ali and the Poetry of Loss and Recovery," in *Reworlding: The Literature of the Indian Diaspora*. Emmanual S. Nelson, ed. (pp. 63–76). New York: Greenwood Press, 1992.

Ondaatje, Michael. *Running in the Family*. New York: Vintage International, 1982.

Phukan, Shantanu. "Through a Persian Prism: Hindi and *Padmavat* in the Mughal Imagination." Dissertation, University of Chicago, 2000.

Radhakrishnan, R. "Postcoloniality and the Boundaries of Identity." *Callaloo*, 16: 4 (1993): 750–71.

Ramazani, Jahan. *The Hybrid Muse: Postcolonial Poetry in English*. Chicago: University of Chicago Press, 2001.

Shankar, Lavina Dhingra, and Srikanth, Rajini. "South Asian American Literature: 'Off the Turnpike' of Asian America," in *Postcolonial Theory and the United States: Race, Ethnicity, and Literature*. Amritjit Singh and Peter Schmidt, eds. (pp. 370–87). Jackson: University Press of Mississippi, 2000.

Simon, Bruce. "Hybridity in America: Reading Conde, Mukherjee, and Hawthorne," in *Postcolonial Theory and the United States: Race, Ethnicity, and Literature*. Amritjit Singh and Peter Schmidt, eds. (pp. 414–44). Jackson: University Press of Mississippi, 2000.

Zhang, Benzi. "Identity in Diaspora and Diaspora in Writing: The Poetics of Cultural Transrelation." *Journal of Intercultural Studies*, 21: 2 (2000): 125–42.

13 Writing Otherwise than as a "Native Informant"

Ha Jin's Poetry

Zhou Xiaojing

IN A RECENT INTERVIEW, when asked the question "Aren't you tempted to cash in on the current craze for flashy novels that try to 'explain' Asian cultures to the West?" Ha Jin replied: "No. I work on similarities. At heart we are all the same." He added, "If I emphasize cultural difference too much, the writing will have less depth" (Rennicks, "Conversation," n.p.). Although the interviewer's question points to familiar problems of Orientalist ethnography, Ha Jin's reply offers a provocative perspective, especially in the context of much emphasis on difference for varied purposes, such as those for marking the Other or for resisting assimilation, and for recognizing and including diversity. Differing from predominant claims and strategies of identity politics, Ha Jin insists on common humanity. "Unlike most academics," says Ha Jin in an interview with Cynthia Liu, "I do believe in universals and that there is truth that transcends borders and time" (Liu, "Interview," 2000, 78). Jin's claims to universality may sound outdated and even problematic, especially when the concept of universality is embodied by the white male subject. But it is precisely because of the construction of the white male as the embodiment of universality that Jin's representation of "universals" through the particulars of the Chinese is especially subversive.

The monopoly of the white male as the signifier of the universal underlies sexist and racist representations of women and people of color as the abject Other locked in their particularities. The containment of the Other in differences as fixed particularities defined in a binarized, hierarchical construction of man versus woman, the West versus the East, and universality versus particularity characterizes Orientalist discourses. In this sense, Ernesto Laclau's critique of particularism and his emphasis on challenging universality as a closed totality is especially provocative and useful for a better understanding of the significance in Ha Jin's refusal to use cultural difference as the premise and end of his writings. Laclau argues that breaking down the binary relation between universality and particularity is a necessary step toward undermining unequal social relations: *"The universal is an empty place, a void which can be filled only by the particular, but which, through its very emptiness, produces a series of crucial effects in the structuration/destruction of social relation"* (emphasis in original;"Identity," 2000, 58). For the particularity of the Other to be included in the universal, Laclau suggests, the signifier of universality must be conceived and kept as an empty one. In addition, in seeking to change unequal social relations, the oppressed and marginalized must intervene in the monopoly of the universal by the white male. Laclau notes that "politically speaking, the right of particular groups of agents—ethnic, national or sexual minorities, for instance—can be formulated only as *universal* rights" (emphasis in original; 58). This logic points to the problem of containment of Asian cultures and Asian American literature in a fixed position of particularity as the opposite of universality in a binary construct of identities. As Linda Zerilli points out, while speaking of Laclau's critique of particularism, for Laclau, "pure particularism is self-defeating" in asserting one's differential identity because it unwittingly sanctions the status quo. Hence Zerilli further notes: "Multicultural groups which cling too closely to a fantasy of pure difference risk at once ghettoization by and complicity with the dominant community. That is why 'a particularism really committed to change,' Laclau concludes, 'can only do so by rejecting both what denies its own identity and identity itself'"("Universalism," 1998, 9). Ha Jin's writings break away from identity construction based on racial and ethnic differences and offer an alternative, viable strategy for disrupting Orientalism and for challenging the status quo of power relations underlying representation.

Even though Ha Jin resists the Orientalist ethnographical tendency to articulate and explain Chinese cultural difference for the West, he uses Chinese history and culture extensively and relies heavily on his experience in China as the primary source for his writing. However, I would argue that his work offers insights into Chinese history, culture, and subjectivity not despite, but because of, his attempt to write about what transcends borders. "I wanted to write about the soul," says Jin in the same interview with Liu. "A lot of writings about China focus on the flesh, the surface of life" (quoted in Liu, "Interview," 2000, n.p.). By diving below the surface of cultural differences to explore the Chinese "soul," Ha Jin has produced compelling poetry about China, which contributes to altering Eurocentric characterizations of American literature and broadening the spectrum of Asian American literature, while showing possibilities of writing about a people and culture of the East without falling into the trap of Orientalism.

The agency of intervention Jin's work enacts resides not only in his goal of exploring the interiority of the Chinese, but especially in the aesthetic effects produced by his negotiations with lyric poetry. "The inner life is the unique *way* for the real to exist as a plurality," Emmanuel

Levinas contends (*Totality*, 1998, 58). The significant effects of Jin's employment of the lyric—the genre of inner life—cannot be understood fully in terms of border-crossing, antihegemonic characteristics of identity differences described by critics such as Lisa Lowe and Shirley Geok-lin Lim. Lowe stresses Asian American "heterogeneity, hybridity, and multiplicity" in terms of "class, gender, and national differences among Asians," as "a strategy to destabilize the dominant discursive construction of Asian American as a homogeneous group" (*Immigrant*, 1996, 66–68). This strategy, she contends, can also be used to unsettle "the dichotomy of nativism and assimilation" in Asian American debates over identity politics (80). Besides socially constructed identity differences among Asians, Lowe notes that cultural representations such as Peter Wang's film *A Great Wall* (1985), which performs "a continual geographical juxtaposition and exchange between the national spaces of the People's Republic of China and the United States," can disrupt "the nativism/assimilationist dyad" (80). Developing the concept and implications of border-crossing and geographical location outside the U.S. nation-space, Shirley Geok-lin Lim in her essay, "Immigration and Diaspora," endorses Lowe's reading of "diasporic writing as interrupting or challenging the hegemony of metropolitan cultures" ("Immigration," 1997, 298; see also Lowe, "Heterogeneity," 1991). Lim contends that "[t]he tradition of writing by transnationals of multiple diasporas resists . . . nationalistic appropriation" (298). For Lim, resistance as such is rendered possible by the diasporic writers' subject position between national and cultural borders (299). Ha Jin's poetry, with its predominantly Chinese speakers, materials, and geographical locations, however, cannot be comfortably placed under the category of "diasporic writing" as characterized by Lowe and Lim. Aiming to explore what transcends national and cultural borders, Jin's poems do not assume differences of national and ethnic identities as the locus of their articulation. Thus, Ha Jin's writings constitute a transformative force in American literature, as well as Asian American literature, not so much because he locates his characters and narratives outside the U.S. national borders, or performs a geographical juxtaposition and exchange between the United States and China, but because of the way he handles his materials.

Border-crossing and juxtaposition or exchange between the United States and China in representation do not necessarily guarantee intervention in Orientalist discourses that construct the Chinese and Chinese culture as a homogeneous Other of the West. In order to better understand Ha Jin's strategy for going beyond cultural difference—the "surface of life"—so as to give voice to the interiority of the Chinese, it seems necessary to briefly compare Ha Jin's poems about the Chinese with those by a contemporary poet, Wang Ping, who like Ha Jin is an immigrant, an academic, and a writer living in the United States. I am not suggesting that all of Wang's poems are Orientalist; what I am trying to establish is how Ha Jin's lyric poetry offers an alternative to ethnographical representations of cultural differences, which some of Wang's poems about China exemplify.

Wang Ping's autobiographical poems, written from a feminist perspective and a shifting position between being an insider and an outsider to Chinese culture, illustrate some typical problems of what Laclau calls "particularism" in ethnographical representations of cultural difference outside of history. In her title poem of *Of Flesh and Spirit* (1998), Wang writes in fragmentary narratives and comments about her experience of growing up in China. Although the fragmentation gives Wang much freedom, enabling her to cover a wide range of materials, experiences, and time-space, it also prevents her from focusing on a single event or concentrating on a particular emotion so as to achieve an in-depth portrayal of any of the incidents she refers to in the poem. These effects help produce the ethnographical knowledge her poem offers through cultural translation by a "native informant." Speaking in the autobiographical voice of the poet-I, this prose poem assumes a confessional mode. But it moves quickly from personal "secret" to apparently cultural oddities:

I was a virgin till twenty-three, then always had more than one lover at the same time—all secret.

In China, people go to jail for watching porno videos while condoms and pills are given out free.

For a thousand years, women's bound feet were the most beautiful and erotic objects for Chinese. Tits and asses were nothing compared to a pair of three-inch "golden lotuses." They must have been crazy or had problems with their noses. My grandma's feet, wrapped day and night in layers of bandages, smelled like rotten fish.

The asshole in Chinese: the eye of the fart.

A twenty-five-year-old single woman worries her parents. A twenty-eight-year-old single woman worries her friends and colleagues. A thirty-year-old single woman worries her bosses. A thirty-five-year-old woman is pitied and treated as a sexual pervert.

The most powerful curse: fuck your mother, fuck your grandmother, fuck your great-grandmother of eighteen generations.

[. . .]

Women call menstruation "the old ghost," science books call it "the moon period," and refined people say "the moonlight is flooding the ditch."

[...]

Chinese peasants call their wives: that one in my house; old Chinese intellectuals: the doll in a golden house; in socialist China, husbands and wives call each other "my lover."

The story my grandma never tired of telling was about a man who was punished for his greed and had to walk around with a penis hanging from his forehead.

We don't say "fall in love," but "talk love." (Wang, *Spirit*, 1998, 14–15)

Although the voice in this poem is autobiographical and confessional, the poem is not simply about the self; rather the personal stories serve to establish the speaker's authority to speak as a "native informant," whose ethnic authenticity in translating the Chinese culture and language for readers of English is implied. Thus the narratives about personal experiences in the poem have the function of providing the Western reader in English "authentic" information about Chinese sexuality and mentality without any historical contexts. The closing paragraph drives this point home: "When I left home, my father told me: 'never talk love before you're twenty-five years old.' I waited till twenty-three. Well, my first lover was a married coward. My first marriage lasted a week. My husband slept with me once, and I never saw him again" (15).

Although the father's warning seems to allude to the oppressive patriarchal policing of the female body and sexuality, the daughter's confession reveals a rebellious individual. This confessional, autobiographical writing enacts the kind of "specific strategy of authority," which, James Clifford notes, characterizes a mode of "ethnographic writing." Clifford explains that this strategy "has classically involved an unquestioned claim to appear as the purveyor of truth in the text. A complex cultural experience is enunciated by an individual" in ethnographies such as *We the Tikopia* by Raymond Firth, and *Coming of Age in Samoa* by Margaret Mead (*Predicament*, 1996, 25). By beginning her poem with a confession of personal secret ("I was a virgin till twenty-three, then always had more than one lover at the same time—all secret"), Wang assumes an unquestioned claim to authority through this apparently truth-telling individual who switches between "I" to "we" the Chinese. This confessional poem raises political-epistemological questions about the authority in speaking as the Other and for the Other through a range of eclectic information across historical periods and translation of language as cultural translation. Wang's apparently authentic literal translation, however, is consciously selective. In translating literally a Chinese phrase for having a love-relationship that is expected to lead to marriage as "talk love," Wang represses the actual culturally and historically contingent meaning of the phrase in Chinese that emerged with the practice that broke away from arranged marriage. Thus her literal translation enhances the apparent oddity of the Chinese way regarding "love" and sexuality. Similarly, her translation of the Chinese characters for "asshole" as "the eye of the fart," chooses "eye" instead of "hole," and "fart" instead of "ass" out of plural contingent meanings of the characters so that the Chinese language seems to reveal a peculiar mentality and culture in juxtaposition to the English phrases. Moreover, amassing fragmentary references out of specific historical contexts in a confessional voice that reveals personal and cultural "secrets," Wang renders her experiences in China with multiple inscrutable lovers sensational, rather than engaging in a meaningful cultural critique as the defiant female autobiographical voice might suggest. As a result, the insider's exposure of the Chinese sexuality becomes a cultural spectacle for readers of English in the West.

But Wang's poet-I in this confessional, autobiographical poem does not speak as a Chinese only. She is speaking also as a Chinese American who grew up in China. One paragraph in the same prose poem tells the reader that she came to New York City through the sponsorship of a cousin of her first lover, a married man who dreamed of coming to New York but whose cousin decided to sponsor her instead. Hence the speaker assumes more than one position in the poem, representing Chinese people and culture as both an insider and outsider, through the eyes of the West as an American, from a feminist stance and with a focus on what are presumed to be "cultural" differences. Just as her Chinese identity allows her to claim ethnographic authority as an insider, her American identity indicates her distance from the other Chinese—a distance that puts the poet-I in the strategic position of the ethnographic fieldworker as a participant observer. According to Clifford, "participant observation," which assumes a "scientific" methodology and neutrality, was established as "a professional norm" of modern ethnography (*Predicament*, 1996, 28). By employing a seemingly neutral strategy of "participant observation," which is characterized by descriptive narratives from the double position of the insider-outsider, Wang's autobiographical narrator simultaneously translates and interprets the raw materials of Chinese culture. This positioning of an authoritative female speaker as the Other and speaking for the Other on grounds of personal experience, also assumes a critical distance without raising questions about how its positioning of the speaking subject problematizes representation of cultural difference out of historical contexts. The result is a reproduction of typical Orientalist knowledge of the absurdity, strangeness, and millennia-old oppression of women in the East through the gaze of the West. Wang's other poems such as "Born in the Year of Chicken" and "Female Marriage" are written in the same mode and produce similar effects. Thus Wang's apparently feminist cultural critique falls into the trap of Orientalism—the kind of representation Sheng-mei Ma deploys as "ethnographic feminism" in her book *Immigrant Subjectivities in Asian American and Asian Diaspora Literatures* (1998, 12).

Feminist critics have recognized the problems of overlooking "cultural imperialism" in addressing feminist concerns across national boundaries. Inderpal Grewal and Caren Kaplan, in their introduction to a critical anthology *Scattered Hegemonies: Postmodernity and Transnational Feminist Practices* (1994), warn against the assumptions and practices embedded in "global feminism" that have "stood for a kind of Western cultural imperialism" (17). From a different perspective, Chandra Talpade Mohanty in her essay, "Under Western Eyes: Feminist Scholarship and Colonial Discourses," discusses similar problems provocatively. "An analysis of 'sexual difference' in the form of a cross-culturally singular, monolithic notion of patriarchy or male dominance," she contends, "leads to the construction of a similar reductive and homogenous notion of what I call the 'third world difference'—that stable, ahistorical something that apparently oppresses most if not all the women in these countries." She adds that "it is in the production of this 'third world difference' that Western feminisms appropriate and 'colonize' the constitutive complexities which characterize the lives of women in these countries. It is in this process of discursive homogenization and systematization of the oppression of women in the third world that power is exercised in much of recent Western feminist discourse, and this power needs to be defined and named" (1991, 53–54). Terms such as "Ethnographic feminism" and "global feminism" could be considered attempts in naming such discursive homogenization of the "third world difference," as Mohanty has noted.

In addition to power relations, the politics of representation is bound with the poetic of writing, as Wang's confessional autobiographical poems indicate. In his introduction to a critical anthology, *Writing Culture: The Poetics and Politics of Ethnography*, Clifford calls critical attention to the fact that culture is "composed of seriously contested codes and representations," and that "the poetic and the political are inseparable." Putting to crisis the ethnographic authority of "participant observation," he foregrounds "the constructed, artificial nature of cultural accounts." Rather than claiming "transparency of representation" for ethnography, he calls attention to the fact that ethnography "is always caught up in the *invention*, not the representation, of cultures" (emphasis added; 1986, 2). Clifford points out that ethnographic writing "is determined," at least contextually, rhetorically, institutionally, generically, and historically (6). Hence he contends: "Ethnographic truths are thus inherently *partial*— committed and incomplete" (emphasis in original; 7). Drawing on

Clifford's theoretical and critical perspective on ethnography, feminist critics such as Kamala Visweswaran propose to situate "feminist ethnography in the specific ideological context of its production" by tracing the influence of a "master narrative" on women's individual narratives and identifying "other sources of ideological subject positioning," and "locating the temporality of speech" in examining "the constitution of subjectivity" ("Betrayal," 1997, 92, 99). Although Ha Jin does not write ethnographic poems about China as Wang does, Clifford's and feminist critics' perspectives help shed light on what is at stake in writing about China and the Chinese and the challenges entailed.

Jin's poems have resolutely broken away from Orientalist ethnographic representation of the Chinese, offering an alternative mode of writing "as an attempt to hear the Other, the Others," to borrow John Yau's words. Indeed Jin shares Yau's credo of writing "as a form of attention and responsibility" ("Between," 1994, 41). Rather than using the autobiographical poet-I as the locus of narrative and voice as Wang does, Jin employs dramatic and interior monologues to allow multiple voices and speakers to be heard. One crucial strategy in Jin's poems about China is specific historical contextualization of narratives, particularly the speakers' feelings and thoughts. In the preface to his first book of poetry, *Between Silences: A Voice from China* (1990), Ha Jin provides the reader with a particular historical context for his poems:

> The poems contained in this book mainly present some experience of the 60s and 70s in China. The experience is not strictly personal, although in most cases I was stimulated by my memory of those hard facts which cannot be worn away by time. There were many things more terrible in the Cultural Revolution. I do not mean to tell horrible stories in this book, and instead I want to present people's feelings about and attitudes towards these events. The people in this book are not merely victims of history. They are also the makers of the history. Without them the history of contemporary China would remain a blank page. (1)

Unlike Wang, who attempts to speak for the Chinese, Ha Jin wants to give voice to "those unfortunate people who suffered, endured or perished at the bottom of life and who created the history and at the same time were fooled or ruined by it" (2). In seeking to give voice to those who are deprived of a voice, Ha Jin makes sure that the voices he presents in each poem are situated in a particular historical context. By providing a particular context for the feelings and actions of the characters in his poems, Jin renders the people and their lives of a vastly different time and place, compelling and provocative. At the same time, his poems reveal the ideologies of an autocratic state and their effects on individuals. Thus the speakers in Ha Jin's poems are concrete subjects interpellated by particular dominant ideologies at a specific historical moment, rather than representatives of cultural and racial difference.

"The Dead Soldier's Talk," for example, is contextualized not just by Ha Jin's preface to the book, but also by his introductory note under the title of the poem. The note informs the reader of the year of the soldier's death, why and how he died, and what happened after his death: "In September 1969, in a shipwreck accident on the Tuman River, a young Chinese soldier was drowned saving a plaster statue of Chairman Mao. He was awarded Merit Citation 2, and was buried at a mountain foot in Hunchun County, Jilin" (*Between Silences*, hereafter cited as BS, 5). In addition to providing a context for the dead soldier's speech in the poem, the note serves as a background for the changes taking place in the poem. These changes help enhance both the irony and tragedy of the soldier's pointless death. The poem begins with the dead soldier speaking of his loneliness and his longing for home, then it turns into a dramatic monologue, as the soldier speaks to his sister who is visiting his grave:

> I saw you coming just now
> like a little cloud wandering over grassland.
> I knew it must have been you,
> for no other had come for six years. (BS, 5)

Jin tactfully indicates profound social changes through the soldier's reference to the fact that no one has come to visit him for the past six years except his sister. Mao died in 1976, and the political events following his death had contributed to the Chinese disillusionment about Mao and the communist leaders, as well as the communist ideology. Although the soldier's speech reveals his historically shaped subjectivity, it also indicates the changes taking place in the society and the people. The soldier chastises his sister for bringing him wine and meat and paper-money, and asks her if she has brought the collection of Chairman Mao's quotations, the "red treasure book," as the Chinese used to call it:

> I have forgotten some quotations.
> You know I don't have a good memory.
> Again, you left it home.
> How about the statue I saved?
> Is it still in the museum?
> Is our Great Leader in good health?
> I wish He live ten thousand years!
> [. . .]
> Why are you crying?
> Say something to me.
> Do you think I can't hear you?

In the early years
you came and stood before my tomb
swearing to follow me as a model.
In recent years
you poured tears every time. (BS, 5–6)

The changes in the sister foreground further the dead soldier's interpellated subjectivity and the historical conditions. Therefore, the poem not
only reveals the absurdity of the soldier's heroism, it also helps the reader
understand why such martyrdom was possible.

Despite the dehumanizing ideological conditioning of the Chinese as
concrete subjects, there is some irreducible individual humanity that remains in the poem, which Ha Jin portrays through references to the soldier's feelings of loneliness and homesickness, and to his thoughts about
his mother and little sister:

Last week I dreamed of our mother
showing my medal to a visitor.
She was still proud of her son
and kept her head up
while going to the fields.
She looked older than last year
and her grey hair troubled my eyes.
I did not see our little sister.
She must be a big girl now.
Has she got a boy friend? (BS, 6)

These details render even more horrible the destruction of individual lives
by the dominant ideology and the state power. Moreover, details like
these, though rooted in a particular time and place, can transcend their
temporal-spatial limits to reach a wide audience through similarities of
humanity across national and cultural borders.

In poem after poem, through similar methods, Jin portrays the formation of and actions by concrete subjects in a totalitarian society. Many
of the poems are about the various ways in which children are constituted by ideologies both at school and at home. These poems serve as a
backdrop for those about grownups and their thoughts and actions, including their cruelest and most brutal acts of destruction. In other words,
Ha Jin's poems about childhood help shed light on his poems about the
Chinese in their adulthood, showing the process of subject formation and
the operations of ideology through concrete subjects. Poems such as "A
Page from a Schoolboy's Diary," "Because We Dare Not Be Ambitious,"
and "A Thirteen-Year-Old Accuses His Teacher" make the brutality in
"The Execution of a Counter-Revolutionary" understandable though no

less horrible. Taught to obey absolute power completely, to regard people as either comrades or enemies according to a monolithic standard, and to consider a person's deeds in terms of absolute good and evil, the young men's execution of a so-called counter revolutionary, who is only eighteen years old, is not surprising. Facing immanent execution by his peers, the young man's only worry is "I'm not nineteen yet / and my parents will never know / how their son disappeared" (BS, 45). He was shot in the penis because that was "the best way to save the skin" for the hero who "risked his own life / saving horses from the burning stable" (BS, 44).

Understood within the context of the totalitarian rule of an autocratic regime, the monstrosity of the Chinese, like their ordinary grace, transcends its particularities of time and place in its implications for any nation or people regardless of the difference of race, ethnicity, or culture. Jin's poems about China and the Chinese during the cultural revolution reveal not so much an alien world, as how a nation and its people can become the way they are. Nevertheless, the speakers and characters in Jin's poems are not simply representatives of a collective identity, or homogenous subjects constituted by the same dominant ideology. Jin reveals the complexity and humanity of individuals by employing interior and dramatic monologues to reveal the inner life of the Chinese who lived during the radically totalitarian regime. As Emmanuel Levinas points out, "The inner life is the unique *way* for the real to exist as a plurality" (emphasis in original; *Totality*, 1998, 58). Through the interiority of the speakers and characters in his poems, Jin shows that even though individuals are constituted by the dominant ideologies as concrete subjects, they are more than ideological subjects. In a number of poems Jin employs the dramatic monologue to reveal the characters' or speakers' unutterable feelings because even they would deem these feelings unacceptable according to the communist party's ideologies. In "Promise," for instance, the son's speech addressed to the mother confronts the mother's fear for her fourteen-year-old son who has joined the army when military conflicts broke out along the border between China and the former Soviet Union. Through the son's observations of intimate details about the mother, Jin tactfully reveals the mother's unspoken concerns. The mother did not eat the most delicious dumplings she had made for dinner. After her other children had gone to bed, she sat face to face with her fourteen-year-old and broke the silence, asking him to promise her that if he were caught by the enemy, he would never "betray our country and our people" (BS, 15). But her son could hear what the mother dared not utter:

Your demand was so weak
that I did not have to promise you.

"Go to bad, Mom. Please don't
think of such a bad thing.
I will be all right."
[. . .]
But before you went away
you murmured, as if to yourself,
"I hope they put you in a headquarters.
You are too young, just fourteen.
They should treat you differently
and assign you to be an orderly
or a telegraph operator
or to do any kind of service
far away from the frontier." (BS, 16)

Here motherhood is implicated in patriotism, in service to the nation as it often is in helping sustain patriarchy. Jin uses the son's perception of his mother's love for him to indicate simultaneously the regulation of human relationships by state power and the human "soul" that resists the totality of the ideological domination. Similarly, Jin's use of the dramatic monologue enables him to reveal the son's own fears, which he could speak of to his mother only years later:

For many years I couldn't promise you, Mom.
I was not sure whether I could endure
the wolfhounds the Russians would sent upon me
if I refused to tell what they wanted to know. (BS, 18)

This perfectly understandable fear of a fourteen-year-old boy ironically echoes the fear of other boys in another poem, who "decided to go to the army" because they were afraid of being "roasted at home / like little pigs" in case the Russians dropped an atom bomb in China (BS, 13–14). The fears of these boys contrast the heroism of another in the poem "Again, These Days I Have Been Thinking of You," in which the dramatic monologue speaker remembers his young comrade-in-arms, who "burst into tears on the train" when leaving home for the army, saying "I will miss my parents. / I have never travelled that far." But this soldier-to-be declared that "it was everyone's duty to defend the country," and that he "would fight the Russian Revisionists to the dead end."[1] Yet, he is badly injured during a military training exercise and falls silent. In the eyes of the monologue speaker, this heroic boy who chose "that tank / with a revolving barrel like a gigantic scythe, / to lay an explosive package at its back," now "sluggishly turned into your ward / like a startled turtle." Although this young soldier's heroism and sacrifice belong to a past "epoch," for the speaker, he remains "a little dog, abandoned,

/ often groaning at the door / of my conscience" (BS, 9–11). Through these contrasts and contradictions, Jin dives below "the surface of life" to explore what shapes and troubles the souls of these individuals. By using the capacity of the dramatic monologue for narrative and lyricism, and for assuming situations and multiple characters with particular identities, Jin is able to break the silence of those who could not speak of their innermost feelings, which would undermine the political ideology of their time.

Dramatic monologue also enables Jin to situate the subjectivities of different speakers, characters, and addressees in specific social and historical contexts. Although these particularities indicate that what they reveal is "partial truth," and that subjectivity is historically and culturally contingent, they paradoxically enhance the "universals" and "truth that transcends borders and time"—love, fear, courage, anxiety, conscience, vulnerability, and even foolishness—through multiple individuals and their experiences. It is worth noting that in seeking to write about the "soul," Jin relies on particularlized persona of the dramatic monologue, rather than a disembodied lyric "I" without any specific identity. In discussing the differences between the lyric "I" and the "I" of the dramatic monologue, Elisabeth A. Howe notes that the "I" in poems such Wordsworth's "Daffodils" is a typical lyric "I" for it "does not necessarily, or not absolutely, represent the poet himself, it also does not represent anyone else, either—unlike the 'I' of 'My Last Duchess' or 'Ulysses' or other dramatic monologues. A characteristic feature of the lyric 'I' is precisely this vagueness that allows the reader to equate it with the poet, perhaps; to identify with it himself, or herself; or to see it as a universal 'I' belonging to no one and to everyone" (Dramatic, 1996, 6). This distinction between the particularized "I" of the dramatic monologue and the universal "I" of the lyric seems to correlate with what Helen Vendler defines as the differences between "selves" and "souls." Vendler contends, "Selves come with history: souls are independent of time and space. . . . The lyric is the gesture of immortality and freedom; the novel is the gesture of the historical and of the spatial" (Soul, 1995, 5). But in Jin's poems, the selves and souls are not mutually exclusive, just as the personal and the social, the particular and the universal are inseparable.

It is precisely the historically and spatially conditioned selves and their socially specific identities that demonstrate that the souls of the selves can transcend the conditions of their time and place. "An Old Red Guard's Reply" is another example that shows what the soul says does not have to be stripped of the social and ideological, as Vendler claims. The lyrical in this poem is grounded in the historical, as the speaker, one of the Red Guards who worshiped Chairman Mao like a god, examines what "we"—the Red Guards—have become.[2]

Having been wrecked so many times
we will not set sail once more.
Having been deceived again and again
nobody could care whether there is any truth.
[. . .]
Our old hearts, burnt out by dreams, fell
like meteors on the shore
and cannot be shaken by the great waves.
Our legs were amputated on the tables
which we once mistook as stages
where we enacted the Dance of Loyalty.

Now we cannot move,
either toward the sea or toward the land.
Whatever you say, our tongues,
which finally have learned how to voyage,
will reply, "Yes sir." (*BS*, 77)

This is the voice of the disillusioned Red Guards who realized that they were used for political ends and felt bitter about the loss of idealism and faith in any beliefs. These Red Guards sometimes refer to themselves as the "lost generation" who has lost not only innocence, idealism, and faith in communism, but also the most precious, productive years of their lives for a false cause. Jin examines their inner lives and expresses them through their voices, which are part of the history of China, but what they articulate is not reducible to the time and place that give rise to them.

This historically specific voice, however, does not become "abstract" as Vendler says of the lyric voice. "In lyric poetry," Vendler claims, "voice is made abstract" (*Soul*, 1995, 3). She argues that "When the soul speaks, it speaks with a number of voices. . . . But the voices in lyric are represented not by characters, as in a novel or drama, but by changing registers of diction, contrastive rhythms, and varieties of tone." She adds that "the life of the soul lives when it is present to itself and alone with its own passions" (6). This version of the lyric voice is characteristic of the "lyric I" in Wordsworth's "I Wondered Lonely as a Cloud," who experiences a joyful moment when he is alone with himself and his "pensive mood" changes into joy as his "inward eye flashes" upon his memory of the sight of daffodils—"the bliss of solitude" (1965, 191). This autonomous, self-enclosed moment of pleasure exemplifies what Vendler defines as the lyric moment when the self is "alone with itself, when its socially con-structed characteristic[s] (race, class, color, gender, sexuality) are felt to be in abeyance." For Vendler, the "biological characteristics" of the self's identity "can be reconstructed in opposition to their socially constructed form, occasioning one of lyric's most joyous self-proclaimings: 'I am I, am

I; All creation shivers / With that sweet cry' (Yeats)" (*Soul*, 1995, 7). This is the lyric voice "made abstract" by stripping the "I" of its particularities of biological and social identities. But how can an abstract lyric voice as such reconstruct the characteristics of the self's identity "in opposition to their socially constructed form" when there is no socially constructed identity attached to this voice to contend? If solitude, self-reflection, and passions are the conditions for sustaining the life of the soul, and by extension, of the lyric, as Vendler claims—"the life of the soul lives when it is present to itself and alone with its own passions"—what then generates self-reflection and passions? The stuff that keeps the soul alive must be more than Wordsworth's daffodils and Yeats's self-consciousness, as Jin's poems suggest. Indeed, Jin's poems challenge the separation of the lyric voice from dramatic monologue, of what the soul says from the social conditions that impinge on it.

The closing poem, "Because I Will Be Silenced," of Jin's first volume *Between Silences* demonstrates that the passions of the soul arise from the weight of history and from the speaker's sense of urgency in response to specific social conditions. Unlike many of Jin's other poems, this poem is not a typical dramatic monologue. It does not assume a situation or a character; nor is the speech addressed to a particular listener. However, the lyric "I" identifies himself as a poet who is also a social critic and a political dissident:

> Once I have the freedom to say
> my tongue will lose its power.
> Since my poems strive to break the walls
> that cut off people's voices,
> they become drills and hammers.
>
> But I will be silenced.
> The starred tie around my neck
> at any moment can tighten into a cobra.
>
> How can I speak about coffee and flowers? (BS, 79)

This and Jin's other poems break away from the centrality of the self enclosed in its autonomous consciousness in the lyric model defined by Vendler. The passions of the speaker result from his or her social position and identity and from his or her sense of response to social, political issues as responsibility of a poet. It would be impossible to isolate this soul's passions from the social circumstances, or to erase the particularity of this lyric "I" from his or her lyric utterances. For this lyric "I," what the soul says risks his or her freedom and perhaps even life. Thus it is not simply how, but also what, the soul says that matters. As the speaker asks: "How can I speak about coffee and flowers?"

The sense of responsibility and urgency conveyed in this poem helps explain Jin's frequent use of the dramatic monologue, which allows the voices of the Other(s) to be heard, and the plurality of inner life to resist totality. The displacement of the centrality of the poet's sensibility and self-consciousness in Jin's poems makes it possible for his poems to be a means to "hear the Other, the Others," and to be "a form of attention and responsibility," to borrow again John Yau's words ("Between," 1994, 41). In "An Apology," collected in Jin's second volume *Facing Shadows* (1996), the speaker asserts Jin's reasons for rejecting the centrality of the autobiographical poet-I as the subject of his poems. The poem begins with reference to the speaker's remarks that "it would waste my time / to write an autobiography" in response to a friend's suggestion. Although it is written as an apology, the poem is an argument for poetry—not an autobiographical poetry of self-indulgence, but one that opens up the self to the world and others:

> Though my words tumble,
> my pen can't help
> redrawing my circumference.
> On paper I dare to laugh
> or weep like a free man.
> On paper I can reach
> for a hand, a face,
> a cloud, or thunder.
> The "I" ought to be conquered
> when we cage stars on the page. (*Facing Shadows*, hereafter cited as FS, 55)

For the speaker, writing poetry means achieving a form of freedom for deeper, fuller, and more passionate experiences. It also means making connections with others and reaching for the unthinkable and the unattainable. In this complex endeavor and encounter, the egotistical self—the "I"—must not be the center of all experiences or the locus of words.

As the title of Jin's second volume, *Facing Shadows*, suggests, the lyric for Jin is not simply an inward-turning of the self in solitude to be wrapped in the "here and now," but also a turning to face shadows of the past of a people and a country. In "I Sing of an Old Land" Jin articulates passionately the profound connections of his poetry to China and the Chinese. The diction, tone, rhythm, and emotional intensity of this poem indicate that the lyric "I" is not talking about the cultural differences of China or the Chinese defined in relation to the West for an audience of English. He is singing of the atrocity, misery, and majesty of China for the sake of China and the Chinese:

I sing of an old land
where the gods have taken shelter underground,
where the human idols eat human sacrifice,
[. . .]
where words imitate spears and swords,
where truth is always a bloody legend.

I speak of the old land not
out of love or wonderment.
Like my ancestors who were scattered into the smoky winds,
who scrambled to leave home
or rushed towards the approaching enemies,
I join those who fled and returned,
    who disappeared in other lands
bearing no hope but persistence, no honor but the story,
    No fortune but parents and children,
singing a timeless curse,
a curse that has bound us together
and rooted us deep in the wreck
    of our homeland. (FS, 19)

The speaker's singing is not motivated by nationalism or nostalgia. Rather, his singing of China is compelled by the devastation of the land, by the tribulation of the people, and by the urge to tell the story he and others like him are destined to carry and make known. Rather than assuming the ethnographic authority of the "native informant," the speaker identifies himself as one of the writers in exile who are bound by their conditions of displacement in exile and their persistence in singing the wreckage and endurance of their homeland.

This position of the writer in exile has significant ramifications. It refuses the geographical containment of the "natives" and dislodges the binary construct of self versus Other in polarized locations of the East and West, thus unsettling the dichotomy in which the East is reduced to the object of knowledge for the episteme and pleasurable consumption of the West. Jin's lyric speaker reclaims the agency of the Chinese who become muted objects of knowledge in Orientalist discourses. Moreover, the displacement of the lyric speaker in exile who confronts the history of China from outside of China, foregrounds the position of the speaker outside national boundaries—a position that entails multiple subject positions and perspectives for examining a national history. Jin's song about China, written from the exile's perspective, counters the official history of China, while resisting idealizing or Orientalizing China. In singing the paradoxes of China, the speaker confronts his own and other Chinese people's conflicted feelings about the land. The complexity of the speaker's

emotional and psychological ties to China matches the political entangle-
ment and historical intricacies of China, rendering both the singer and his
song irreducible to any simple categories of identity politics:

> I dream of myself in that land,
> not for happiness or harvest.
> I dream of suffering together with my people,
> of being understood and useful,
> [. . .]

> I weep for the old land,
> for its vast narrowness,
> for its profound stupidity,
> for its chaos and tenacity,
> for its power to possess those of my kind
> to devour us to nourish itself
> to seize our hearts and throats
> and mix our moans with songs—
> songs of monstrous grandeur
> and merciless devotion,
> songs crazed by the cycle of that land. (FS, 19–20)

This singing from the position of the exile breaks the containment of the
speaker from a different culture as a "native informant" in the "fieldwork" of ethnography. Lyricism that conveys the speaker's passion for
singing and his devotion to what he sings renders it impossible for the
speaker to assume either an ethnographic authority or a cynically critical
distance from the West, as Wang's confessional autobiographical "I" does
in her narratives of Chinese cultural differences.

In his second volume, Jin often continues to employ dramatic monologues from the exile's position to reveal the complexity and humanity of
the Chinese and to articulate social critique. For instance, "June 1989"
with the subtitle, "To a Poet in China" is an epistolary poem addressed
to the speaker's friend in China. Both the poetic form and the different
locations of the correspondents enable Jin to respond to the massacre on
June 4, 1989, from the perspectives of the Chinese in China and outside of
China. Although the Chinese who did not know what actually happened
on Tiananmen Square on the night of June 4, 1989, mourned "for the
deaths of murderers" and celebrated "the murder of themselves," those
in "the foreign land" watched how "the capital was darkened / by a red,
red night"; how "A small girl hid in a rickshaw, / but thirty-nine bullets
smashed / the vehicle and the life inside"; and how "a young man stopped
eighteen tanks / with two bags of groceries" (FS, 26, 27, 26). Watching
the event unfolding from outside of China, with his knowledge of and

connections to China, the speaker concludes his poem/letter with a fore-
boding remark that articulates Chinese people's courage, indomitable
spirit, and defiance of state-power: "From curses behind doors, from
groans in dreams, / an eyeless typhoon is gathering" (FS, 27).

Dramatic monologue, moreover, also enables Jin to show that those
communist party officials are not a monstrous, homogeneous unity. "A
Former Provincial Governor Tells about His Dismissal" is another epistolary poem, addressed by a former provincial governor to his son, who
is living in the United States. This dramatic monologue reveals that the
governor was ousted and put under house arrest because he asserted
criticism of the central government for using military force on June 4,
1989:

> I said those above were fools and thugs
> who had ruined the Party and the country
> in one night. Why couldn't they have talked
> with the demonstrators? Why did they
> have to pull in tanks to crush the people
> who didn't have an inch of iron in their hands?
> You don't shoot a sparrow with artillery.
> Now the Party has lost the people's trust
> simply because a few old urchins were scared,
> so they tore the nation up
> to keep their skin unscratched. (FS, 29)

Despite his personal misfortune of political downfall, this former provincial governor remains devoted to his country and people. The corruption
and intrigue within the party did not make him lose hope or embrace
Western ideas of democracy. He advises his son not to plan to return to
China soon, "or live in America for good." Noting that "A billion people
must be fed. / An impoverished country must be developed. / Only we
Chinese ourselves can solve / these problems [,]" the father urges his
son not to waste his time "with those there / who only talk of empty
democratic theories" (FS, 30). By giving voice not only to Chinese soldiers, mothers, and poets, but also government officials through dramatic
monologues, Jin is able to foreground the complexity of China and the humanity of the Chinese, which are often repressed or erased in Orientalist,
ethnographic representations of cultural differences.

Ha Jin's poems enact his belief in "universals and that there is truth
that transcends borders and time." His employment and development
of lyricism, particularly dramatic monologue, offer a viable strategy for
countering Orientalism and for resisting the kind of reductive and problematic models of ethnographic representation of cultural difference based
on authenticity and authority of the "native informant," which Clifford

challenges. It seems that Jin's poetry accomplishes what Ihab Hassan calls "the *resistance of literature* to power, the resistance of literary texts to contexts" (emphasis in original, "Globalism," 1999, 65). It is precisely the "transhistorical, transcultural element" of literature, Hassan argues, that "compels our reading" of "Homer, Dante, and Shakespeare, Sappho, Austen, and Morrison, *Gilgamesh*, the Bhagavad Gita, and *The Tale of Genji*, which come to us from other times, other places" (65). Hassan goes on to urge us to recognize the fact that "literature, like all other art, possesses us" through "individual, cultural, or historical singularities" (65). He adds: "For it is simply untrue that nothing survives cultural translations and that no pragmatic universals exist—universals like language, ritual, gods or spirit, social status, matrimonial customs, the pursuit of satisfactions, as well as hunger, copulation, and death. Excessive particularism not only stymies value judgments but also, more drastic to human communities, inhibits the faculty of human empathy, without which no reciprocity is possible" (65–66). For Hassan, literature breaks our confinement of historical circumstances and connects us through its textual appeal to the reader. "The globe may endure its vast discontents," he argues, "but a reader or teacher or writer of literature can still experience the 'truth of the text.' This truth is a felt force in the work, a stubborn moment experienced as transcendence or emptiness (*kenosis*), at once deeply private and cosmically impersonal" (66). Ha Jin's poetry embodies the possibilities of literature in reclaiming the humanity of those who have been dehumanized, not by denying particularities of cultural difference or historical specificities, but by showing what transcends these particularities.

NOTES

1. During the 1960s, the Communist Party of China accused the Communist Party leaders of the Soviet Union of betraying the communist principles and called them "revisionists."
2. The Red Guards are those high school and college students who were mobilized by Chairman Mao to carry out the cultural revolution through a series of radical, violent, and destructive actions during the 1960s and 1970s.

WORKS CITED

Clifford, James. "Introduction: Partial Truths," in *Writing Culture: The Poetics and Politics of Ethnography*. James Clifford and George E. Marcus, eds. (pp. 1–26). Berkeley: University of California Press, 1986.

———. *The Predicament of Culture: Twentieth-Century Ethnography, Literature, and Art*. Originally published in 1988. Cambridge: Harvard University Press, 1996.

Grewal, Inderpal, and Kaplan, Caren. "Introduction: Transnational Feminist Practices and Questions of Postmodernity," in *Scattered Hegemonies: Postmodernity and Transnational Feminist Practices* (pp. 1–33). Originally published in 1994. Minneapolis: University of Minnesota Press, 1997.

Hassan, Ihab. "Globalism and Its Discontents: Notes from a Wandering Scholar," in *Profession 1999* (pp. 59–67). New York: MLA, 1999.

Howe, Elisabeth A. *The Dramatic Monologue*. New York: Twayne, 1996.

Jin, Ha. *Between Silences: A Voice from China*. Chicago: University of Chicago Press, 1990.

———. *Facing Shadows*. Brooklyn, NY: Hanging Loose Press, 1996.

Laclau, Ernesto. "Identity and Hegemony: The Role of Universality in the Constitution of Political Logics," in *Contingency, Hegemony, Universality: Contemporary Dialogues on the Left*. Judith Butler, Ernesto Laclau, and Slavoj Zizek, eds. (pp. 44–89). London: Verso, 2000.

Levinas, Emmanuel. *Totality and Infinity: An Essay on Exteriority*. Trans. Alphonso Lingis. Originally published in 1969. Pittsburgh: Duquesne University Press, 1998.

Lim, Shirley Geok-lin. "Immigration and Diaspora," in *An Interethnic Companion to Asian American Literature* (pp. 289–311). New York: Cambridge University Press, 1997.

Liu, Cynthia W. Interview with Ha Jin. "Writing in Solitude." *International Examiner*, 2000. n.p.

Lowe, Lisa. "Heterogeneity, Hybridity, Multiplicity: Marking Asian American Difference." *Diaspora*, 1: 1 (1991): 24–44.

———. *Immigrant Acts: On Asian American Cultural Politics*. Durham: Duke University Press, 1996.

Ma, Sheng-mei. *Immigrant Subjectivities in Asian American and Asian Diaspora Literatures*. Albany: State University of New York Press, 1998.

Mohanty, Chandra Talpade. "Under Western Eyes: Feminist Scholarship and Colonial Discourse,"in *Third World Women and the Politics of Feminism*. Chandra Talpade Mohanty, Ann Russo, and Lourdes Torres, eds. (pp. 51–80). Bloomington: Indiana University Press, 1991.

Rennicks, Rich. "A Conversation with Ha Jin." Retrieved from http://go.borders .com/boutiques.

Vendler, Helen. *Soul Says: On Recent Poetry*. Cambridge: Belknap Press of Harvard University Press, 1995.

Visweswaran, Kamala. "Betrayal: An Analysis in Three Acts," in *Scattered Hegemonies: Postmodernity and Transnational Feminist Practices*. Inderpal Grewal and Caren Kaplan, eds. (pp. 90–109). Minneapolis: University of Minnesota Press, 1997.

Wang, Ping. *Of Flesh and Spirit*. Minneapolis: Coffee House Press, 1998.

Wordsworth, William. "I Wondered Lonely as a Cloud," in *Selected Poems and Prefaces*. Jack Stillinger, ed. (pp. 191–92). Boston: Houghton Mifflin, 1965.

Yau, John. "Between the Forest and Its Trees." *Amerasia Journal*, 20: 3 (1994): 37–43.

Zerilli, Linda M. G. "This Universalism which Is Not One." *Diacritics*, 28: 2 (1998): 3–20.

About the Contributors

LIAM CORLEY completed his Ph.D. in American literature at University California Riverside in 2004. He received a B.A. in rhetoric from UC Berkeley and an M.A. in English from San Jose State University. His dissertation is a cultural biography of Bayard Taylor, a nineteenth-century American travel writer, novelist, poet, journalist, and diplomat.

ROCÍO G. DAVIS is an associate professor of American and postcolonial literature at the University of Navarre (Spain). She has published *Transcultural Reinventions: Asian American and Asian Canadian Short Story Cycles* and is currently finishing a full-length study of Asian American autobiographies of childhood.

JOHN BLAIR GAMBER is a doctoral scholars fellow in the English department at the University of California, Santa Barbara. He received his B.A. from UC Davis and his M.A. from California State University, Fullerton, both in comparative literature. His research includes examinations of pollution in contemporary U.S. minority literature.

ROBERT GROTJOHN is an associate professor of English at Mary Baldwin College in Staunton, Virginia. He has published essays on Asian American poetry in *Western American Literature*, *Amerasia Journal*, *Southeast Review of Asian Studies*, and *Shenandoah*. His current work extends his interest in interlingual Asian American poetics to writers such as Arthur Sze, Walter Lew, Myung Mi Kim, and Cathy Park Hong.

CHERYL HIGASHIDA is an assistant professor of English at the University of Colorado at Boulder. She is currently working on a book about U.S. ethnic literary radicalism from the Depression to the Cold War.

RUTH Y. HSU is an associate professor of English at the University of Hawaii at Manoa. She teaches and writes about Asian American, Asian diaspora, and postcolonial literature. Her research interests include examining the ways that prevailing discursive constructions of race, ethnicity, gender, and sexuality are being refigured by the intersections of local and global forces.

MAIMUNA DALI ISLAM is the assistant professor of world literature and of creative writing and fiction at Albertson College and the literature advisor to the Asian studies minor at the college. Most recently Dali was the recipient of a full fellowship at the Vermont Studio Center, a residency program for writers and artists, and her poetry was shortlisted for the Emily Dickinson Prize in Poetry.

KATHERINE HYUNMI LEE is an assistant professor of multicultural American literature at Indiana State University whose research interests also include feminist theory, film, and cultural studies. Her essay is excerpted from her dissertation, "North American Orientalism: The Career and Works of Winnifred Eaton (1875–1954)." In addition to her work on Eaton, she has also authored essays about Asian American authors Helena Kuo and Marie G. Lee.

SHIRLEY GEOK-LIN LIM, professor of English, University of California, Santa Barbara, recipient of the Commonwealth Poetry Prize and two American book awards, has edited *Reading the Literatures of Asian America*, *Approaches to Teaching Maxine Hong Kingston's* The Woman Warrior, and other Asia Pacific American cultural studies volumes. Lim was chair professor at the University of Hong Kong (1999–2000) and received the 2002 UCSB Faculty Research Lecture Award. Her first novel, *Joss and Gold* (Feminist Press), appeared in 2001.

SRIMATI MUKHERJEE is a visiting assistant professor in the English Department at Temple University in Philadelphia where she teaches courses in composition; American, Asian American, and postcolonial literatures; and women's studies. She has presented papers at various national and international conferences and published essays on American and diasporic Indian authors. She is currently completing the introduction to an edited anthology on Asian American women writers.

JOSEPHINE NOCK-HEE PARK is an assistant professor of English and Asian American studies at the University of Pennsylvania. She is currently working on a study titled "Apparitions of Asia: Modernism's American Orient and Asian American Poetry."

GITA RAJAN is an associate professor of English and director of the literature program at Fairfield University. She is the Jane Watson Irwin Visiting Endowed Chair at Hamilton College for 2004–2005. She publishes and teaches in Asian American and South Asian literatures, in visual culture, and in victorian and globalization studies. She has co-edited *New Cosmopolitanisms: South Asians in the U.S.* (forthcoming),

An Introduction to Cultural Studies: History, Theory, Practice, Postcolonial Theory and Changing Cultural Contexts, and *English Postcoloniality: Literatures from Around the World.*

STEPHEN HONG SOHN is a graduate research fellow in the English Department at University of California, Santa Barbara. He currently is researching postmodern representations of city space in Asian American literature. He received his B.A. in biological sciences and creative writing at the University of Southern California and is currently pursuing his Ph.D. His work has appeared in *Studies in the Literary Imagination* (SLI) and *Southeast Asian Review of English* (SARE).

ELEANOR TY is a professor of English at Wilfrid Laurier University in Ontario. Author of *The Politics of the Visible in Asian North American Narratives* (2004), *Empowering the Feminine: The Narratives of Mary Robinson, Jane West, and Amelia Opie, 1796–1812* (1998), and *Unsex'd Revolutionaries: Five Women Novelists of the 1790s* (1993), her latest book is a collection of essays, *Asian North American Identities Beyond the Hyphen*, coedited with Donald Goellnicht (2004).

GINA VALENTINO is a graduate research fellow at University of California, Santa Barbara. She writes on class and contemporary U.S. literature in the new economy. She earned her B.A. and M.A. in English, specializing in American studies, at California State University, Fullerton.

ZHOU XIAOJING is an associate professor of English at University of the Pacific. Her publications include *Elizabeth Bishop: Rebel in Shades and Shadows*, a number of articles on Bishop's poetry and Asian American poets that appeared in critical anthologies and scholarly journals and her coedited anthology *Asian American Literature: Form, Confrontation, and Transformation.*

Index

Abjection, 142–43, 150–53, 194
Abuse, 33, 173
Accomando, Claire, 170, 174
Agha, Dr. Iqbal, 271n9
Ahmed, Rukhsana, 123
Alarcón, Norma, 8
Alexander, Meena, 15
Alger, Horatio, 50n8, 190
Ali, Agha Shahid, 15, 17, 21, 257–77
Ali, Monica, 123
Alien Land Acts, 32
Alienation, 72, 80, 142, 259
Alquizola, Marilyn, 50n8
Alsaybar, Bangele, 156n3
Althusser, Louis, 81
Amatarya, Sen, 139n3
"ambassadors of goodwill" (Kim), 166–67
American Dream, 76, 82, 134, 142–43, 156
Anderson, Benedict, 128, 140n8
Angelou, Maya, 177n2
Anti-Japanese Immigration Act (1924), 32
Appadurai, Arjun, 97n7, 124, 126, 128, 138, 140n6
Assimilation, 64, 66, 75, 156, 173, 276
Authenticity, 193
Autobiography, 17, 19–21, 161–96, 280–81

Bahri, Deepika, 13, 14
Baker, Houston A., 7, 13
Bangkok, 106, 110–12, 117
Bao, Quang, 103
Barthes, Roland, 17, 30
Basch, Linda, 145
Bauman, Zygmunt, 19, 126, 130–33, 135, 137–39, 140n10
Beauvoir, Simone de, 185
Behl, Aditya, 271n11, 272n14
Benjamin, Walter, 97n8
Benstock, Shari, 20, 185, 195n6
Bergland, Betty, 163, 176, 177, 178n10
Bernard-Donals, Michael, 195

Bhabha, Homi, 21, 62, 69, 72, 169, 171, 208, 260–61, 270n4, 270n5
Biraciality, 69, 144, 170–71
Birchall, Diana, 181, 194n1, 194n2, 194–195n3
Boelhower, William, 163, 164, 169–70, 171, 177
Bow, Leslie, 10, 18
Brada-Williams, Noelle, 13
Brazil, 75–76, 95
Brazil-Maru, 75, 95
Bulosan, Carlos, 1, 2, 14, 17, 22, 29–54
Butler, Judith, 101, 183–84

Cambodia, 174, 178n14
Campomanes, Oscar V., 51n11
Cao, Lan, 14
Capitalism, 30, 32, 33, 36, 45, 49, 111; as global, 75, 79, 142–143, 145, 149, 152; as late capitalism, 66, 106, 112, 118; as print capitalism, 140n8
Cartography. See maps
Caruth, Cathy, 206
Cather, Willa, 194n3
Cha, Theresa Hak Kyung, 8, 11, 14, 15, 16, 17, 20, 21, 22, 197–213, 235, 242, 246, 249, 254n1
Chan, Jeffrey Paul, 6
Chang, Julia, 21
Chang, Juliana, 219, 213n22
Chee, Alexander, 120n2
Chen, Da, 170, 178n13
Cheng, Anne Anlin, 9, 10, 187, 189, 193, 213n22
Cheung, Kin-Kok, 5, 6, 7–8, 11, 13, 17, 30, 31, 49–50n2
Chew, Kristina, 211n13
Childhood, The, 161–80
Children's literature, 177
Chin, Frank, 6, 7, 11, 13–14, 22n4
Chin, Justin, 14
Chin, Marilyn, 232
China, 167, 174, 178n13

Chinatown, 168, 169, 171–72
Choi, Susan, 15
Choudhari Amit, 123
Chow, Karen, 13
Choy, Wayson, 168, 169, 172
Chu, Patricia, 10, 18, 173
Chua, Lawrence, 1, 14, 16, 100, 106–20
Chuh, Kandice, 3–4, 12, 13
Chung, C., 102
Class, 14, 16, 31, 44, 48
Cleary, Thomas, 227
Clément, Catherine, 220, 231
Clifford, James, 278, 279, 280, 292–93
Clinton, Bill, 56
Coe, Richard N., 20, 161, 162, 164, 165, 170, 176, 177n1, 177n2, 177n4, 178n5, 178n7, 178n11
Cole, Jean Lee, 12
Colonialism, 7, 20, 77, 80, 83, 86–87, 106, 112–13, 117,139; as neocolonialism, 21, 42, 83, 142, 156n1, 198, 200, 210n6, 248
Colorum Party, 41
Commodity, 63, 65–66, 100, 68, 82, 152, 155; as commodity fetishism, 115–16; on commodities and queer sexuality, 101, 106–11, 114–15, 117, 120
Cook, Captain James, 85
Cordova, Fred, 50n4, 51n12, 52n14,
Corley, Liam, 18
Covi, Giovanna, 213n22
Creef, Elena Tajima, 11
Cultural memory, 238
Cultural Revolution, 281

Davis, Bette, 154
Davis, Mike, 88, 96n3, 97n3, 97n8
Davis, Rocío, 11, 13, 19–20, 171, 172
Demilitarized Zone (DMZ), 247
Denning, Michael, 30, 51n10
Devi, Mahasveta, 202, 211n11
Dhalla, Ghalib Shiraz, 14, 120n2
Diaspora, 1, 6, 8, 10, 12, 13, 15, 16, 19, 21, 72, 123, 128, 258, 259, 269, 276, 280
Diasporic voice, 236
Diaz de Revera, Lina B., 52n22
Dickinson, Emily, 265–67
Dimok, Wai Chi, 139n3
Dinkins, David, 5

Dirlik, Arif, 142
Disability, 173
Diseuse, 235, 246
Divarakuni, Chitra, 15, 123
Dolan, Chris, 78
Domestic sphere, 201
Doyle, James, 182
Dramatic monologue, 284–89, 292
Duncan, Patti, 11, 18
Dwyer, June, 70

Eakin, Paul John,161
Eaton, Edith, 13, 14, 15, 190
Eaton, Richard, 271n14
Eaton, Winnifred, 12, 17, 20, 22, 181–96
écriture feminine, 220
Effeminate, 136
Eng, David L., 10, 13, 14, 101, 103–04, 106, 147, 148, 156n4
Engles, Tim, 70
Enlightenment, the, 85
Ethics, 124–25, 128–30, 132–39
Eviota, Elizabeth Uy, 38, 40, 52n14, 52n15, 52n16
Ewha Haktang, 197
Exile, 56, 72, 80, 146, 156, 258, 259, 260, 261, 264, 268, 269, 271n12, 290, 291
Exploration, 85–85

Fabula, 31
Fairy Tale, 182, 187–91
"false consciousness," 183
Family in autobiography, 168–69
Fa Mu Lan, 187, 190–93
Far, Sui Sin. See Edith Eaton
Feminism, 8, 10–11
"Feminist ethnography" (Visweswaran), 281
Fenkl, Heinz Insu, 168, 170, 175, 177, 178n12, 178n15
Fenollosa, Ernest, 240
Fictions in Autobiography: Studies in the Art of Self-Invention, 161
Fifth Chinese Daughter (Wong), 167, 168, 172
Firth, Raymond, 278
Fixer Chao (Ong), 142–43, 144, 150–56
Flashback, 107–09
"flexible citizenship" (Ong), 1
Ford, Ford Madox, 62
Forster, E.M., 131

Foucault, Michel, 101
Franklin, Benjamin, 184
Freeman, John, 150
Freud, Sigmund, 130, 131
Frost, Elisabeth A., 212n16
Fujikane, Candace, 101
Fung, Richard, 103

Gao, Yan, 12
Gernes, Todd S., 51n11
Ghazals, 268
Ghosh, Amitav, 123, 257, 260, 263
Gilbert, Sandra, 220
Gilmore, Leigh, 192, 195n8
Giuliani, Rudolph, 60, 68
Globalization, 3, 5, 8, 9, 11, 12, 15, 19,
    22, 128, 138–39, 142, 144, 150,
    152–53
Godfrey, Thomas, 85
Goellnicht, Donald C., 50n3, 50n7, 147,
    177n3
Golden Venture, 55–59, 67–68, 73n1
Graphic novels, 11
Grewal, Inderpal, 280
Grice, Helena, 11, 18
Grotjohn, Robert, 21
Gurin, Patricia, 156n5

Hagedorn, Jessica, 15, 16, 105–06
Hahn, Kimiko, 17, 21, 219–32
Hamid, Mohsin, 123
Hanh, Thich Nhat, 64
Hapa, 15–16
Harischandra, Neshantha, 195n7
Harpham, Geoffrey Galt, 139n3
Harrison, John, 85, 98n12
Harvey, David, 97n6
Hassan, Ihab, 293
Hattori, Tomo, 183, 186
Hau'ofa, Epeli, 87
Hegemony, 65, 81, 96, 148; as
    counter-hegemony, 96
Heian period, 220, 226, 228
Hemingway, Ernest, 47
Higashida, Cheryl, 17
Hindi, 258
Ho, Wendy, 10, 18
Hohokam, 264–65
Holloway, Karla F., 139n3
Hom, Alice Y., 103
Home, Alice Y., 13

Homogenization, 198, 205, 207, 209
Homosociality, 35, 42, 108
Hong, Grace Kyungwon, 50n3
hooks, bell, 212n16
Houston, Jeanne Wakatsuki and James,
    168, 169, 172, 176–77
Howe, Elisabeth A., 286
Hsu, Kai-Yu, 6
Hsu, Ruth, 18
Huk rebellion, 51n11
Huntley, E. D., 12
Huo, T. C., 14, 120n2
Hurtado, Aida, 156n5
Hustler, 105, 149
Hwang, David Henry, 11, 13, 14
Hybridity, 9, 13, 62, 67, 69, 72, 260, 261,
    270n2, 270n4, 270n5, 270–71n6,
    271n7, 276
Hyphen, 260, 261, 263

Illegal immigration. See Golden Venture
Imagism, 21, 238, 240, 241
"Immediate immigrants," 264
Immigrant visas, 263
Immortal Sisterhood, 229
Inada, Lawson Fusao, 6, 22n4
Ingram, Gordan Brent, 118
Intergenerational conflict, 31
Internalized colonialism, 270n3
Internationalism, 260
Internment camps, 171–74, 176
"Interpreter of Maladies" (Lahiri),
    129–33
"interstitial spaces" (Bhabha), 171
Intersubjectivity, 129, 134, 136
Irigaray, Luce, 230
Islam, 267, 268, 271n14
Islam, Maimuna Dali, 21
Itinerary of selfhood/socialization/
    adaptation, 162, 167, 168, 170, 173,
    174

Jackson, Peter A., 118–19
Jacobs, Harriet, 185–86
Jagger, Alison M., 139n3
Japan, 76, 95; on Japanese Brazilian, 76
Japanese Americans, 79
Japanese American internment, 168, 169,
    171–73, 174, 176
Japanese colonization of China and Korea,
    174

Jayawardena, Kumari, 20, 197, 201–02, 210n3, 210n4
Jen, Gish, 2, 73n3
Jin, Ha, 17, 22, 123, 274–94
Julien, Isaac, 148–49

Kafka, Phillipa, 10, 18
Kain, Geoffrey, 13
Kang, Laura Hyun Yi, 10–11, 18
Kang, Younghill, 170
Kaplan, Caren, 280
Karim, Abdul, 271–72n14
Kashmiri secession, 269
Kashmiri Uprising, 1996, 269
Kazin, Alfred, 177n2
Keller, Nora Okja, 11
Kenner, Hugh, 239
Khusrao and Shirin, 267
Kim, A., 102
Kim, Elaine H., 6, 7, 8, 22n2, 49–50n2, 166–67, 183, 186, 198, 208, 212n21, 235–37
Kim, Myung Mi, 15, 17, 21, 232, 235–55
Kim, Richard, 168, 170, 174, 177
Kim, Suki, 15
Kim, Willyce, 14
Kincaid, Jamaica, 213n22
Kingston, Maxine Hong, 6, 7, 10, 11, 12, 13, 17, 20, 177n2, 181–96
Kogawa, Joy, 11, 14, 177n2
Kolodny, Annette, 97n7
Kondo, Dorinne, 65
Korea; as country, 55, 171, 174, 178n15; on culture, 61, 70–72; on Korean War, 58, 238, 239, 241, 254
Korean Americans, 55, 56
Koreatown, 79
Koshy, Susan, 9, 140n5, 140n7
Kristeva, Julia, 51n13, 151
Kundera, Milan, 184
Kuramoto, Kazuko, 170, 174
Kwa, Lydia, 14, 120n2

Laclau, Ernesto, 275–75, 277
Lahiri, Jhumpa, 19, 123–39
Lai, Larissa, 14
Lakhana, Peou, 102
Lama, Dalai, 64
Language acquisition, 167–68
Lapidus, Ira M., 272n14

Lasker, Bruno, 50n4
Lawrence, Bruce B., 272n14
Layla and Majnoon, 267–68, 271n11
Le Thi Diem Thuy, 14, 15
Lean, David, 131
Lee, Chang-rae, 15, 17, 18, 55–74, 123
Lee, Josephine, 11
Lee, Katherine Hyunmi, 20
Lee, Li-Young, 16
Lee, Rachel C., 10, 18, 36, 37, 41, 42, 46, 47, 49, 51n9, 51n13, 65, 73n8, 96n2, 120
Lee, Robert G., 108, 120n3, 147
Lee, Yan Phou, 20, 22n2, 161, 166, 167
Lei-Lanilau, Carolyn, 232
Lemeshewsky, A.K., 102
Leong, Russell, 13, 14, 103
LeRoy, Pierre, 85
Levinas, Emmanuel, 275–76, 284
Li, David Leiwei, 9, 151
Libretti, Timothy, 51n11
Lim, Genny, 11
Lim, Shirley Geok-lin, 3, 6, 8, 13, 231–232, 259, 276
Lim-Hing, Sharon, 102
Ling, Amy, 6, 7–8, 13, 22n3, 182, 183, 186
Ling, Jinqi, 12, 14
Linmark, R. Zamora, 104, 120n2
Lippi, Rosina, 123
Liu, Aimee, 173
Liu, Catherine, 14, 120n2
Liu, Cynthia, 274, 275
Lorde, Audre, 185–186
Los Angeles, 77, 79–80, 83, 88–91, 93–95, 144; riots, 208–09, 249–50
Lothrop, Lee, and Shepard Publishing Company, 166
Louie, David Wong, 104
Louima, Abner, 60
Lowe, Lisa, 3, 4, 9, 51n8, 57, 211n14, 212n16, 212n17, 212n19, 276
Ludwig, Sämi, 13
Lukács, Georg, 32, 34
Lyotard, Jean-Francois, 138

Ma, Sheng-mei, 9, 280
Magic realism, 78
Mah, Adeline, 173–74
Manchuria, 170
Mandelbrot, Benoit, 98n13
Mao, 282, 286, 293n2

Maps, 75, 77, 88–90, 96n; as cartography, 80, 84, 90–91
Mar, M. Elaine, 175, 176
Marital crisis, 135–37
Marquez, Gabriel Garcia, 78–79
Marx, Karl, 115
Masculinist, 197
Masculinity, 10, 11, 134, 142–43, 147–50, 152
Mass media, 131
Massey, Doreen, 97n7
McBride, James, 63
McClintoock, Anne, 20, 184–85, 186
McDonald, Dorothy Ritsuko, 22n4
McDowell, Linda, 97n7
McWilliams, Carey, 32, 34
Mead, Margaret, 278
Meer, Ameena, 14
Mehta, Ved, 173
Meissenburg, Karin, 22n5
Mental illness, 173
Mercer, Kobena, 148–149
Merisami, Julie Scott, 271n11
Mexico, 79, 80–81, 89, 93–94
Mignolo, Walter, 97n7
Miller, J. Hillis, 139n3
Miller, James E., 241
Min, Anchee, 11
Minuit, Peter, 72
Miscegenation, 147
Mistry, Rohinton, 123
Modernism, 9, 21, 235, 240, 241, 242, 255n1
Mohanty, Chandra Talpade, 280
Momaday, N. Scott, 177n2
Moore, Ward, 29, 49n1
Morrison, Toni, 77, 97n8
Moser, Linda Trinh, 188, 189
Mostern, Kenneth, 36, 50n8
Mukherjee, Bharati, 15, 123
Mukherjee, Srimati, 20
Mullen, Bill, 30
Multinationalism, 258
Mura, David, 104
Murdza, Therese, 112
Murray, Stephen O., 113

Naipaul, V.S., 123
Nakashima, Daniel, 175
Naming, 174–75
Nationalism, 6

Nation-state, 62–63, 80, 101, 103, 145
Native American, 127, 264–65, 267
Navigation, 78, 81, 85–86
Needham, Lawrence, 268
New, Ilhan, 161, 166, 167
New Masses, 52n21
New York, 55–69
Ng, Fae Myenne, 10
Ng, Franklin, 8
Ng, Wendy, 13
Nguyen, Kien, 14, 15, 161, 170, 174
Nguyen, Viet Thanh, 12, 19, 119
Noh play, 226, 233n7
Norris, Kathleen, 64
Nuñez, Sigrid, 14
nu shu script, 221, 222, 223, 225, 227, 228, 232n2, 232n4
Nussbaum, Martha, 139n3

Odyssey, The, 247
O'Keefe, Georgia, 266–67
Okihiro, Gary, 17, 37, 42
Okubo, Mine, 11
Olney, James, 184, 195n6
Ondaatje, Michael, 123, 261
Ong, Aihwa, 1, 112
Ong, Han, 15, 19, 120n2, 142–44, 149–50
O'Reilly, Helen, 52n22,
Orientalism, 5, 6, 21, 102, 128, 136, 182, 235, 241, 274, 275, 276–77, 279–81, 290, 292
"Our Sea of Islands" (Hau'ofa), 87–88

Palubinskas, Helen, 6
Palumbo–Liu, David, 9, 11, 13
Panethnic coalition, 59
Parikh, Crystal, 104
Park, Josephine Nock-Hee, 21
Parmar, Pratibha, 101
Parreñas, Rachel, 145
Partition, 268
Passage to India, A (Forster), 131–32
Passing, 146
Patriarchy, 30, 35, 36, 45, 47, 49, 50n5, 188, 191, 192, 222, 228
Pearl Harbor, 174
Peng, Timothy, 156n5
Persian, 267
Petersen, Susan, 63
Phallocentrism, 45, 47, 49

Pham, Alex W., 15
Philippines, 142, 145, 155, 177; as
    Filipinos, 142, 145, 147, 150,
    154–156; as Filipino youth, 143; as
    Filipino immigrants, 143–44; as
    Filipino American, 143–44, 146,
    156n3
Photography, 11, 178n9
Phukan, Shantanu, 271n11, 272n14
Polynesians, 87
Popular Front, 17, 30, 48, 49, 49n1
"positions of subjectivity" (Paul Smith),
    162
Postcolonialism, 3, 4, 6, 7, 8, 13, 14, 16,
    19, 20, 21, 100, 113, 123, 127, 139,
    140n9, 257, 258, 260, 263, 268, 269,
    270n2
"postmodern autobiography" (Bergland),
    163
Postmodernism, 4, 8, 16, 78
Postnational, 4
Poststructuralism, 4, 8, 164
Pound, Ezra, 233n7, 235, 239, 240, 241,
    242, 250, 255n2
Power, Susan, 123
prem-kahanis, 267, 271n11
"Promise" (Jin), 284–86
Prostitution, 42–46, 52n17, 52n20, 105,
    108, 110–20, 149, 150–51,
    153–54
Psychoanalysis, 8, 9–10
Publication, 56, 63–66
Pulitzer Prize, 123–124, 139n1
Pynchon, Thomas, 89

Quan, Shirley N., 106
Queer anthologies, 100, 102–04
Queer sexuality, 100–20, 150–53
Queerness, 9, 10, 13, 14, 16, 18–19

Rabinehas, Leslie, 46
Rabinowitz, Paula, 46
Racial struggle, 60–62
Radhakrishnan, R., 271n12
Rainsford, Dominic, 139n3
Rajan, Gita, 19
Ramazani, Jahan, 21, 259, 270n2, 270n3
Readable text, 30, 35
Realuyo, Bino, 14, 156n2
Refugee camps, 178n14
Remarque, Erich Maria, 97n5

Renan, Ernest, 63
Resnais, Alain, 206
Revoyr, Nina, 120n2
Reyes, Norman, 170, 174, 176, 178n8
Ricou, Laurie, 162
Riverhead Books, 63, 73n5
Rody, Caroline, 73n3
Rolden v. Los Angeles County, 44
Roley, Brian Ascalon, 19, 142–44, 150,
    156
Rolf, Robert T., 49–50n2
Rooney, Doris, 194n1
Roth, Philip, 177n2
Roy, Arundhati, 124
Rushdie, Salman, 123

Said, Edward, 84, 97n7
San Juan, Jr., Epifanio, 34, 37, 43, 51n11,
    51n13, 52n20, 142
Sansei, 175
Santos, Bienvenido, 156n5
Sassen, Saskia, 97n3
Sawney, Deepak Narang, 97n3
Scarry, Elaine, 101
Schiller, Nina Glick, 145
Sedgwick, Eve Kosofsky, 101, 108
Sei Shōnagon, 233n9
Selvadurai, Shyam, 14, 120n2, 123
Sex tourism, 100, 105–07, 110–20
Shankar, Lavina, 259, 270n1, 270n3
Shimakawa, Karen, 11, 13
Shipwreck, 57, 58, 67. See also Golden
    Venture
Shohat, Ella, 143, 156n1
Sidhwa, Bapsi, 123
Silber, Cathy, 223, 225, 229, 232n6
Simmons, Diane, 12
Simon, Bruce, 270n6
Sin, Caroline, 182
Sinophobia, 182
Skandera-Trombley, Laura E., 12
Slash, 9, 11
Slavery, 127
Slotkin, Joel, 51n11
Smith, Neil, 60, 73n1, 73n4
Smith, Paul, 162, 165
Smith, Sidonie, 185, 186, 193, 209,
    213n23
Sociopolitical, 201
Sohn, Stephen Hong, 18–19
Soja, Edward, 97n3

Sone, Monica, 168, 169, 172, 175
Song, Cathy, 8
Sonora Desert, 264–65, 269
Spectacle; of media, 55; of Asian immigrant exploitation, 66; of shipwreck, 67
Speech/writing, 205, 206
Spivak, Gayatri Chakravorty, 20, 202, 203
Srikanth, Rajini, 259, 270n1, 270n3
Stallybrass, Peter, 97n11
Stam, Robert, 143, 156n1
Stanwyck, Barbara, 154
Statue of liberty, 62, 63
Stehle, Philip, 98n13
Student visas, 263–64
Sufi, 267, 271n11, 271n13, 271n14
Sumida, Stephen H., 6, 7
Sunni, 268
Suri, Manil, 123
Syuzhet, 31

Tabios, Eileen, 220, 221, 222, 229, 230
Tables of content, 92–94
Takagi, Dana Y., 14, 101
Takaki, Ronald, 32, 147, 212n17
Takei, George, 168, 169, 172, 175–76
Tan, Amy, 6, 8, 10, 12, 13, 14, 182
Tan, Cecilia, 103
Tan, Joel, 103
Taussig, Michael T., 115
Tayug Revolt, 41, 52n19
Taxi cab drivers, 58–59
"terrain" (Bhabha), 169
"Third Space" (Bhabha), 261, 270n4, 270n5
"Third World child" (Coe), 164
"third world difference" (Mohanty), 280
Through the Arc of the Rainforest (Yamashita), 75, 95
Tiananmen Square, 291
Transgressive discourse, 220
Transimmigrant, 260, 264, 269, 270n4, 270n5
Transnationalism, 1, 2, 3, 4, 5, 6, 8, 10, 11, 13, 15, 16, 22, 37–38, 51n13, 60, 72, 100, 105–106, 112, 138, 142, 145, 258, 260, 263, 269, 270n5, 276; on subaltern, 142; on transnational queerness, 117–20; on production, 142–43; on migration, 143; on labor, 142, 145, 152; on trade, 153; as psychic transnationalism, 143; as

emotional transnationalism, 143; as transmigrants, 145, 149, 154–55; as trans-Pacific, 86
Trauma, 197, 198, 200, 204, 206, 207
Triangulation, 108
Tropic of Orange (Yamashita), 75–98
Truong, Monique, 15
Turkic-Persian-Arab expansion movement, 268
Ty, Eleanor, 19

Uchida, Yoshiko, 168, 169, 172–73, 175, 176
Ung, Loung, 170, 174, 178n14
Universalism, 22, 274–75
Urdu, 258, 267, 268

Vasudeva, Mary, 13, 14
Vendler, Helen, 286, 287–88
Vidal, Gore, 15
Vietnam, 171, 174
Vietnamese refugee, 79
Villa, Jose Garcia, 14
Violence, 137, 142, 149, 152
Visweswaran, Kamala, 281

Waldrop, Mitchell, 98n13
Wand, David Hsin–Fu, 6
Wang, Peter, 276
Wang, Ping, 276–81, 291
War, 174, 176
Watson, Julia, 209, 213n23
Weatherwax, Clara, 46, 52n21
Weightman, Simon, 272n14
Welch, Marie De L., 34–35
White, Allon, 97n11
Whitman, Walt, 65, 67–68, 72, 73n9, 241
Winfrey, Oprah, 123
Wolf, Diane L., 143
Wong, Jade Snow, 167, 168, 169, 172, 173, 175, 177, 177n2
Wong, Norman, 14
Wong, Sau-ling, 5, 6–7, 12, 22n1, 35, 50–51n8, 51n13, 105, 118, 147, 166, 167, 172, 173
Wong, Shawn, 6
Wong, Shelley Sunn, 211n13
Woods, Tim, 139n3
Wordworth, William, 286, 287, 288
Wright, Richard, 47
Writable text, 30, 34

Yamamoto, Hisaye, 2, 14, 17, 29–54
Yamamoto, Traise, 69, 73n10, 165, 178n6
Yamashita, Karen Tei, 17, 18, 73n3, 75–99
Yamauchi, Wakako, 11
Yanagihara, Hanya, 103
Yau, John, 281, 289
Yeats, William Butler, 288

Yep, Laurence, 171, 175–77
Yogi, Stan, 5, 50n2
Yu Guan Soon, 20
Yu, Timothy, 212n16

Zerilli, Linda, 275
Zhang, Benzi, 259, 270n4, 271n7
Zhou, Xiaojing, 22, 219
Zia, Helen, 14